Once Around on a Bicycle

By

Michael Clancy

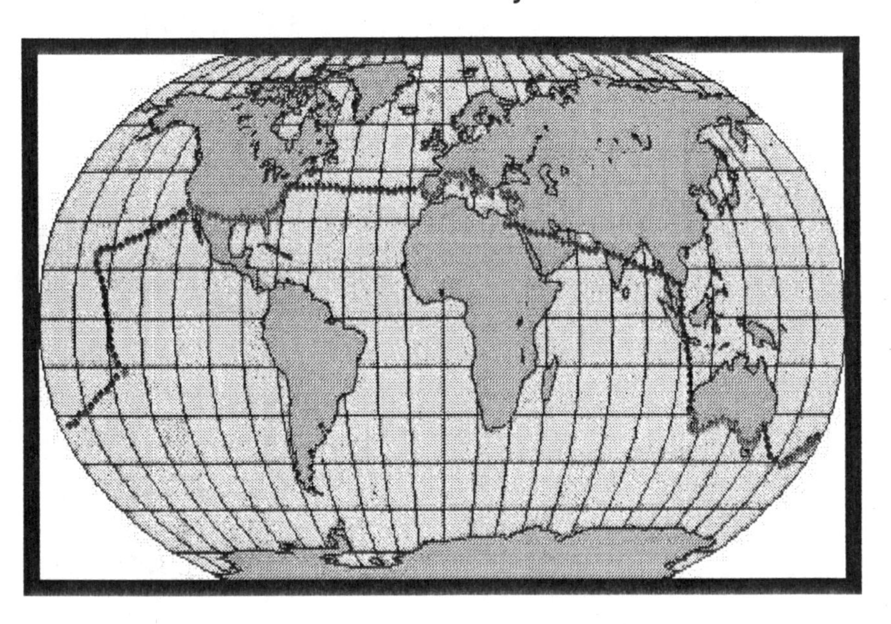

ISBN 0-7414-1769-3

Published by:

519 West Lancaster Avenue
Haverford, PA 19041-1413
Info@buybooksontheweb.com
www.buybooksontheweb.com
Toll-free (877) BUY BOOK
Local Phone (610) 520-2500
Fax (610) 519-0261

Printed in the United States of America

Printed on Recycled Paper

Published October 2003

Contents

Introduction

Once Around on a Bicycle is the journal of my bicycle trip around the world from April 4, 2001 to July 12, 2002. The tone of each journal entry reflects my demeanor on that given day. The entries were typed into a Pocket PC inside a sweaty tent, on heaving ferries, in greasy restaurants, and in almost every style of lodging known to man. They were written after days of pure pain, sheer joy, and utter boredom. So, if you don't like the tone of any entries, keep reading. The next entry will likely be less offensive.

The distances traveled each day were recorded in kilometers (Km) for all metric countries, that is, everywhere but the United States. Distances in the U.S. were recorded in miles. Prices were recorded in U.S. dollars, unless otherwise noted.

Thank you to the hundreds of thousands of drivers who stayed on their side of the white painted roadway stripe. Thank you to all of the good people that I met on the road who offered me encouragement and assistance when I was in need. Thank you to all of my friends and co-workers who kept my spirits up when I was a world away. Most importantly, thank you to my family for everything.

Portugal

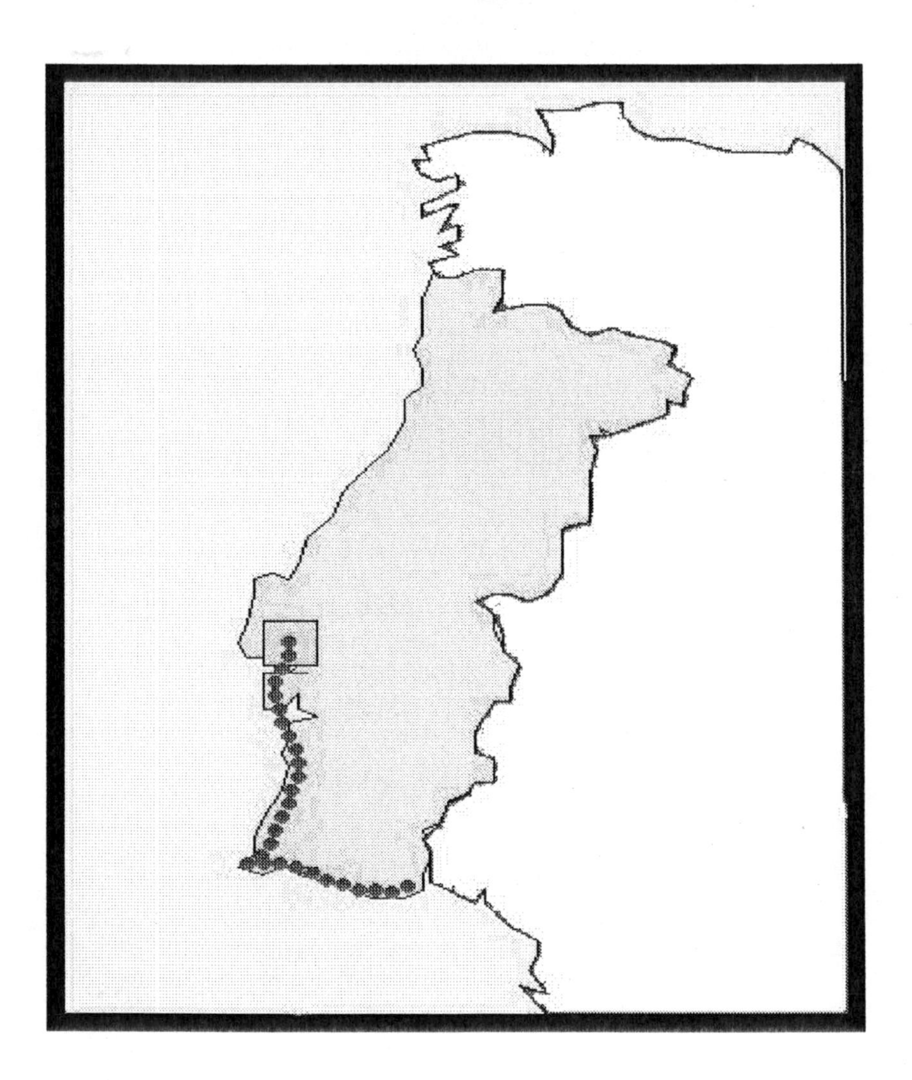

Wednesday & Thursday, April 4th & 5th
Philadelphia to Boston to Paris to Lisbon - 1.5 Km

I've finally begun the "big trip." After years and years of dreaming about bicycling solo around the world, I am actually doing it today. Since 1985 I've taken many two-week bicycle trips in Europe and North America, but they've paled in comparison to this one. When I originally planned this trip ten years ago, I felt that it could be done in 18 months, over 18,000 miles, for $18,000. I've already revised the budget up to $25,000. If I've learned anything from my previous bike trips, it's to be flexible. Flexibility and a gold credit card will see me through the most difficult days of this trip, wherever they may occur.

It wasn't easy to say goodbye to the folks yesterday. Eighteen months is a long time to be away from family. I'll stay in touch with them via daily Short Message Service (SMS) e-mail and weekly telephone calls, but I'll still miss the holidays and big family events. This trip won't be easy for any of us.

Dad drove me to Philadelphia International Airport at 9:30 AM on Wednesday, the 4th. Airports are the natural enemy of bicycles. Things rarely go smoothly when you travel with a bicycle. So, I was pleasantly surprised when Delta Airlines produced a bicycle box for me to transport my 1984 Specialized Expedition. I had called the airline two days ago to confirm the availability of bike boxes, but that's never an ironclad guarantee that one will be available when you arrive at the airport. After packing the bike, I spent almost an hour at the check-in counter arranging to pay for this flight with 50,000 frequent flyer miles. The one-way ticket to Lisbon that I booked a couple of weeks ago is now a roundtrip ticket, returning from Zurich on January 1, 2002. If there's a waiting list in Zurich next January, one lucky air traveler should be happy to know that I'm in Australia.

I left Philly around 2:00 PM and arrived in Boston at 3:30 PM. The next few hours were spent working the phones in the Delta lounge at Logan Airport. It was my last opportunity to work out some technical problems with Motorola, Compaq, Earthlink, and Voicestream. My GSM phone, Pocket PC, international Internet Service Provider, and global mobile phone service are not yet interacting seamlessly. I left Boston at 8:30 PM with most of the technical issues still unresolved and arrived at Charles de Gaulle Airport in Paris at about 9:00 AM Thursday morning. After a boring six-hour layover in Paris, it was on to Lisbon. I arrived around 6:00 PM and then took my time assembling the bike in the baggage claim area. I even videotaped some of the assembly process. By the time I left the airport it was almost dusk. I cycled to the Terminus Hotel just outside of the airport where I had stayed last year. Unfortunately, there were no rooms available. Darn! I hadn't planned on that. Then, I cycled farther into town. After a second turndown, the Hotel Roma took me in. By then it was completely dark outside, and I think that they took pity on me. Or, maybe it was just the $75 that I was willing to pay for the phone booth that they put me in. Either way, I am happy to have a bed. I've been awake for 36 hours now.

Friday, April 6th
Lisbon to Carvalhal - 81.7 Km

This was my first day on the bike in over six months. I didn't get any training in prior to this little adventure. I spent all of my time handling the details of the trip. I sold the house, put my belongings into storage, quit a great job, arranged my finances, bought supplies, had appointments with my doctor and dentist, endured a dozen shots, and made up a will. I am now in the enviable position of having no responsibilities and no attachments, other than a small plot of land that I recently purchased in St. Denis Cemetery. I may not be prepared physically, but I'm prepared in every other way.

I woke up at 9:50 AM, thinking that it was 6:00 AM. After 10 hours of sleep I was still bone-tired. But, that didn't keep me from rushing down to the hotel dining room for my free continental breakfast (available 7:00 AM-10:00 AM). I'll try not to pass up too many free meals on this trip. By noon I was on the road. After an exhilarating (i.e., death-defying) ride through the congested streets of Lisbon, I decided to get out of town immediately. I saw most of Lisbon last year on another cycling trip. I've been there and done that. I'm sure that I'll have plenty of opportunities to risk life and limb cycling through other capitol cities in the next year and a half. I just didn't want to get run over on my first day in the saddle.

Like all ferry rides, the ferry across the Rio Tejo was fun. I think that's because I'm gaining ground but not expending any energy. Later this afternoon, after cycling the N10 to Setubal, I had another ferry ride across the Rio Sado. That's two ferries in one day. Yippee! The real fun began after the second ferry ride when I missed the campground in Troia. I continued south on the N253 and N261, looking for any kind of lodging. For the second day in a row I was forced to use my headlights. Twenty-eight Km later I reached Carvalhal where I was directed to the town's pousada located above a taverna. The owner of the taverna was a great help in getting me the room and a good steak meal. Since I didn't speak Portuguese well and he didn't speak English well, we conversed in Spanish. For about $18, I now have a comfortable room. I'll sleep like a baby tonight.

Saturday, April 7th
Carvalhal to Vila Nova de Milfontes - 82.7 Km

I got on the road a little earlier today, 9:00 AM. There was a good tailwind all day. I passed a lot of familiar sights from last year's trip, like Sines and Porto Covo. I even stopped for refreshments at a couple of establishments that I had patronized last year. The left knee was a little sore in the morning, but after a few Km it warmed up. I fine-tuned the bike while en route. The seat seems to be at the correct height now, but the chain is already a bit dirty. Before this trip is over I'm going to become a great bicycle mechanic, or else.

I finished cycling around 4:30 PM and I'm staying at a fairly nice campground. It's only costing me about $5. The U.S. dollar is strong versus most foreign currencies right now. That bodes well for my finances throughout the trip. Thank you Mr. Alan Greenspan. It's getting cold and windy. I hope I can get a good night's sleep in the tent tonight.

Sunday, April 8th
Vila Nova de Milfontes to Odeceixe - 54.3 Km

This was a shorter day than I had hoped. I got a late start out of the campground, explored the town of Vila Nova de Milfontes, and then took a less than optimal route south. Vila Nova de Milfontes is well situated at the mouth of the Rio Mira. It's a very photogenic town. I spent well over an hour shooting video from different locations in the town. In one plaza there is a monument to a local hero who flew a biplane in 1928 across the Middle East, India and Asia, to Macao. The preparations for that jaunt must have rivaled, well, my preparations for this trip.

I have to remember not to get off of the national roads in Portugal. Those would be the red roads on my Michelin map. The local, or white, roads are extremely rough. In some places they are barely passable. And worse than that, they have nasty farm dogs just waiting to sink their teeth into a solo bicycle-tourist. I left the N393 (red) to ride the coast road (white) for a while. Portugal seems to be bordered by cliffs along most of this coast. Despite another good tailwind in the afternoon, I was toast by the time that I joined the N120 (red) at Sao Teotonio.

Right now I'm in the cafeteria of a very nice campground. I've just finished a steak and rice dinner. I'm watching a football match (soccer game) in the campground's TV room as I type this journal entry. I'm also charging my Pocket PC on the sly in a nearby electrical socket. Campers normally have to pay to have electrical service turned on. I'm going to have to keep my eyes peeled for available sockets over the next 18 months. The Pocket PC, mobile phone, and camcorder will all need to be charged twice a week. I used the phone tonight to call home and let Mom and Dad know where I am. It's always good to let the folks know that I'm still alive.

Monday, April 9th
Odeceixe to Sagres - 69.1 Km

This wasn't a bad day. I slept fairly well at the campground last night. I'm camping again tonight. I hope to do even better in the sleep department. Once again, I passed through familiar territory on the N268. The riding was pleasant. There were no dogs. The road surfaces were decent. And, there was a strong tailwind near the end of the ride. I did have a few tough hills, but "slow and steady wins the day." I think that's the old saying. I stopped at the village square of Vila do Bispo for a snack, just like last year. I also shot some videotape around the town. If any of this tape turns out to be viewable, it'll be a miracle.

Since it's still early in the tourist season, some places are not open yet. This campground in Sagres will not open their market until next week. Aaargh! All I have is my last Met-Rx bar and some water. It's far too windy to make the three Km trip back to town for a meal. Tomorrow will be an off day, so I'll try to work out some of the technical glitches that have been haunting me. If I can get this phone, Pocket PC, and camcorder to work as promised, that will also be a miracle.

Tuesday, April 10th
Sagres to Cape St. Vicente to Sagres - 19.1 Km

This was my first rest day of the trip. I still put in a few tough Km to go out to Cape St. Vicente to see the famous lighthouse at the edge of the medieval world. The fortified lighthouse was the last sight of Europe seen by Portuguese explorers as they set sail down the west coast of Africa in search of a sea route to India. As you would expect, the wind is extremely strong out on the Cape. I had to pedal most of the way in the granny gears just to reach the lighthouse.

I arrived at 10:05 AM, just as the first tour bus pulled up and as the vendors were setting up their tables outside of the lighthouse. There were a few tourists standing beside their cars, making no moves toward the fortified entrance. Being the bold, adventurous-type, I cycled right through the front gate. That's when I realized why no one had entered yet. Two very angry dogs were guarding it. As they came at me I jumped off of the bike (gracefully, I'm sure) and put it between them and me. While they barked and showed me their incisors, I looked around for their owner to step forward. The dogs must have been strays. After about 30 seconds one of the old ladies sewing lace doilies for the tourists yelled something at the dogs. They seemed to listen to her and reluctantly backed off. Then, the less bold and adventurous tourists entered. The dogs knew that the tour bus crowd outnumbered them, so they retreated back to their corners, content that they had at least scared the daylights out of one intruder.

I spent five more minutes in the lighthouse, shot a little videotape, and then got the heck out of there. I didn't even stop outside of the fortified entrance to look at the display of authentic Algarve handcrafts (made in Morocco). I went back into Sagres and toured the fort there. Prince Henry the Navigator established a school about 1420 inside the fort to study cartography, navigation, and shipbuilding. The well-preserved chapel inside the fort walls was built for Henry. I shot lots of videotape there in the hope that some of it might turn out.

Later, I found a room in the middle of town for about $40. It was a third floor walk-up, but had a terrace with a great view of the ocean. The owner had just opened it up for the season. I was her first guest. After doing my wash in the room, I stepped out to a small café on the Village Square for a whole pizza margherita. I'm ready to head east tomorrow.

Wednesday, April 11th
Sagres to Praia da Rocha - 69.4 Km

As I was leaving the front door of the guesthouse this morning, an athletic girl with her own bike in hand asked me if I had stayed in the room on the third floor adjacent to her. This could have been a trick question. I don't think that I was laughing too loud at the *Green Acres* reruns last night. And, no one has ever proven to me that I snore. So, I hesitantly said, "Yes." She explained that her friend couldn't hear her from the locked front door of their room because she was probably sunning herself out on their balcony. I gave her the key to my room and waited downstairs while she ran up and yelled to her friend from my balcony to open the door. When she came back down she explained that she and her friend were Canadians, cycling much of the same territory that I was cycling in Portugal. The encounter lasted less than two minutes, but I can now say, "Yes, Mom. I did meet some new people on my trip."

The wind was not quite so strong as I left Sagres for the return trip to Vila do Bispo. But, just like last year, the wind seemed to turn from the northwest to the southeast as I headed down the coast on the N125. The ride still wasn't too difficult. One of the links on my chain did start to freeze up, but I did a little roadside maintenance and continued on. I've started to look out for bike shops to replace the chain. I had the same problem last year, so it probably needs to go.

I'm in Praia da Rocha tonight where I found a McDonalds and a $25 hotel room one block back from the beach. What more could I ask for? The fancy Hotel Rocha on the beach probably costs about $100/night. I went directly to the Hotel Rocha II (a wholly owned subsidiary of Hotel Rocha) to get my room. This place is dead. They were happy to have my business. I just have to go across the street tomorrow, to the Hotel Rocha, to get my complimentary breakfast. Rick Steves, eat your heart out. I walked the length of the beach this afternoon. It's a bit like Miami Beach, but with just a few more Europeans. And, the hotels are on cliffs above the beach. I finished the day writing a few postcards. I have a feeling that those won't be the last postcards that I mail home during this trip.

Thursday, April 12th
Praia da Rocha to Olhao - 81.1 Km

I had a good night's sleep and a good breakfast at the hotel in Praia da Rocha. Cycling out of Portimao was difficult, just as I remembered from last year's visit. Early in the ride today a dog jumped at me as I cycled past. I veered away, into traffic, and got honked at. That pretty well ruined my day. For the rest of the day I was scanning the horizon, looking for other dogs that might want a piece of me. That was more physically draining than the headwinds.

I stayed on the main road, the N125, in order to see the fewest stray dogs. Most of them are afraid of cars. Not all, though. I did see a couple unfortunate ones by the side of the road that had been hit. I passed Faro and looked for the campground in Olhao. It was at the end of a street that looked like it was right out of the Gaza Strip. I just knew that there were dogs waiting in the rubble to pounce on unsuspecting cyclists. I turned around, went back to the other side of town, and booked a $20 room in an average hotel. At least I'm indoors tonight. Dinner was what I could scrounge from a BP gas station mini-market.

Friday, April 13th
Olhao to Monte Gordo - 45.7 Km

I cycled hard today, Good Friday, in hopes of getting to the post office at Monte Gordo to pick up my first mail drop. I thought that they might close at noon. There were a lot of cyclists on the road today. Nobody was at work. I started to worry that it might be a national holiday in this very Catholic country. It turns out that it is a national holiday. I arrived around 11:30 AM. Two local cyclists led me past the post office, explained that it wouldn't be open until Monday, and then led me to the nearby campground. It looks like I'm going to stay here for three nights. It's a little frustrating because I'm just five Km from Spain, but I'll wait it out. There's a nice beach across the street, so I'll work on evening out the tan. I walked a few Km on the beach in the afternoon. I'll try to find the church for Easter mass. Then, Monday, I'll stop by the post office at 9:00 AM to ask for my package of maps and books for Spain and beyond.

Saturday, April 14th
Monte Gordo - 0 Km

What did I do today? Not much. I went to the beach for a couple of hours. Then, I went into town exploring. The centerpiece of the town is the casino, but it didn't appear to be open. There are a few hotels, lots of shopping, and many places to eat. When I walked back into town later in the day, I bought a pizza. I seem to be getting by on just one big meal per day. Other than that, I didn't do anything. And, there's nothing wrong with that.

Sunday, April 15th
Monte Gordo - 0 Km

Easter Sunday. Again, I did very little today. I got up at 8:00 AM to go into town for the 9:00 AM mass. When I got to the church, it was closed. It actually looked like it was de-commissioned. It was very old, small, and plain. The surroundings were less than desirable. There was only a stray dog asleep on the front steps of the church. I walked back to the campground, convinced that all of the Catholics in Monte Gordo had to go to mass in the next town. I asked at the front desk of the campground and at a nearby hotel. They both said that there would be a 10:30 AM mass at the church that I had just visited. When I got back to the church, it was 9:50 AM and people were pouring into the little structure. Thinking that the mass started at 10:00 AM, I stood in the back and watched the last five or ten seats get filled.

The mass didn't start at 10:00 AM. The ritual of squeezing twice-a-year Catholics into a too-small church began then. By 10:30 AM, the 250-seat church had about 500 people in it, and spilling out the back. They put seats on the altar. They brought the children to the front to sit on the floor. They brought out footstools for the parishioners to sit on. I was glad that I took the time to shower this morning. I wish others had.

These Portuguese are a sturdy lot because I only saw one woman faint during the hour mass. They lifted her up and carried her out like she had just passed out in the front row of a Beatles concert. When it came time for the collection, the sack was passed right out the back door. Even more surprising, it was passed back in a few minutes later. There were no processions up the main aisle. That was also filled with parishioners. When the priest said that we should "go in peace", we all sort of fell out of the place. Christmas mass must be a real treat in this town.

After mass I was ready for some beach time. I went down to one of the hotel beaches and sprung 1,000 escudos ($4.50) for my very own lounge chair and umbrella. Normally I would have just used my shirt as a beach towel and lay on the sand. But, I decided to splurge today since I was only spending around $5/night for the campsite these three nights. After four hours vegetating on the beach, I made use of the campground's washing machine and dryer. They are a rarity around here, so I took advantage of them.

Spain, Gibraltar & Morocco

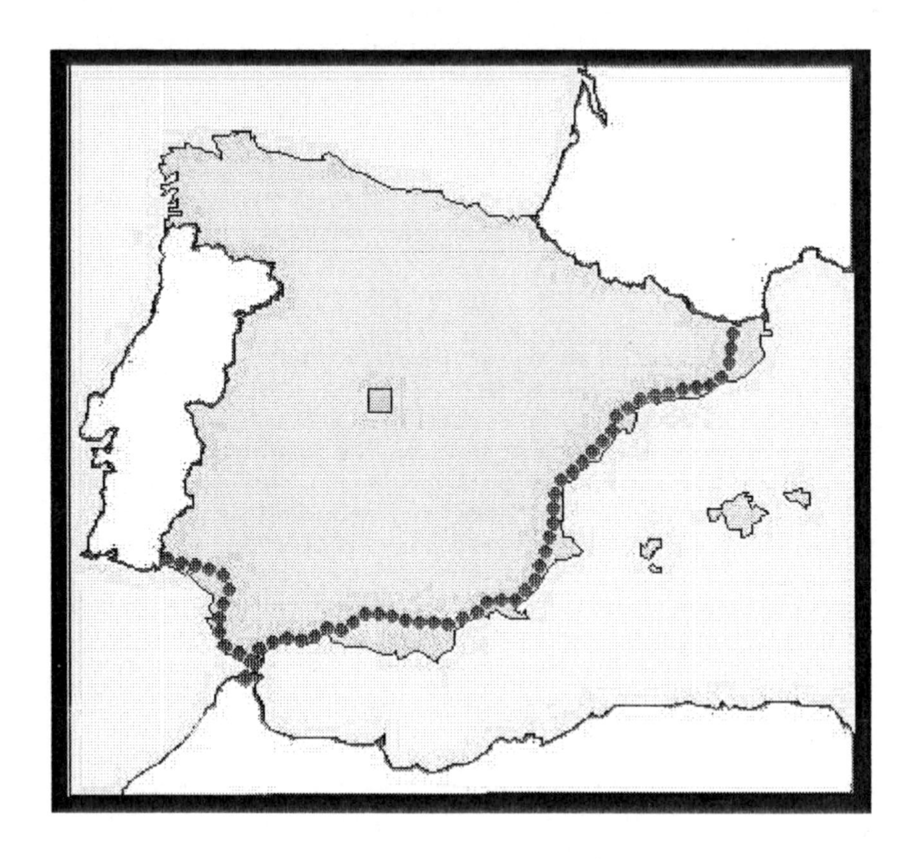

Monday, April 16th
Monte Gordo to Huelva - 66.2 Km

I couldn't believe my eyes when I saw the package that I had sent to myself Poste Restante two weeks ago from the United States being pulled out of a filing cabinet in the Monte Gordo post office. I had imagined a dozen different scenarios for the fate of that package of books and maps, but none of them involved me receiving it as soon as I entered the post office. So, I decided to push my luck. I bought a small box and mailed back a few extra items. I didn't even pay to register the package. I'm putting the global postal system to the test. If they can't find my parent's home, my spare maps and clothes will be returned to the Monte Gordo Campismo, where I imagine they will be divvied up amongst the staff.

By 11:30 AM I was on my way to the border at Vila Real de Santo Antonio. A 15-minute ferry ride across the Rio Guadiana took me to Ayamonte, Spain. I could immediately sense the better standard of living on this side of the river. The Spanish take better care of their cities and seem to have a more vibrant economy. I didn't do Ayamonte justice because I was anxious to put some Km behind me. It had a nice main plaza and lots of unique shops on the haphazard streets radiating out from the plaza. I did meet another Canadian woman who admired my bike and told me about her bike-touring trip in the Pacific Northwest. As soon as I left town I could tell that I wasn't in Portugal anymore. The N431 had wide, smooth shoulders. And, there wasn't a stray dog to be seen. I even had a tailwind. I was in heaven.

Besides the Canadian woman, I met a few more people today. I spoke to three retired ladies from the U.S. doing a bus tour while I exchanged my escudos for pesetas. One of them asked if I was a college student. Being 20 years out of college, I took that as a compliment. Then, I spoke with some laborers at a gas station. They advised me on the fastest route to Huelva, and then cheered for me a few minutes later as they drove past me on the A492. I also met a retired Dutch gentleman in Huelva who I had spoken with on the ferry ride four hours earlier. He was also on a bus tour and gave me directions to the Tourist Information office in Huelva. I'm in a newly refurbished hotel in Huelva tonight. I lost an hour in the time zone change at the border crossing, so I need to get some sleep.

Tuesday, April 17th
Huelva to Seville - 90 Km

That 90 Km is just an educated guess. The cyclometer died this morning. I then wasted about five Km trying to get out of Huelva on the correct road. The signs to Seville said it was 85 Km away. So, 90 Km sounds about right.

I had tea and toast in the hotel restaurant before leaving. Then, I spent about an hour in a mobile phone store trying to get e-mail transmissions to work with my Motorola Timeport. Finally, after another overseas call to Voicestream Customer Service, I apparently have the ability. I tested it tonight and will wait to see if there is any response from the recipients.

By mid-morning I was rolling. It was a little cool and cloudy, but still pleasant riding weather. For the first time I went without the sunscreen and sunglasses. I'm peeling nicely now, thanks to the strong sun in the Algarve. The terrain was rolling, and the A472 needed some patching in places. But, it was better than the Portuguese roads. At one point in the day, while I was in a tuck position on my aerodynamic handlebars, a bee flew down the neck of my shirt. I must have been a sight to see as I hurried to un-tuck my shirt to let the bee out before it stung me. Too late. It got me at the collarbone.

As the day progressed, the tailwinds picked up. I got stronger throughout the day and was really moving by the time that I hit Seville. I rode right to the Hotel Inglaterra in the center of town to claim a "care package" from home at the attached American Express office. Amex directed me to the central post office to retrieve the box. Wonder of wonders, they had my package. I was two for two in this global mailing game.

I cycled around town a little, trying to find the right hotel. I settled on the Hotel Venecia. I don't know where they get off giving this place three stars, but I'll take it for $45/night. I'll play tourist tomorrow and visit the must-see sights.

Wednesday, April 18th
Seville - 0 Km

I toured the Cathedral, Giralda, and Alcazar today. I saw where Columbus and his son are entombed, and where Magellan's trip around the world was planned, in the Cathedral. Magellan never survived his 1519 expedition around the world. Natives in the Philippines murdered him in 1521. Only 18 of 270 men, and one of the original five ships, returned to Seville in 1522. I'm hoping for a better outcome to my trip. Just to be safe, I'll avoid the Philippines.

My back was sore from all of the walking, so I went back to the hotel to stretch for a while in the afternoon. I did buy and install a new cyclometer on the bike. Later, I went back out in search of pizza. I had no luck, so I ate at McDonalds for the third day in a row. Some things never change. Tomorrow I'll try to cycle past the Gold Tower and the bullfighting ring as I leave town.

Thursday, April 19th
Seville to El Cuervo - 78.65 Km

I didn't get all the way to Jerez, as I had hoped. But, I did well considering the circumstances. I cycled to Dos Hermanas on the A4, and then got onto the N4. About half of the distance was over a rough road surface that severely increased rolling resistance and affected my hands and wrists. I hope that I don't run into that gravel topcoat on too many other roads in Spain. The headwinds were also pretty stiff today. The ride was mostly through flat farmland. There's very little to see or do here. There are only truck stops along the way. I had a ham sandwich at one truck stop for lunch. I did shoot some video of the bullfighting ring and Gold Tower before I left Seville.

I stopped today around 5:15 PM at this little truck stop hotel because I knew that I had another hard hour and a half ahead of me to reach Jerez. This place will cost me about $15. I've got a plan to save 100 Km by ferrying to Tangier from Cadiz, and returning to Spain at Algeciras. I may even return directly to Gibraltar. I could be in Morocco tomorrow night. More likely, it will be Saturday.

Friday, April 20th
El Cuervo to Cadiz - 50.03 Km

It was another tough 50 Km on the N4. The headwinds coming up from the Mediterranean were relentless. I had some more of those rough surfaced shoulders to bounce over. I cycled around the western edge of Jerez instead of cutting through the center of town. I was in no mood to sightsee. When I finally got to El Puerto de Santa Maria to take the ferry to Cadiz, I saw a class of young students from the American naval base school at Roto disembarking. The kids and their parents must have taken a field trip. I spoke to one of the parents to ask about laundromats in Cadiz. She suggested that I use the one at the base, but I was anxious to keep moving south. It was nice to speak English again, though.

The bike sat at the bow of the tiny ferry to Cadiz catching a lot of the sea spray. There was no other spot to place it. Not good. I sat inside, out of the wind. When I finally got to Cadiz, I decided to splurge and take a room in a parador, an upscale hotel administered by the Spanish government. This place costs about $60, but I was able to wash all of my laundry in the tub. Now, I have to find out when the next ferry to Tangier departs.

Saturday, April 21st
Cadiz to Tahivilla - 81.71 Km

Well, the company that ran the ferry service between Cadiz and Tangier either went bankrupt or doesn't sail that route any more. I couldn't completely understand the guard at the port entrance gate. But, I understood the key points. 1) They did sail that route last year. 2) They don't sail that route this year. 3) I wasn't going to Morocco today.

The day started with me watching my clothes slowly dry on the balcony of my room in the Cadiz parador. There was no sense in stuffing wet clothes into my panniers. I had until noon to checkout, so I waited until 11:45 AM to pack. While paying my bill in less-than-arid cycling shorts, I realized that I was automatically charged for breakfast. So, as a matter of principle, I ran down to the parador restaurant and asked when they stopped serving breakfast. When the answer came back "in five minutes", I sat down and ordered tea and toast. I stuffed a sugar packet in my pocket as I left.

Today was one of those days when I could have done either 50 Km or 100 Km because there appeared to be a 50 Km stretch on the map where there were no towns or services. At 50 Km I came upon Vejer, a hill-town dating back to long before bicycle touring was ever popular. I took one look up at that town and decided I would rather cycle another 50 Km on the N340 than try to climb that hill. I should have known that it was a hill-town because the map had viewpoint symbols printed on three sides of the town.

So, I took the risk and got lucky when I came upon this town, Tahivilla, 25 Km down the road. I'm paying $11 for a decent room in the Hotel Apollo XI. Dinner in the attached restaurant (steak, fries, and ice cream) costs more than the room.

Sunday, April 22nd
Tahivilla to Gibraltar - 75.38 Km

I'm back in an English speaking territory again. The day began with a mass that did not start at 10:00 AM, as promised by the Apollo XI innkeeper, but at 11:00 AM. It was held in a second-floor classroom of the town's elementary school, not in the nearby locked church. There were only about 50 of us attending, mostly women and grade school children. The men waited in the courtyard for their wives and children. After mass I got back on the N340 heading south to Tarifa. On the way to the southern tip of the Iberian Peninsula I passed many campgrounds, hotels, and shops catering to windsurfers. The winds squeezing through the Straights of Gibraltar can be very strong. Fortunately, they were at my back and side most of the day. I needed the tailwinds to push me over the difficult 310-meter high hump from Tarifa on the Atlantic coast to Algeciras on the Mediterranean coast. It must have taken me well over an hour of stiff climbing in my lowest gear to reach the top. The views were great, though. I stopped a few times to videotape the view across the Straights to Africa.

I continued through Algeciras and around the bay to Gibraltar. Gibraltar has a passport checkpoint upon entry. Then you walk or drive right across their only airport runway to get into town. I found the Queen's Hotel to be fairly well situated for all that I needed to accomplish here. I may stay for three or four nights. I need to have my chain repaired or replaced. I need to work on my PC/phone problems. I need a haircut. I need to mail back a few items. I want to take a daytrip to Morocco. I also want to tour Gibraltar. That should all take a few days.

Monday, April 23rd
Gibraltar - 0 Km

I played tourist today. But first, I walked up and down Main Street looking for help with my Pocket PC and mobile phone. Unfortunately, there are no Compaq reps in Gibraltar. I did leave the bike with a shop that had a part-time repairman, to take care of the bad chain. Then, I took the gondola ride up to spend the afternoon on the Rock's Upper Nature Reserve. I walked a few Km up there and shot a lot of videotape of the Rock Apes, St. Michael's Cave, and the Moorish Castle. The weather was great for photographing the awesome panoramas. The apes, Barbary macaques actually, were a lot of fun too. They're the last 243 free-ranging primates on the European continent. They've learned to "Yogi", or beg for food, where the tourists congregate. They do have an aggressive streak, but they will never be removed from the Rock. Legend has it that when the last ape leaves Gibraltar, Britain will loose this strategic possession. So, the locals are willing to put up with a little monkey business.

I finished up the day with a pizza back at sea level. I arrived at the Pizza Hut just as a parade started down Main Street. I think that they were celebrating St. George's Day. Anyway, there were a lot of bagpipers and scout troops marching up Main Street.

They say that bagpipers are always marching when they play because they're trying to get away from the racket. I enjoyed it, though. It was a nice way to end an enjoyable day.

Tuesday, April 24th
Gibraltar to Tangier to Gibraltar - 0 Km

I can now add Africa to the list of continents that I've visited. I took the 8:30 AM ferry to Tangier. The crossing took only 1½ hours on an ultra modern catamaran. I had paid for the guided tour and lunch. Somehow, I got my very own personal tour guide. Hassan was 71 years old (maybe it was 81) and spoke five languages. I don't know if English was one of the five because I only understood every other word. Hassan slowly led me around downtown Tangier, occasionally taking me into stores where he would rest after introducing me to a friend/salesman. He took me into a rug store where the salesman had two assistants unfurl about 15 rugs for me to view. After the hard sell I told the salesman that I had no home and would be on a bicycle for the next year and a half. I think that was the first time that he heard that excuse, so he let me leave his store without purchasing anything.

Then, Hassan took me to a spice store where I was taught about the wonders of saffron and other magical spices. After the 15-minute tutorial where jar after jar of spices was stuffed in my face, I was asked how much I wanted to purchase. I explained that I don't cook and don't suffer from the embarrassment of psoriasis, but the salesman wouldn't take "no" for an answer. So, I admitted to having a possible snoring problem and purchased some sort of snuff for $4. I later dumped the snuff on the catamaran back to Gibraltar, convinced that it was hashish and that there were Customs officials just waiting for me to step off of the boat.

After the spice store Hassan took me to an authentic Moroccan restaurant, full of authentic American tourists, for my complimentary lunch. Hassan stayed outside with the other tour guides. I hardly ate anything. Thank goodness. As I got up to leave, a large cockroach scurried across the floor. A waiter deftly stepped on it and kicked it under a table before any of the other tourists saw it. As American tourists go, I think that I was a disappointment to my guide, Hassan. I had spent only $4 all day. So, I gave him a dollar tip when I said goodbye. Maybe that would help him save face with his fellow hustlers.

Back in Gibraltar there was another parade. You have to love the British for their sense of pomp and tradition. This was my second parade in as many days here. This one accompanied the monthly ceremony that recreates the locking of the gates during the Great Siege of 1783. I just happened upon the event when I saw all of the tourists milling about the main square late in the day. The Chief Minister arrived in a Rolls Royce with the license plate "G 1". He was dressed in full Horatio Hornblower regalia. He inspected the troops. The band played *God Save the Queen*. They set off some cannons up on the Rock. It all took about 45 minutes. The Gibraltarians can once again sleep safely tonight knowing that the marauding Spanish hoards outside of the gates will be unable to storm across the border and destroy their Marks & Spencer.

I learned later tonight, as I watched the news on the Gibraltar Broadcasting Corporation station, that I missed an opportunity to meet Monty Python's Michael Palin today. He was interviewed at the ceremony by the GBC. He's in Gibraltar preparing for a television series about traveling around the Sahara. I would have loved to tell him about my plans to go around the world, since he did just that in his first travel series.

I also got the bike back. The chain was cleaned, oiled, and un-kinked for about $7.50. I hope that's all it needed. I'll find out soon enough.

Wednesday, April 25th
Gibraltar to Torre Real - 96.83 Km

I've finally, reluctantly left Gibraltar. But, before I did, I got a haircut and mailed home some more dead weight. I also sent off a few postcards and spent the last of my Gibraltar pounds at the BP station as I left "Little England."

I'm on the Costa del Sol now, so the traffic has definitely picked up. There aren't too many choices of roads to take up the coast. I ended up on the N340, which is signed to be off-limits to bikes. But the locals rode it, and they told me that I could. So, I did. The road was OK, but the one tunnel that I went through was a little nerve-wracking. It was about 300 meters long, and the noise from passing traffic was deafening. I'm staying in a campground just past Marbella tonight.

Thursday, April 26th
Torre Real to Malaga - 66.87 Km

I broke camp this morning and continued along the coast on the N340. There was heavy traffic most of the way to Malaga. It was a fairly cloudy day. I stopped at one beach to have a quick snack, but most of the way I just kept to the highway.

I went through the usual hassles of trying to find a laundromat to wash my clothes. I ended up getting a room in a hotel in Malaga and hand-washing again. The problem is that it's too cool for the clothes to dry, and I'm too late to hang them in the sun. I have a big climb tomorrow, and I'll probably be carrying five extra pounds because the clothes are still not dry. I can't win.

Friday, April 27th
Malaga to Villanueva del Rosario - 44.97 Km

It took four hours of climbing to get off of the Costa del Sol and over the Sierra Madres. My knees are jelly tonight. This sets me up for arrival in Granada tomorrow night, if I have the strength to do the 85 Km.

As expected, the clothes did not dry overnight in Malaga. I had to carry the extra weight up a killer hill. I took the N331 north along the Rio Guadalmedina and through the Puerto de las Pedrizas at 804 meters. I veered off towards Loja on the A359 at that point. That route had me on autovias all day. Bikes are supposedly prohibited, but none of the passing Guardia Civil stopped me. There are no other roads that go this direction. Since I was last in Spain ten years ago, they took all of their long-distance roads and upgraded them to autovias. The only new roads that they've built are autopistas, which definitely don't allow bikes. So, if I want to go long distances, I'm forced to use the autovias. They have gradual grades and nice wide shoulders, but the traffic can be heavy and fast. I cycled through a couple more tunnels today. There are small sidewalks in the tunnels on which to ride. For claustrophobic, squeamish, or wobbly cyclists those little sidewalks are not ideal.

I stopped for dinner in a roadside rest stop and realized after eating that there was a brand new hotel added to the complex. I booked a comfortable room for $25 and am, at this moment, watching my clothes dry on the heater. Now, it's on to Granada and a much needed rest day.

Saturday, April 28th
Villanueva del Rosario to Granada - 108.64 Km

I stayed mostly on the A92 autovia today. The Guardia Civil still haven't stopped me for cycling on these autovias. I exited once in Loja to check out a parallel local road. There was no shoulder, the traffic moved just as fast, and the road was poorly graded. I got back on the autovia ASAP.

I didn't read the map well enough before entering Granada and added about another hour to my ride. Aaargh! Then, I wasted well over an hour trying to find a hotel in the middle of town. No luck. After being turned down at about ten hotels, I cycled out to the edge of town to the campground. Here at the campground, an

Australian couple told me that it is a festival week in Granada and people are streaming in from all over. I set up camp and prepared to spend a cold night in the tent.

Sunday, April 29th
Granada - 6.6 Km

It was bone-chilling cold last night. I'm definitely in the hills. The weather report that I got on my mobile phone yesterday said that the overnight low would be 44 degrees. I believe it. It was hard to get out of the sleeping bag and into the cold air this morning, but I did. I ventured into the city to see the Alhambra. I was at the ticket office by 11:00 AM and waited in line for an hour to get an afternoon ticket with access to the Nazerene Palaces at 7:00 PM. They limit the number of tickets sold each day, so I was lucky to get what I did.

I walked down to the city for a little sightseeing while I waited for my 2:00 PM entry time at the Alhambra to arrive. Just before 2:00 PM I trudged back up the hill to wait with the other afternoon ticket holders. These rest days are going to kill me. I spent the next five and a half hours exploring every nook in the Alhambra, the Generalife, the Palaces, and the Alcazar. There is even a four-star parador and a one-star hotel within the walls of the Alhambra. I wish I had booked ahead at one of those places. The parador probably would have set me back over $200/night, but it would have been worth it.

While I was looking over the city from the highest tower of the Alcazar, I got a call from my younger brother. He was concerned about the message that I left on his answering machine last night during my frantic search for a hotel. I assured him that I survived the night and that I would stay at the campground again tonight. He's going to see if it's possible to book ahead via the Internet before I hit the next big town. Before hanging up I had to tell him about the great view and give him a vicarious travel thrill before he started his workday back in Philadelphia.

After viewing the opulent Palaces in my allotted half-hour, I headed back to my simple campsite for the night. I grabbed a burger and fries from a Burger King across the street and got into the tent just as it started to rain. It wasn't much more than a drizzle, but it's the first that I've seen on this trip.

Monday, April 30th
Granada to Baza - 85.93 Km

I was back on the A92 autovia this morning, riding to Gaudix. The plan was to ride only 50 or 60 Km because the legs were not fully recovered from climbing all over the Alhambra. Of course, I ended up going much farther. The road out of Granada took me farther up into the hills. I was sweating profusely due to the effort, but freezing because of the frigid temperatures. After an hour of out-of-the-saddle climbing in just a T-shirt and windbreaker, I took off the soaked T-shirt and put on a polypropylene turtleneck shirt, a wool turtleneck sweater, and the windbreaker. I was much more comfortable after that. Dropping out of the hills also helped. The temperature rose as I descended. At Gaudix I cycled past the exits to the town. Any possible hotels there would have been off of the road by one or two Km. I continued on to where the autovia splits in two, hoping to find accommodations there. No luck. So, I continued on the A92N into an area that looked a lot like the American Southwest. It was wide-open country. I ended up riding another 35 Km before I found this little hostel/restaurant. It's only costing me $20 for the night. The dinner in the restaurant cost nearly as much. At least I'm inside and warm.

Tuesday, May 1st
Baza to Puerto Lumbreras - 122.12 Km

It was a day of extremes. Extreme cold. Extreme tailwinds. Extremely long descents. It all contributed to my biggest mileage day so far on this trip.

When I finally got rolling this morning at 10:00 AM, the weather was frigid. After a few Km I stopped to put a pair of socks and sandwich Baggies over my hands to keep them warm. I was pushed along all day by the fierce tailwind. The A92N runs between two mountain ranges, and the westerly wind was funneled right between them. Today was a national holiday in Spain, so there wasn't much traffic on the autovia. I did see a few cars with snow skis on their roof racks. Snow in the south of Spain in May? Who would have thought that it could get that cold? Certainly not I.

Like yesterday, I had to stop to remove a soaked cotton T-shirt and replace it with a polypropylene turtleneck. I had a sit-down lunch at that point. That's a rare occurrence, but I needed to dry my wool sweater and windbreaker. After lunch I had my longest descent ever. It seemed to be about 30 or 35 Km long. And, I still had the killer tailwind. I wasn't pedaling at all and was still cruising at 40 Km/hour. At one point I reached 73.9 Km/hour. That's "dangerous" fast.

Near the end of the day, I stopped to buy a quick snack and a new map. As I got back on the bike I realized that I had a flat rear tire. It was my first flat of the trip. A half-inch nail had found its way around the side of the Kevlar belt on the tire. I took the opportunity to replace both the tube and tire. The old tire is now my reserve. I was fortunate to discover the puncture at a rest stop, rather than on the road at 73.9 Km/hour.

This town has a parador and campground. The campground on one side of town appears to be closed, and the parador on the other side of town looks too expensive. So, I compromised. I took a $35 room in a nice three-star hotel in the middle of town.

Wednesday, May 2nd
Puerto Lumbreras to Cartegena - 115.91 Km

It was another good mileage day. And, this was without the aid of tailwinds or long descents. I'm just getting a little stronger. A good bit of the day was even into a headwind.

I rode from Puerto Lumbreras to Totano on the N340 in the morning, and then finally got off of the autovia. The secondary road, MU602 to Cartegena, was not bad. The riding was a fairly uneventful. At the end of the day I did some extra cycling around Cartegena looking for a good hotel. The campground signs were nowhere to be found. The town has some history to it, and a decent port. But, it's rough around the edges. I think that I'll be happy to get out of here tomorrow. I won't even check out the Roman Amphitheater.

The weather has been cool and partly cloudy for many days now. I'm anxious to cycle up the coast and find a campground on a beach to relax for a day. I need to get my wash done in the worst way. The weather will change for the better on Saturday, but I'll need to stop tomorrow afternoon for the wash.

Thursday, May 3rd
Cartegena to Los Alcazares - 39.9 Km

This was a wasted day. After only two and a half hours of riding on the N301 and N332, I stopped when I came across a campground with a washing machine. Then, I had to hang everything out and wait for it to dry. While I waited I cleaned the bike and checked for any mechanical failures. I did catch a loose nut on the front wheel's quick-release hub. Other than that, I didn't see or do much.

Friday, May 4th
Los Alcazares to Santa Pola - 71.45 Km

There was a tough headwind all day. It was also cloudy and cool. So, the elements were not in my favor today. And, as I reached Santa Pola, it began to rain. I spent the first half of the day cycling on a portion of the N332 that is under construction. I even cycled through a newly constructed tunnel. It was about a half Km long, and very dark. My front light seems to have failed. I may need a new bulb. It's been taking a beating on the rough surfaces.

When I reached Santa Pola, I found myself cycling for a few minutes towards this hotel up on a hill, trying to decide if it was worth splurging for a night in a posh room. When I saw a bolt of lightning, I quickly made up my mind. I cycled into the shelter of the back lobby just as a heavy rain hit. For $40, I have a very nice room with a panoramic view for the night. I even had a steak dinner in the hotel restaurant.

This is a popular area for British and German tourists. Many of them retire to the Costa Blanca. At dinner I spoke with a British gentleman who had just purchased his retirement flat and had come down to inspect the progress on its construction. I was alone in the restaurant, playing on the piano, when he walked in and immediately recognized the tune, *Pictures at an Exhibition* by Mussorgsky. It felt good to practice both my piano playing and my English. Since I don't plan on any rest days in the near future, the good meal and a good night's sleep should help.

It's now one month since I started. There are only 17 more to go. I've ridden 1,700 Km, or 1,050 miles, so far. I'm right on schedule.

Saturday, May 5th
Santa Pola to Benidorm - 62.6 Km

It's funny how what you eat affects the way you feel. For the first time in this trip I hit the wall. And, it's all because of the second bag of candy that I ate late in the day. I ride, more or less continuously, for five to six hours every day. I don't stop for lunch. But, I often stop for cold drinks and snacks at gas stations. They all have mini-markets, just like in the States. My regular purchases are Gatorade or Aquarius (a similar sports drink), a croissant, and some candy. I would only buy candy once each day, even though I stop four or five times. Today I bought a second bag of candy late in the afternoon. The second half of the day had been strenuous on the N332. The road went up and down hills along the coast and into the wind. Almost immediately after the rest stop where I had the second bag of candy, I bonked. I had to pull off to the side of the road, behind a windbreak and regain my strength. About 10 minutes later I got back on the bike and wobbled into Benidorm.

This town has a great beach in front and an amusement park in the hills behind it. They are building high-rises all along the crescent shaped beach. It looks a little like Rio de Janeiro from the air. I'm on one of the top floors in my hotel. There's a great view from my balcony up here. I'm going to stay for two nights and hopefully regain some strength in the legs.

I'll be able to attend mass tomorrow in the church down the street. The first mass is at noon. They do everything later in Spain.

Sunday, May 6th
Benidorm - 0 Km

The mantra for today was, "Relax." I tried not to exert myself too much in an effort to let the muscles recover. I feel like I've been really working the quads lately. Even on my off days in Granada and Gibraltar, I was climbing hills all day. My back was also a little tender yesterday because I had been using my whole body to climb some of the hills lately. When I get out of the saddle for the tougher hills the muscles in the lower back get a workout.

I went to the noon mass in the ultra-modern glass-walled church near my hotel. Despite five years of Spanish classes in Catholic schools, I didn't understand most of the mass. I did stand and sit on cue, though. Then, I took a short stroll along the beach road. I stopped into an Internet café for a half-hour of access. Dinner was a pizza.

But, the big news of the day was that I was finally able to access the Internet from my Pocket PC over a landline. Oh, happy day! I can't make the connection via infrared with my mobile phone, but I'm still thrilled. I immediately started to browse the web. There are many PC things that I still can't do. But, at least I'm on-line now and can e-mail various tech-support departments for help.

Monday, May 7th
Benidorm to Mareny de Barraguetes - 129.67 Km

The rest yesterday really helped. I felt strong throughout the day. It was a great day to ride. The weather was almost perfect. Lots of sun. Not too hot. Not too cold. Not too windy. The two hills that had me worried were not a problem. The first one, coming out of Benidorm, I had been looking at all day yesterday. It turns out that the road leaving town skirts it. The second hill, as shown on the map, had a very gradual climb. It went on for many Km but was never too steep.

The rest of the day was relatively painless. It did drag on, though. I had gotten a late start and finished late trying to find a campground. I didn't find one until I got off of the N332 at Cullera. I cycled through orange groves on the local coast road until I reached the Mareny de Barraquetes campground. This place is almost deserted. There's just one other couple in an RV here for the night. Dinner was a loaf of bread and a bottle of Coke, and a Kit Kat for dessert. Just like at home.

Tuesday, May 8th
Mareny de Barraguetes to Benicasim - 117 Km

I went right past Valencia without so much as a glance at the city center. I stayed right on the coast and cycled past the port. I know from experience that I lose time and patience in large cities. I'm sure that Valencia has some interesting sites, but not for me today. Besides, Valencia is playing Leeds in soccer tonight and I wanted to be out of town before the British hooligans began to tear it apart.

I left Valencia on the N221 and headed a bit inland to Sagunto. I spoke for about 15 minutes with an old Spanish guy at a gas station there about my bike, the road north, and the Valencia - Leeds match. From what I could understand, the price of tickets and hotel rooms has been jacked up for this game. He thought that I was wise to get out of town.

After Sagunto the road north ran parallel to the A7 autopiste, crossing over it a couple of times. I felt strong again. I seem to gain strength throughout the day. It could be that the legs go on autopilot after a few hours. Or, it could be that the occasional Kit Kat, Twix, and Snickers bars are real energy boosters. Either way, I went farther than I had planned. The old Spanish guy suggested that I stay in one of the many hotels in Castellon Beach. Well, of the two that I found, one was booked solid and the other was a one-star. I continued cycling north another pleasant six Km to this hotel. It's on the beach and full of pensioners. It turns out that they're here tonight to hear the Hammond Organ Wizard of the Costa del Azahar. I'm one floor above the festivities. This guy had the bass pedals pumping and the Magic Chords Accompaniment going. And, he sang the greatest hits of the Castellon region...for two sets...until midnight. The pensioners seemed to enjoy the Wizard because they were dancing and clapping and singing right along with him...for two sets...until midnight.

Wednesday, May 9th
Benicasim to Peniscola - 67.28 Km

Those were 67 difficult Km today. It was another dreary morning, so I didn't get started until 11:00 AM. It was cool, so I wore the polypropylene turtleneck, the wool sweater, and the windbreaker. The windbreaker acted like a sail in the stiff headwinds that I encountered all day. I had to pedal *down* many hills because of the wind resistance. I couldn't see any sights. I was in an aero tuck all day with my chin in my chest.

I had to go up into the hills on the N340 for much of the day. When I came down in Benicarlo, I looked around for a hotel room. All three hotels were booked solid. It was recommended that I go south four or five Km to Peniscola to find a room. As much as I hate to backtrack, I did go south along the beach. I found the entire town of Peniscola to be a construction site. After snaking my way south through the torn up streets, I found a nice condo complex where rooms were available for $25. I'm on the 8th floor, looking out at the Mediterranean Sea. And, it's raining. I had the opportunity to camp out, but decided against it. Good decision. I did my laundry and had a snack in the complex bar. I conversed with the Romanian bartender for a half-hour in Spanish. Maybe the five years of Spanish classes weren't a total waste after all. I'm happy to be indoors tonight.

Thursday, May 10th
Peniscola - 0 Km

It rained all day. I saw on the news that it was clear all day in Valencia, about 100 Km south of here. The weather farther up the coast in Barcelona has been unsettled for weeks it seems. Saturday in Barcelona looks to be sunny. So, if I can get through tomorrow, I should have a good ride Saturday into the city. It looks like more rain is expected on Sunday, though. That might be another good day to rest. I would be in Barcelona on a Sunday. I could go to mass and see some sights. Then, I could get back on the road Monday, hopefully. I've got a feeling that I might have started this trip about a month too early, based upon the weather I'm experiencing. I may have to slow down a little as I head north into France to let the good weather catch up.

As I approach the French border, the urge to continue along the Mediterranean Sea through France and right into Italy grows. The weather should be fine in Italy, and that is ultimately the direction that I need to go in order to complete the goal. I could beat the July and August crowds in Rome and the Greek Islands. But if I do that, I might run into the monsoon in India and cold spring weather in Australia and America. I'll see if I can get my world weather spreadsheet sent to me from home before I have to make that decision.

I sent out long e-mail messages to the family today. I feel good about doing that. I may try to send out a few more tonight to friends. I ventured out into the rain twice today, once to have tea and a croissant for breakfast, and then to have a pizza for dinner. I picked up some essentials at a supermarket before dinner (Oreo's, a Kit Kat bar, and hamburger buns). So, breakfast and lunch for tomorrow have been taken care of.

I've also seen too much European television today. Both the German and Spanish versions of *Big Brother* dominate the uncluttered airwaves. The Spanish version is pretty funny because all of the contestants wear sunglasses inside and smoke constantly. They look like the Hollywood stars of the 1940's, except with a euro-trash twist. On the EuroSport channel, the only English-speaking channel that I could get, they had a charity Pro-Am modern pentathlon meet. I didn't recognize any of the European celebrities other than the pole-vaulter Sergie Bubka and Prince Albert of Monaco. I missed the first event. I believe it was running. The next four were pistol shooting, fencing, horse show jumping, and swimming. Fortunately, no one was injured in the pistol shooting or fencing events. Some of the celebs that couldn't ride a horse were pulled around the course like little kids on a pony ride. Other celebs had trouble competing the 100-meter swim. As for Prince Albert, I think he finished in a very respectable second place. Still, I think a future head of state shouldn't be seen in public in a Speedo. But, that's just one man's opinion.

Friday, May 11th
Peniscola to Montroig - 99.68 Km

What a difference a day makes. I woke up to bright sunshine and much warmer temperatures. The wind even seemed to subside a bit in the morning. I quickly got ready and checked out. I was on the road at 10:00 AM, early for me these days. I felt strong again, after the day off. I had planned on stopping at a spot 100 Km down the N340 where there were five campgrounds in the span of about ten Km. As it turns out, that's just how far I went. And, I had the luxury of passing the first campground and choosing the second that I encountered. This campground is easily the best, and most expensive, campground that I've ever visited. It costs $20 for the night. I spent $25 the last two nights in the hotel room/condo. But, I will get to see Gladiator with the other campers in the TV salon tonight for free.

Early in the day a local cyclist joined me. He was on a one-day tour. We rode hard for about an hour into the wind. He pointed out all of the interesting sights: the cement factory, the rice fields, and the highest mountain in the province. His name was Paco, which somehow translates to Francis in English. It was a pleasure riding with Paco. I was a little envious when he turned around and headed home with the wind at his back.

Later on in the day I saw a sad sight. In the distance I could see one dog on its back, moving its legs, but unable to right himself. He was in the middle of the road and had probably just been hit by a car. I'm guessing that his back was broken. Another dog was next to him, unable to do anything to help his friend. I was still approaching the scene when the injured dog got hit in the head by the undercarriage of a truck. I think, and hope, that that was the blow that put him out of his misery. I passed him right after the second hit and he looked like he was just about to die. I kept moving, knowing that I couldn't help. I was a little nervous about the second dog. I didn't know if he would go after me, or also go out into traffic and get hit. It was a sad scene all around, just because some people let their dogs run free. I've seen many dead animals on the side of the road, but this was the first that I saw die in front of me. Very sad.

On the brighter side, I'm one day away from Barcelona. If I'm lucky, I'll get a nice cheap room in the city tomorrow night and tour the city on Sunday. I might even avoid riding in the bad weather predicted for Sunday. That's it for now. It's time to go and watch *Gladiator*.

Saturday, May 12th
Montroig to Gava - 115 Km

Today was my second day in a row with good weather. That may be a record since I've been in Spain. There were some hills, especially at the end of the ride, but nothing too taxing. I even did some boardwalk riding. That's the best. It's flat, sunny, full of places to eat, and the scenery is nice. I hugged the coast most of the day from Tarragona to Sitges. Near Torredembarra there is a Roman triumphal arch in the middle of the road. The Bara Arch is very impressive, situated between the north and south lanes of the N340. I had to stop and shoot some video of the 2,000-year-old structure. After Sitges, the hills were extremely dangerous. I could tell by reading the map that they were almost cliffs that dropped right down to the Mediterranean, but there was only one road for me to take, the C246. The nearby railroad and autopiste tunneled through the mountains. The C246 just hung off of the cliffs. It went up and down and around the coves. There was hardly any shoulder to speak of. The guardrails seemed a little too low for comfort. And, there was a lot of Saturday afternoon traffic. The drivers were all extremely courteous. But, there were times when I was holding up seven or eight cars behind me. There were no places to pull off and let them pass. Eventually we all got through the hills. I found a campground soon after that.

While I was setting up at the campground, a girl came over and introduced herself. She was an American, also on a solo bicycle tour. She had come through the same dangerous stretch of road the day before and enjoyed it. She compared it to the Pacific Coast Highway in California. I told her that I was much more nervous today than when I rode the PCH in 1990. We compared gear and routes, and then agreed to cycle the 15 Km into Barcelona tomorrow together.

I called home today and asked to have the next care package put on hold until I decide which direction I'll be taking when I reach France. I also asked to have my world weather tables sent to me as an e-mail attachment. That spreadsheet, created to show monthly average temperatures and precipitation in all of the cities that I planned to visit, will be the deciding factor in my decision.

Sunday, May 13th
Gava to Barcelona - 13.79 Km

I got up early and was ready to ride into the city by around 9:00 AM. But, I had promised to ride in with the American girl that I met at the campground last night. She wasn't ready until 10:30 AM. Oh, well. I still enjoyed the company for the ride. She had taken the bus into town yesterday and knew the way well. When we arrived, we ran right into a charity walk-a-thon. They had shut down many of the streets in the city center. We just blended right in with mothers and fathers and baby strollers and dogs on the walk-a-thon. The route took us to the Placa de Catalunya, the Times Square of Barcelona. It must be because it has a McDonalds, Burger King, and Planet Hollywood surrounding the square.

We said goodbye there and went our separate ways. It was almost noon, and I was anxious to find a church with a late mass. I found the Basilica de Santa Maria del Mar, a 14th century gothic masterpiece. It shows its 700 years, but its sheer bulk is still impressive. The masses started at 1:00 PM, so I found the nearby Park Hotel and agreed to pay $75 for the night. I dumped off my stuff in the room and went back to the basilica for mass. It was celebrated in Catalunyan, not Castillan, Spanish. I understood even less of the sermon than usual. The organ sounded great, though.

Next, I went out on the town in the standard double-decker tourist bus. In about four hours I saw the exterior of all the major sights, half that were closed anyway. Antonio Gaudi designed the other half. I did get off the bus to walk Las Ramblas with the rest of Barcelona. That's the cool pedestrian walkway cutting through the old part of the city. The newest section of the walkway is on a pier with shops, restaurants, cinemas and an IMAX theater. Like I said, cool. It was a full day. I am dead tired tonight.

Monday, May 14th
Barcelona to Pineda de Mar - 60.49 Km

I started out the day by going back to the Basilica de Santa Maria del Mar to shoot some video and buy a few postcards. Then, I went to an Internet café on Las Ramblas to do some e-mailing. I spent 90 minutes there. Once again, I got a late start on the riding. I ended up only doing 60 Km, despite great conditions. I stopped at 5:30 PM at one of the last campgrounds before I turn inland to go over the Pyrenees into France. Now, I may not hit France until Wednesday because of today's late start. I'm staying very well connected to friends and family, but I can't let it cut into riding time.

A good bit of the riding today was along the Costa del Maresme on the N11. In most places there were no boardwalks, but gravel paths. That's not good for the bike. I should have stayed on the road on the other side of the train tracks. There wasn't much of a shoulder on that road, though. The area north of Barcelona is very industrial, congested, and a bit rough. On the plus side, I didn't exert too much energy today. That will be helpful tomorrow. I'm going to try to break camp early and make every effort to get to France tomorrow night, 120 Km away. They're predicting rain in Perpignan on Wednesday. I don't want to ride in that.

France & Monaco

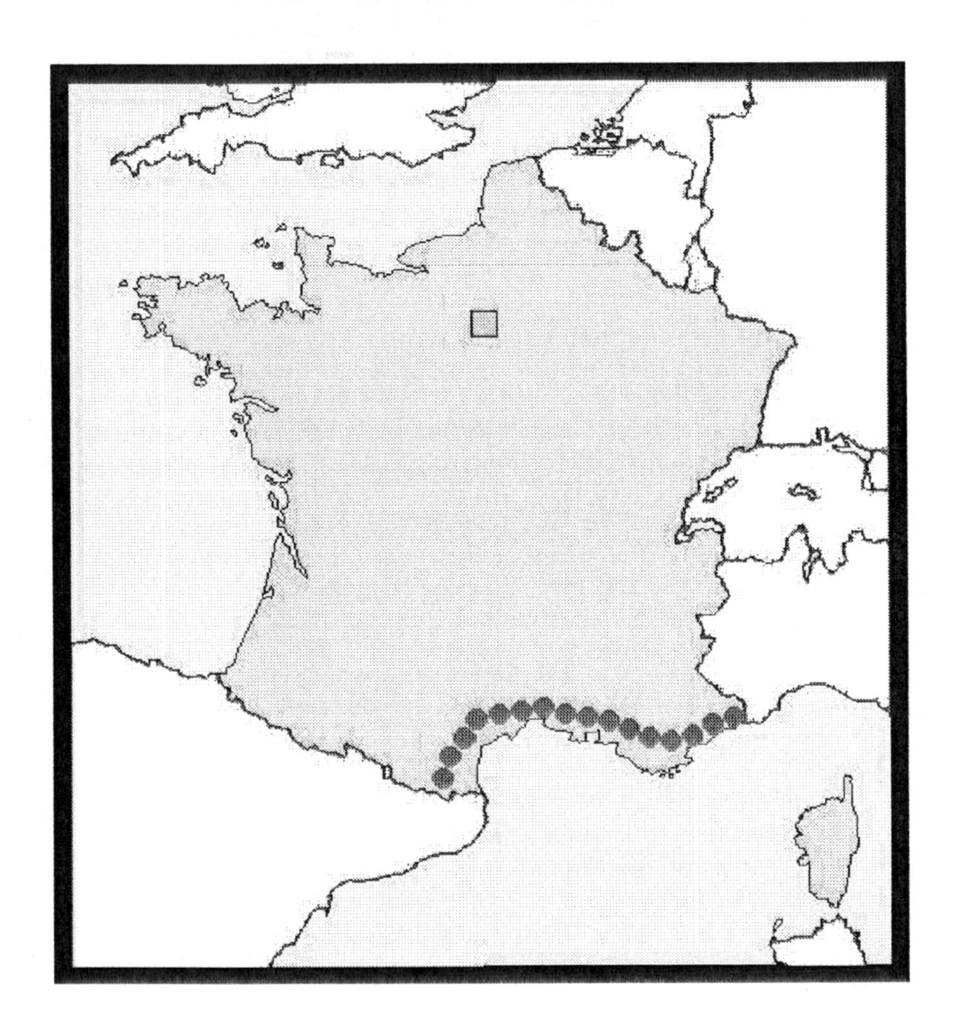

Tuesday, May 15th
Pineda de Mar to le Boulou, France - 120.36 Km

Another day, another country. I finally left Spain behind and entered France. I did it by crossing the Pyrenees at the Col du Perthus where it's only 290 meters above sea level. I started the day on the Mediterranean, so I know that I climbed at least that far. In reality, I climbed much farther because the N11 rose and fell a few times during the trip up from the coast. The middle stretch was relatively flat, as long as I stayed on the national road around the towns of Girona and Figuera. The more direct route through those towns would have taken me over some difficult terrain. The N11 has three tunnels that cut through the hills surrounding the towns. It was a much easier route.

The border town of La Jonquera was what you would expect. It had numerous hotels, restaurants, gas stations, and moneychangers. And, it was overflowing with truckers waiting to cross the border. After passing through the control point without incident, I continued riding for another couple of Km until I reached the French border. I thought that that would be the end of the climbing today, but I still had to get through the French border town of le Perthus. The main street seemed to go straight up, past shops, restaurants, and more moneychangers. I was completely drained by the time that I reached the top. There was a hotel there, but the front desk wasn't open for another hour. A sign in the window indicated that they only had six rooms. I was sure that, if I waited the hour, I would have been told that the rooms were already occupied. In my mind the glass is always half-empty, and Murphy was an optimist. So, I got back on the bike and headed farther into France. On the way to the next town I found a hotel set up on an old tree farm. I took a room here and collapsed.

Dinner was at 8:00 PM in the hotel restaurant, and I think that I was the only hotel guest eating here tonight. Maybe I was the only hotel guest, period. I sat down in an area of the dining room filled with locals who were well into their meals. A waiter then came out of the kitchen and asked me to follow him to another room. I was the only person seated in the second dining room. I ordered the entrecote du boef and wondered why I was separated from the others. I had showered after the day's ride. Who knows? I'm learning not to let those types of things bother me anymore. As an American bicycle-tourist in Europe, I'm going to be "different." I can't avoid that.

Tomorrow I'll be back on the coast for more beach riding, hopefully.

Wednesday, May 16th
Le Boulou to Torreilles - 61.59 Km

I rode almost half as many Km as I did yesterday. It was a leisurely day cycling down from the hills to the coast. In the city center of le Boulou I found my first laundromat of the trip. I had to stop and wash everything. While I did the wash, I worked on e-mail with the Pocket PC. A little boy and his sister came in to do laundry and were fascinated by the Pocket PC. I let them play Solitaire and tried to show them how I get on the Internet. Of course, the infrared connection failed. Still, they were suitably impressed. They asked about the mirror on my glasses, as so many others have. I asked them how to say rear-view mirror in French so that I can answer the inevitable question for the next few days. "Retroviseur" was the answer.

I also changed my money and withdrew more francs in le Boulou. Then, I continued a little farther on the national road #9 before turning to the coast on the D612. The road through Elne and St. Cyprien was not as well surfaced, but did have less traffic. As soon as I hit the coast at St. Cyprien-Plage, I stopped for a cheese sandwich at an outdoor café on the beach. Then, I continued my leisurely ride up the coast through Canet-Plage and Ste. Marie-Plage. If there was a boardwalk, or "maritime passage", I took that. Otherwise, I went back inland a couple of Km for the main coastal road. I eventually stopped here in Torreiles-Plage because it had six different campgrounds. I knew that at least one would be to my liking. Camping Les Dunes was right on the beach (obviously "plage" in French), so that's the one I chose. It was too late to take advantage of the beach, but I might take a day off tomorrow. I'll decide in the morning.

Thursday, May 17th
Torreilles - 0 Km

I probably made a bad decision by taking today off. I didn't really need it, but I wanted to spend a day relaxing on a beach. As it turns out, the weather was better suited to cycling than sun tanning. It even drizzled a bit in the morning. I did get a couple of good hours on the beach in the afternoon. I felt that, if the next set of care packages sent from home didn't arrive at the travel agency representing American Express in Montpellier by Saturday, I didn't want to spend my time in a hotel room in the city. Tomorrow I'll call the agency in Montpellier to see if they've received anything yet, and if they have Saturday hours. I've got the feeling that I won't see the packages until Monday. C'est la vie.

Friday, May 18th
Torreilles to Beziers - 104.79 Km

It was definitely a bad decision to take yesterday off. For the second night in a row I had trouble sleeping in the tent. Two nights ago it was the sound of snails crawling all over the outside of the rain fly that woke me up. I thought that they were rats trying to get in. I moved the tent yesterday to get away from them. Then last night a weather front blew in. It rained hard, and the wind was dangerously strong. I spent an hour holding up the tent poles from the inside against the force of the wind. I thought that there was a chance that the poles might break due to the strength of the gusts.

Before getting out of the tent this morning, I could tell that it was going to be windy all day. I just hoped that it would be at my back. Boy, was I disappointed when I stepped out and felt the wind coming from the northeast. It was a dry and sunny day, but the wind proved to be relentless. I was in the granny gears for hours, doing less than 10 Km/hour. One stretch of the road near the village of Leucate was beside a bay that is popular with windsurfers. Dozens were out on the water, taking full advantage of the conditions. Even though that road was flat, I had to get off of the bike and walk it because the gusts were almost throwing me off. And, every time that a tractor-trailer passed, I was tossed around. I had to pedal *down* some hills because the wind was so strong.

As I struggled north on the N9, I kept telling myself that I would stop for the day at the next town, but didn't finally stop until I hit Beziers. The wind had moderated a little by the end of the day, but it was still an enormous effort getting into Beziers. I rewarded myself for all of the hard work with a cheap hotel and a McDonalds dinner.

Saturday, May 19th
Beziers to Sete - 50 Km

I knew that I probably wouldn't get to Montpellier in time this afternoon to see if my packages arrived from home. So, I decided to split the cycling to Montpellier over two days. Today was a great day for riding. It was sunny, warm, and not too windy. I headed towards the Mediterranean on the N112. The plan was to go through Agde, then on to Sete. In Agde I tried to find an Internet café or mobile phone store. The infrared port on my mobile phone has apparently stopped working. The 56K modem may also be broken. It didn't work the last time that I tried it in Spain. I haven't picked up a French phone jack adapter yet to test the modem again. I had no luck finding a café or phone store. Still, it was a nice old town to explore. There was a flea market operating in the main square this Saturday morning. I spent some time browsing the stalls, checking out French knick-knacks. They're surprisingly similar to American knick-knacks. After lunch I continued on to Sete on the beach road. I stopped a couple of times to lie out in the sand with the locals. I probably spent two hours on the beach in total. Finally, I hit Sete and found a hotel right next to a church. I arrived in time to shower and attend the Saturday night mass. Three weeks in a row now I've heard mass in different languages (Castilian Spanish, Catalonian Spanish, and French). If I ride hard in the next week I can hear it in Italian. But first, I have to get my care packages in Montpellier.

Sunday, May 20th
Sete to Clapiers - 54.72 Km

Today would have been an even shorter day if I had been able to find a hotel room in Montpellier. Of course, there was a convention in town and all of the rooms were already booked. That's just my luck. The one room that was available was a dive. The front desk at the downtown Ibis Hotel directed me to a hotel eight Km out of town. I took the room sight unseen, and without knowing the price. It turned out to be about $70. The room is very plush, but the hotel is at the top of a killer hill. There is no way that I am going back down that hill for dinner, and I'm not anxious to spend a lot of money in the hotel restaurant for a chichi meal that doesn't appeal to my bland tastes. So, I just had a Coke and potato chips in the bar. I did get onto the hotel iMac Internet connection. That was an extremely frustrating hour because the keyboard was not QWERTY-compatible. Not only do the French have a different word for everything, as Steve Martin points out, they also have a unique keyboard with seemingly misplaced letters for typing those words. To make matters worse, while I was slowly pecking out e-mail messages, the iMac randomly deleted paragraphs and dumped the cursor into other sections. I got off two messages in an hour.

During the day I did get into town to see the Havas Voyages travel agency. Now I know where the packages were sent. I'll go back tomorrow to see if they have arrived.

Monday, May 21st
Clapiers to Lattes - 17.74 Km

I began the day by getting out of the expensive hotel on the hill. Before I left, I asked the guy at the front desk to call Havas Voyages on my behalf. He did, but got the same runaround that I did, only in French. I thanked him for his efforts anyway and cycled into Montpellier. On the way I stopped in a smaller town to withdraw cash, buy some baked goods, and do my laundry. While the laundry was being done, the only rain of the day fell. I took the opportunity to catch up on my writing.

When I got into Montpellier I went right to the Place de la Comedie and Havas Voyages. As soon as I walked in and told them my name, they handed me three boxes that had just arrived. I got on the phone and called home to confirm that there should have been four packages. The count of four packages was confirmed. The most important item in this shipment is my U.S. passport. You guess which box it is in. I went back into Havas Voyages to explain that there will be a fourth box delivered. They told me that the next delivery would be tomorrow between 10:00 AM and 11:00 AM.

I am able to travel without my U.S. passport because I also possess an Irish passport. I am a dual-citizen, registered as a foreign birth with the Republic of Ireland. I did not bring the U.S. passport to Lisbon because it was still being passed around embassies and consulates in New York City and Washington, DC for visa approvals when I left home. Most of my applications have now been approved.

I went to an Internet café in town and tried to read and send e-mail for an hour. Once again, the non-QWERTY French keyboards hindered my efforts. I was only able to send one feeble e-mail message. Then, I was on the road again, heading south of town for the cheap hotels. They all seemed to be clustered around Lattes. France has these self-service hotels that allow you to book a room with your credit card at an ATM-style machine at the front door. The machine dispenses a card for you to use as your key. The rooms cost around $20 to $25 and are small, sterile cubes. The bathrooms are small modular units that were probably easily installed in these rooms. The beds are usually two singles side by side, and a bunk bed across the top of the singles. They do have small television sets. They're very Spartan, but clean. They're only twice the cost of a campsite, so I'm going to try to take advantage of them while I'm in France.

Tuesday, May 22nd
Lattes - 24.74 Km

Another day has passed, and my fourth package from home has still not arrived at Havas Voyages. I'm going to give it one more day, and then I have to move on.

I found out today that the post office in Montpellier has been on strike for the past two weeks. That's their explanation for the missing package. I stood in line at two post office branches and had no luck. One branch gave me four telephone numbers to call. The person answering the first number did not speak English. The other three numbers were never answered. The English-speaking lady at Havas knows me by sight now. She has my card with my SMS Internet ID. She promises to send a message to my mobile phone if the package arrives.

I did get through to Motorola in Paris. They gave me the number of a company near Marseilles that repairs mobile phones. I don't think that's going to happen. I've heard bad things about Marseilles. I may have to buy a new phone for $300 to get a working IR port. I'll give it another shot in Italy. Maybe Motorola in Italy will be more understanding. I did pick up the phone jack adapter that I needed to work with my modem in France. I tested it out in the hotel tonight. The modem and adapter both work fine. I spent an hour on-line answering e-mail. This hotel is right next to the one that I used last night, but it has direct-dial phone access. I paid an extra $1.50 for that luxury. I'll also have to pay around $4 for the hour on the phone.

That's it for today. There was nothing else of interest. I'm leaving Montpellier tomorrow, with or without my U.S. passport.

Wednesday, May 23rd
Lattes to Aigues Mortes - 53.83 Km

Well, the box with the U.S. passport did not arrive today. I've worked out the details with the nice people at Havas Voyages to either forward it to me in France, or return it to the States, depending upon when it does arrive.

By noon I was finally leaving Montpellier. It felt good to get back on the road and start heading east again. First, I cycled south to the beach towns of Palavas, Carnon, la Grande-Motte, and le Grau-du-Roi to ride leisurely along the water. Then, I turned inland towards Aigues Mortes, a medieval walled city. I almost passed by this town, but I'm glad I didn't. The history of the place kept me occupied for hours. It was the departure port for the Crusades of 1248 and 1270. The walls and towers appear to be very well preserved, considering they were built in the early 13th century. The ancient church dedicated to St. Louis in the middle of the town was also in great shape. I had to wonder how much of what I was seeing was original and how much was rebuilt. Of course, I was too cheap to buy a guidebook.

I didn't climb the main tower or walk along the top of the walls, but I did cycle through the town. I considered getting a room at one of the hotels within the walls, but they were too expensive.

So, I cycled outside of the walls and found a reasonably priced hotel.

Thursday, May 24th
Aigues Mortes to Salon-de-Provence - 97.11 Km

This was a good day of riding. I got in almost 100 Km and saw some great Roman ruins. I left Aigues Mortes around 10:00 AM and headed into the plains of the Camargue. The D58 and D570 were perfectly level, and surrounded by salt flats. I believe that Aigues Mortes literally means "dead waters" in Latin. The high salt content in the water probably doesn't support too much aquatic life.

Many of the roads through the Camargue had bike paths, and I saw more bicycle-tourists today than I had seen on the trip thus far. At mid-day I crossed the Rhone River and headed into Arles. I had lunch at a McDonalds and then explored the Roman Theatre and Amphitheater. These ancient structures are also very well preserved. I paid the minimal entrance fee at both sites to wander around and shoot lots of videotape.

Around 2:30 PM I was back on the N113 heading due east. I had thought about going all the way to Aix-en-Provence, but by the time that I had reached Salon-de-Provence the skies looked threatening. I rushed around from hotel to hotel while thunder rumbled off in the distance. At the fourth hotel, the most expensive in the area, there were vacancies. So, I paid the $45 and took a room. An hour later the skies opened up. It was worth the money to stay inside tonight. I'd be swimming in my tent otherwise.

Friday, May 25th
Salon-de-Provence to Brignoles - 97.16 Km

It could have been a horrible night tonight, but I think that St. Christopher was looking out for me. It was a great day for riding, sunny and warm all the way on the N7. It was probably the warmest day that I've had so far. I'm guessing that it was in the low 80's. I passed through Aix-en-Provence and stopped in St. Maximin for a McDonalds lunch/dinner around 4:00 PM. I probably should have found a room there, but I wanted to get closer to the Riviera to have a shorter ride on Saturday. So, I continued on to Brignoles, my original destination for the day. When I arrived around 6:00 PM the weather was still great. After being refused at three hotels outside of the city, I headed into the "centre ville." By the time that I reached the middle of town I was in a thunderstorm. I cycled right into an open foyer of a building off of the main square. I stayed there for about 45 minutes, watching torrential rains flood the storm drains. Then, one of the building's residents came down and suggested that I talk to the owner of a nearby restaurant. We both ran up the street to talk to the restaurateur. We told him about my predicament in English and in French. He quickly called the only other hotel in town and got me the last room. I was told to hurry to the hotel down the street because the owner was about to leave. I was there in a minute. The owner was waiting for me at the doorstep. While I was checking in, he turned down two other people. The storm continued for another two or three hours. The electricity almost went out after a couple of huge lightning strikes. I was never so happy to get into a three-story walk-up hotel room with a sagging bed than I was tonight.

The moral of the story is to try to get checked in before 4:00 PM. By then, most of the rooms in busy towns are taken. If I have the opportunity to book ahead, I may start to do that also. I can always cancel a reservation.

Saturday, May 26th
Brignoles to St. Raphael - 80.35 Km

It was another good day, weather-wise. I started out at 9:00 AM, but got sidetracked at a laundromat and bike shop. It's a real pleasure to have laundromats available in almost every town in France. They're a rarity on the Iberian Peninsula. At the bike shop I complained about my chain, which continues to freeze at a couple of the links. I showed the mechanic what I was using on the chain. He explained that what I had only protected the chain, but did not lubricate it. I bought a lubricant from him that seems to make a difference. Only time will tell.

Then, I headed on the N7 towards Frejus and St. Raphael, the beginning of the Cote d'Azur. I think that I cycled this same route a decade ago, but nothing looked familiar. It was an uneventful ride. I got to the coast by around 3:00 PM. As seems to be the case too often, the first hotel was fully booked. I continued on to a campground where I might have stayed the last time that I passed through here. On one side of the campground is a lighthouse atop a large hill. On the other side are a little church and a monument to General Eisenhower and the American troops that stormed this beach in August 1944. Off the coast is a castle on a small island. I'll hit the 9:00 AM mass tomorrow and then decide if I want to continue up the coast. The Monte Carlo Grand Prix takes place tomorrow, and I don't want to be caught without a room again. I'm leaning towards cycling up to Nice. There are lots of hotels around Nice, and the race-goers may leave town before sundown. I can only hope.

Sunday, May 27th
St. Raphael to Villeneuve-Loubet - 79.08 Km

The day started out with a 9:00 AM mass at the little chapel next to the campground. It looked to be about 200 years old and probably held about 100 parishioners. The chapel was so small that they never moved the altar forward enough for the priest to stand behind it and face the congregation. So, as he celebrated the Eucharist with his back to me, speaking a language that I didn't understand, I thought that this was what attending mass was like before the Second Vatican Council.

After mass I hung around Dwight Eisenhower Square shooting more videotape. Then, it was time for me to attack the French Riviera. Between St. Raphael and Cannes, the red cliffs of the Massif de L'Esterel are the dominant geological feature. The N98 twists and turns around the coves formed in the Massif. It's a bit like Highway 1 in California, around Big Sur. It's fun to cycle, but it can be tiring. I saw lots of weekend cyclists out there today. That's always a good sign. It means that the cars are aware of us, the dogs don't care about us, and the bike repair shops are there for us (blatant and senseless use of rhyme).

After going around the Massif, you hit Cannes and its long, crescent-shaped beach. The beach promenade was a blast to cycle. There were lots of other tourists out walking. Many congregated around the hall where the film festival was held last week. Several of the tourists climbed the famous steps, emulating the walk that the movie stars took in front of the paparazzi. There's also a series of handprints in the pavement of people that the French think are important to the film industry, like Brooke Shields and Diana Ross. I couldn't find the handprints of Jerry Lewis.

After Cannes I cycled around the Cap d'Antibes. There is some serious money in that neighborhood. Many of the homes had high fences and gates. Some even had full-time security guards. I decided that if this is how the other half live, I want to join their club. If it's just a matter of filling out a membership application, count me in.

I finished up the day at one of those automated McHotels two Km inland. It only cost me about $35, including breakfast. I'm going to miss these hotels when I leave France.

Monday, May 28th
Villeneuve-Loubet to Menton - 61.32 Km

It was another day of hob-nobbing with the idle rich on their home turf. The cars that were passing me became increasingly more exotic as I approached Monaco. It wasn't

Renaults or Citroens any more, but Ferraris and Lamborghinis. Everybody seems to have a Porsche for his or her around-town car. Three Ferraris in one 10-minute stretch passed me. There probably aren't three Ferraris in all of South Dakota.

In Nice I cycled into the old section of the city for a little while to browse the flea market. Then, I cycled the increasingly more congested and dangerous roads to Monaco. Monaco was like a construction site. It's the day after the Grand Prix, and hundreds of men were dismantling the stands, guardrails, and other temporary structures all over town. I sent off four postcards with Monaco stamps and frank marks.

At the end of the day I booked a room at the last McHotel before Italy, the ETAP in Menton. I'm definitely going to miss these places. I'm about a half Km away from the border. Tomorrow I enter my seventh country on this trip, if you count Gibraltar and Monaco. And, I'm sure the Gibraltarians and Monegasques would. The others are Portugal, Spain, Morocco, and France.

Italy & Vatican City

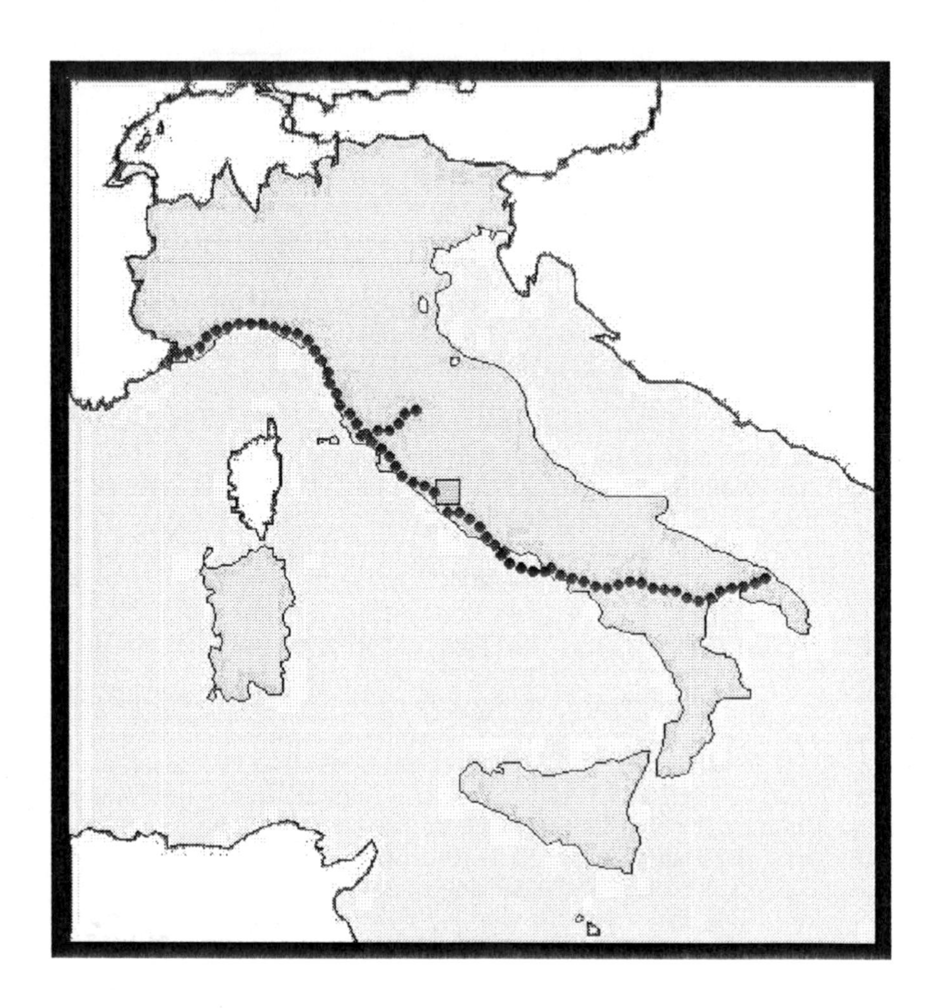

Tuesday, May 29th
Menton to Diano Marina, Italy - 59.01 Km

It was another short ride today. They seem to be getting shorter and shorter. That means that I probably need to take a day off soon. I need a good meal to build up the strength again. The scenery and terrain around here has had a negative effect on my daily mileage as well.

The big news today, besides entering another country, was that my U.S. passport arrived safely at the Havas Voyages travel agency in Montpellier. I was just about to leave France when I received the phone call. For a split second I considered having them forward the box to the Havas Voyages travel agency in Menton, but I didn't want to wait another day for that thing. They agreed to mail the package back to the States. I'll continue traveling on my Irish passport for now.

I cycled through three tunnels in the first few Km today. The Italian Riviera is very hilly, and engineers have tunneled through those hills to build the roads and lay the train tracks. This stretch of coast is very congested. It's not as much fun to cycle as the French Riviera because you rarely get to see the Mediterranean. There are the train tracks and an endless row of buildings between the main road that I cycle and the sea.

There are a lot of cyclists out on the SS1, so I feel safe despite the traffic. There are also many good bike shops. I shouldn't have any trouble repairing the bike in Italy.

I got off of the SS1 at the end of the day when I found a paved bike path closer to the sea. The scenic path led me to this town, Diano Marina. This is the first quiet place that I've been on the Italian Riviera, so I took a room in a hotel that is owned and patronized by British. I feel comfortable here. I had a T-bone steak for dinner. That should help tomorrow. I don't think that I've been getting enough protein at the McDonalds. I'll shoot for a town just short of Genoa tomorrow. If I can find a nice place, I'll take a day off there.

Wednesday, May 30th
Diano Marina to Albissola Marina - 76.35 Km

The weather today was gray. For the most part the scenery was also uninspiring. So, I just put in the Km. The road that I've been riding in Italy is called the Via Aurelia, a.k.a. the SS1. The Romans built this road two thousand years ago, and I think it hasn't been repaired since. It's also considered part of the ancient pilgrim's trail from Rome to Santiago de Compestello in northwest Spain. It is well traveled, to say the least.

I'm staying at the Hotel Garden, a four-star hotel, for around $70. I booked a room here because I wanted to see what makes a hotel worthy of a four-star rating. The service was pretty good, but the room isn't spectacular. And, the hotel is a block back from the beach. I've determined that the star system is administered randomly.

Thursday, May 31st
Albissola Marina to Santa Margherita Ligure - 80.18 Km

It was kind of a frustrating day because I couldn't get some things done. I wanted to find a laundromat, but I haven't seen one since entering Italy. Maybe they're illegal here. On a related note, the stench around Genoa is strong. It smells just like you would expect an industrial port city to smell.

I also wanted to get the infrared port on my mobile phone working, but I couldn't find the shop in town that could do the work. Once I left the old port in the center of Genoa, I got lost. My map isn't detailed enough, and the street signs are few and far between. I was unsuccessful in my search for a hotel in town, so when the weather turned bad I high-tailed it out of there.

The rain held off as I flew down the coast. After many Km I came across a hotel, but they wanted $90 for a room. I had already decided that I needed to take a day off tomorrow, and I wasn't going to spend $180 for a room. So, back on the bike I went. Unfortunately, that meant going over a large, steep hill to get to the next town. I was toast at that point, so I had to walk the bike a couple of times. I haven't pushed the bike much on this trip, so that confirmed my need for a rest day. The last few Km were downhill into Santa Margherita Ligure, a tourist town popular with the yachting set. They actually have stores here that sell the whole Thurston J. Howell III outfit, including patches. I saw quite a few American yachties strolling around the port. It's always comforting to see my fellow countrymen, no matter how they're dressed.

I'm in a nice, cheap hotel a block back from the water, and I got my laundry into a dry cleaner before it closed. I'll do some sightseeing tomorrow, and then pick up the clothes at 5:00 PM. I think that I hit my furthest point north on the trip today just before entering Genoa. I should have the prevailing northwest winds at my back the rest of the way to Australia. Ha! That's wishful thinking.

Friday, July 1st
Santa Margherita Ligure - 0 Km

I started out the day by going to an Internet café to catch up on my e-mail. I've been sending SMS messages from my mobile phone to my younger brother every night since beginning the trip. He was away on vacation the past few days, so I've been sending daily updates to my father at his AOL account. The first two e-mail messages that I opened at the Internet café today were from my two older brothers telling me that Dad hadn't received any e-mail from me, and Mom was imagining the worst. I immediately sent off messages to let everyone know that I was alive and well. Later, I took a ferry to Portofino for some sightseeing, but I kept worrying about Mom and Dad. I walked around Portofino, waiting for the hour when they would both be awake and I could call them. They were relieved to hear my voice when I finally did telephone. I reminded them that they could call me anytime they wanted, day or night. The one thing that I've tried to do on this trip with all of the computer and telephone equipment that I'm carrying is stop others from worrying about me.

I finished the day with a nice steak dinner. My legs should be in better shape for tomorrow's ride.

Saturday, July 2nd
Santa Margherita Ligure to Ameglia - 98.89 Km

As I suspected, this was a difficult day. The map showed many chevrons on the SS1, indicating climbs. There was even a mountain pass shown on the map. The day started with some riding around coves. That type of terrain can be draining. Then, there was a long climb to the 615 meter high Passo de Braco. I met a local on the way up who was also cycling over the pass. He didn't speak English, but he stayed with me and tried to tell me what to expect. He was a great help, and after almost an hour of climbing we reached the pass. On the way down he turned off at the first road heading down to his town on the coast. I barely had time to thank him. He pulled me up a hill that would have beaten me otherwise.

I continued on around Rick Steves' Cinque Terre towards La Spezia, my goal for the day. Since it was 5:30 PM on a Saturday when I reached La Spezia, every hotel was already booked. I inquired at five or six hotels before leaving town in search of a campground. It took a while, but eventually I found this place. My legs were like rubber when I finally arrived here. I pushed hard all day. It almost feels like I never had the steak or day off yesterday.

Sunday, June 3rd
Ameglia to Pisa - 68.74 Km

This was not a difficult day, despite the fierce wind coming off of the Mediterranean. Since it was Sunday, there were many weekend athletes out on their bikes. The first half of the ride was through seaside tourist towns. I only know that they were seaside towns because I see on the map that I was riding right alongside the Mediterranean. You wouldn't know it because the entire coast is built up, and the road is set back from the beaches. The wind was kicking up a very fine dust off of the beaches. They don't have the typical sandy beaches here. It's either stones or dirt. Most of the ride was still on the SS1. I did get a little lost near Viareggio, but got back onto the SS1 eventually for the final push into Pisa.

Just outside of Pisa I came across the first McDonalds that I had seen in days. Of course, I had to stop. Then, after a quick burger and fries, I entered Pisa through the northwest corner of the walled city. The famous Leaning Tower, Cathedral, and Baptistery are all located around their well-manicured "Field of Miracles" in this quadrant of the city. Unfortunately, they are finishing up a two-year project to bring the tower back into the position that it held 300 years ago, not too cockeyed and not too vertical. It's just far enough off kilter to keep the tourists coming, but without crashing down on them. So, it looks like a construction site with an ugly metal fence around the base of the tower.

I didn't pay to go inside the Cathedral or Baptistery (they also lean, but get no press) because I was anxious to find a hotel. I passed on the first hotel at $35 because it didn't include a shower in the room, but took a room in the second hotel for $70. I probably paid too much, but it was getting late and I wanted to get inside after camping out last night. It was a smart move because there was a bad storm late in the afternoon. After the storm I rushed out to a 6:00 PM mass. All things considered, it was a successful day.

Monday, June 4th
Pisa to Florence - 97.06 Km

I got a late start, as usual, but it didn't matter today. I had to be out of the hotel at 10:00 AM. I paid the bill at 9:59 AM. Then, I went in search of help for my mobile phone. I found the Motorola authorized repair shop just outside of the Pisa city walls. A technician took a look at the infrared port in the backroom, then came out and said that it was working fine. I retrieved my Pocket PC from the bike, tested the infrared connection between the two devices, and found that he was correct. I don't know why it didn't work a week ago, but I'm happy just to be connected again. Since they were also a Compaq authorized repair shop, I asked if they could load another e-mail program onto my Pocket PC. They couldn't, but they suggested a store where I might find the software that I needed. It was on the way to Florence, so off I went. Of course, that store didn't have what I needed, but at least it got me moving towards Florence.

By noon I was rolling in earnest. The wind that was pounding my face yesterday was now at my back. I followed the SS67 the whole way to Florence, except for the few Km where I got onto an expressway by accident. There is no distinction between local roads and highways on the signs here. While I was rolling along towards Florence many times today I saw signs that tried to direct me off of the SS67. I soon realized that these signs would put me onto the expressway.

By 5:00 PM I was in Florence. I found a cheap pensione near the action and set up shop. The bike is stored in the room with me. It's a small room with shower and sink, but the toilet is down the hall. What do you expect for $50? I took a quick walk around town to see the Ponte Vecchio and few other sights tonight. I'll do the real sightseeing tomorrow.

Tuesday, June 5th
Florence - 0 Km

I played tourist today. I took the camera and explored the historic section of Florence. I meandered on the Ponte Vecchio, sauntered down to the Pritti Palace, and strolled up to the Duomo. I stood on line to climb to the top of the Duomo, but decided against waiting on line to get into the Ufizzi Gallery and the Academy of Fine Arts (where Michelangelo's *David* is displayed). In addition to climbing the 463 steps to the cupola on Brunaleschi's dome, I went down under the Basilica to see his tomb. So, you could say that I saw the Basilica from top to bottom. I also climbed the 414 steps to the top of the Bell Tower adjacent to the Basilica. Once again, I've worked as hard on my day off as I would on a cycling day. I called home from the top of the Bell Tower to describe the view of Florence and the nearby Tuscan hills just to make the folks jealous. I didn't do the view justice, but I think I still made them jealous.

This marked the end of two months on the road. I'm well ahead of my 1,000 miles per month target pace. My $1,000 per month target budget is probably shot by now. I'll have to cycle faster or spend less to come in under budget for the trip.

Wednesday, June 6th
Florence to Pisa - 90.94 Km

The rain covers on my new Madden panniers were given a good test today. It was a miserable day to ride a bike. When I left Florence I didn't expect rain. The SMS forecast on my mobile phone said nothing about rain. But, 20 Km into the day's ride it started. The intensity varied throughout the day, anywhere from drizzles to downpours. As I sensed a downpour coming, I would rush for the next available shelter. When the rain eased up, I would rush out and ride a few more Km. It was like playing musical chairs with the storm clouds. I was only caught once in a drenching downpour, but once is enough to soak you to the bone. By 3:30 PM the rain had stopped.

I had trouble finding a hotel all day. Near Pisa I passed on one that I thought was too expensive. I headed into town and found this hotel, three stars for $50. It's a bargain. I stayed up until 2:00 AM watching *The Sixth Sense*. Then, I woke up at 3:30 AM and watched the 2nd quarter of Game One of the NBA Finals between the Philadelphia 76ers and Los Angeles Lakers. And then, I woke up around 5:00 AM to see the overtime. The Sixers won, but I lost a lot of valuable sleep. I'll pay for that tomorrow.

Thursday, June 7th
Pisa to Follonica - 113.69 Km

If only every day was like today. I cycled the Via Aurelia the whole day. The road was straight and flat for Km. It was lined with shade trees on either side. The wind was at my back, and by the end of the day I was easily averaging 30 Km/hour. The late night last night hardly affected me.

I did cycle through Livorno, a port city, but it wasn't too bad. Then, the road hugged a slightly rugged coast south of Livorno, but it wasn't too difficult either. The views along the coast were very nice. I probably should have pulled the video camera out of the panniers a few more times. I finally stopped outside Follonica at a truckers' hotel. In Spain I could get a room in one of these places for $12. Here it cost me $30. Italy is going to destroy my budget.

Friday, June 8th
Follonica to Grosseto - 52.99 Km

Any hopes of getting to Rome by Saturday evening were quickly dashed this morning. First, I found that the route I chose to Grosseto was a bit more difficult than expected. Second, the wind that had been at my back yesterday had swung around 180 degrees. Third, I got my second flat of the trip this morning. I could just tell that it wasn't going to be my day.

The scenery was pleasant and the sun was out. But, the roads had no shoulders and were very rough in spots. When the tube on the front wheel went, I replaced both tire and tube. Now I have two new tires on the bike. I feel pretty good about that. I need to buy a couple more tubes, though.

As I was leaving Grosseto I realized that I wasn't going to ride 110 Km as I did yesterday, so I decided to start looking for hotels. I knew from my map that the next campgrounds were 30 Km away. Minutes later I came across this hotel and decided to stop early for the day. The only drawback to choosing this $40 hotel room is that it doesn't get the channel with the NBA Finals broadcast. I'll get a full night's sleep tonight.

Saturday, June 9th
Grosseto to Albinia - 38.63 Km

This was possibly the worst day of the trip so far. The headwinds were extremely strong. The Via Aurelia was like Route 22 in northern New Jersey: no shoulder, two narrow lanes each way, and high-speed traffic. To top things off, I left the hotel without my passport. I didn't realize it until I stopped here in Albinia. Due to the difficult cycling conditions, I stopped for the day at a group of campgrounds around 1:30 PM. I soon realized that last night's hotel still had my passport. I called them, and they immediately knew what I wanted. They offered to drop it off at a restaurant nearby by 4:00 PM. At 4:10 PM they still hadn't arrived. I called and they said that they forgot and would be there in 20 minutes. I didn't tip the guy because the hotel was partially to blame for not giving me my passport back at checkout, and they didn't have to make me wait three hours in a restaurant for a 20-minute drive on their part. Besides, the service in the hotel was awful. During the wait I cleaned up the bike. It looks as good as it did the day I hit Lisbon.

I did break 4,000 Km and 2,500 miles today. So, even a little progress is good, I guess. I'm in a $10 campground tonight. It's crowded because it's Saturday night. I hope I can get some sleep. I may try to get out very early to avoid the winds. Or, I may stay another day if it's just as bad tomorrow. I hope this road becomes safer. Early Sunday morning has to be the safest time to cycle on a road like this.

Sunday, June 10th
Albinia to Tarquinia - 66.95 Km

All roads may lead to Rome, but this one is making the journey difficult. For the third day in a row the headwinds were brutal. I got up early in hopes of getting in some Km before the winds picked up. I also hoped to do some riding without the traffic. I was disappointed on both counts. I was on the road at 7:00 AM, and the wind was as strong then as it had been the previous afternoon. By 8:00 AM the cars and trucks were out there buzzing past me in a hurry to get somewhere. The Italian drivers all seem to be late for some appointment. How Mussolini ever got the trains to run on time is beyond me.

It rained off and on throughout the day. It looked like it might get worse when I reached Tarquinia, and it was a long way to the next town, so I pulled in here. I asked at five hotels if they received the satellite station with the Sixers-Lakers NBA Finals game. No luck. So, I took a room at the last hotel. It's a nice place, and fairly empty. Tonight I walked around Tarquinia, another hill-town. I wished that I had my camera with me because there was a great panoramic view of the countryside at the far end of the town where the main street stops at the edge of a cliff. I didn't go to see the Etruscan necropolis just outside of town because I had to get back for an evening mass. Those Etruscans won't be going anywhere. I'll visit their necropolis the next time that I'm in Tarquinia.

Monday, June 11th
Tarquinia to Rome - 95.97 Km

I finally made it to Rome. It took longer than expected, but it's good to finally get here. The day didn't start well. The minute that I stepped out of the hotel it began raining. It wasn't so heavy that I couldn't ride, though. I covered the equipment and myself with the appropriate rain gear and began riding. It rained most of the morning and didn't clear up until I was just outside of Rome.

I traveled the Via Aurelia the entire way into Rome. The road was much better today because there were other parallel roads that siphoned off most of the traffic. I traveled almost every Km of the Via Aurelia from the French border, just like a true pilgrim.

Along the way today I purchased a couple more tire tubes and had the battery pack for the helmet-cam fixed in Santa Marinella. The connecting wires needed to be soldered back onto the pack. A local electrician did the work for free.

The Via Aurelia dumped me right onto St. Peter's Square in Vatican City. I took a few pictures and then went looking for a hotel. I found a very nice room in a two-star hotel with private bath down the hall for about $70/day. This is home for the next few days. It took a little effort, but I found a McDonalds for dinner. All is right with the world.

Tuesday, June 12th
Rome - 0 Km

I did the Vatican today. I spent five hours touring the Museum. There is just so much to see. The last part of the tour takes you into the Sistine Chapel. I spent a half-hour in there, standing shoulder to shoulder with a few hundred other art lovers, just staring at the ceiling. No one wants to leave. Everyone comes to see Michelangelo's *Creation* frescoes on the ceiling, but his *Last Judgment* on the wall behind the altar is more spectacular, in my uneducated opinion. Raphael's *The School of Athens* in the Stanza della Segnatura in the Vatican Palace is also very impressive. All in all, it was worth the price of admission (15,000 Lira, or around $6). While I was in the museum I checked out the gift shop, mailed home some postcards, and had one of my "political prisoner" lunches (bread and water).

Then, it was on to St. Peter's Basilica. On the right, as you walk in, is Michelangelo's *Pieta* sculpture. The famous dome over the Basilica is also Michelangelo's handiwork. You get the impression that the Vatican would have looked a whole lot less inspiring if it weren't for Signor Buonarroti. Just as in Florence, I saw the Basilica from top to bottom. First, I went underground to see where St. Peter and other early pontiffs were buried. Then, I visited the Basilica's museum. Finally, I went up to the roof and onto the cupola. There is an elevator to take visitors to the roof, thank goodness. I climbed up the steps inside the dome to the cupola for a bird's eye view of Rome. There happens to be another gift shop and post office on the roof, probably not designed by Michelangelo.

Wednesday, June 13th
Rome - 0 Km

I started out the day in St. Peter's Square with a few thousand other pilgrims for the Pope's weekly address and blessing. If I had gotten into town early on Monday, I could have picked up a ticket to sit closer to the Pope. Instead, I stood about 300 meters back with the ticket-less heathens. The event was very well orchestrated with the Pope being driven around the ticket-holders' sections in the pope-mobile, then up the steps of the Basilica to a small stage. He addressed the crowd in a variety of languages, and then a group of visiting priests read the list of pilgrim groups in attendance from the stage. There was also some music and prayer. All the while, the Pope's every move was displayed on the Jumbotrons in the Square, like Mick Jagger at a Rolling Stones concert. It all took about 90 minutes.

Afterwards, I walked through central Rome to see the Pantheon, Trevi Fountain, Piazza Navona, Forum, Palatine Hill, and Coliseum. My back and feet were so sore by the end of the day that I took the subway back to my hotel. Tomorrow I'm back on the bike.

Thursday, June 14th
Rome to Ostia - 58.81 Km

Well, I'm on the road again. I didn't get in many Km because I ran a few errands in Rome before leaving. I went to the Vatican to mail postcards. I couldn't mail back maps and books because the Vatican post office doesn't offer boxes for sale. Then, I found out where the American priests study in Rome from a young novitiate in the Square. It's called the North American College ("the NAC", to the students) and is located near St. Peter's, but at the top of a hill, of course. I went up to the NAC guardhouse and asked about two friends from high school who might be studying there now. I wasn't allowed on the grounds without a host, so I gave up the search. It might have been fun to meet them though. Lastly, I made two purchases at a gift shop just off the Square. I bought a Vatican Museum pen for Father's Day and a framed Papal Blessing for Mom and Dad's 50th Wedding Anniversary. I had to fill out a form that included my current parish and pastor. I went with my previous parish in Connecticut, as I haven't registered with any others yet. I wonder if I could have registered to be a parishioner of St. Peter's in Vatican City? The Blessing will arrive in Philadelphia in two months, God willing.

Finally, I cycled out of Rome. But, I soon stopped at Ostia Antica to see the ruins. Ostia was the port of Rome before the River Tiber silted up. It's the place that is mentioned in the movie *Gladiator*, where the Spaniard's men were waiting to attack. I didn't stop to explore Ostia the last time that I cycled through Italy due to a tight schedule. I have the time now. It took a few hours just to rush through the ruins. Ostia seems to be as big as Pompeii. I would have enjoyed the quick tour more if I had a guidebook and a comfortable pair of shoes. Still, it was a worthwhile diversion.

Afterwards, I made it back to the coast again. I had dinner at McDonalds and found a campground for the night. I'm back in the swing of things.

Friday, June 15th
Ostia to Sabaudia - 100.48 Km

I broke the 100 Km mark for the first time in a week today. Early on I stopped at a post office in Anzio to mail home my extra stuff. Forty-five minutes later the package was on it's way. The Italians work hard, but they don't work smart. While standing in one of the lines I heard other customers talking derisively about the "progress" of their postal system. I couldn't agree more. I think that the clerks were behind bulletproof glass to protect them from the angry mob trying to buy stamps. Actually, most of the customers were there to cash some sort of pension checks. If my package arrives in the States, I'll be pleasantly surprised.

I had passed signs for the U.S. military cemetery 10 years ago when I cycled through this area. But, after seeing the U.S. military cemetery in Henri-Chappelle, Belgium a couple years ago, I thought that I had to see this one. It also offered me the opportunity to step onto U.S. soil again. I wasn't disappointed with the decision to visit the World War II cemetery. It is as well maintained as Henri-Chappelle. The lawn and monuments are immaculate. I think that it sends a good message to all who visit: The U.S. is the greatest country on Earth, and it remembers those who fought and died to make it that way.

After leaving the cemetery I tried a different route back to the coast. Of course, I got lost. It was a nice ride, but I hated wasting the effort on an indirect route. I'm all about getting from Point A to Point B right now. No dilly-dallying. At a supermarket somewhere in Latina an elderly clerk gave me directions back to the coast and good information about the towns there. I eventually made it back and found a four-star campground. Once again, this was no four-star accommodation.

The interesting thing about my ride through the back roads of Latina is that I was riding on roads that the 84th Giro d'Italia just passed through in the last two weeks. There were messages written on the road in support of various teams and riders. They probably cycled through the area a little faster than I did.

Saturday, June 16th
Sabaudia to Formia - 77.64 Km

I had hoped to make this a short day, find a hotel near a church, and do my wash. No such luck. As is the case on most

Friday and Saturday nights, there is never a room available in the tourist areas. So, I ended up camping out again.

The scenery did get better today. There was a large hill, similar in shape to the Rock of Gibraltar, at Cape Circeo. The beaches after the Cape were sandy and crowded. They appear to be privately owned by people who charge admission to get onto the sand. And, many make money from bars on the beach and private parking on the street. It makes them a tad exclusive, and less natural. I prefer the public beaches where any fool on a bicycle can just stop and put his feet in the water.

I visited three bike shops today. The third was able to clean my chain while I waited. The bike had picked up a lot of sand yesterday as I slogged through one beach road that was more like a sandy path. The owner of the shop spoke English. He confirmed that I'd need to replace my chain and freewheel soon. I'll try to do that before I leave Italy.

Sunday, June 17th
Formia to Isola d'Ischia - 79.77 Km

This portion of the Italian coast is just as I remembered it. Horrible! There are a whole lot of very angry people living here. I thought that by cycling this area on a Sunday morning I might avoid some of the nastiness. No such luck. The Italians here drive with one hand on the wheel, one hand on the horn, one hand on their mobile phone, and one hand on a cigarette, with both feet on the gas. They've turned off the traffic lights here, so the right of way goes to the vehicle with the loudest horn. It's pure mayhem. I had a close call in the morning as I passed behind a car that was hung out entering traffic. The driver suddenly realized that he couldn't get into the flow of traffic and threw the car into reverse. I swerved away from his rear bumper just in time. He didn't seem fazed by it. I imagine he's hit many a cyclist in his day. The roadside in this area has many small monuments to people who died in traffic accidents. Still, the "go fast" mentality of the Italian driver hasn't changed. I saw a motorcyclist with a passenger pop a wheelie down the main road. They might as well start chiseling his tombstone right now.

Somehow I managed to arrive at the port of Pozzuoli to begin my ferry rides around the Bay of Naples. Past experience has told me that cycling through Naples would be suicide. The ride to the port confirmed that it was a good decision to avoid any further cycling in this area. I arrived just in time to board the ferry to the island of Ischia. The island is a summer resort for the Italians, just like Martha's Vineyard is for New Englanders. The town around the main port on Ischia is very touristy, and there's a lot more of this island paradise to explore beyond that. I had some trouble finding a room, but eventually a hotel offered me an interior room for $40. I took it because I had no other choice. The room is small and hot, and has one window out to the hallway. I'm glad to have any place to lay my head tonight, even this broom closet. But, tomorrow I'll ask if an exterior room has become available.

I went to mass at the nearby church, but it was overflowing. I stood in the vestibule, shoulder to shoulder with many others for as long as I could, and then left early. I'll sleep well tonight.

Monday, June 18th
Isola d'Ischia - 0 Km

I didn't sleep well. The room was too hot. I checked around at a few other hotels, but they are all fully booked. I went back to my hotel and requested an exterior room. It will cost $30 more, but I can't spend another night in the broom closet.

I found out that there is a ferry on Tuesday mornings that will take me directly to the Amalfitano Coast, bypassing Capri. I was ready to buy the ticket right then and there, but didn't. I'm glad that I didn't because a mix-up at the cleaners will cause me to stay another day on Ischia.

I took my clothes to Lavanderia Anna at 8:00 AM this morning and asked for the four-hour service that she had posted in large block letters outside her establishment. Like most conversations I've had here, this one was conducted in a mixture of English and Italian. When asked about the "rapid service" she said what I thought, in English, was "No, no. Double the money." I replied "OK. Double the money." In my mind, a 100% surcharge on laundry service was an acceptable expense if it got me off the island tomorrow morning. You know, it's amazing how two things that sound so similar can have such different meanings. What Anna actually said to me, in Italian, was "No, no. Dopo Domani." That literally means "double tomorrow", or "the day after tomorrow." Oops! I realized this at 5:00 PM when I arrived to pick up my clothes. After some hand gestures and calendar pointing by Anna, I realized the mix-up. She promised to get the clothes back to me by 5:00 PM tomorrow night. I rushed back to the hotel to see if my room was available for one more night. It was. Then, I ran out to buy another shirt for tomorrow. All of my clothes are with Anna. So, I get to stay on beautiful Ischia, wearing my new shirt, in my hotel room with a balcony for an extra day. And, I get to pay through the nose for all of this. Paradise can be expensive, especially if you don't know the language.

I called home to tell the folks the story of the day, and to work out the arrangements for my next mail drop in Athens. I also found out that my phone bill last month was $350. I've got to get out of Italy as soon as possible and cut my expenses.

Tuesday, June 19th
Isola d'Ischia - 0 Km

Well, I got taken to the cleaners today. Anna charged me $47 for the wash. I was too stunned to say anything. Besides, she wouldn't have understood me anyway. I managed to stay upright, pay the bill, and walk out. Then, I caught my breath, went to the bancomat, and withdrew another $150. I think the lesson here is for me to go to the more expensive western hotels like Holiday Inn and Best Western when I need to get my wash done. I may be able to do the wash myself, or use their same-day service. The only problem with that is that those hotels are probably the first to be fully booked.

I did get out this morning to see the Aragonese Castle at Pointe Ischia. It's built on an island about 100 feet from the main island, and connected by a stone bridge. The first fortification here dates back almost 2,500 years. The modern fort goes back 550 years. The weather today was great, and I shot lots of good video footage of the castle. Tomorrow I ferry to Capri and, hopefully, the Amalfitano Coast. Then, I begin riding towards Potenza. From Potenza it's all downhill to Greece.

Wednesday, June 20th
Isola d'Ischia to Capri to Salerno - 43.25 Km

All went according to plan. I got the 8:30 AM ferry from Ischia to Capri, then the 1:40 PM ferry from Capri to Amalfi. I had about an hour layover on Capri. Everything of interest is at the top of a killer hill, so I waited at the dock. I'm sure Capri is a nice island, but you can't tell much about an island by its port.

I'm glad that I didn't ask to get off of the second ferry at Positano. Positano doesn't have a dock, just a launch that motors out to take passengers off of the hydrofoil. My bike would have certainly been at the bottom of the Mediterranean if I had attempted that transfer. Also, it's straight up from Positano to the coast road. Amalfi was a great point to start my abbreviated ride on the Amalfitano Coast. There was a nice little town around the port, and the coast road rose gently from there. I saw a couple of cyclists resting on the dock as soon as I arrived, so I knew that the S163 coast road was do-able, at least to Amalfi.

The ride to Salerno was great, some of the best coastal riding I've ever done. The scenery was awesome. The narrow coast road hugs the side of a cliff hundreds of feet above the Mediterranean. With Formula 1 tour bus drivers squeezing by on my left and a three-foot high cement barrier on my right, the cycling was exhilarating, to say the least. I shot lots of video, including some helmet-cam stuff. There's a 10-minute helmet-cam video of me going downhill that has to be the best I've shot. It shows what a really good day on the bike looks like.

I found a $25 hotel room just past Salerno. I paid cash. Tomorrow I start the ride that I've been planning, and dreading, for weeks. I go over the Apennine Mountains, the spine of Italy.

Thursday, June 21st
Salerno to Picerno - 94.36 Km

As expected, it was a tough day, but I was well rested and up to the task. First, I had to get off of the coast and head into the hills. The first 20-30 Km on the S19 was not too difficult. Then, it gradually got steeper and steeper. By the time I reached this hotel in Picerno, my quads were completely dead.

I didn't use the route suggested in my cycling book, because it looked to be a bit circuitous. Instead, I chose a direct route that linked the S19 and the S94 with a back road that I found on the map near the town of Zuppino. Just before reaching Zuppino I stopped at a bar for a couple of Gatorade drinks and some potato chips to replace the electrolytes that I had been sweating out all day. The owner was thrilled to have an American in his bar and insisted that I sit down for a few minutes while I drank my Gatorade. He really wanted to talk to me. He brought over his son and we talked about my route, the Giro d'Italia, and the interesting history of his town during World War II. He told me that the townspeople hid from the Germans in caves in the hills above town. They stayed there until the Allied forces liberated Zuppino.

I had hoped to make it all the way to Potenza, but that wasn't going to be possible. It was farther than I had thought. The hotels and campgrounds are few and far between in the Apennines. So, when I saw a hotel at the top of a hill near Picerno, I rushed up to it. I probably looked a little disappointed when the man at the front desk said that the hotel wasn't open. They were renovating the interior. Another man who overheard the conversation suggested a hotel that was six Km away. He was heading that way and told me to follow him. Fortunately, it was all downhill as I sped around the hills following this guy's car. He took me to a new four-star hotel just across the valley from Picerno. I thanked him for his help and took a $50 room for the night. I have a great view of Picerno, another ancient hill town, outside of my window. Dinner was roast pork in the hotel restaurant. There are no other restaurants, supermarkets, or convenience stores nearby for a meal.

I'm having more trouble with e-mail. Earthlink changed their e-mail system and it's not allowing me in, probably because of some limitations of the Pocket PC operating system. I set up an Excite account in order to reply to some e-mail. The technology hassles never end.

Friday, June 22nd
Picerno to Metaponto - 137.43 Km

Well, I lost a credit card. I left my Visa credit card at the hotel on Ischia two days ago. I realized this when I went to pay last night's bill. I remembered the last place that I used it. I telephoned and, sure enough, the man at the front desk had it. After consulting with Visa and Fleet, I told him to destroy the card. Visa promised an emergency replacement card for me in Patras, Greece on Monday. Fleet was not very customer-friendly throughout the whole ordeal. I'll be happy to close my account there when I return from the trip. I used my Visa debit card to pay the bill.

Because of the credit card hassles, I got a late start. The first hour was all uphill on the S94 to Tito, the industrial area outside of Potenza. The rest of the day was downhill to the coast on the S407. I even had a tailwind most of the day. I really flew after passing through Potenza, and it was a good thing. The S407 was sort of a highway. Before Potenza, bicycles weren't allowed on it. Afterwards, we were allowed on at our own risk. In some places the shoulder was minimal. I also passed through a number of tunnels on the ride to Metaponto. The longest was over 800 meters. That's a long way to go in a poorly lit tunnel with traffic going past at 50 mph.

I ended up at a campground near the beach. After a few more calls to Fleet and Visa, I finally got some sleep. Without the credit card hassle, and the first hour of climbing, I could have easily done a century today. Yesterday was the summer solstice, so I had the daylight to do it. I'll just save those 100 miles for another day. Tomorrow I need to reach Brindisi and get on a ferry for Patras, Greece.

Saturday, June 23rd
Metaponto to Brindisi - 127.78 Km

It was another big mileage day. The first half of the day was into the wind on the S106. After cycling through Taranto, I had the wind hitting me sideways on the S7. Fortunately, the terrain was fairly flat and the roads smooth. I entered Brindisi on the Via Appia around 4:00 PM, bought a ticket on an 8:00 PM ferry, and said goodbye to Italy.

I got myself a private cabin with shower for only $100. There are some American backpackers on this ferry, but most of the passengers are Greek and Albanian families. They're a noisy bunch, so I'm happy to have my own cabin. I think that a hamburger from the ship's self-service restaurant made me a bit queasy. It just didn't taste right. I'll stay out of there for the rest of the voyage. It will take 18 hours to get to Patras. I should arrive around 3:00 PM Sunday. Greece is one hour ahead of Italy. Yippee! Another time zone.

Greece

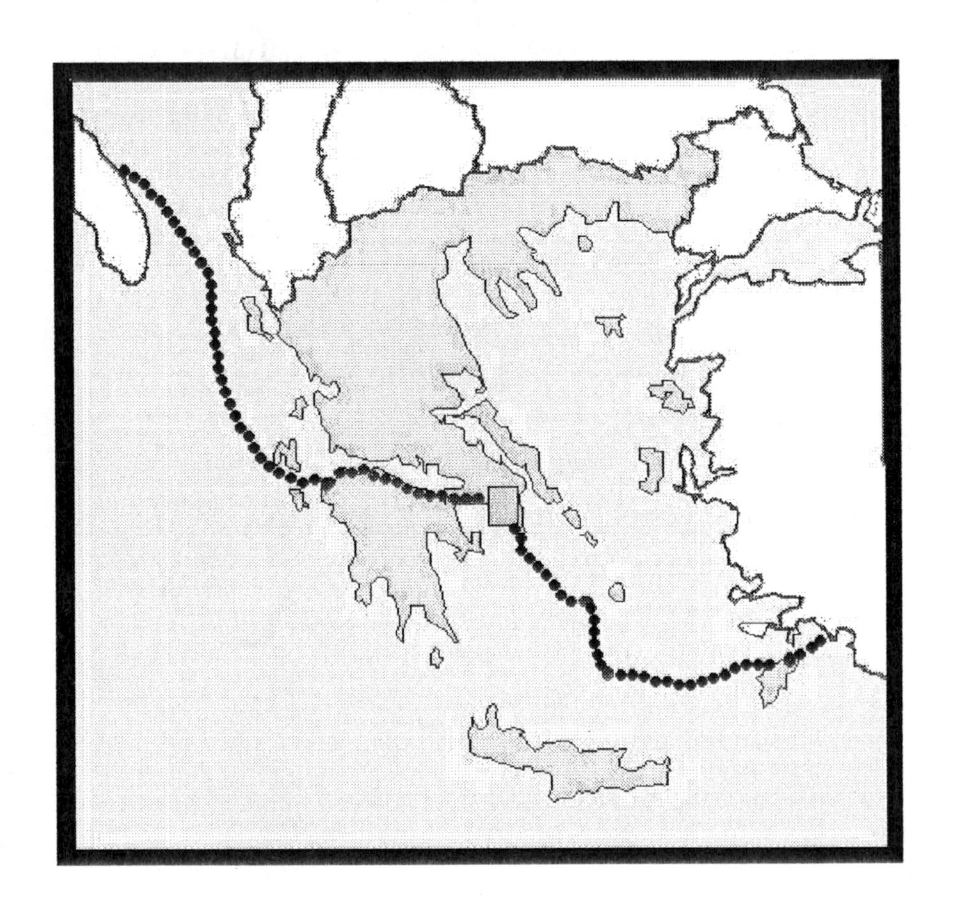

Sunday, June 24th
Brindisi to Patras, Greece - 0 Km

It was a lazy day, just relaxing on the ferry to Patras, Greece. At 8:00 AM the ferry docked at Igoumenitsa, near Corfu, to drop off most of the passengers. We cruised quietly the rest of the way to Patras. The remaining passengers were almost all backpackers.

Unlike my 1992 ferry trip to Patras, there was no Greek Customs to pass through today. I cycled out of the docks and found an ATM, a hotel, and a burger joint. At the ATM I miscalculated the new exchange rate and withdrew almost $400. Oops! I found a $25 room at the El Greko Hotel, which was undergoing renovations. There are no McDonalds in Patras, so I settled for a Hambo hamburger. It was OK. I can't find Gatorade here either.

Monday, June 25th
Patras - 9.4 Km

It was another lazy day. I checked out of the hotel and went to a laundromat to get the wash done. When the attendant said that it would take two hours, I decided to go to a nearby bike shop to look into replacing my chain and sprockets. The shop sold me a chain and freewheel, but couldn't do the work just then. They sent me to another shop a few blocks away. The mechanic there, Stavros, did the work quickly. When Stavros handed the bike back to me he warned that, due to excessive wear, I needed to replace one of the chainrings immediately. So, I went back to the first shop downtown where I had to order a whole new crank/chainrings combination. It won't be available until tomorrow morning. I rushed back to the El Greko hotel and got another room. Then, it was off to Hambo for another burger.

My replacement Visa card was never delivered to the bank in downtown Patras, as I requested a few days ago. I was told today that Visa needs an address, phone number, and contact person for delivery of a new card. I spent some time in an Internet café searching for a hotel in Athens where I could direct Visa to deliver the card. Ultimately, I ended up booking a room at the Hotel Cecil listed in my guidebook. That's the first reservation that I've made on this trip. After calling Visa with the contact information, they promised to deliver the card tomorrow. Other than that, I didn't do much today.

Tuesday, June 26th
Patras to Xilokastro - 109.31 Km

The bike and I were at the downtown bike shop at 9:00 AM to have the repairs completed. Around 10:00 AM I was told that I needed a new front derailleur to work with the new crank. The old derailleur did not travel far enough to shift the chain over all three chainrings. I had to come back in ninety minutes. So, I spent the time getting a haircut and working back at the Internet café. It looks like the e-mail problems may have been resolved.

When I returned at 11:30 AM, the bike was good to go. My drive train is almost entirely new now. I feel good about that. By noon I finally left Patras. I had to work hard because it was 230 Km to Athens, and I had hotel reservations in two days. The first 30 Km were a little hilly and into the wind. The rest of the ride was very pleasant cycling along the Corinthian Gulf. The weather was 85 degrees, sunny and calm. I passed the last campground before Corinth, so I took a $22 room in an average beach hotel here in Xilokastro. Athens is now 121 Km away.

Wednesday, June 27th
Xilokastro to Athens - 121.19 Km

I worked hard today to reach my hotel in Athens by 6:00 PM. I had booked a room for two nights and told the guy at the front desk that I would arrive between 5:00 PM and 6:00 PM. I arrived at 6:30 PM and was informed that they gave my room away because I was late. Rather than blow my stack, I asked them to find me another room, and they immediately did. At least they didn't give away my replacement Visa card, too.

The ride to Athens wasn't too strenuous. I cycled along the coasts of the Corinthian and Saronic Gulfs most of the way. The Corinth Canal connects the two gulfs. I shot some video at the canal, and then moved on through some industrial areas on the Saronic Gulf. Near Athens the old national highway gave way to the new super highway. It was congested, and more than a little dangerous. The Greeks have a nasty habit of driving on the shoulder of roads. I was looking in my rear-view mirror more than I was looking forward. I crested the last hill before Athens near Delphi, and then it was all downhill into the smog, congestion, and haphazard streets. I shot a little more video with the helmet-cam to show what it's like entering a big city by bicycle. It's some hair-raising video. I just wish that I could record sound with the helmet-cam to give the full effect.

The hotel that I'm in is not bad, but they could only take me in for one night. Tomorrow I have to begin searching for a room for two more nights.

Thursday, June 28th
Athens - 0 Km

I spent most of the day doing the tourist thing at the Agora and Acropolis. Near the entrance to the Acropolis is a large rock/small hill where Saint Paul supposedly addressed the Athenians. It's extremely slick now from years of tourists scampering all over it. I climbed it with a few other foolhardy souls. Getting down was more dangerous than getting up. In my cycling shoes I'm lucky that I didn't twist an ankle, or worse.

At 3:30 PM I called the AmEx office in Syntagma Square to check on the status of a care package from home but got the standard run-around, only this time in Greek. The AmEx office closed at 4:00 PM, so I hopped on the bike, raced up a pedestrian shopping street, attempted to ride over a 1" sloped curb, and fell. It was a slick marble curb, and I slid much farther than I thought possible. I got road rash around the left knee, but my ego was thoroughly crushed. After 5,200 Km of mostly back road riding, I had to fall off of the bike at 3:45 PM, on one of the busiest streets in Athens. I quickly got up and straightened the front wheel and handlebar. Some lady was trying to say something to me in German like, "You should be careful on these slick marble streets." I kept saying to her, "I'm OK. I'm OK." I hurried out of there and got to the Amex office just in time for my next disappointment. The package from home did not arrive yet. As Yogi Berra would say, it's like deja vu all over again. "Priority Mail" – now there's an oxymoron for you. With the prices that they charge, the Postmaster General should come up to my hotel room and hand deliver the package.

Fortunately, the day ended on an up note. The guy at the front desk of my new hotel, the redundantly named Hotel Jason Inn, told me that Vangelis was giving a big concert at the Temple of Zeus tonight. Tickets were $125, and all of the best people would be attending. Down the street from the temple was the old Olympic Stadium where the concert would be simulcast on a big screen for free. That seemed a better venue for me. I got to visit another monument and see one of my keyboard heroes in a rare concert appearance. It was worth the long walk to the stadium.

Friday, June 29th
Athens - 0 Km

I walked to the top of Filopappou Hill and shot some panoramic video of Athens this morning. Then, I walked through the ancient Plaka shopping district and didn't buy anything, other than Gatorade, lemonade, and Coke. I get very thirsty in the dry heat here. I also tend to sweat just a tad, like Charlton Heston in *Ben-Hur*.

I took a walk through the National Gardens and saw Hadrien's Arch, the Olympic Stadium, the presidential palace, and the changing of the guard. I also visited my friends at the Amex office again. Still, there is no package. Somewhere in the global postal system there is a Cliff Claven toying with me. I'm not waiting around for this package. I'm off to the islands tomorrow. I'll keep calling my friends at AmEx and decide what to do when/if it finally does arrive.

Saturday, June 30th
Athens to Naousa, Paros - 20 Km

I left the hotel around 10:00 AM to go to the port of Pireus. It was way too early because the ride was short and the ferries didn't leave until around 4:00 PM. I bought a ticket on a catamaran to Paros because it would get me there about 7:30 PM, giving me some daylight to cycle across the island to Naousa, find a campground, and set up camp. As it turns out, I needed every minute. I got a little lost around Naousa looking for my favorite campground from my 1992 visit here. The road signs and directions from the locals sent me in circles. By the time I got to the Surfing Beach campground and set up the tent, the sun was going down. No shower tonight.

Sunday, July 1st
Naousa, Paros - 10 Km

The mileage today is estimated because I never reset the odometer on the bike this morning. This is the campground where I stayed ten years ago. There are a few more new homes nearby now, and they no longer have saltwater for the showers. They now get fresh water piped from Naousa, which isn't much of an improvement.

I went to the 6:00 PM mass in Naousa at a church that was so small that they could only fit 60 wooden chairs inside. Not to worry, though. Only twelve people showed up for the mass, including the priest. I think he said the mass in Latin. He encouraged us to use a missalette that had the liturgy printed in Latin and five other languages. I did pretty well, following along with the mass. I'm getting quite an education on this trip.

Monday, July 2nd
Naousa, Paros - 10 Km

I cycled into Naousa this morning and dropped my wash off at the launderette. I cycled back in the early evening to pick up the clothes and to have dinner at one of the many outdoor cafés around the little port. The rest of the day I just hung out at the beach. That's not a bad day.

I did a dumb thing late tonight with the Pocket PC. I reset it before ever backing up my contact information and programs to the CompactFlash card. I was trying to get onto the Internet via an infrared connection with my mobile phone, but the PC hung up. It gave me an error warning and suggested that I do the reset. It was late at night in a dark tent, and I wasn't thinking straight. So, now I can't use the Targus Stowaway keyboard because I lost the driver. And, I can't send postcards to a lot of people because I lost their addresses. It's going to be a lot harder to remedy this goof while on the road. But, a valuable lesson has been learned; late at night in a dark tent I should be sleeping, not working on the Internet.

Tuesday, July 3rd
Naousa, Paros - 0 Km

Today I did a very touristy thing. I rented a motor scooter and went around Paros. I didn't want to bicycle around the island because it's hilly, the roads are bad, and some of the dogs are left free to chase unsuspecting cyclists.

The guy who rents the scooters didn't want to rent me one because of my limited experience (three days in Bermuda). He kept trying to get me into a "nice air-conditioned car." I had to take a quick spin around the block to prove my road-worthiness. I guess three straight months balancing on a bicycle wasn't good enough for him.

I stayed mainly on the coast and checked out a lot of the little fishing villages that, like Naousa, are beginning to cater to tourists. I drove over a few roads that eventually became rough tracks. At times I thought that the scooter might not be able to handle the abuse. But, that little 80cc scooter was tough.

Near the end of the day I took a ferry over to the little island of Antiparos. The Greeks have a habit of naming smaller cities and islands across from major cities and islands as "anti_____". So, they would have named Camden: Antiphiladelphia, and Hoboken: Antinewyorkcity. Antiparos seemed even more remote than Paros. As they say, it wasn't the end of the world, but you could see the end from there. I got the scooter back by 8:00 PM, and then had dinner at another outdoor café. I'm in the Pension Anna near the center of town tonight. Three straight nights in a tent is my limit.

Wednesday, July 4th
Naousa, Paros - 0 Km

I finally got a chance to visit a place that I've dreamed about for years, the island of Santorini. It is, as advertised, one of the most beautiful islands in the world. The capital of Fira and the village of Oia are particularly spectacular, dangling off cliffs high above the deep blue Mediterranean.

I took a one-day ferry/bus excursion with a lot of other tourists. It was a novel experience for me, and probably old-hat for my fellow travelers. On these organized tours you wear tags indicating the tour group that you're with. You get on and off the bus at designated times. And, you tend to move in a pack through the narrow streets of the old towns, like a rat through a snake. It's almost like a grade school class trip. Instead of chaperones though, each bus has a multi-lingual guide telling you everything that they know about the history and culture of Santorini. The whole thing took 12 hours. By 8:00 PM we were back at the docks in Naousa, in time for a dinner at another outdoor café. I can get used to this kind of travel.

Thursday, July 5th
Naousa, Paros - 0 Km

I moved out of the Pension Anna and into a nice hotel next door. The mosquitoes in the pension were eating me alive. In addition, there was no hot water this morning. The hotel room costs about $40 but is worth it for one night. I got some computer work done in the morning and relaxed by the pool in the afternoon. Dinner? It was at another outdoor café around the port, naturally.

Friday, July 6th
Naousa, Paros - 15.74 Km

I returned to Surfing Beach Campground again. The people in Reception didn't realize that I had left for three nights. There's really not much to report on these days at the beach. I just hang out for hours, watching the windsurfers and listening to the techno music blaring out from the bar. Of course, the tent site only costs me $3.75/day. Still, I can't wait for the care package to arrive in Athens.

Saturday, July 7th
Naousa, Paros - 0 Km

I've decided to return to Athens tomorrow and hope that the package arrives on Monday. By Tuesday I want to be on Rhodes. I just can't wait any longer. I'm getting fat and lazy here, but I'm tanning nicely. There's nothing else to report.

Sunday, July 8th
Naousa, Paros to Athens - 28.45 Km

I have to keep moving. Otherwise, I could grow old and die on Paros before the Greek postal system delivers my package from home. So, today I cycled across the island to the port in Parikia and bought a ticket on the slower 12:05 PM ferry back to Pireus. The tickets for the high-speed catamaran had sold out. The port was chaotic because all of the ferries were late today. My ferry was almost two hours late.

I got into Pireus around 7:00 PM and immediately headed northeast to Athens to find a hotel. It was only about a 10 Km ride from Pireus to Athens, and mostly straight as an arrow. When the Pireus road was laid out, it was aimed directly at the Acropolis. Despite the heavy traffic, I couldn't help but admire the view of the Parthenon as I cycled up to Athens. It was a simple ride back to the Hotel Jason Inn off of Ermou Street. They had a room available for $50, and I gladly took it. I'm a regular here now. Tomorrow I'll run a few errands in preparation for the next leg of the trip.

Monday, July 9th
Athens to Pireus - 17.47 Km

I had a late start, but still got a lot accomplished today. I sent off postcards, bought a Middle East guidebook in an English-language bookstore, bought a ticket for the 7:00 PM ferry to Rhodes, and looked into visa requirements for Turkey. But, most importantly, I got my package from home. Of the four inner boxes, Greek Customs only opened the box with the maps, books, and Sports Illustrated. I imagine it took Customs a few days to translate the articles in SI, searching for any derogatory remarks about their national soccer team. Still, I was like a kid at Christmas opening up all of the boxes on the sidewalk outside of the post office depot. I could barely fit everything in my panniers. I'll have to weed out a few spare items before I start traveling in Turkey.

Tuesday, July 10th
Pireus to Rhodes - 14.63 Km

The ferry ride was an overnight affair. I shared a cabin with two other guys, both truckers I think. They snored something fierce. I was in the top bunk, and I worried myself to sleep about falling out in rough seas. It was not a restful night.

The ferry made a few stops throughout the night. At 7:45 AM I asked one of the truckers in my cabin when we would arrive at Rhodes. I thought that it was supposed to be around 10:30 AM. He said "No, 8:00 AM." I quickly got dressed and hustled up to the Reception area where one of the crew told me that arrival at Rhodes was expected to be at 12:00 Noon. I went back to the cabin and relayed the message to my cabin-mate. He mumbled, "Sorry."

The old town of Rhodes is completely surrounded by castle walls. It's a well-preserved historic city. At the old port I saw where the Colossus of Rhodes once stood. It was one of the Seven Wonders of the Ancient World, but all that remains are two monuments on either side of the port entrance. The newer section of town is filled with hotels and clubs. It's a rockin' place at night. I was happy to get a room above the noise, on the roof of a six-story hotel. I have to climb to the top of the hotel stairwell, step out onto the tarred roof, and tiptoe through the pigeon droppings to get to my "penthouse suite." My single room up on the roof was probably not on the original architectural drawings. I don't mind, though. I have a bird's eye view of the castle walls. I took a quick spin around the old town in the afternoon and had a pizza for dinner. I'll hit the sack early. I want to be well rested for my first day of riding in Turkey.

Turkey & Northern Cyprus

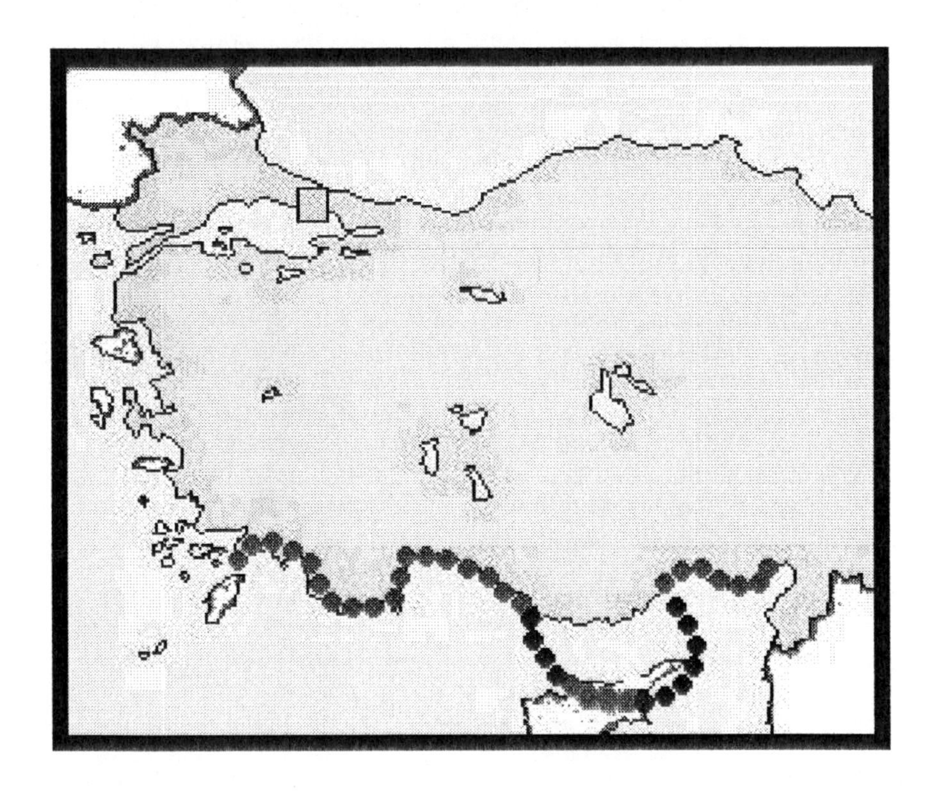

Wednesday, July 11th
Rhodes to Ortaca, Turkey - 87.14 Km

I took the 9:00 AM ferry from Rhodes to Marmaris. Although I was 15 minutes early for the hydrofoil, I didn't get my passport stamped at the Customs office near the entrance to the port. So, I reluctantly handed over the passport and 8,000 drachmas to a ferry company employee who rushed back on a motorbike to handle the paperwork. One passenger complained to the ferry guys at 9:00 AM that we hadn't left yet. They lied, telling him that there were more passengers coming. I felt a bit uncomfortable standing out there on the dock those last five minutes until the man on the motorbike returned with my stamped passport.

Marmaris is a nice town for yachties. I didn't want to spend too much time there. I used a $20 travelers check to pay the visa fee, then went looking for a bank. I withdrew 50 million Turkish lira, and then started to question my calculation of the exchange rate. Did I just take out $40, or $400? I immediately sent an e-mail home to have more money transferred into my checking account. By the end of the day, after buying a few grocery items, I realized where the decimal point was in the exchange rate.

My first impression of Turkey is that the roads are rough and poorly graded, the weather is hot and dry, and the people are overly friendly. Every kid I passed yelled "Hello", some many times, over and over. The adults all wanted me to sit down and talk with them. When I stopped at a gas station for a bottle of water, the employees came over and asked the usual questions: Where are you from? Where are you going? Are you married? Are you traveling with friends? What is your job? How do you like Turkey? I had to gracefully extract myself from these conversations in order to keep moving. It's not going to be easy to do 100 Km per day in Turkey.

Thursday, July 12th
Ortaca to Fethiye - 60.39 Km

In the immortal words of Mr. Nipsey Russell, "Spring has sprung. Fall has fell. It's the middle of July, and hotter than usual." This place is scorching. It's at least in the high 90's, if not over 100 degrees. Fortunately, I am in an air-conditioned hotel tonight. The Turkish lira is doing so poorly against the U.S. dollar in recent months that I can get a top-of-the-line hotel room for under $20.

The ride today was a killer. I've been on Route 400 since departing Marmaris. I did one 1,000-foot pass and a couple other big hills. After the 1,000-foot pass I rolled into the next town,

Gocek Gec, completely spent. I must have looked like a zombie stumbling into the market to buy a liter of Pepsi, a sport drink, and a loaf of bread. I consumed them right on the steps of the market and then went back for a liter of bottled water.

In hindsight, I should have taken a ferry from Rhodes to Fethiye, instead of Marmaris. I could have avoided two very difficult days of riding. There hasn't been much to see, and Route 400 has been very bumpy. I'm just torturing the bike and myself. Since it's so hot here they can't use regular asphalt for the roads. That would buckle too easily. They have to lay down tar and cover it with stones. As the stones wear away it leaves a bumpy surface. I'm worried that it will be like this all of the way across Turkey, and beyond.

Friday, July 13th
Fethiye to Patara - 79.35 Km

I'm on the outskirts of the town where the real St. Nicholas was born. I didn't go all the way into Patara because it was down a nearly impassable road. At least, it seemed impassable in my state. I am zapped again. The hills weren't as bad, but the roads were just as bumpy. And, I had headwinds the last 45 Km. I think that the heat may also be stealing some of my energy. I drink liters of water and soda, and I sweat it out almost immediately. I feel like I'm back in football camp doing two-a-days.

I'm staying in a hotel that caters to German tourists. There's no air-conditioning, and dinner is served buffet style in the restaurant. "Buffet style" means that you have no choice but to eat whatever they've cooked. I'm staying in my room tonight with two fans running, eating a Met-Rx bar for dinner. The hotel is not near any other restaurants or stores. There's just farmland outside. Oh, well. That's the joy of bicycle touring.

Saturday, July 14th
Patara to Kas - 41.08 Km

Wow! This was supposed to be an easy day. Instead, I ended up pushing the bike again within the first 10 Km. There is a combination of factors for this difficulty that I'm having. First, after my drive train was overhauled in Greece, I lost my lowest gearing. I can no longer just spin my way up any hill, no matter how steep. Second, because of the rough road surfaces in Turkey, the rolling resistance is very high. I have to work for every inch. Third, the heat is oppressive, even at 9:00 AM. It's in the high 90's every day. I think that I may have lost some leg strength during my time off of the bike in Greece, too. That should be enough excuses for now.

The last 25 Km on Route 400 today was along a very scenic coastline. I saw a couple of the old wooden boats that ferry tourists around here to the different coves. I had to stop and take a picture. That's the way to tour Turkey.

I must have lost weight since starting the trip because the receptionist at the hotel today looked at my passport photo and immediately said that I looked thinner. An unsolicited compliment. I think that I may stay here for three nights, and not just because of the compliment. For $16/night I will have air-conditioning and a nice pool. I need to rest before the next leg to Finike, too. I'm dreading it. I was seriously thinking about ferrying around it.

I found an Internet café in town and downloaded the driver for my Stowaway keyboard successfully there. Now, I need to catch up with my journal entries. I'll return to the café tomorrow to upload some pictures, send off a few more e-mail messages, and start a web page. I may even download some more software for the Pocket PC.

Sunday, July 15th
Kas - 0 Km

I'm taking today and tomorrow off in order to rest up for some tough hills after Kas. I'm not looking forward to the ride up from this seaside town. The hotel is very nice, and I spent a couple hours relaxing poolside this morning. I set up the beginnings of a web page this evening at the Internet café. I'll return tomorrow to enhance it a bit. I don't imagine that it will be as comprehensive as my previous personal web page, but it will give the folks back home a chance to see some of the places that I have visited.

I had a steak for dinner, trying to get as much protein as I can before cycling out of here. I also called home to discuss a few trip details. It was great to hear about things back there.

Monday, July 16th
Kas - 0 Km

I was kicked out of my hotel this morning, just like Keith Moon in the 1970's. I didn't throw the TV set off of my balcony or drive a car into the pool, but I committed the sin of not paying for all three nights up front. The lady at the front desk was very apologetic and got me into a sister hotel down the street right away. It's not as nice, but it's still a three-star hotel. I spent the afternoon sleeping. Tomorrow I start riding again. Oh boy!

Tuesday, July 17th
Kas to Finike - 80.14 Km

I got through a day that I was dreading. I knew that the road out of Kas was going to be difficult. I had been looking up at it from the hotel pool for the past three days. I was on the road at 8:20 AM, and by 10:00 AM I finally reached the top of the pass out of Kas, nine Km away. There were a few more hills to climb, and then a descent into Kale at the 50 Km mark. Route 400 from Kale to Finike was mainly coastal cycling and not too challenging.

Throughout the course of the day I sweated more than the entire crew of *Das Boot*. Every chance that I had, I bought bottled water and sodas. I was forced to accept un-bottled water a few times because of the scarcity of markets with the bottled kind. Some of it came from public fountains and some from old two liter Coke bottles that the locals had filled with water and refrigerated. They drank the stuff in front of me. So when I was offered some, I drank it too. I'm very nervous about catching any bugs. I don't want to be laid up in a hotel for seven days while one passes through me.

I'm in a nice air-conditioned hotel room tonight for 11 million Turkish lira. At an exchange rate of 1.4 million lira to the dollar, that translates to an $8 room. I watched a show tonight on TV, in Turkish, about the falling lira vs. the dollar. I'm feeling compelled to buy something here. What are the odds that someone in Finike will offer to sell me an original 1967 3C Moog Modular synthesizer?

Wednesday, July 18th
Finike to Kemer - 84.36 Km

There was only one hill today. Of course, it took half of the day to reach the top. There is a pattern to my days lately. I start in port towns and spend my cycling hours going inland, up and over a mountain to the next port town. There are very few markets or restaurants inland, up in the hills, so I have to make sure that I have enough water to get me over the hill. On a long hill like today, in 100-degree heat, that's not possible. I have to hope that I come across some place to get water in the middle of the climb. It took a while today before I came across a restaurant near the top of the hill. I downed two large Cokes and a large glass of water, and then filled all three water bottles with ice water. I stopped a few minutes later farther up the hill for another Coke. I know that the Cokes promote dehydration, but they also give a quick energy boost that I need in the mountains.

At the end of the day I thought that I had pulled into Kemer, but it was a resort area just south of Kemer that caters to Germans. I was turned away from five or six hotels. It's high season around here, and the resort was fully booked. I left thinking that I had to cycle another 50 Km to Antalya for a room. Fortunately, a traveler at a gas station outside of the resort told me that Kemer was only two Km up the road. After two rejections in Kemer, I finally found a hotel room for the night. The German holidaymakers in this hotel looked at me as if I had just arrived from Mars. The kids asked me the usual questions, and a few unusual ones. One kid asked me if I was a star back in America. Another asked if I was making a film. It's amazing what a pair of sunglasses can do for your image. I finished the day with a big pizza. I'm looking forward to the Burger King in Antalya.

Thursday, July 19th
Kemer to Antalya - 53.07 Km

The terrain wasn't too bad today, but the road surface was lousy. They must have recently poured the tar and stones because they were painting lines today on a long section of Route 400. I did cycle through two unlit tunnels, the longest being 300+ meters. The last 10 Km into Antalya is lined with beaches and hotels. I saw a McDonalds as I approached the city center, always a good sign. I'm in a hotel a few blocks away from the action for $20/night. Tomorrow I'll look into alternate plans to avoid the worst of the Turkish Coast. I'm thinking of taking a ferry to Northern Cyprus and then back to Turkey farther up the road, past the most difficult section. I'll see what the travel agencies have to say tomorrow.

I saw the movie *Pearl Harbor* tonight. It was in English with Turkish subtitles. That was fine with me, until the scenes with Japanese-speaking characters were also subtitled in Turkish. Still, I could follow the plot, and it was a good diversion. I think I was supposed to sit in an assigned seat in the near-empty theater, but I just sat in the front row and stretched my legs. The usher made a half-hearted attempt to get me into my assigned seat but gave up when he realized that I didn't speak Turkish. Ignorance truly is bliss.

Friday, July 20th
Antalya - 16.22 Km

I was unsuccessful with the travel agencies today. The language barrier became a real deterrent to my gathering any ferry info. I'm going to continue cycling to Alanya, and then probably take a ferry to Northern Cyprus. From there, who knows? Besides three different ports farther down the Turkish coast, I'm also considering returning to the mainland at Haifa, Israel. That would cut out a lot of difficult Km. I could also avoid Syria, which still hasn't granted me a visa. Entry into Syria is strictly controlled. They require a full itinerary from a traveler before they will approve a visa application. How would I know when I'd reach the Syrian border on this trip? My second application is at the Syrian embassy in Washington, DC right now with a guestimated itinerary. It doesn't look promising.

I had my third and fourth flats today. I had a slow leak for a few days, so when I removed a pin from the tire casing I thought that I had fixed the problem. I found out a few Km later that only half of the problem was fixed. A shard of glass was also stuck in the tire casing. Who would have thought to look for two different objects poking through the Kevlar tires? Not I.

I finished off the day with my second Burger King dinner in as many days. The forecast for tomorrow is 100 degrees again. I can't wait to get back on the road.

Saturday, July 21st
Antalya to Manavgat - 101.7 Km

I'm sitting in a $165 hotel room typing this journal entry. It's amazing how similar the $165 room is to the $20 rooms that I've been in lately. A buffet style dinner by the pool is included in the price, so maybe the burger and two hot dogs that I ate account for the $145 difference. I still had to pay for my post-dinner ice cream. "All-inclusive" does not include ice cream or hard liquor. If it were, it would be unfair to the guests who have no desire to be fat and drunk.

The ride here from Antalya was surprisingly enjoyable. For the first time in Turkey, I spent most of the day on smooth asphalt. And, the terrain was fairly flat. I don't even think that the temperature hit 100 degrees today. I can't complain about the headwind because it kept me cool.

I had hoped to go to the town of Side at the end of the day to see the Greek ruins, including a massive amphitheater by the sea. But, I decided against it when I saw that the four Km "side-road" (pun intended) was poorly paved. Why cycle an extra eight Km on bad roads just to take a few pictures and be turned away at a few hotels? So, I continued on.

I knew that Dad was going to call me at 7:00 PM, so I became a little anxious around 6:00 PM when two seaside resort villages had turned me away. I had seen, and been turned down at, similar resorts near Kemer. They are guarded, fenced-in holiday camps for German tourists. I decided to try a little deception to get into this camp. I called them from a couple of Km away, said that I was an American (implying wealthy), and that I needed a room for the night. No mention of a bike was ever made. Bingo! They had a room for me. "Great", I said. I gave them my name and said that I would arrive shortly. You should have seen the look on the security guard's face when I arrived at the gatehouse on my bike and said that I had a reservation. I doubt that he had ever seen a guest as sweaty and dirty as me pull up. He immediately called in to the front desk and said something about a bicycle. Then, the guard put me on the phone and I explained to the front desk that I was just guaranteed a room. They asked for the guard again, and more discussions ensued. I felt like Richard Pryor at a Klan rally. They wanted me to leave so badly. Eventually the guard let me through the gates and I cycled down the long driveway, past the manicured lawns, to the Reception building. There was no bike rack out front, so I just leaned the bike against a post, giving it a prominent position in front of the building for all to see. I knew what the cost was at the resorts near Kemer, so I didn't flinch when they told me the price here. I think that I even gained some respect from two bellboys when I told them how far I had come. Maybe it was worth the money just to strike a blow and gain some respect for bicycle-tourists the world over. Or, maybe not. At least I was able to tell Mom and Dad that I was safely in a hotel for the night when we spoke on the phone. And, I get to wear a cool red wrist bracelet for the duration of my stay at the Majesty Club - Palm Beach.

Sunday, July 22nd
Manavgat to Alanya - 52.49 Km

Another Sunday has passed and I was unable to find a Catholic Church. I don't think I've seen one in Turkey since arriving. The cycling today should have been fairly easy, but I am running out of steam. The road surface was very rough again, and I had some headwinds. Fortunately, some of the riding was on a service road beside Route 400. I think that the heat is beginning to take its toll.

Alanya has a large fort at the top of a hill jutting out into the Mediterranean. Had I been a little less tired, I might have climbed to the top. Instead, I have to be content to enjoy the view from sea level. I was so tired when I reached Alanya that I forgot to ask if the hotel that I'm in had air-conditioning. Of course, it doesn't. That means I'm in store for another hot night. I've got a 7:30 AM wake-up call tomorrow because I'm taking the 9:00 AM ferry to Girne, Northern Cyprus. I bought a ticket today, with a return to Tasucu, Turkey. The return was an extra $5. I probably will not use it, but it seemed like a wise investment at the time. I was informed that the return is good for a year, in case I should find myself in Northern Cyprus again. I'll have to find a safe place to store that ticket.

Like many of the port cities in Turkey, this place comes alive at night. There is live music in many of the bars by the waterfront. It seems like the whole town strolls down here when the sun goes down. I took a stroll around myself. I don't think they watch much prime time TV in these towns. Everybody is out and about, making the scene and being seen. I told you I was tired.

Monday, July 23rd
Alanya to Girne, Northern Cyprus - 6.02 Km

My wake-up call was done in person. I guess, like the A/C, the phones in this hotel don't work. It took an hour and a half to get about 50 passengers past Customs and onto the ferry. I have to laugh at the formalities involved in going from Turkey to the Turkish Puppet State of Northern Cyprus (T.P.S.N.C.). Turkey is the only country in the world that recognizes Northern Cyprus as a sovereign nation, yet they try to legitimize that state status by forcing you through Customs and stamping your passport. You would have thought that I was passing from North Korea to South Korea.

The ferry ride was very comfortable and we arrived at Girne, Northern Cyprus (Southern Turkey) around noon. Girne isn't a large town, but it has a very picturesque old harbor and fort. I took a room with a balcony at the Hotel Atlantis facing the harbor. I made sure that it had A/C this time. My room is on the top floor (elevator turned off by the way), and I noticed that the management had hung large flags of Turkey and Northern Cyprus from the railing on my balcony. The two flags are reversed images of each other. Turkey has white symbols on a red field. Northern Cyprus has the same symbols in red on a white field. They're probably both sewn in the same factories. In this way there would be no wasted fabric from the red and white bolts of cloth.

I mention the flags because, after going on walkabout in Girne, I returned to my room to find the flags removed, the balcony door left open, the used towels in the bathroom placed back on the rack, and the A/C not working. I told the guy at the front desk that the A/C in my room had mysteriously stopped working while I was out. He gave me another remote control for the A/C. When that didn't work, I drug him up to the room. He tried both remotes and failed, as expected. Then, this guy miraculously knew to reach under a night table and flick a hidden switch to get the A/C unit working again. These people are so keen to save electricity that they turned off my A/C while I was out, just like they turned off the elevator. I guess they had hoped that I wouldn't complain so diligently. Ha! I'll teach them a lesson. I'll set the thermostat to 60 degrees and sleep under two blankets tonight.

Tuesday, July 24th
Girne to Gazamagusa - 84.7 Km

I woke up this morning with the sound of water dripping from my A/C unit onto the night table. I had cranked it up so much that the huge bottle on the balcony that collects all of the condensation from the unit had been completely filled. The water had backed up and started dripping in the room. No problem. I wanted to get up then anyway. And, I got a great night sleep.

The guy at the front desk asked for $US 30 for the room. So, I went to a couple of banks to exchange some of my American Express travelers' checks for U.S. dollars. The second bank gave me Turkish lira and said that the Hotel Atlantis would accept it. Fortunately, they were right. If I had known that I wouldn't have gone to the trouble of trying to get U.S. currency. As a final insult, the crack Hotel Atlantis staff put my bike outside overnight. I was more than happy to check out of there.

One of the reasons that Girne is such a scenic town is that it has a mountain range as its backdrop. The mountain range runs the length of the island and separates Girne from the other major port of Gazamagusa. I climbed over that range this morning on the main road. I know it was the main road because 1) it was paved, and 2) every ten minutes a car or truck passed me. Man, was it hot. When I reached the top I actually had to wring the sweat out my shirt and cycling gloves. There was a restaurant at the top where I replaced the fluids that I sweated out on the climb. Then, I enjoyed a wild descent down the other side of the range. By the time I reached the plains at the bottom, my shirt and gloves had completely dried. The last 50 Km was across flat farmland. Better still, it was on a newly paved road that had not yet been open to traffic. So, while the cars going east and west had one lane each, I was on the other side of a grass median strip with two lanes to myself. If it weren't for some headwinds, it would have been perfect riding conditions.

In Gazamagusa I bought a ferry ticket to Mersin, Turkey where three different Cypriots assured me that I could get a ferry to Haifa, Israel. The ferry for Mersin departed at 9:00 PM, so I didn't get a hotel room and shower. It wouldn't matter because I bought a deck class ticket. That means just what it says. I would spend the night on the deck with the rest of the tired, poor, and huddled masses while first class passengers basked in the opulence of an air-conditioned lounge.

The few hours that I spent in Gazamagusa were more than enough. It is a town that has never recovered from the war that split the island. I've never seen so many ruined churches in one city. The military presence is overwhelming. I even saw a UN jeep on the way into town. It's probably the most depressing place that I've visited so far, other than Tangier. I couldn't imagine living there.

Wednesday, July 25th
Gazamagusa to Mersin - 1.72 Km

The seas were rough, my friend. This added to the enjoyment of 12 hours of deck class. Many of my fellow passengers suffered from "mal de mer", seasickness. Fortunately, I was not affected. Unfortunately, I couldn't find a place to stretch out during the trip, so I wandered about the ship looking for comfortable places to rest. There were none.

Just before we docked in Mersin I went below deck to the area of the ship where the cars, trucks, and my bike were held. The door to the hold was locked and, before I knew it, the rest of the passengers had followed me down the passageway and blocked me in. If the ferry started to sink then, I would have been a dead man. I literally sweated that one out for 15 minutes while the ship was docking. Afterwards, I got my first taste of corrupt officials demanding bribes. While waiting in line to go through customs, one of the port police said, "Give me your passport and one million lira, and follow me." We went into the hall. He spoke with one of the police checking passports, and then came back and said, "Go to the first policeman." I went to the first policeman, was handed my passport, and was sent on my way. Baksheesh and bureaucracy are why Turkey will never be a world economic power.

As surprising as it may seem, I was apparently misled by the three people in Northern Cyprus who said that there was a ferry from Mersin to Haifa. Abdullah at the Flash Travel Agency confirmed what I had heard from other authorities in Mersin today. There is no such ferry. I also could not rent a car for a trip across Syria or take a train. I even checked the marina to see if any American yachts were in town. Maybe I could help crew a yacht to Israel, I thought. No luck. I could fly over Syria to get to Israel. Even that had to be done in a backward fashion. I would have to fly from Adana to Istanbul, then Istanbul to Tel Aviv. At this point I still do not have a visa approval from the Syrian embassy in Washington, DC. I have no choice. I booked the flight for $344 cash with Abdullah. He also used his contacts to get me a good room in Mersin tonight, and a four-star room in Adana tomorrow night, for great prices. He was a great guy, and we talked for an hour about the Turkish economy, his family, his business, and his dream of coming to America to sell boiled corncobs on South Beach in Miami. It's a popular product for street vendors to sell in Turkey. Maybe there's a market for it in America. I wished him good luck and prepared for a final day of cycling in Turkey.

Thursday, July 26th
Mersin to Adana - 72.56 Km

I cycled through Tarsus, Saint Paul's hometown, today. What a dive. Adana isn't much better. I'm in a four-star hotel tonight for 30 million lira, instead of the standard 80 million lira, courtesy of Abdullah at Flash. Once again, I have to wonder how stars are awarded to hotels. I suppose it's handled similar to the way the IOC awards Olympic games to host cities, that is "money talks."

I had an incident today when I stopped at a small store to buy water, soda, and some crackers. The owner's entire extended family cornered me, had me sit down, and asked a variety of questions. I had a sense that, while I was speaking with some of them, others were outside looking through my panniers. I tried to gracefully get out of the store, and they all but tackled me. I took off as soon as I got out, without even waiting for my change. When I got down the road I took a complete inventory of the panniers. Everything was accounted for. I think I got out of there just in time.

Then, in Mersin, I was walking the streets looking for supplies to transport my bike, and for some food. While I answered questions from a few local kids I attempted to extract myself from the usual conversation by pointing to a cafeteria and saying, "I need to go there to eat." The smartest kid in the bunch cheerfully said, "OK. Follow me." We walked across the street together, and then another 30 yards to the cafeteria. I was surprised when this kid, who impressed me with his knowledge of English, then turned towards me, put out his hand, and said, "Money. Money." I had pictured this kid being first in his class at Mersin Elementary School, and here he was, sinking to the level of a common beggar. There were a lot of things that I wanted to say to him. Instead, I just gave him my spare change and walked away, disgusted. If Turkey's best and brightest have no sense of pride...

Israel & the West Bank

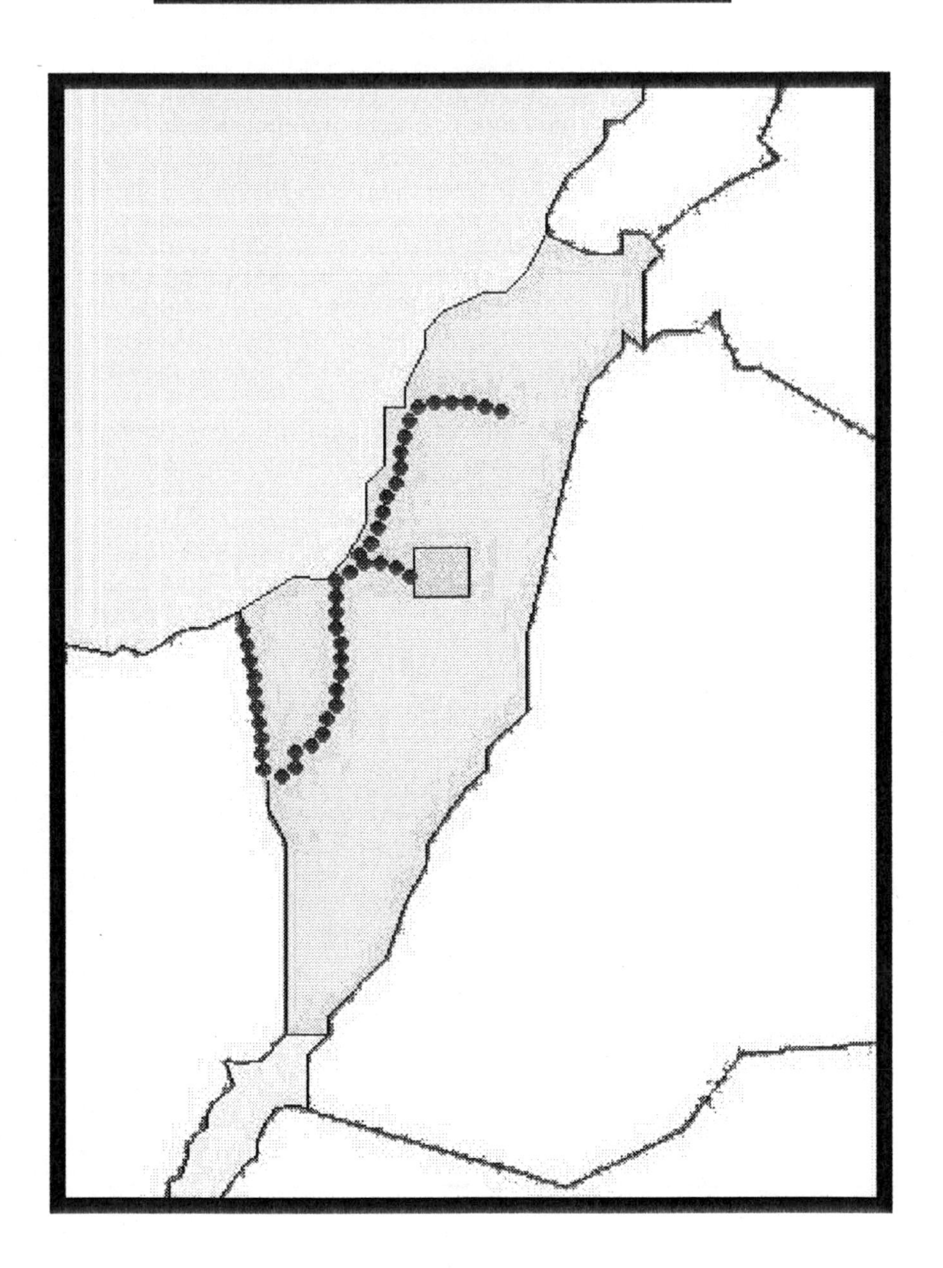

Friday, July 27th
Adana to Tel Aviv, Israel - 34.57 Km

Note to self: If the opportunity should arise again, *do not* mention failed attempts to obtain Syrian visa to Israeli border police. I spent 20 minutes today explaining to airport security about my plans to bicycle around the world. No, I do not have a job or a home address. Yes, I had hoped to go through Syria first, but they had refused my visa request. No, I have nowhere to stay tonight and no friends in Israel to help me. Yes, I realize that there is a heightened state of tension in Israel now. Yes, I bought my one-way Turkish Air ticket with cash only three days ago. They kept asking "Why Israel? Why now?" I tried to explain that it was on the way to Egypt. I made reference to the challenge of adventure travel. I even quoted mountaineers Sir Edmund Hillary and George Mallory: "Because it's there." I can't believe they let me in.

All of the pieces of the bike fit back together again. Soon, I was out of the airport and getting lost in a foreign land with no money, no water, and no knowledge of the local language. Things were back to normal. After some invigorating highway riding on Route 1, I arrived in Tel Aviv proper. At the first hotel that I came across, I booked a room for the night. That appears to have been a mistake. This place is mighty seedy. I'll be happy if I don't catch any diseases here.

Saturday, July 28th
Tel Aviv to Haifa - 113.92 Km

I had a good time on the bike today. The wind was at my back and the roads were fast and flat. I didn't stop to do any sightseeing along the way because I knew that I would probably be returning this way after visiting Nazareth tomorrow. Since it was the Sabbath, the streets of Tel Aviv were completely empty at 10:00 AM. It was an eerie *Twilight Zone* sight, but it made the cycling that much easier. On the way out of Tel Aviv there are a lot of hotels on the beach where I could have stayed last night. When I return I'll choose one of them.

Finding a hotel room in the coast town of Haifa was a challenge. The town rises up from the Mediterranean dramatically. There didn't appear to be any hotels at sea level. I had to work my way up some switchbacks before I found the Haifa Tower Hotel. Staying here tonight will put me back $60, but the view from the 12th floor is spectacular. Luxury has its price. Dinner tonight was menu item #1, Biggie sized, at Chez McDonalds.

Sunday, July 29th
Haifa to Nazareth - 60.39 Km

Jesus must have been in great shape growing up around the hills of Nazareth. There are very few flat places here. If you're not going uphill, and you're not going downhill, then you're standing still to catch your breath. I did all three at the end of my ride today while searching for a room. There aren't many choices for a simple pilgrim on a bike. You have to show up with a busload of fellow-tourists before they'll open a hotel for business. July doesn't seem to be the high season for religious pilgrimages.

The ride from Haifa on Route 75 was relatively short, but had a couple of difficult climbs. I really miss the lowest gearing that was lost when I had my freewheel and chainrings replaced in Greece. But, the climbing didn't bother me too much because I knew that Nazareth was close. Even the fifth flat of the trip didn't faze me. It wasn't until I got to Nazareth and couldn't find a hotel that I started to feel fatigued. It took three hours to find this one, the Grand New Hotel. It's way up in the hills, away from the action, if there is any action in Nazareth. At least the room has A/C. Tomorrow I'll take a day off and tour the city on foot, the way Jesus would have.

Monday, July 30th
Nazareth - 0 Km

It's 1:00 AM, July 31st, and I'm still awake because of the live music blaring from a rooftop party a few streets over. Middle Eastern music is an acquired taste. The uninitiated might not appreciate the janglely, repetitive nature of the music after midnight. I count myself among the uninitiated.

The Grand New Hotel seems to be empty tonight. Last night's busload of Italian pilgrims has moved on to the next site on their Holy Land checklist. The hotel staff must have been given the day off because my room wasn't made up while I was out seeing the sights. I'm surprised that they didn't just leave me the hotel's master key and instructions for the circuit breakers and water heater.

I did spend about four hours walking through the old city of Nazareth. I saw where Mary and Joseph lived and worked. I saw the well where Mary got her water and the angel Gabriel appeared to her. I saw where Jesus ate with His disciples after the Resurrection. I also walked through the souk, the labyrinth of alleys that constitute the old Arab marketplace. Nazareth is almost 70% Arab today, and that's most evident in the souk where falafel stalls abound. If I was so inclined, I could have picked up a wood carving of a camel or a brass hookah pipe. I was not. Instead, I went back to the hotel and did my laundry. Even in Nazareth I still had mundane tasks to perform.

Tuesday, July 31st
Nazareth to Netanya - 112.5 Km

This was originally planned to be a short day of coasting downhill to Haifa. Then, I got ambitious. I arrived at Haifa around 12:30 PM and decided to continue down the coast towards Tel Aviv. Six hours later I was cycling hard to find a place to stay before nightfall. Ambition, not sloth, should have been one of the seven deadly sins.

There are two roads heading down the coast, Routes 2 and 4. Route 2 is closer to the Mediterranean. It's almost a super-highway with narrow shoulders along many stretches. Route 4 is the old national highway. It's inland a bit and has wider shoulders. It's a more bicycle-friendly road. Naturally, I ended up on Route 2. By the end of the day I was sharing my personal space with most of Israel's tractor-trailers. All of the hotels are on the coast, and that's where I needed to be.

I had wasted too much time in Caesarea looking at Roman and Crusader ruins. Herod established Caesarea in 22 B.C. to honor Augustus Caesar. It is now a large tourist complex with lots to see, most notably the Roman amphitheater and Crusader castle. The guy selling tickets to the complex suggested that I check out the amphitheater first, since it would be closing at 6:00 PM. It turns out that they are holding a rock concert in the amphitheater tonight, and the band's roadies had already built the stage. They were doing the sound check when I arrived. I strolled around the grounds trying to imagine life 2,000 years ago, while pre-recorded Red Hot Chili Pepper tunes blared from the speakers. My illusions of the glory of Rome were further shattered when I went under the seating and saw the modern cement supports that were keeping this relic standing. I felt as though I had just looked behind the Wizard's curtain. I suppose the supports are necessary. Otherwise, the Chili Peppers would have leveled whatever was still standing.

I made it to Netanya, an Israeli summer resort, with a half-hour of sunlight to spare. There are many cheap hotels available here. I took a room one block back from the beach for $25. The rest of the night was spent addressing the bureaucracy of moving my money from one financial institution to another. There are bills to pay back home, and my checking account needs a cash infusion immediately. After a few international phone calls, e-mail messages, and faxes, I am back in business.

I passed the 4,000 mile and 6,500 Km marks today. That called for a celebration at Burger King.

Wednesday, August 1st
Netanya to Jerusalem - 105.71 Km

Today's ride was one of the toughest so far. The rides to Granada, Spain and Potenza, Italy may have been steeper, but not by much. The day started out innocently as the first 50 Km paralleled the coast on Route 4. Then, I turned inland through Ramla, home of Joseph of Arimathea (don't ask). Near Latrun I got onto Route 1 and began the real work. Route 1, as the number implies, carries more than its fair share of traffic. Along some stretches there is no shoulder. There are almost no services along the last 20 Km into Jerusalem. And, it's almost all uphill. Two Km from the city I hit the wall. I had no water left, and just a few cookies. I sat by the side of the road eating the cookies, hoping to regain some strength for the final push. It took about 20 minutes to recover. Eventually, I made it to Zion Square in West Jerusalem. I rested the bike against the wall of the Kaplan Hotel just off of the Square and ran inside to request a room. Sixty seconds later, when I went outside to retrieve the bike, a crowd had formed across the street. They thought that the fully loaded bike could have been a bomb, and they let me know it. Sufficiently chastised, I apologized for the security breach and then took the bike into the hotel.

People come to Jerusalem to be closer to God. I think the altitude has a lot to do with that. It's not heaven, but you can reach it from here.

Thursday, August 2nd
Jerusalem - 0 Km

I walked around the Old City of Jerusalem today. On the way to the Jaffa Gate I stopped at the Amex office and picked up a package from home that included a new Visa card, $100 cash, and my elusive U.S. passport. Then, I passed through the traditional pilgrims' gate into Jerusalem. The "guides" and "independent salesmen" were waiting inside the gate to pounce, just as I imagine they were centuries ago. They're a persistent lot. They try to engage you in a conversation, find your weakness, and then go in for the kill. The trick to getting away from these guys is to keep moving and to volunteer no personal information. Revealing so much as your name could lead to the purchase of a huge stuffed camel doll.

The Old City is divided into the Christian, Muslim, Jewish, and Jehovah's Witness quarters. I could be wrong about that last one. Anyway, I wandered through all four. It's a bit of a sensory overload. The sights, sounds, and particularly the smells are very real. This isn't Disney's ReligionLand. The market streets (alleys really) are claustrophobic, scary, and more than a little unhygienic.

I walked most of the Via Dolorosa, one of the main market streets now. I toured the Church of the Holy Sepulcher and the Wailing Wall. I paid a little Muslim boy to "guide" me to the Dome of the Rock. On the way some elderly Muslim men stopped us and chastised the boy for taking a heathen to see the Dome. They told me that if I wanted to see the Dome I would have to come back when they weren't praying, hire a real guide, and convert to Islam. Again, I could be wrong about that last one.

Anyway, it was a successful day of sightseeing. Despite the rising tensions here I was able to walk through all four quarters of the Old City without being harassed. And, you know how militant those Jehovah's Witnesses can be. At the end of the day I returned to my hotel just off of Zion Square (the Fast Food Quarter) where relations between McDonalds, Burger King, and Pizza Hut have never been better.

Friday, August 3rd
Jerusalem - 0 Km

There's too much of Jerusalem to see in just one day. So, I went sightseeing again. Besides, I still hadn't recovered from the ride up here. I decided to explore outside the walls of the Old City today. There was some trouble last Friday in the Old City. I thought it might be safer outside of the walls. I felt as though I was the only tourist in Israel as I walked the deserted road up to the Mount of Olives. On the way back down I saw that demonstrators praying in the street had blocked one of the major thoroughfares on my right. So, I turned left and walked to the church built over the site of the Last Supper. I finished the day of sightseeing by walking the ramparts of the Old City.

It felt bizarre to be walking around Jerusalem with a camcorder and guidebook, while the entire Israeli Army was out there with automatic weapons. While walking from the Garden of Gethsemane to the Tomb of the Virgin Mary, one female soldier armed to the teeth asked, "Can I help you?" We were standing between two of Christianity's holiest sights, so I couldn't say that I was lost. I just replied, "I guess it's not a good day to be a tourist." She gave me the "all clear" signal and I continued on my way, careful not to make any sudden movements. I'm sure that my every move was recorded and documented by the security forces. Thank goodness I didn't have to use the public restrooms.

Saturday, August 4th
Jerusalem to Bethlehem - 12.42 Km

It wasn't enough to watch the tensions between the Israelis and Palestinians escalate every hour on the BBC World News. I had to go out and get in the middle of it. I decided to ride the 10 Km to Bethlehem to see the Church of the Nativity and Manger Square. It didn't matter that Bethlehem was inside the West Bank. I was determined to see where Jesus was born, stay the night, and attend mass tomorrow morning in the oldest, continuously used church in Christendom.

The ride was a pleasure, flat and little trafficked, until I got to the eight-foot high cement barrier behind the sign stating, "Military Zone - No Admittance". It became decidedly less fun after that. I turned around, rolled back half a block and asked some locals how to get to Bethlehem. They pointed back at the cement barrier and said, "Just stay to the left." So I did. There was room to the left of the barriers that I hadn't seen originally. After passing the barriers there was a short street with two-story buildings on either side. On top of one of the buildings was, what appeared to be, a bunker. I remember a lot of sandbags and barbed wire, but I didn't stop to take pictures. I just kept rolling, once again, careful not to make any sudden movements. When I came out of the other end of the gauntlet, I was in the West Bank. The final two Km was well signed, and I was in Manger Square in minutes.

Again, I felt like the only tourist in town. It's becoming clear to me that armed conflicts are bad for a region's tourist trade. I changed into a pair of long pants and entered the church. Naser, a licensed tour guide, immediately offered a 45-minute tour for about $5. I accepted. Naser did a great job explaining the history of the church and then offered to take me to one of the few souvenir shops still open in Bethlehem. In the small shop behind the church the sales pitch was relaxed. The stock of olive wood crosses and nativity scenes was of a high quality. I made a few purchases for shipment to the folks back home. I'm confident that these gifts will not be returned, as doing so would require entering a war zone. Naser then helped me get into one of the few hotels in town that is still open. I'm only paying $40 for a spacious, modern room in the four-star Shepherds' Hotel. The hotel is only one year old, has a restaurant in the basement, and is a ten-minute walk to Manger Square. I am the only guest tonight. The front door is locked. Entry is only through the restaurant.

I suppose that if I had any complaint about the hotel it would be the noise from the battle between the Israeli Army and the Palestinian militants that took place just four Km away this evening. The hotel management probably could not have stopped the battle, but the noise did keep me awake. Around 10:00 PM I heard the pop-pop-pop of automatic weapons, and then a couple of booms. I turned out the lights, opened the window, and hesitantly raised the metal blinds a few inches. The gunfire and bombs sounded sporadically for the next hour. I videotaped one exchange. Then I lowered the metal blinds, closed the window, and went back to the safety of the bathroom to call the U.S. Embassy. I thought that it would be wise to let them know where I was staying tonight. I explained to the Marine who answered that I was checking in because there was some action outside of my hotel. He said that that was normal around these parts, but he took down my name anyway. I guess that makes me feel better.

Sunday, August 5th
Bethlehem to Jerusalem - 9.96 Km

Well, the one-hour battle that I witnessed last night made the news. It was the big story on CNN. I can't believe that the Marine at the U.S. Embassy made it sound like it was a normal occurrence around here. I also think that my footage of the battle was better than that shown on CNN. Anyway, I slept well last night, considering there was a war going on outside my window.

It took 10 minutes to walk to the Church of the Nativity this morning where I planned to attend a Latin mass in the small cave where Jesus was born. The Church of the Nativity is actually a complex of churches built by various Christian denominations. Masses are said in a variety of languages in the different sections of the complex. There are always a few masses being offered at any given time on Sunday mornings. I just had to find a Roman Catholic mass offered in a language that I could understand. The best that I could do today was the 9:00 AM mass offered by the Franciscans in Arabic. I didn't understand a word. I did stand, sit, and kneel on cue, though.

After mass I cycled out of Bethlehem and the West Bank to return to the relative safety of Jerusalem. After the short ride I spent the rest of the day hanging out around Zion Square. They have a great camping store here with an extensive books and maps section. I did some "free" research there, then bought a book on India and a map of Egypt. Although I'm feeling a little boxed-in by the political problems here, I'm still preparing for the future legs of this trip.

Monday, August 6th
Jerusalem to Tel Aviv - 72.01 Km

It's not all downhill from Jerusalem to Tel Aviv. In the first 20 Km there are two long uphill climbs. The first is the more difficult because it has a very narrow shoulder and three lanes of traffic, all rushing to get out of Jerusalem. At the end of the second hill I got my sixth flat of the trip. Of course, it was on the rear wheel. I couldn't find the object that punctured the tube in my tire tread, so I just put in a new tube and continued on my way. I hope the tire isn't getting too thin. I may go through these expensive Kevlar tires faster than I would like.

I generally followed the same path down from Jerusalem as I did on the ride up. I took Route 1 down to Latrun, then a local road through Ramla. Finally, I rode Route 44 into Jaffa. It's the fastest way to the coast. I cycled around the ancient port and flea market at Jaffa. I asked a couple of security guards at the port if there were any ferries leaving from Jaffa for Egypt. I didn't understand what they said in Hebrew, but I knew that their laughter meant "no." So, I cycled up the coast to Tel Aviv and found the marina. I posted a note on the marina bulletin board stating that I was a U.S./Irish citizen looking to crew or passenger on a yacht traveling to Egypt. I left my mobile phone number and Internet ID. I don't expect anything to come of it, but it's worth a try.

I'm in a nice hotel one block back from the beach for $50/night. It will be my base of operations for the next three days. Within a few minutes walk are the U.S. Embassy, the sea-front promenade, an indoor mall, a laundromat, an Internet café, fast food joints, travel agencies, and a bike store. I'll try to accomplish a few things here before continuing on to Egypt.

Tuesday, August 7th
Tel Aviv - 0 Km

I had the bottom bracket replaced on the bike with a nice Shimano LX model. The store mechanic gave my bike a thorough check-up. It's good to go for another 6,000 Km. Next, I found out that a cabin on the overnight ferry from Haifa to Cyprus would cost me $140. I still don't know if there is a ferry from Cyprus to Egypt. I'll continue exploring other options.

I spent about three hours in the Internet café, responding to e-mail and downloading website construction software. A regularly updated site would keep the folks back home up-to-date on my travels. I should be able to maintain the site from my Pocket PC anywhere in the world. The $15 HTML editor is a real bargain. The $25 image viewer won't save scaled down images, as I had hoped. Still, it has some value.

Wednesday, August 8th
Tel Aviv - 0 Km

It was another productive day in Tel Aviv. First, I walked over to the U.S. Embassy to ask about border crossings. After a very thorough security check, I got in and went to the American Citizen Services room. The man at window #2 told me that the Rafah crossing was closed but that I could cross at Nitzana. Rafah is in the Gaza Strip and would have been my first choice because it is the most direct route to Egypt, along the coast. Nitzana is about 45 Km south of Rafah in the Negev Desert. I would have to cycle through Be'er Sheva, but it beats the other alternatives. I'm not confident about ferrying through Cyprus or crossing at Elat, the southernmost city in Israel. A travel agent in Tel Aviv had told me that the Nitzana crossing was only open to commercial traffic, but the Egyptian embassy in Tel Aviv told me that I could cross there.

Next, I did a load of wash and hit the Internet café again. The website is coming along nicely. Earthlink makes it more difficult than it has to be, but I was able to upload the pages that I designed on my Pocket PC. I would like to do a little more tweaking before I let everybody know that the site is up and running.

Finally, I finished the day with a Pizza Hut pizza and a walk along the promenade. The Pizza Hut restaurant is in a three-story mall, directly across the street from the promenade and beach. Security is tight all over, especially here. Somebody attacked one of the Ministry buildings in Tel Aviv a couple of days ago. All bags are checked at the one mall entrance, and every street performer on the promenade seems to have their own personal security guard. Nobody heckles the performance artists here.

Thursday, August 9th
Tel Aviv to Nir Am - 78.91 Km

Well, it was bound to happen. Somebody set off a bomb in the heart of Jerusalem today. It was at the Sbarro's, just a block from the Kaplan Hotel on Zion Square. The blast killed 16 people and was heard all over the city. I remember walking past the Sbarro's four nights ago and being surprised to see another American pizzeria in Jerusalem. I had eaten at the Pizza Hut on Zion Square, so I didn't have a desire to eat at Sbarro's. Still, that's too close for comfort. It's definitely the time to get out of Israel.

So, what did I do today? I got as close to the Gaza Strip as I could. I'm on a kibbutz in Nir Am (short for Near Ambush), just a stone's throw from the border. During the Intifada it's not smart to be a stone's throw from Palestinians. I'm watching CNN tonight and Jim Clancy is reporting that Israeli tanks are rolling into Gaza in response to the bomb attack. And here I am, just a Km from the border, in one of the most Jewish of all institutions, a kibbutz. I'm more than a little nervous. The other residents? They're outside having a cookout. I want to yell out the window, "Extinguish the fire, head for the shelters, maintain radio silence." But, they're too absorbed in cooking their "chicken bits on a stick." So, I'm hunkered down in my room watching CNN, hoping that Jim Clancy doesn't mention Nir Am.

Friday, August 10th
Nir Am to Nitzana - 116.47 Km

I couldn't leave Nir Am fast enough this morning. With every pedal stroke I got farther away from the conflict...and farther into the Negev Desert. Cycling through a desert in August is not advisable. Moses and his followers spent 40 years lost in this one. I can't carry that much water. I had to rely on my superior orienteering skills to get me from Nir Am to Be'er Sheva to Nitzana. I took Routes 34 and 25 to get to Be'er Sheva. After Be'er Sheva the civilization thinned out along Route 211. There are no convenience stores out this way. I would have killed for a Slurpee this afternoon.

The rear wheel had two flats between Be'er Sheva and Nitzana. Fortunately, they both occurred as I was approaching gas stations. I couldn't find what was causing the flats. So, after the second one, I switched to my backup tire.

Around 5:00 PM I rolled into Nitzana, which isn't a town but a bus stop. My hopes of choosing between a Hilton and a Hyatt tonight were dashed when I saw the dusty little shelter along the side of the main road. As luck would have it, there was an American waiting at the bus stop. He had an acoustic guitar in hand and was trying to hitch a ride north. His name is also Michael. He teaches web page design and studies Hebrew at the school just up the hill from the bus stop. He had actually lived in Norwalk, Connecticut for a while, just a few miles from my last job. He was having no luck hitching a ride to Tel Aviv, so he offered to help get me into one of the visiting student rooms.

The school is a little village, completely enclosed and behind a guarded gate. Foreign students are taught Hebrew here. There are groups of Ethiopians and Russians here this month. Michael hooked me up with the administrator, and then took off to hitch a ride to Be'er Sheva to see *Planet of the Apes*. The administrator said that they currently had 400 students in a school built to handle 300. He did have one room left, though. Like every other room in Israel, it cost $50. It's a dorm room for six students that I have all to myself. One of the two air-conditioners even works, so I'm in heaven.

The only snag is that it's Friday night, and I have nothing to eat. Wal-Mart hasn't opened a Nitzana Supercenter yet. For an extra $10 I was allowed to eat the Sabbath meal with the student body. The meal started with a five-minute ceremony that took ten minutes. It had to be translated into Ethiopian and Russian. Then, carts filled with chicken, roast beef, rice, and potatoes were rolled out. At least that's what I think it was. There were pitchers of red water to drink. Needless to say, I did not get my $10 worth. I would most definitely kill for a Slurpee right now.

Saturday, August 11th
Nitzana to Al-Arish, Egypt - 97.62 Km

Both the Egyptian and U.S. embassies lied to me. Tourists cannot cross from Israel to Egypt at the Nitzana crossing. The two Israeli soldiers at the crossing told me that it was for commercial freight only. They did not have the facilities to process my exit from Israel. There was no reason to be upset, though. It just meant that I wasted a day cycling through the Negev Desert in scorching heat, spent the night in a Spartan dorm room, and had a meal that an Ethiopian would complain about.

The soldier who spoke the best English told me that the Rafah border crossing was open. It was 45 Km to the north on Route 10, the "border road." First, the soldier told me that I couldn't take the border road. Then, he told me how to get on it. Then, he told me that he, and presumably the entire Israeli government, could not take responsibility for my safety on the border road. That conversation gave me a warm, fuzzy feeling. So, I assured him that my family wouldn't fly to Israel and beat the daylights out of him if a crazed Egyptian border guard did shoot me. Then, I was on my way again, into the desert.

A barbed wire fence ran the entire 45 Km on my left. The only other sights were sand dunes and border guard towers. Egypt seems to be leading in the border guard tower race. That makes them either more paranoid or more fond of high places. In 45 Km I only saw three cars, smugglers probably.

A gate and an Israeli bunker marked the end of the road. The soldiers in the bunker all had a good laugh when I rolled up. They treated me to some ice-cold water and explained how the border crossing is handled. I had to put my bike on a bus that drove the Km or two to the terminal on the Israeli side. The bus had an armed soldier in the front seat and was escorted by an

Egyptian diplomat's car. Besides the bus driver, the soldier riding shotgun, and me, there were two other passengers. I don't know where they were going because they never crossed the border with me. The only excitement on the bus ride was that it took three Israeli soldiers from the bunker to push start the Egyptian diplomat's car.

I got personalized attention as I was processed through the Israeli terminal. I don't think they've had many customers passing through lately. At the end of the process an Israeli official took me to the door and pointed to the Egyptian terminal across the street. He said that I could just ride my bike over there. I got the distinct feeling that he did not want to step out of the building. Yet he was willing to send me out there. Once again, I had the warm fuzzies.

The Egyptian terminal was just like any other third world marketplace, but without the livestock. It was a dark, sweaty hanger with people and luggage strewn about the open floor. The officials had fans in their offices. The rest of us were left to perspire at our own pace. The science of air-conditioning has not yet reached this part of the world. A half-hour after entering the Egyptian terminal I was back on the road again.

I tried to ride the 40 Km to Al-Arish quickly to get a hotel room, but at each of the military road stops (there were three) I ended up talking to the soldiers. They asked the standard questions, and I answered them all. One guy was fascinated by my mobile phone and asked to call his parents. I let him, and then I ended up on the phone talking to his father. Then, another asked to do the same. A third was getting up the courage to ask for the phone when the soldier in charge got a little nervous and handed it back to me. I think one of his superiors might have been driving by.

Al-Arish isn't as nice as I had hoped. It's a little rough around the edges. I'm in a five-star hotel, safe from the two-star riff-raff. I'll hang out here for two nights. I need to work on the rear wheel (another flat as I entered town) and rest for the big ride to Al-Ismailiya.

Egypt

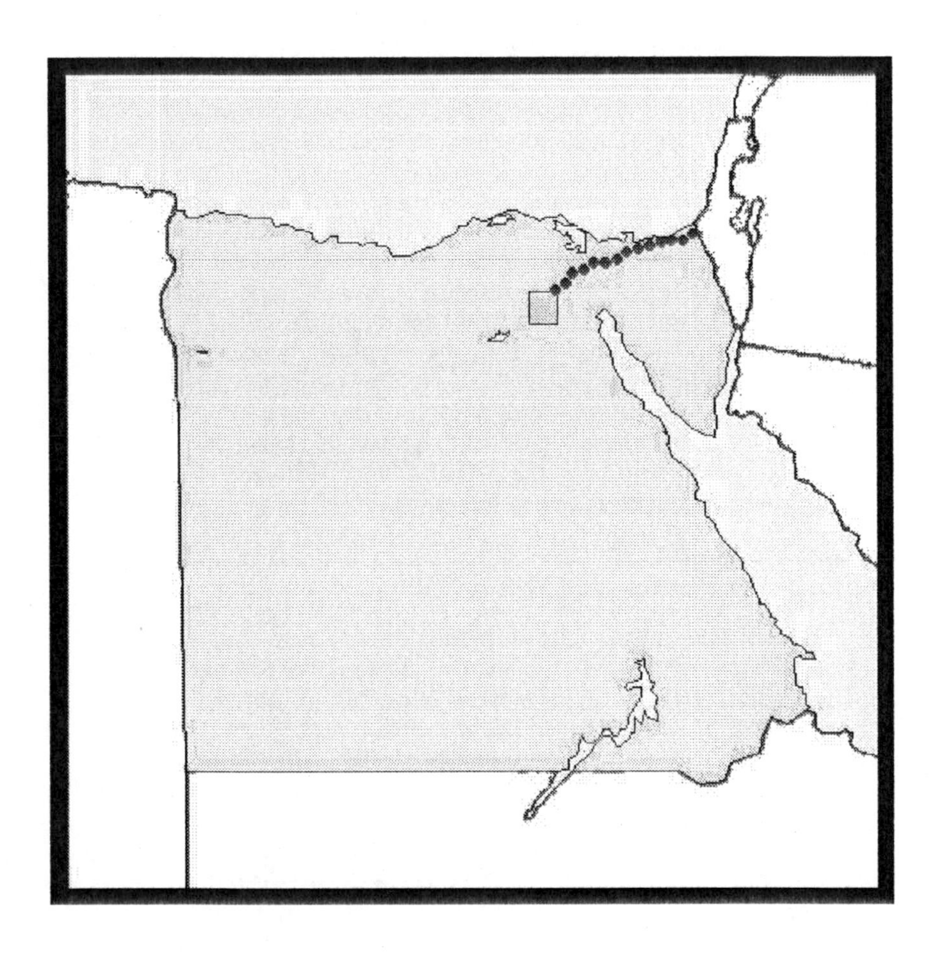

Sunday, August 12th
Al-Arish, Egypt - 0 Km

I took advantage of the day off to hopefully fix the rear wheel's problematic propensity to puncture (blatant and senseless use of alliteration). Then, I ventured out of the Hotel Oberoi compound to buy some AA batteries for my shaver. Al-Arish is very dirty, not what you would expect of a resort town. Although the main roads are paved, not much else is. It's the kind of place that would become unbearably muddy if it were to ever rain here. I had to visit a few of the street stalls on my shopping trip. I didn't know the word for "battery" and the shopkeepers didn't understand "Duracell" and "Eveready." It was hot and sticky, and the flies were out in force. So, after I eventually found the batteries, I immediately walked back to the hotel compound.

I took a quick dip in the hotel's salt-water pool but didn't like the taste it left in my mouth. I spent the rest of the day back in the room ordering room service. Even my laundry was done without leaving the room. I just hope I have the strength to reach the Suez Canal tomorrow. Otherwise, I'll be camping out in the desert. And, there's no room service out there.

Monday, August 13th
Al-Arish to Ismailiya - 202.72 Km

Far and away, this was the longest day that I've ever spent riding a bicycle. Ten years ago I cycled 162 Km in Spain on a day when all of the elements were in my favor. I knew that I had to do at least 175 Km today in order to reach a possible hotel in Al-Qantara. So, I got on the road, Route 55, by 7:00 AM and kept a steady 20 Km/hour pace all day. I took five minutes breaks at 50, 100, and 150 Km to stretch and eat a snack.

The plan started to fall apart around 1:00 PM when I got another flat on the rear tire. Miraculously, I was near a gas station when I noticed the flat. I'm starting to wonder if gas station owners are placing sharp objects on the roads nearby in order to pull in customers. I pulled into the station and went through the routine of replacing the tube twice. The first spare tube had a puncture somewhere. The whole time I had to keep moving around because an item at rest tends to attract flies in the desert. I've never seen so many flies. They swarmed all over my panniers, my water bottles, and me. Refugee camps in Ethiopia have fewer flies. While the flies attacked every orifice in my body, I cursed and flailed and ran around the pumps. The gas station attendant must have thought that I was mentally challenged. He wouldn't be half wrong. Eventually, I got back on the road.

Because there are very few 7-11's in the desert, I was forced to accept untreated water from the locals. They would take my water bottles into their homes and fill them, or bring out old two-liter cola bottles filled with suspect water. I was very nervous accepting this water. I am taking tomorrow off, mainly in preparation for the possibility of getting sick. I don't want to be on the road to Cairo if ill effects should hit me.

I did finally get to see the Suez Canal. At Al-Qantara I got to the ferry point and waited about 30 minutes while a tugboat pushed a temporary, Bailey-type bridge into place spanning the canal. I spent the half-hour amusing the local security force with tales of my adventures. They, and some locals, thought that there might be a hotel on the other side of the canal, but I never did find one. So, with no gas in the tank and little light left in the day, I continued on Route 44 to Al-Ismailiya, 25 Km away.

You don't know what fear is until you cycle in the dark on a major Egyptian highway. The last 10 Km into town were spent dodging potholes and listening for passing vehicles. My rear-view mirrors were useless because most Egyptian drivers do not use their headlights at night. Apparently, they are blessed with super-human nighttime vision.

I was greeted in Al-Ismailiya by mayhem in the streets. Every mode of transportation known to man in the last three millennia was out there, blocking my path and making a wicked stench. I made my way slowly through the maze of streets in search of the elusive Hotel Mercure. After a half-hour of touring the city, I finally found the Mercure. It was a beautiful sight. I apologized two or three times to the lady at the front desk for my look and smell. The hotel probably lost one of its four stars when she took me in. She did ask that I leave my bike outside. The armed soldier standing post at the front door would keep an eye on it. How could I refuse? I quickly showered, went down to the hotel restaurant for a steak, and then hit the sack.

Tuesday, August 14th
Al-Ismailiya - 0 Km

I slept well last night. Today is a rest day, and I took full advantage. I never left the grounds of the hotel. It's a modern high-rise on the banks of the Suez. There is a little beach on the canal and some water-sport activities for the guests. I'm a little nervous about swimming in the canal water.

From my spacious balcony on the fifth floor I can see the hotel gardens, soccer field, and outdoor café. There is live music in the café at night. There is also a whole rack of bikes for rent to any guest who would like to tour the gardens. I don't even want to look at a bicycle today, though I did check on the welfare of my bike in the afternoon. The soldier from last night was still on post out front. He assured me that no locals had attempted to destroy my god-less vehicle of Yankee imperialism. I felt strangely comforted by his assurances.

Wednesday, August 15th
Al-Ismailiya to Cairo - 139.2 Km

As I had feared, getting out of Al-Ismailiya was confusing. I probably added 10 Km to the ride unnecessarily. There are no bike paths meandering alongside the Suez Canal to follow south. There's only the mayhem of the city streets, and the mayhem of Route 44. The ride through the desert to Cairo was fairly flat and the wind variable. The flies were out for the first half of the ride, so I put on my mosquito head net. I may have looked stupid, but I didn't get any flies in my mouth, nose, or ears.

As I approached Cairo's outer environs there were more places to buy water and snacks. The traffic on the final 30 Km into the city was brutal. Cairo is not a bicycle-friendly city.

Thursday, August 16th
Cairo - 0 Km

Do you know how to tell when a Cairene is lying? His lips are moving. That's an old joke, but it sums up my feelings about the people of this city today. There are no honest Cairenes, just Cairenes with a better rap.

Typical rap: "Hello my friend. Where are you from? What city? I have been to America. I have a friend in America. It is a great country. What is your name? My name is Mohammed. Please accept my hospitality. Come in here. Sit down. Would you like an Egyptian coffee or tea? Please, there is no charge. We are like brothers. Do you like the papyrus paintings? I have a special one for you." There are similar raps for oils and pyramid tours.

I fell for the pyramid tour scam, and then a papyrus salesman got my money back. Then, I probably fell for the papyrus scam from him. If two legitimate papyrus paintings arrive back home, I'll be amazed. I don't even want to think about all of the other scams that were attempted. It just makes me mad. I couldn't even stroll around the city without being accosted. One kid bumped me from behind at a street corner and I accused him of trying to steal my money. I wasn't 100% sure that he was a pickpocket, but I let him have it anyway. That's the mood that I was in today. I was forced to hunker down in the hotel room to avoid the constant barrage of con artists. In short, Cairo SUCKS. As Randy Newman sings, "Let's just drop the big one now."

I wonder if this journal entry will hurt the sales of my book in Egypt. It's probably best to not even translate it into Arabic.

Friday, August 17th
Cairo to Giza to Cairo - 42.14 Km

I got two things accomplished today: I saw the pyramids, and I booked my flight out of Cairo for 3:00 AM tonight. I've accomplished what I wanted to do, and now it's time to move on.

In order to beat the traffic to the pyramids I had a 6:00 AM wake-up call. I was on the road before 7:00 AM. It was the only way to cycle across the heart of Cairo to Giza and still retain my sanity. I crossed over the Nile, then rode almost 10 Km out of town on a major thoroughfare. I was one of the first tourists to arrive. I bought the $5 ticket and then just cycled through the complex, between and around all of the pyramids. I finished up at the Sphinx. I didn't try to go into the pyramids or ancillary buildings because I was afraid to let the bicycle out of my sight for even one minute. The place was swarming with flies and shysters. You could shoo the flies away, but the con artists were more persistent. One old guy offered to videotape me in front of the Sphinx and then asked for money. I expected that and didn't give him a thing. I'm glad that I didn't because I just looked at the twenty seconds of sand and sky that he shot, complete with narration, and laughed out loud. A drunken Stevie Wonder could have shot better footage. Then, for the last time, a Cairene suckered me. I was standing in front of the Pyramid of Cheops when two guards at the museum began speaking to me about my bike. After a while one of them offered to take my picture in front of the pyramid. I said, "OK." After handing the camera back the first word out of his mouth was "baksheesh." I burst into laughter. He wanted $5 for pushing a button. I'm afraid that there is no hope for Egypt. The phrase, "an honest day's pay for an honest day's work" doesn't translate here because there is probably no word for "honest" in Arabic. Someone should come hear and explain the Puritan work ethic, and why it's made the United States the greatest country in the world. I gave him $2.50.

The booking of my flight to Mumbai, India went smoothly at the Egypt Air office in downtown Cairo. The ticket agent had my reference number on file from a previous phone call. He suggested that, if I wanted to fly business class direct, Air Egypt could get me onto tonight's flight. The price was even cheaper than the connecting flight through Dubai. I accepted. So, here I am, after a hair-raising taxi ride to the airport, awaiting the boarding call for the 3:00 AM flight to Mumbai. I am tired.

India

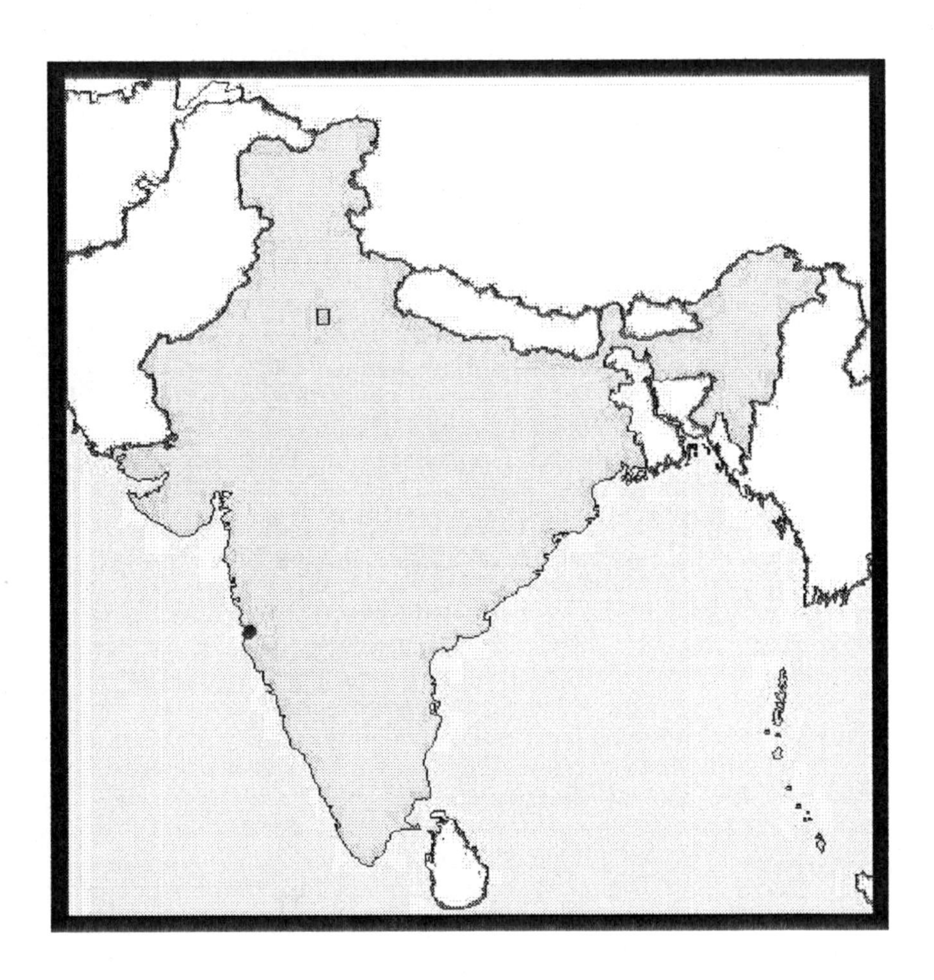

Saturday, August 18th
Cairo to Mumbai, India - 0 Km

The Cairenes had the last laugh. They gave me food poisoning yesterday, made me wait in their airport an extra three and a half hours until just before the effects hit me, and then sent me on my way to get sick at 30,000 feet.

Yesterday had been a long day. I had been up for 24 hours when they finally started to board my 3:00 AM flight at 6:30 AM. I waited around the airport for seven hours prior to the boarding call. I couldn't wait to get into my comfy business class seat and get some sleep. Fifteen minutes after take-off I began to feel a bit ill. Soon after that I was lightheaded, nauseous, and clammy. The next thing that I remember was a flight attendant asking me if I was OK. I had fainted. It wasn't long before I fainted again. This time when I came to, there was a doctor sitting next to me. He had me drink a very sugary concoction and then get wrapped up in a couple blankets. I have no idea where the doctor came from. I hope they didn't announce that there was a sick passenger in business class. I can just imagine the passengers in coach snickering.

For the remainder of the flight I managed to keep appearances up, and my last meal down. My first thought of what caused this reaction was the untreated water that I accepted from the people in the Sinai Desert six days ago. Now, I think that it was the well-done steak that I ordered at the restaurant in the Cairo Grand Hotel last night. I should have been suspicious when the steak arrived at my table one minute after I ordered it.

After a short stopover in Oman, we landed in Mumbai in the early afternoon. As we were landing I got my first, unhealthy glimpse of life in Mumbai. Between the runway and the shantytown outside of the airport was an overgrown grass median strip. The first Indian that I saw was a completely naked old man getting up from a squat. Farther down the runway I saw other residents of the shantytown in the median strip. It had become their very public privy. And, this was not an isolated incident today.

I gathered up the energy to get through customs and retrieve my checked baggage. As usual, the bicycle had been manhandled. I changed my money to rupees, and then looked for a taxi driver to take me to a western hotel. I figured that all of the western hotels had doctors on call. I also figured that they might have standards of hygiene acceptable for a sick man. A crowd of taxi drivers immediately surrounded me. It's not hard to gather a crowd in Mumbai. You just have to stand still. I said I wanted to be taken to one of the "H" hotels: Hyatt, Hilton, or Holiday Inn. I mentioned a few more hotels, and then one of the drivers said he could take me to a Best Western nearby. Bingo! We strapped the bike onto the top of his taxi and took off.

The ride out of the airport to Juhu Beach was extremely depressing. The traffic was deadly. The roads had no shoulders, just rutted dirt paths that were filled with people, animals, and carts. There were dogs running free. There were children begging at the intersections. I saw just one cyclist. I knew right then that I was not going to be able to cycle in India, especially in my condition.

The Best Western Emerald hotel was an oasis of civility in Juhu. The staff was great. I told the front desk that I was sick and they sent for a doctor. Twenty minutes later I was examined and pills were prescribed for gastroenteritis. Anthony, the bell captain, ran out to get my medicine and a few bottles of water. I will try to take the pills, drink an electrolytic solution, and eat some toast. It's becoming harder to swallow anything, though. I'm becoming de-hydrated. If I don't drink the solution I may have to be admitted to a hospital or clinic and put on an IV. I am not fond of hospitals to begin with. Indian hospitals scare the heck out of me.

Sunday, August 19th
Mumbai - 0 Km

Well, I'm in Breach Candy Hospital. I asked for an ambulance to take me here because it's supposed to be the best hospital in Mumbai. The ride was painful. The ambulance was a very small van with a hard cot in the back. The shocks were non-existent, and the driver didn't miss a pothole. I don't know how long the ride took. It might have been thirty minutes, or it might have been three hours.

Anthony, the bell captain from the hotel, stayed with me throughout the ordeal. I was shifted from the Emergency Room to ICU to Ward C Room 303. I'm on an IV now, and feeling a little better, but I still have trouble eating or drinking anything.

Monday, August 20th
Mumbai - 0 Km

I had a few visitors today. A representative from the U.S. Consulate stopped by to check on my condition and drop off some reading material. I called the Consulate before entering the hospital, just to let them know that I was sick. The visiting representative was very helpful and offered to keep my family informed of my progress. I am now officially a big fan of the U.S. State Department.

Later, Anthony from the Emerald hotel came over. He's been a big help handling the standard hospital bureaucracy for me. Thanks to Mumbai's notoriously bad water system, Anthony recently spent some time in the hospital. He told me that he only drinks the bottled stuff now. He brought me another couple of bottles today.

Finally, my doctor stopped by. He said that yesterday's tests showed that I had gastroenteritis and a hypoglycemic reaction. He expressed surprise that I didn't feel more pain in the belly because the food poisoning was severe. He also told me to plan on staying two more nights in the hospital.

Dad called me after the Consulate gave him my direct line in Breach Candy. I assured him that I would live, unless the hospital food killed me. I'm taking no chances with the food. I'll eat the toast, mashed potatoes, and rice. Nothing else.

Tuesday, August 21st
Mumbai - 0 Km

I had no visitors today, so I spent time reading and speaking with my roommate. He's an elderly gentleman who spent many years in England. His British/Indian accent is so thick that I'm straining to pick up every other word. I'm in no mood to work hard just to hear about his extended family and their many accomplishments. I listened quietly and muttered the occasional, "Is that so?"

Breach Candy continues to try to kill me with their hospital food. I'm not going to let them. I'm drinking the bottled water that Anthony brought and eating the toast. Anything else might be fatal.

Wednesday, August 22nd
Mumbai - 0 Km

I was released from the hospital today. Anthony got a taxi and took me back to the Emerald in Juhu. He also helped with all of the hospital bureaucracy, again.

When we arrived back at the hotel I asked to speak with the General Manager to express my gratitude for the help that I received during my illness. The hotel had stored all of my equipment while I was in the hospital. They brought in the first doctor on Sunday night. They organized the ambulance ride. And, their bell captain Anthony was my Man Friday all week. I thanked the General Manager and told him that I would be leaving a significant tip for the staff when I checked out.

I've decided to leave India as soon as possible. I'll spare no money in my effort to get to Australia. I don't know how quickly I can leave, but I hope it will be within the next two or three days. I'm working with the travel agent in the hotel on possible flights. I've got to get out of here. I'm afraid to eat or drink anything. This is not a safe environment for a sick man.

Thursday, August 23rd
Mumbai - 0 Km

I've got a line on a flight to Perth this Saturday. While the travel agent worked on the flight details, I took a quick tour of the city. The agent hooked me up with a car and driver to take me downtown. I saw a few remnants of the British occupation of India, like the Gate of India and the Victoria Terminus train station. I also took care of some business at the Mumbai World Trade Center. I picked up a care package from home at the American Express offices, and then went to the Australian embassy to pick up a visa. Since I want to enter Australia so soon, I had to apply for a three-month electronic visa. I'll pay to have the visa extended another three months when I'm in Perth.

Dinner was a bowl of dry cereal and toast. I'm probably losing a lot of weight, but I'm not going to take any dietary risks. I can maintain my "political prisoner" diet for a few more days. I'll be in Australia soon enough.

I spoke with friends back at the old job for an hour tonight on the phone. We all had a good laugh at my recent misfortunes. Misery certainly does love company.

Friday, August 24th
Mumbai - 0 Km

Today I stepped out of the safe confines of the Emerald and walked to a nearby supermarket to buy some sealed, imported snacks. I figured that an Oreo cookie packaged overseas would be safe to eat. I was back in my hotel room within an hour.

I had to get a taxi to take me to another travel agency near the airport to purchase my ticket to Perth. The driver hardly spoke English and had to stop to ask for directions three times. Inside the travel agency I was told that the Australian government would like proof that I will eventually leave their country, so I purchased a round-trip ticket. I'll stash the return ticket with all of my other unused returns. Maybe at the end of this trip I can go around the world again, in the opposite direction.

My taxi driver had graciously, and unexpectedly, waited an hour for me while I conducted business inside the travel agency.

So, I gave him a nice tip and asked if he would return to my hotel tomorrow at 4:00 PM to take me to the agency once again to pick up the printed ticket, and then drive me to the airport. His taxi has a rack on the top that's perfect for carrying the bike. He now knows the way to the travel agency. What could go wrong?

Saturday, August 25th
Mumbai to Perth, Australia - 0 Km

Nothing went wrong. In fact, my driver was an hour early. I left a tip and note of thanks for the staff at the Emerald. The travel agency had my ticket ready for me when I arrived. The airline accepted my bike without a box. I had plenty of time in the airport to relax before my flight. I even bought Dad some tea from the Assam province of India at the duty-free shop. During World War II he spent some time up in the jungle with the Army Airways Communication System.

I was very selective about what I ate at the airport cafeteria. I don't need a repeat of last week's flight. This flight will have a stopover in Singapore. I'm not sure if you're even allowed to be sick in hyper-clean Singapore. At this time tomorrow I'll be south of the equator for the first time. Hallelujah!

Western Australia

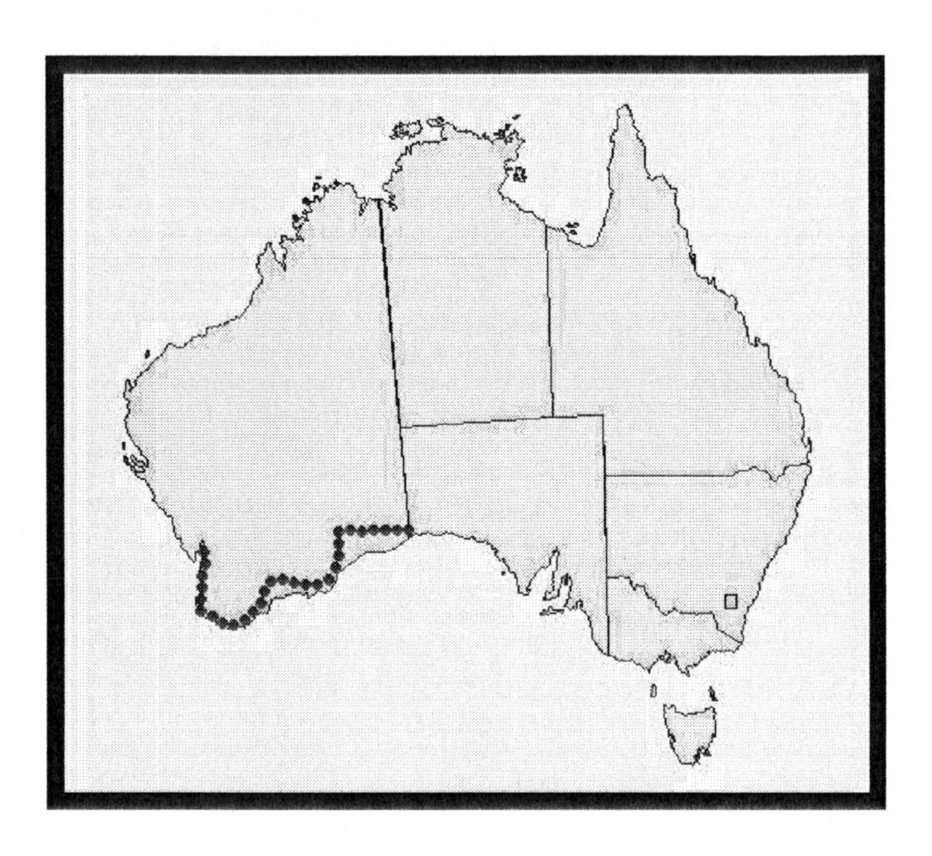

Sunday, August 26th
Perth Airport to East Perth - 23.35 Km

Getting off of the plane at Perth International Airport today was the greatest feeling in the world. I had left the Third World behind and re-entered the First. The airport was a clean and modern facility. There was an unhurried pace, surprising for an international airport. I lingered around the lobby for a while, getting Australian dollars and changing into my riding gear.

There were two things to adjust to when I got outside, a brisk temperature and cycling on the "wrong side" of the road. It was mid-afternoon and the skies were clear. It was probably about 65 degrees. It felt a bit like early fall in Philadelphia, great football weather. After the heat of the Middle East and the humidity of India, it was invigorating. I shifted my rear view mirror from the left arm of my glasses to the right, only to find that my right eye is a bit lazy. I cycled cautiously out of the airport and into suburbia while I practiced spotting passing traffic with my lazy eye. I followed a route from the airport to Perth city center detailed in my cycling guidebook. It took me through pleasant middle-class neighborhoods and alongside the Swan River. I even had a late lunch at a McDonald's. I was in heaven.

I eventually stopped here at the Perth City Hotel. It's close to the city center and advertises its rate with a big banner across the front of the building. I figure that, if they're that keen to tell people their rate, it must be one of the cheapest in town. I could also see that the hotel was nearing the end of some major construction. Maybe I would get a new room. As it turns out, I got a recently refurbished room. Very modern. Very clean. I'm one happy camper tonight.

Monday, August 27th
East Perth to Scarborough - 29.68 Km

After two days, it's official; I want to live here. The weather is perfect. The people are laid back. The city is clean. The prices are reasonable. The only snag is that Perth is half a world away from Philly. The cost alone of shipping Tastykakes to Perth would bankrupt me.

I began the day by going to a bike shop on Hay Street and buying a new helmet and a regional bike map. This is definitely a bicycle-friendly city. I cycled through the Hay Street pedestrian mall and along a bike path near the river. I shot some video of the Swan Bell Tower and the Supreme Court gardens. Then, I cycled out of the city to the coast in search of an apartment.

On the flight to Perth I spoke with a couple from Kenya who told me that friends in Perth had found them a nice apartment in Scarborough for a reasonable rate. Scarborough is a beach resort town, and this is the off-season. I decided to check out the accommodations there as well. I cycled due east to City Beach, then north on a bike path parallel to the Indian Ocean coast. When I arrived here in Scarborough, I found a company that rented cars and offered free apartment referrals to tourists. They got me a great rate ($140/week) for a two-bedroom garden apartment a half block back from the beach. There's a supermarket down the street, plenty of fast food joints in the neighborhood, and a couple of places to get on the Internet nearby.

I plan on staying here for two to four weeks. I need to fully recover from the food poisoning. I also need to wait for the days to get a bit longer and the temperatures a bit warmer. I have to remind myself that it's wintertime here. In the meantime, I'll sit around my new home away from home, watching TV and getting fat. That's the plan, and I'm sticking to it.

Tuesday, August 28th to Sunday, September 23rd
Scarborough - 0 Km

Watched TV. Got fat.

Monday, September 24th
Scarborough to Mandurah - 85.6 Km

Finally, I did something today. After five weeks of inactivity, I finally started bicycle touring again. Since arriving in Perth four weeks ago, I've probably only put 250 Km on the bike, and most of that was without the gear strapped on. My most strenuous activities in the past four weeks were growing a beard and changing channels with the remote.

As expected, it took some effort this morning to fall out of bed and get on the bike. I started riding around 10:30 AM. It was a cool day. The temperature never reached 70 degrees. I wore the sweater and Gore-Tex jacket all day. The bulky jacket didn't help any in the headwinds.

I didn't do any sightseeing. I just pushed as far south as I could. I probably should have spent more time exploring Fremantle, Perth's old port on the Indian Ocean, but I was too anxious to start exercising again. What I did see wasn't very impressive. I was too close to the docks and didn't check out the market or any other historic sites in the middle of town. I spent most of the day cycling down Route 1. I'll stay on the same road tomorrow for 107 Km to Bunbury. The road has a wide enough shoulder, but it's not very smooth macadam. After I reach Bunbury I'll follow a route to Albany described in my cycling guidebook for a few days.

I'm relaxing in a nice $42 hotel room tonight. I ate a big sirloin steak in the hotel restaurant, hoping to build up some leg strength again. The temperature is going to be in the 70's tomorrow. Let's just hope the wind dies down.

Tuesday, September 25th
Mandurah to Bunbury - 114.56 Km

This was a long, tough day. I started riding at 10:30 AM and finished just as the sun was setting around 6:15 PM. The major difficulty was the rough road surface. It was stones over tar, just like the roads in Turkey. It's probably the fastest and cheapest method to pave roads, but it is literally a pain in the butt for cyclists. It also increases rolling resistance, requiring more effort to keep the forward momentum going. For someone like me who was hoping to coast around the world, this type of surface is horrible. The civil engineer that invented this paving method must never have ridden a bicycle.

Although it was a sunny day, I wore both the sweater and jacket again. I was tired most of the day. I don't think I've been getting enough sleep lately. I've been staying up late to watch the news from America. I took a rare lunch break in order to have a bite to eat and shut my eyes for a few minutes. It felt good to sit out in the sun with my eyes closed, like some Florida retiree. I think it helped, too. I had a little more energy in the afternoon. Lunch, by the way, was a Gatorade, potato chips, and a hot dog. If you don't request otherwise, they put a sauce on the hot dogs and butter the buns here. What do you expect from the people who gave the world Vegemite?

I'm staying at the Lighthouse Beach Resort in a room that opens up to an indoor pool and whirlpool. I want to hoist my old aching muscles into that whirlpool, but I'm just too tired to get off the bed. I wonder if anyone has ever drowned in one of those?

Wednesday, September 26th
Bunbury to Busselton - 61.53 Km

I knew right away this morning that I wasn't going to be doing 100 Km today. My right knee was too sore. Yesterday's ride really ripped the muscles good. I wasn't prepared for such an effort after five weeks off, and I paid for it today. I should have ridden to Dunsborough, but I stopped 25 Km short at Busselton. I'm staying in a cheap motel for $19. I hope the knees feel better tomorrow morning.

I had more of the same rough road surface to deal with today. I got off Route 10, the Bussell Highway, about halfway through the day and cycled through the Tuart Forest and the

Vasse Estuary wetlands. In the forest I saw my first two kangaroos of the trip, both dead on the side of the road. If I were the superstitious type, I would consider that bad luck for me. Instead, I realize that it was just bad luck for the two kangaroos.

I'm planning on a short day of riding tomorrow to Margaret River. I might also try to get some wash done. There's rain in the forecast over the next few days. I might stay in Margaret River for two nights if I find a nice place, and if the weather does get bad. I know that I need a day off to let my knees recover.

Thursday, September 27th
Busselton to Margaret River - 49.89 Km

I got a late start and cycled to Margaret River on the main road, Route 10, rather than follow the guidebook's suggestion to go by way of the coast road. I shaved off some Km by doing that. I don't think I missed much.

Margaret River is a quaint little tourist town. Lots of B&B's, wineries, and fudge shops. This is the beginning of a three-day weekend (the Queen's birthday), so room rates are a little higher than usual. Still, I will need to stay here until Monday because of the bad weather forecasted. My knees need a rest anyway. I asked a local if the Queen's birthday always falls on a Monday. It does. That's a pretty amazing feat. Even Jesus' birthday is sometimes celebrated on a Wednesday.

Friday, September 28th
Margaret River - 0 Km

Boy, am I glad that I decided to stay indoors today. The last time it rained like this Noah started building an ark (I got a million of 'em, folks). I just stayed indoors and watched four consecutive in-house movies, including *Crocodile Dundee in Los Angeles*. I would have thought that the Australians would be embarrassed to show those Paul Hogan movies. I did rush out to stock up on food for the next three days.

Saturday, September 29th
Margaret River - 0 Km

I spent most of the day reading a book called *Shimmering Spokes* by an Australian who cycled completely around the continent. I did that because 1) it rained all day, 2) I thought that I might gather some insights about the geography from the author, and 3) the book was too heavy to stick back in my pannier and carry to another town. The one thing that this guy kept complaining about was the headwinds. He's really got me concerned about cycling west to east through the Nullarbor during the spring. Oh well, I'll worry about that when I get there.

I also lost heat in my room tonight because the circuit breaker that controls all of the sockets kept tripping. I have nowhere to plug my complimentary mini-heater. They never had these kinds of problems at the Ritz-Carlton.

Sunday, September 30th
Margaret River - 0 Km

My big accomplishment today was doing a load of wash. I also walked around the town when it wasn't raining, watched a couple of the free in-house movies, and spent some time in the local Internet café. I was hoping to upload changes to the website, but I was unable to configure the café's PC to sync with my Pocket PC. So, instead I just read the latest news from back home.

Football season is well underway back in the States, and I've been trying to follow the success of the team that my oldest brother coaches. Surprisingly, Strath Haven High School's 35th consecutive win isn't big news down here. Instead, the Aussies just had their big AFL and NRL Footy Finals this weekend. I wish I had put some money on the Brisbane Lions and Newcastle Knights. Maybe then I could afford to stay in these nice hotels every night.

Monday, October 1st
Margaret River to Augusta - 54.62 Km

It was a fairly easy day today. I'm determined not to push too hard until I get myself into better shape. I think I rushed things a little last week, and that's why I had knee problems. Today I got off of the Bussell Highway and cycled near the coast on the quiet Caves Road. The road rolled and meandered a bit, and I did some climbing out of the saddle, but it was still an easy ride. I finished up here at the Augusta Hotel Motel. What's the difference between the hotel rooms and the motel rooms? The hotel has a view of the river; the motel has a view of the hotel. For a savings of $10 I'm happy to stare at the old hotel.

Augusta is just nine Km from Cape Leeuwin, one of four places in the world where two oceans meet (Indian and Southern, in this case). It also has a very famous 100-year-old lighthouse. It's a site not to be missed. So, I stayed in my comfy motel room overlooking the Augusta Hotel and relaxed. There's no need to do an 18 Km round-trip to some old lighthouse. I'll check it out next time I'm in southwest Australia. Besides, I have a headache.

Tuesday, October 2nd
Augusta to Nannup - 91.2 Km

I started out the day by retracing some of the terrain that I had just covered yesterday on my way into Augusta. That's a mortal sin for bicycle-tourists, but I had to do it to get onto the Brockman Highway and head east. The highway, which is still Route 10, passes through a very desolate area. Early on, I bought some snacks at a very lonely general store. The owner told me about a shortcut to Pemberton on a back road that would allow me to avoid Nannup. I considered taking the shortcut but decided that the ride would have been too long for one day. I was happy to split it up into two days of riding.

Nannup is a one-horse town, and the horse is on life-support. The hotel looks to be about 100 years old. The guest rooms are on the second floor, over the bar. Although I got here early in the afternoon, I could see that some of the citizenry of Nannup had already begun drinking themselves stupid. Around 9:00 PM the shouting and cursing in the street began. Then there was the glass breaking and the car tires squealing. By 11:00 PM the drunks had left downtown Nannup, and I could go to sleep. It'll be a shame to see this slice of authentic rural Australia disappear.

Wednesday, October 3rd
Nannup to Pemberton - 79.66 Km

It was all up and down hills today. Eighty Km isn't too far for one day, but it was strenuous. If I wasn't chugging up a steep hill, I was screaming down the other side. There was no flat stretch of road on which to coast for a while. It's hard to get into a rhythm and relax on a ride like that.

Twice today, black and white birds attacked me, magpies I think. The first one came at me from across a field and repeatedly dive-bombed me for 500 meters. The second only took a couple of runs at me outside of the hotel. I don't know what they were protecting, or if they just don't like cyclists. Maybe my new beard scared them. Whatever the reason, it was very distracting and could have been dangerous if I was in traffic. I was swerving all over the road.

On the bright side, I'm getting a bit more relaxed around dogs during this trip. I realize that most of them are behind fences or are on chains. If they aren't secured I give them a lot of room as I slowly pass, ready to hop off the bike at a moment's notice.

I'm in a Best Western hotel tonight. The room is in a very modern addition to the old Pemberton Hotel. The lady at the front desk gave me a reduced rate for a very nice room. I think she took pity on a destitute traveler. I spoke to my younger brother, who has my Power of Attorney during this trip, and to my stock fund Help Desk about transferring more cash from my money market account into my checking account. I am going through money at an alarming rate. I hesitate to think what the final cost of this trip will be. It's getting a little scary.

Thursday, October 4th
Pemberton to Northcliffe - 35.57 Km

I cut the ride short today because I didn't feel like cycling 135 Km to Walpole. Besides, the terrain is still rough. Like yesterday, there are no flat stretches on Route 10 between Pemberton and Northcliffe. This is lumber country, specifically jarrah wood. So, I spent the morning peddling up and down hills through the forest.

I stopped a little after noon in this small town of Northcliffe and checked out the old hotel. They didn't have en suite bathrooms or TV, so I booked myself into a little six-unit motel down the street. I'm comfortable here, and it only cost me $21. After 6:00 PM everything in town is closed. I walked outside to see if I could find a place open to get a snack around 7:00 PM. No luck. It was eerily dark and quiet. No cars driving by, no people out walking, very few street lights on. It appears that a late night rave-scene has not yet been established in Northcliffe.

I have a big day tomorrow. I'll finally get back to the coast. I always enjoy riding along a coast more than riding inland because it's often flatter and has better scenery. You can also see your progress. Whereas, inland you could be riding in circles and not even recognize it. Also, when you're on the coast, dogs will only attack you from the inland side.

Friday, October 5th
Northcliffe to Walpole - 100.71 Km

It was a lousy day to ride. I had rain, wind, cold, hills, and dogs. On the bright side, I wasn't run over by an 18-wheeler. There's not much else positive to say about the day. It started to rain as soon as I stepped out of the motel in Northcliffe. It was a cold rain, and a southerly wind made it worse as I was headed south on Route 1. I put the neon orange rain covers over the panniers for the first time since Italy. Maybe it was those florescent rain covers that protected me from the 18-wheelers. They almost didn't protect me from a couple of young dudes in a beat up Holden a few Km outside of Walpole. For some reason, the driver jammed on the brakes and veered onto the dirt shoulder just 50 feet behind me. When I heard the screeching I also turned onto the shoulder, then hopped off of the bike, ready to dive behind a tree if necessary. Another car directly behind the dudes almost rear-ended their Holden. I looked to see if there was going to be any explanation for the sudden maneuver, but all that I got from "Bill and Ted" was some nervous laughter. So, I got back on my bike and left them to their excellent adventure.

Walpole, like Nannup and Northcliffe, does not have GSM digital mobile phone service. Before I booked my room in the Tree Top Walk Motel, I found the only public PC in town with Internet access and sent a message home. As I get farther away from Perth, it becomes harder to find mobile phone coverage or Internet cafés. This must be a hardship similar to those endured by the early explorers.

Saturday, October 6th
Walpole to Denmark - 68.14 Km

The rain stopped overnight, but I had some serious headwinds to deal with today. I was all business on the bike. I knew that today was a relatively short ride, and I considered stopping off at the Valley of the Giants to walk 40 meters above the forest on 600 meters of suspended walkways. But, when I realized that the headwinds were going to slow me down, I plowed on.

One of the nice things about cycling in Australia is the courtesy of the drivers. In the past few months I had been honked at so many times that my nerves were on edge. In places like Egypt and India the horn is used to say "Hello", "I'm passing you", "Get the #&@! out of my way." Here, the drivers passing me give a wide berth. And, I just noticed that the drivers going in the other direction are almost always waving to me. No obnoxious horn, just a pleasant wave.

Sunday, October 7th
Denmark to Albany - 69.91 Km

Denmark to Albany. Sounds like a trans-Atlantic flight, not a half-day bike ride. Despite more headwinds, it was still a fairly easy ride. There were only two stores along the route, and one of them was closed. When I stopped into the other store, the owner warned me about snakes and bandicoots. His advice to me if I was about to run over a snake sunning itself on the road was to lift up my legs. Country-wisdom like that you just can't get in the city.

Just a couple of Km outside of Albany I broke one of my toe-clips. It felt strange to ride with one foot free to just wander off the pedal at any time. I carefully pedaled into town and into the strongest winds of the day. I stopped at a replica of the Amity (the ship that delivered the first settlers to Albany) and shot some video. The town has some history to it. It was established 30 months before Perth, making it the first permanent European settlement in Western Australia. While Perth became capitol of the state and a modern city of skyscrapers, Albany still has the skyline it had in the early 1900's. Many of the buildings on the waterfront look like they belong on the Universal Studios back lot.

I cycled up from the bay and found a cheap motel that's not too far from a McDonald's and an Internet café. It's the first McDonald's that I've seen in two weeks. Guess what I had for dinner?

Monday, October 8th
Albany - 0 Km

After seven days of riding, I needed a day off. I thought that I might spend the day exploring Albany's historic sites. Instead, I went to a bike shop and bought new toe clips and had the chain cleaned. Afterwards, I went to the Internet café to upload changes to my web page. The connection was way too slow, so I had no success there. Then, the skies opened up and I rushed back to the motel. It rained the rest of the day. I'm not ready to start riding again tomorrow. I'll wait at least one more day. At $30/night, I'm in no hurry to move on.

Tuesday, October 9th
Albany - 0 Km

I'm glad that I decided not to ride. It rained most of the day. I needed this time to catch up on my journal and plan for my next couple of days. I'm pretty nervous about tomorrow's ride because I don't really know where I'm going to sleep. The next real town, Jerramungup, is 180 Km away. The few towns in between do not have any hotels or motels. I may end up in a B&B or a caravan park. Even that isn't a sure thing. I don't know what tomorrow's weather will be. I don't know how bad the wind will be. I don't know how the terrain of the South Coast Highway will be. This doesn't bode well.

While I was lounging around in my motel room this afternoon, there was an automobile accident just outside my window. I didn't see the accident, but I did hear the crash. And, I saw the dazed passengers getting out. The driver of one car needed to be extracted with the Jaws of Life. The emergency response was quick and it appeared that everyone, even the injured driver, would be all right. It was just another worrisome event on this dreary day.

Wednesday, October 10th
Albany - 0 Km

It rained again this morning. I knew before I started this trip that my daily state of mind would be most affected by the weather. I just knew from experience that I was more willing to ride farther and longer on sunny days than I was on rainy days. So, I didn't leave Albany today.

I spent most of the morning dwelling on the difficulties that I was likely to encounter over the next stretch of Route 1. Mostly I was concerned with the apparent lack of accommodations. I started to investigate alternate methods of getting from Albany to Adelaide. I got pricing on car rentals, as well as on bus and train tickets. I was getting ready to take some action to avoid this tough stretch ahead when the sun finally came out. Then, I saw a bike touring couple pull into the caravan park across the street. I went over to talk to them about their plans. Although they were finishing their tour in Albany, they mentioned that there were two other cyclists in the campground. I took that as encouraging news, that I wasn't the only idiot trying to bicycle tour in this desolate area. I went back to my room and, after a few calls, found a B&B on a secondary road heading to Esperance that had room for me tomorrow night.

So, with the promise of better weather, I'll be doing around 100 Km tomorrow. I'm happy about that because I feel like I've been skipping over too much of my original route around the world (Northern France, Syria, UAE and Oman, India and Sri Lanka). I've had legitimate reasons for passing over each of those regions (dwindling funds, visa problems, terrorist activities, poor health), but I still feel as though I've short-changed the dream by missing them. Although I will not be able to cross the Nullarbor, I want to get as close to the start at Norseman before I skip over to the other side of Australia at Ceduna. Who knows, maybe I'll find a way to cross the Nullarbor. That would make me very happy.

I should also report that I saw my first real, live kangaroos at a petting zoo across the street today. There were about 8-10 young ones in the compound with some ducks and an emu. When they get a little older and bigger I guess the owners will release them onto a busy highway nearby.

Thursday, October 11th
Albany to Borden - 106.73 Km

What a difference a day makes. It was a great ride due north to the Yardup Farm Stay Cottage near Borden. I didn't know what to expect today (wind, rain, hills?), so I got an early start. The road was graded very well, climbing gradually up to the Stirling Range from Albany. It was a little cool, but there was no rain. And, I had a tailwind for some of the trip. I can't remember the last time that I had a tailwind. The traffic was light, so I had the road to myself much of the day.

As you approach the Stirling Range you're greeted with a panorama of mountains stretching across your whole field of view, save for one notch near the middle. You pray that the engineers who laid out the road also saw this notch through the Range. Fortunately they did, and I passed through without breaking a sweat.

I took some great photographs today. I'm anxious to get them posted on the website, but I'm in a 100-year-old farm cottage. It's been "lovingly restored", but there is no phone jack available. Go figure. My GSM phone doesn't work out here either. Aaargh! Maybe I'll be back on line tomorrow in Jerramungup. Let's hope.

Friday, October 12th
Borden to Jerramungup - 88.62 Km

It's Friday night in "Jerry", as the locals call it. I'm right in the middle of the action, the Jerramungup Hotel Motel. When I checked in at the bar (always a bad sign) the waitress/bartender/receptionist told me I was lucky to be there tonight because there was going to be a live band playing the hotel/motel/bar/restaurant. I asked what kind of music, and she said, "country." I knew what that meant; good ol' boys would be making noise well into the night. And, I was right.

The day started out well with a great tailwind. It was a little cool, and I did get some rain early on. But, it cleared up and warmed up by noon. Since there is no GSM service around here, I stopped into the telecenter (a government-supported, publicly accessible rural telecommunications space) to send e-mail to the family. My younger brother, who keeps track of my daily progress, probably thinks that I'm back in Perth. During our phone conversation while I was in Albany, I was leaning toward taking a bus back to Perth, and then a train to Adelaide.

I have a big day tomorrow with about 115 Km to cycle to Ravensthorpe. I hope these tailwinds continue. After watching the weather report tonight, I think they will.

Saturday, October 13th
Jerramungup to Ravensthorpe - 118.82 Km

I put in a good effort today. I had a very slight tailwind and the road, Route 1 again, was relatively flat until the last 20 Km. I averaged over 22 Km/hour, which is hyper-speed for me. It felt good to go so far, so quickly. There was nothing out there to stop me or slow me down. Between Jerramungup and Ravensthorpe there is NOTHING. No gas station. No hotel. No restaurant. There were a couple of places to pull off of the road and rest. They had a picnic table and a trash can. That's all. One of the rest areas was on the 120-degree meridian. There was a sign to mark the spot. That means that I am one third of the way around the world from Portugal and the prime meridian. It should be all downhill from here on out, because it has been all uphill to this point.

I'm in a $22 motel unit in the Palace Hotel Motel in Ravensthorpe tonight. It's not bad. It's a little bigger than the phone booth in Jerramungup, but I still have to move the bicycle every time that I want to get into the bathroom. The best thing about the room is that it has a direct line out. I'm finally able to use my 56K modem and dial into the Internet. That's important because the mobile phone won't work out here, and the telecenter is closed until Monday. I'm going to stay here at least two nights.

Sunday, October 14th
Ravensthorpe - 0 Km

I didn't do too much today. I tried to find a Catholic church, but I don't think they have one here. I bought some food and a newspaper at the Foodtown. I spoke to a little old lady manning the Tourist Information booth about accommodations between Ravensthorpe and Esperance. That doesn't look promising. I think that I'm going to have to do over 185 Km tomorrow. I'm dreading it already. I've been told that the hills heading east out of town are worse than the hills to the west. I might also get a little rain. This should be fun.

Monday, October 15th
Ravensthorpe - 0 Km

I got out of bed at 6:00 AM with every intention of cycling to Esperance. As soon as I looked outside though, I knew that wasn't going to happen. It had rained overnight and was still threatening. There was also a stiff wind coming from the southeast. If I were one of those brave adventurers who soldier on despite great obstacles, I would have hit the road and not looked back. Instead, I hit the sack. There's no need to get carried away with this adventure-travel thing, not out here in the "Land of the Far-Between."

It rained off and on throughout the day, at times heavily. It sure was nice to be on the inside looking out. During a lull in the rain I ran over to the telecenter to check my e-mail. I hadn't heard from anyone back home in a few days and I was worried that they hadn't been getting my e-mail. Around 8:30 PM I called my younger brother just to let him know that I was alive.

Tuesday, October 16th
Ravensthorpe to Esperance - 196.11 Km

Well, that was a long day. I got up at 6:00 AM but didn't get on the road until 7:30 AM. I knew that if I could keep to a 20 Km/hour pace I could reach Esperance by 5:00 PM. I took three five-minute breaks during the day, and at 5:15 PM I rolled into town. If there had been headwinds or rain or more hills, I might not have arrived until after sunset at 6:30 PM. But, everything worked in my favor today. I'm sure that I'll feel the effects of ten hours in the saddle tomorrow. But for now, I'm happy with the effort.

If I hadn't been keeping to such a strict timetable, I would like to have videotaped some of the wildlife today. I saw a kangaroo, an emu, and a fox just a few yards away from me. I kept peddling, though. I hope to have other opportunities in the next few days. I finished up the day with an Eagle Boys pizza back in the motel room, where there is some more wildlife...ants. Lots of them.

Wednesday, October 17th
Esperance - 0 Km

I'm 42 years old today, and after yesterday's ride, I feel it. My quads are really tight. I'm going to have to start stretching a bit more now that I'm an old man.

I spent the morning shopping. I didn't buy much, just some water purification tablets and insect repellent (gearing up for the possible Nullarbor crossing). Then, I visited the prestigious Esperance Museum (Open 1:30 PM to 4:30 PM, Monday-Friday). Like all of the other rural museums in Western Australia, they have pictures of the original settlers and a variety of rusty farming implements. But, unlike the other museums, they also have a complete section of authentic space debris. In the summer of 1979, NASA's Skylab crashed down near Esperance. It was the biggest event in the town's 116 year history. Some of the locals became celebrities because they found Skylab parts in their fields.

Later, I found an Internet café where I was able to update my web page. I finished at 5:00 PM, just as they were closing the place. Finally, I finished the day by celebrating with a filet mignon for dinner. All in all, it was a good birthday.

Thursday, October 18th
Esperance to Salmon Gums - 109.94 Km

For the first time in weeks I rode without the Gore-Tex jacket. It's finally starting to warm up. I'm just hoping it doesn't get too warm before I cross the Nullarbor Plain. Hot weather typically brings easterlies to the Nullarbor. I want cool weather and westerlies.

During today's ride I had wind from the south pushing me up Route 1 to Salmon Gums. I'm staying in the Salmon Gums Motel, near the train tracks. There's not much to this town, named after the local variety of gum tree. I picked up a burger at the gas station next door for dinner. There's no TV in my suite, so I guess I'll just hit the sack early. God knows I need the rest.

Friday, October 19th
Salmon Gums to Norseman - 101.44 Km

Tonight I'm in Norseman, "Gateway to the Nullarbor." The Nullarbor (meaning "no trees" in Latin, no kidding) Plain covers all of south central Australia. There is one paved road, the Eyre Highway, and one set of train tracks that cross it. It's about 1,200 Km across to the town of Ceduna (meaning "a place to sit down and rest" in the Aboriginal language, no kidding). Then, it's another

800 Km to Adelaide. By then, I'll be back in civilization. I've decided to take a shot at crossing it. If things don't work out, I'll throw the bike onto one of the buses that occasionally cross the Nullarbor. I've got to give it a try, at least.

I saw my first pair of ostriches today. And, the other birds out here are just as amazing. There are lots of cockatoos, parakeets, and magpies. Lately, the magpies have been attacking me mercilessly. They swoop down right next to my head, and then veer off. It's nerve-racking. I've theorized that it's my yellow helmet that they don't like. It can't be that they just hate me personally. I'm a big fan of the Audubon Society. I gave money to Greenpeace. I had a bird feeder in my back yard. How could they not like me? I've tried swatting the kamikaze magpies with the tire pump hanging from my top tube. I've tried ringing the bell on my handlebar. No luck. They just keep attacking. Imagine driving up behind some nut on a fully loaded bike, frantically waving a pump over his head and ringing his bell. It's a wonder that the local police haven't picked me up.

Today's ride was fairly difficult. The road surface was very rough, and I had a stiff headwind. To compound matters, I didn't bring enough water. There were no stores over the entire 100 Km, and I ran out of water with 30 Km to go. I limped into town and immediately bought a couple of large Powerade drinks. I'm staying in the Great Western Motel for at least two nights. I'll watch the weather reports and gauge my condition before setting out across the Nullarbor.

Saturday, October 20th
Norseman - 0 Km

I felt an earthquake late last night. The bed shifted like a boat passing over a small wave. On this morning's news I heard that it registered 5.3 on the Richter scale. The epicenter was just south of Ravensthorpe. No damage was done, but it was the strongest earthquake in Western Australia in 20 years. If it had occurred five days earlier, I would have felt it much more strongly.

This was a lazy day. I did walk the four blocks into downtown Norseman. On one corner I saw the life-sized statue of Hardy Norseman, the horse who founded the town in 1894. This horse must have been smarter than Trigger, Silver, and Mr. Ed combined. Throughout Europe and America you can see loads of statues of military heroes on horseback. Supposedly, if both of the horse's front hooves are off of the ground, the hero was killed in battle. If one hoof is off of the ground, he was injured in battle. If all of the hooves are firmly planted on the ground, the hero was very lucky. I'm not sure what a riderless horse means, but I'll bet it doesn't say much for the bravery of the early settlers of Norseman.

While I was in town, I did some food shopping and stopped into the Tourist Information Center. It looks like I'm in for a few big mileage days. Based on info that I picked up today, there are three stretches on the Eyre Highway where roadhouses are almost 200 Km apart. I hope I'm up to it.

Sunday, October 21st
Norseman - 0 Km

It rained all last night and most of today. I ventured outside once to order a hot dog from the gas station next door for dinner. When I got back to the room and opened it up, I realized that they had put "sauce" on it. I don't know what the Australians' secret hot dog sauce is, but they've been trying to put it on my dogs since I got here. I let my guard down tonight when I forgot to specify "no sauce" with the order. Why do fast food places want to kill me with condiments? I can't order a burger or hot dog without reciting a litany of things that I do not want on them. My simple orders of only meat on a bun usually leave the clerks dumbfounded. I threw the hot dog in the trash.

The bad weather today was a low-pressure system moving eastward. That should give me westerly winds when it settles over the Great Australian Bight. Low-pressure systems in the Bight rotate clockwise. I'll need some tailwinds to get to Balladonia tomorrow. If the winds persist, I might be able to get to Caiguna on Tuesday. I'm not banking on that happening, but it's possible.

Monday, October 22nd
Norseman - 0 Km

I'm stuck in Norseman. I got up at 5:45 AM and was ready to roll at 6:30 AM. When I stepped outside I realized that this wasn't going to be the day. The sky was cloudy, the winds were coming from the east, and it was starting to rain. Aaargh! I went back to bed. At 9:00 AM I ate breakfast with the couple that operate the motel. They told me that the rain that will fall in Perth today will probably hit Norseman tomorrow. There's some sort of cyclone forming in the Bight. It's the most rain that they've had in quite a while. That's just my luck.

I went into town around 2:00 PM to videotape some of the sights, including the statue of Hardy Norseman who apparently unearthed gold here after a night of digging at the ground where he was hitched. In the middle of a traffic circle down the street, life-sized corrugated metal cutouts shaped like camels are erected. Never one to pass up modern civic art, I committed the metal camels to videotape as well. I tried to get onto the Internet at the telecenter, but it's only open from 11:00 AM to 1:00 PM Monday through Friday. That's a grand total of 10 hours every week. I've had single sessions surfing the Internet that were longer than that.

I finished the day by ordering another hot dog from the gas station next door. This time I specified, "no sauce." What did I get? A hot dog smothered in butter. I can't win.

Tuesday, October 23rd
Norseman to Balladonia - 196.2 Km

In order to get across the Nullarbor without camping I'll have to endure three days when motels are almost 200 Km apart. Today was the first. It's the longest of the three, and hopefully the hilliest. The next leg to Caiguna is the second difficult day. I'll wait a day before I attempt it. The third difficult day will be from the Western Australia/South Australia border to the Nullarbor Hotel Motel. The other legs of the ride across the Nullarbor all average about 100 Km. After surviving today's ride I feel better about my chances of crossing the Nullarbor under my own power.

I started riding at 7:21 AM this morning. I employed the same strategy today that I used on the 200-Km day across the Sinai. I stuck to a 20 Km/hour pace and rarely stopped. The three or four times that I did stop lasted no more than five minutes. Every time the odometer clicked off a multiple of 20 Km I checked the clock on my cyclometer to see if it was 21 minutes past the hour. In the first few hours I gained almost five minutes each 20 Km. These extra minutes were used when I needed to stop for a quick snack or stretch. They also were helpful in the second half of the day when my pace slacked off. I had planned on reaching Balladonia between 5:00 PM and 5:30 PM, leaving me over an hour of daylight, just in case. I arrived in Balladonia at 5:15 PM.

There was more traffic than I expected today, probably because this is the only paved road from Western Australia to South Australia. The traffic was mostly road trains (trucks that pull two or three trailers) and cars pulling camping caravans. At one point I had to pull off of the road because a convoy transporting an enormous mining dump truck passed me. The convoy consisted of a leading and trailing safety car, a police car, and two flatbed trucks hauling the dump truck. The first flatbed had the chassis and the second had the bed. They needed every inch of the two-lane highway to get by.

I saw some more wildlife today. Early in the day I saw a young kangaroo right next to the road, but he took off when I stopped to take a picture. Then, I saw an adult emu crossing the road in front of me. A few seconds later, the emu crossed back to the other side with two baby emus in tow. Near the end of the day, after some heavy rains, I saw three kangaroos on the side of the road. There was an adult, an adolescent, and a baby drinking rainwater from the puddles left on the road.

When I arrived at Balladonia ('big red rock" in the Aboriginal language, no kidding) a spectacular rainbow greeted me. The rainbow appeared to stop right at the edge of the town. There was no pot of gold, but a burger and a warm bed. And that was good enough for me. I was completely zapped. My quads and hamstrings were completely ripped in the ten-hour ride. I could barely walk up the steps from my motel room to the restaurant. I'm going to take tomorrow off to recover and prepare for the next big ride to Caiguna.

Wednesday, October 24th
Balladonia - 0 Km

This may be the most remote place that I will visit on my ride around the world. It's over 190 Km in either direction to the next towns on the Eyre Highway, Norseman and Caiguna. The town here is really just a complex comprised of a motel, backpackers hotel, caravan park, restaurant, bar, and mini-market. The population, written on a chalkboard outside the shower block, is 10. There are four phones in the town. Mobile phones don't work out here. I can't seem to get any reception on my portable radio. The three channels on the TV are pulled in by satellite. Like I said, this place is remote.

I think the chambermaid was surprised to see me when she came to service the room this morning. Very few people stay for two nights in this town. It's a place to rest on your way to another place. About the only thing of interest to see here is the new Cultural Heritage Museum. Besides exhibits on Afghan cameleers and the history of the Eyre Highway, there's an exhibit on the Skylab crash landing. The bulk of the debris fell on the Woorlba Sheep Station 40 Km east of here. Not surprisingly, no one was hurt.

The Eyre Highway exhibit describes the explorer John Eyre's Nullarbor crossing in 1841, the first bicycle crossing in 1896, and Francis Birtle's first automobile crossing in 1912 in a ten horsepower Brush. Only three more cars made the trip in the next 12 years. The highway wasn't completely paved until 1976. Now, anybody with a little extra time on his or her hands can make the crossing. I have nothing but time.

Thursday, October 25th
Balladonia to Caiguna - 187.0 Km

Two down, one to go. The day after I cross the South Australia border will be my last ultra-long day across the Nullarbor. Today's ride was harder than the Norseman-Balladonia ride despite being shorter and flatter. A strong southerly wind and a poor road surface slowed my progress. I arrived here just before sunset. I picked up the pace at the end of the day because I didn't want to be riding on the Eyre Highway after dark. I've seen dozens of kangaroos on the side of the road that probably met their end looking into the headlights of a road train.

One of the employees at this roadhouse allowed me to compose an e-mail to send home. He will send it in the morning when he signs on again. There's no other way for me to communicate with the folks except to use one of the three public phones outside. There are no phones in the motel and no telecenter. I don't know how much a call to the States would cost from the public phones, so I probably need a phone card. I'm not sure if they even sell them out here. I hope nobody is getting nervous about me back home.

Friday, October 26th
Caiguna to Cocklebiddy - 67.69 Km

This was one of my shorter days. Still, I didn't arrive early enough to get a good room. I got a budget room for $20. I had a feeling that there might be a shortage of rooms when, at the very end of the ride, I passed a road crew laying tar and stones. I spoke to one of the road crew while I waited for my turn to pass the construction. He said that they were staying in Cocklebiddy, too. There are usually about 20 rooms at these roadhouse motels. I figure that they took at least half of them tonight, all of the $30 luxury rooms. The bike got very muddy as I cycled through the roadwork. When I finally reached the roadhouse, I spent almost an hour cleaning the bike.

I lost a little time today, as I had to move the clock forward 45 minutes immediately after leaving Caiguna. I'm now in the Central Western time zone. When I cross over into South Australia in a few days, I'll have to move it forward another hour and 45 minutes. This has got to be one of the weirdest time zones in the world. There may only be three towns following this time.

I saw a couple of wedgetail eagles today. I was able to videotape one of them at a distance as it dined on road kill. Their wingspan must be six feet. They're a massive bird. I've also had to deal with locusts for the second day in a row. They seem to come out in the afternoon. The air is so thick with them that I need to wear a mosquito net over my helmet. I know that I look bizarre in the net, but that's preferable to having the locusts hit me in the face for hours. I've been told to expect more of them as I cross the Nullarbor. They're outside my motel room right now, slamming their bodies into the windowpane. It's like a bad Alfred Hitchcock movie out there. No doubt, I'll sleep well tonight.

Saturday, October 27th
Cocklebiddy to Madura - 93.65 Km

Not much of interest to report about today's ride. I pointed the bike east, cranked for about five hours, and here I am in another roadhouse motel. At the very end of the day I went through the Madura Pass, which leads down from the Hampton Tableland to the Roe Plains. I'm at the Madura Pass Oasis Motel halfway down the pass.

I saved myself about $10 when I opted for the budget room. The budget rooms come without heat, other than an electric blanket. It's still pretty cool at night. I think I should have splurged for the room with the mini-quartz heater, aka, the Presidential Suite.

I had another condiment incident at dinner tonight. I asked for a burger to take-away in an almost obnoxious manner, "Just meat and bread." I think the breakdown occurred when the waiter came out of the kitchen to tell me that they were out of hamburger patties but would substitute a steak instead. I accepted the substitution, but did not repeat the list of things that I did not want sharing bun space with my steak. Sure enough, when I took the meal back to my room I found sauces and greens and whatnot surrounding my steak. It all went into the trash. I know when to admit defeat.

On the bright side, I was able to make a direct call home using my MCI WorldCom phone card on the very first attempt from one of the phone booths outside of the roadhouse. It has been my experience that placing a direct international call from a phone booth is slightly more difficult than de-fusing a nuclear warhead. The fact that I got through on the first try speaks volumes about the Australian phone system. Now, if only they could make a plain hamburger.

Sunday, October 28th
Madura to Mundrabilla - 115.0 Km

I was thinking to myself this morning that my muscles have become much more resilient lately. I've been able to recover overnight from any ride. Then, with about 40 Km to go in today's ride, I hit the wall. Between the headwinds, the rough road surfaces, and my left knee turning to jelly, I had to limp into Mundrabilla at under 15 Km/hour. If I weren't so anxious to get onto the Internet at the Border Village, I would take tomorrow off.

I spent most of the ride adjusting the wheel size measurement on my cyclometer. I lost the wheel size after mistakenly removing the battery to change the time of day. Every two Km on the Eyre Highway there are small distance markers. So, at every marker I stopped to fine tune the measurement. It took most of the day to get it just right. Or, maybe not. By the time that I was happy with the measurement I had hit the aforementioned wall. I was swerving all over the road, like a Brat Packer in a new Lamborghini. I was probably cycling two and a half Km to reach each marker. I'll fine-tune it a little more tomorrow.

On the bright side, I ordered a "plain" hot dog for dinner, and I got just what I ordered. I was so thankful that the girl behind the counter must have thought that I hadn't had a hot meal in weeks. She confided in me that she was hoping to visit the U.S. next year. I asked where, and she said North Carolina, Michigan (a Madonna pilgrimage), and North Dakota. I told her that if she liked living out here in the woop-woop, never-never, back o' Burke, she'd love North Dakota. The stress of a week in New York City would probably kill her, though.

Monday, October 29th
Mundrabilla to WA/SA Border Village - 79.68 Km

I'm finally out of Western Australia and into South Australia. Why isn't Western Australia called West Australia? Or, South Australia called Southern Australia? Why isn't the Southern Ocean, which they both border, called the South Ocean? Those questions occupied my mind for the first 30 Km today. Yes, cycling out here can become a tad monotonous. The rest of the ride I concerned myself with Australia's time zone problems. Three days ago I had to move my clocks forward 45 minutes when I entered the Central Western (West?) Time Zone just past Caiguna. Now that I'm in South Australia, I have to move them forward again. This time, by one hour and 45 minutes. Something about this seems odd. I just can't put my finger on it. Maybe the fact that *Friends* starts at 8:15 PM, and not 7:30 PM, is what's confusing me.

I went back up to the Hampton Tablelands through the Eucla Pass near the end of the day. Eucla is only twelve Km from the border, and I considered staying there for the night. But, I decided to move on when I saw a tour bus outside of the hotel, and the giant cement whale out front. A half-hour later I arrived at the Border Village with its giant beer-toting cement kangaroo and "Beware of UFO's" sign. The isolation makes everybody a little loopy out here. I'll stay here for two nights. Any longer and I could become unstable.

Tuesday, October 30th
WA/SA Border Village - 0 Km

This was my first day off since Balladonia. I slept in, despite the chambermaid's best efforts. I lost a dollar on the pokies (poker machines). I played the *Twister* pinball machine. I surfed the Internet. I strolled the grounds and took in the sights (aforementioned cement kangaroo and UFO sign). I even watched *Diagnosis Murder* for the first time on one of the two channels that they get on the satellite. It was a full and productive day.

Wednesday, October 31st
WA/SA Border Village - 37.85 Km

Today was to be a big day, 184 Km to the next roadhouse at Nullarbor. Instead, for the first time on this trip, I had to give up after starting a day's ride. Only one hour into the ride, 18 Km outside of the Border Village, I turned around because I realized that the headwinds were too strong. I was never going to reach Nullarbor before sunset. As disappointing as it was, I made the right decision. The easterlies got even stronger throughout the day. Then, tonight we had a thunderstorm. I was happy to be inside watching *The Simpson's*, rather than lying in a tent counting the seconds between lightning strikes and thunderclaps. One day I'll get out of here, but the conditions will have to be much better than they were today.

Eastern Australia

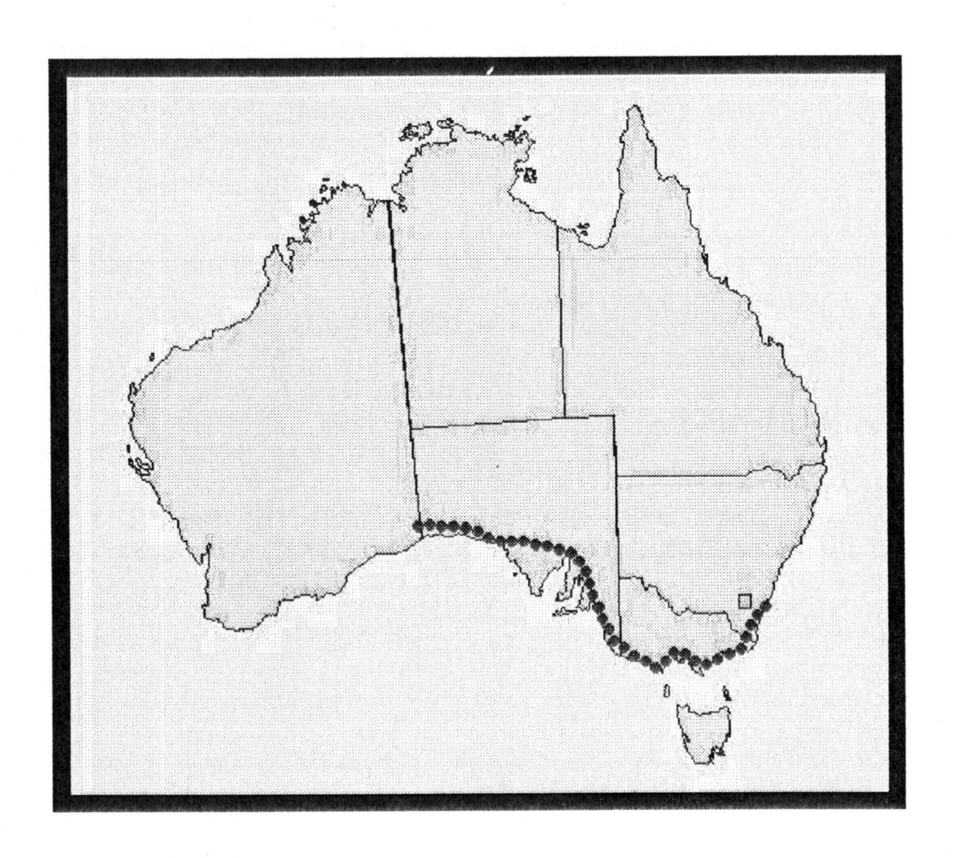

Thursday, November 1st
WA/SA Border Village to Nullarbor - 185 Km

The conditions weren't much better today, but I made it to the Nullarbor Hotel Motel. This may have been my most difficult day of cycling. It certainly ranks up there with the 200-Km day in the Sinai Desert.

I was up with the sun and ready to ride soon after, but waited an hour due to uncertainty about the weather. It was too early to get a report on the television. There was a thick layer of clouds and some thunder. The wind seemed to have died down. There might even have been a slight tailwind. Finally, I decided to chance it. An hour and a half after sunrise I was on the Eyre Highway again, headed due east.

It didn't take long to realize that the tailwind that I felt back at the Border Village was an illusion. Throughout the day I encountered ever-strengthening easterlies weakening my knees, my quads, and my resolve. I tried to keep to a 20 Km/hour pace, but that only lasted the first hour. Then, I tried to stay above 17 Km/hour because that would get me into Nullarbor before sunset. I struggled all day to maintain that pace but was losing the battle in the early afternoon. I was also running out of water. I had drunk over 1.5 liters from my three water bottles and another 1.5 liters of bottled water purchased back at Border Village. With 30 Km to go to Nullarbor I was bone dry. Then, I saw a caravan parked at the side of the road. I cycled into the dirt parking area and got the owners' attention. They were a very nice elderly Australian couple who took pity on me when I asked for water. They happily filled two of my bottles. After five minutes of small talk, I was back on the road with renewed strength.

The road turned slightly to the north and, with the change in direction, my speed increased. I pushed harder, hoping to reach Nullarbor before sunset. I was back up to 18 Km/hour, but that wasn't enough. With 10 Km to go, the sun set.

As I had hoped, out here on "the treeless plain" I was able to see the lights of the Nullarbor Hotel Motel from 10 Km away. It took a half-hour to reach the roadhouse. In that time I was passed by two cars going east, two road trains going west, and two dingoes going south. I don't know what was scarier in the dark, the road trains or the dingoes. My fear of dogs is multiplied ten-fold when it comes to dingoes, the wild dogs of Australia. I was never so happy to get to a motel.

I booked a room for two nights, bought a burger and fries to go, and collapsed in my room. My right knee is a little sore and, for the first time in months, my butt is sore from the 10 hours in the saddle. I'll be happy to relax tomorrow. And, I'll know that I've made it through the toughest section of the Nullarbor. I've completed all three big mileage days. I only have four more average days of riding to reach Ceduna, the traditional end of a Nullarbor crossing. I might even buy one of those hokey "I Crossed the Nullarbor" stickers when I reach Ceduna. I think I'll deserve to display the sticker more than the people who just pressed down on the accelerator pedal for a couple of days.

A complete crossing of Australia is now within reach.

Friday, November 2nd
Nullarbor - 0 Km

This was a much needed rest day. Aren't they all "much needed"? When you stay for two nights at a roadhouse you are something of an oddity there. Most people spend a night and then are back on the road again before 8:00 AM. Anyone who would stay behind is left to sit in his room and look out the window at the scenery. And, the scenery never changes.

I began the day doing the standard rest day activities. I did a load of wash, I sent off a few e-mail messages, and I took a scenic flight over the area in a 1964 Cessna. Actually, the scenic flight isn't standard, but I would like to make it so.

The only public Internet connection in Nullarbor is in the office of Whale Air. After sending off my e-mail, I agreed to a 35-minute flight if the pilot could find another passenger or two. Around 4:00 PM the pilot stopped by my room to tell me that he had another passenger. Ten minutes later we were airborne, taking off from a clay airstrip behind the motel. We flew over the Nullarbor Plain to the Southern Ocean to view the Bunda Cliffs. We also saw a few caves and blowholes on the surface of the Plain. Unfortunately, it was too late in the season to see any whales. In fact, the only wildlife that we saw was a wedgetail eagle soaring at an altitude of over 500 feet with us. It was $25 well spent.

Saturday, November 3rd
Nullarbor to Yalata - 92.23 Km

I'm in a dilapidated mobile home at a roadhouse on an Aboriginal reservation. The mobile home has no sheets, towels, or soap. Still, I was lucky to get it for tonight. The guys who run the roadhouse had no more rooms available in the motel. They're booked solid with aboriginal families who have gathered here for the week. When I told the owners that I wasn't anxious to camp out in the rain, they came up with this alternative.

It rained during much of the morning and early afternoon. I think we're supposed to get more rain tonight. The ride went very smoothly, despite the light rain. I'm definitely past "the treeless plain." After the first hour of riding I saw a sign stating just that. Soon afterward I was cycling up and down hills with trees on either side of me. The change of pace felt good.

I got to see a couple of wild dingoes up close this morning outside of the Nullarbor Hotel Motel. They sat patiently in the parking lot, facing the restaurant, waiting to be fed. The staff gives them some food every morning. They told me that the dingoes are more afraid of me than I am of them. I told them that that was debatable.

Tonight, *Crocodile Dundee 3* and *The Mummy Returns* are being shown in a makeshift cinema in the roadhouse here. The cost is $1.50. The guys running the roadhouse told me that there might be some noise tonight, presumably from patrons of the movies. It's a Saturday night, and I hope they didn't mean that there would be noise from patrons of the bar. I'm not leaving my mobile home tonight.

Sunday, November 4th
Yalata to Nundroo - 52.5 Km

Although it was not a big mileage day, I did reach a couple milestones. I surpassed 10,000 Km and 6,200 miles for the trip. That's a long way to go just for a burger and fries at the Nundroo roadhouse.

I had a strong tailwind today for the first time in ages. I averaged over 25 Km/hour and finished my ride in two hours flat. I considered continuing on to Penong, 76 Km away, but the road turns due east. That would have meant side winds for another four hours. The motel here looked nice enough, so I decided to stay. Besides, there is still a chance for some more bad weather. I'm limiting my exposure to the possibility of getting stuck in a thunderstorm in the middle of nowhere.

A cyclist who was really flying passed me this morning. He wasn't a tourist because he had no panniers. I haven't seen any recreational cyclists since Perth. I thought he might be a local in training. A few minutes later, an RV passed me with a sign on the back saying, "Caution Rider." Now, I figure he must be attempting to ride across or around Australia with a support crew. Lucky guy.

Later in the afternoon three touring cyclists came in and set up their tents in the camping area behind the motel. I spoke to one of them who said he was riding from Sydney to Perth. We exchanged information about the roads ahead and then wished each other luck. Now that it's warming up, I may start to see more bicycle-tourists. Once again, it's reassuring to know that I'm not the only idiot out here.

Monday, November 5th
Nundroo - 0 Km

I woke up to a very dreary day. It was drizzling, and there was a thick cloud cover and strong easterly winds. As anxious as I am to get to Ceduna, I decided to stay in Nundroo for another day. The three cyclists camping out back reached the same decision. I invited them to pop into my room any time during the day to make use of the standard motel electric kettle, which I never use. When I mentioned that I was paying $36/night for the room, they agreed to help me get my money's worth by finishing off the complimentary tea and coffee. Throughout the day, each of the guys stopped by the room for the free beverages, and to watch the weather reports on the local news broadcast.

The older retired cyclist that I spoke with yesterday, Graham from Sydney is the only one amongst us heading west. He considered taking advantage of the easterly, but decided against leaving because of his reluctance to pack up a tent wet from last night's downpour. The other two cyclists were Paul, a parole officer from Washington state, and Andy, a supermarket clerk from Melbourne. I'm not sure how they met up, but they're both cycling around Australia counter-clockwise. They told me that the cyclist I saw yesterday with the RV support also passed them. He is part of a team of riders racing around the country as a tag-team. They're riding 24 hours per day, hoping to break a record.

Tuesday, November 6th
Nundroo to Penong - 79.53 Km

There was a knock on my door sometime before 8:00 AM today. Paul and Andy were already taking off for Penong. Paul said through the door, "If you're still in bed, we'll see you down the road." I muttered, "OK" and rolled over. By 9:40 AM I was on the road and into the teeth of a brutal headwind. Thank goodness it was only a 79 Km leg today. I just took my time. I was in the granny gears almost all of the last 30 Km.

I met another bicycle-tourist heading west three Km from Penong who said that my two "mates" were in the pub at the Penong Hotel watching the Melbourne Cup horse race. When I got to the hotel/pub Paul and Simon were well on their way to getting in the bag with the other patrons. I quickly took a cheap room and got out of the pub.

I find it strange that Australians hold their biggest annual horse race on a Tuesday and their federal elections on a Saturday. Only in the "land down under" would they hold these big events opposite to the U.S. The elections will take place this coming Saturday. Voting is compulsory. If you don't vote, you're fined. How's that for an incentive to vote?

Wednesday, November 7th
Penong to Ceduna - 80.28 Km

Today was a repeat of yesterday. I was out of the hotel by 9:30 AM and immediately into a brutal headwind. I spent almost the entire day in the granny gears. The Eyre Highway seems to be getting narrower every day. Or, maybe the road trains and caravans are getting wider. Either way, I'm getting a little uncomfortable with the tight squeezes that I'm encountering on the road. Just outside of Ceduna some wide load (the driver and his payload) forced me off of the road and onto the gravel shoulder. He almost did the same to an elderly gentleman in a compact car coming the other way. He never touched the brakes. The little old man pulled up next to me and let out a stream of colorful obscenities about the driver. All I could say was, "You're absolutely right." You go, Pops.

When I finally got into Ceduna, I went directly to the Tourist Center. For the second time in as many days I met the old couple that gave me water near the Nullarbor roadhouse. I think they've adopted me. They're following my progress closely. It's a small world out on the Nullarbor Plain. Cyclists are an oddity and are recognized in the towns by the people who have passed them on the desolate Eyre Highway. Four separate people in downtown Ceduna asked me about my trip. They had all seen me on the road earlier in the day.

Based on the information that I picked up in the Tourist Center, I decided to get a room in the East West Flag Motel. The motel receives six television stations, not the usual two. It also offers direct telephone dialing. I've already connected to the Internet via the 56K modem tonight. There is GSM mobile phone coverage here in Ceduna, so my Motorola Timeport is working again. It would be great if there was coverage all the way to Sydney, but not likely. I had a pizza for dinner, the first in about three weeks. Now I know that I'm back in civilization.

Thursday, November 8th
Ceduna - 0 Km

I tried to get a haircut today, but the beauty parlor was fully booked. It's just as well. I felt funny asking for a simple haircut where other clients were getting primped and pampered like prized poodles (more senseless alliteration). I just want some guy named Sal or Tony to cut off the excess hair and send me on my way in ten minutes. There are no Sal's or Tony's Barbershops in Ceduna. I know; I checked the Yellow Pages. I'll let my freak flag fly for another week, until I hit Adelaide. I should be able to find an immigrant there willing to cut my hair.

The rest of my busy day was spent writing postcards, sending e-mail, and preparing updates for my web page. I'm lost without a good Internet café in town. I still need to connect my Pocket PC to a desktop PC in order to transfer files to my Internet Service Provider's file server. I may have to wait until I get to Adelaide to get my Nullarbor pictures posted. Bummer.

Friday, November 9th
Ceduna - 0 Km

I woke up today still undecided about the route that I should take to Port Augusta. So, I went back to sleep. There's no reason to rush an important decision like that. Besides, I wanted to be fully rested when I decided. After careful consideration of all the facts, I've decided to take the shorter route directly across the Eyre Peninsula, rather than the Flinders and Lincoln Highways along the coast. The accommodations are just too far apart in certain places on the coast.

The weather was nice today. It would have been a good day to ride. Oh well, it wasn't a bad day to sleep either.

Saturday, November 10th
Ceduna to Wirrulla - 92.72 Km

Despite the possibility of rain, I got back on the Eyre Highway today. Fortunately, the rain held off. The headwinds didn't. I had to work hard for these 93 Km. The countryside is slightly rolling and covered with wheat farms, not scrub land like in the Nullarbor. I'm hoping that, as I get farther inland, the winds will ease.

As I left Ceduna, the old couple that seems to have adopted me passed with their camper in tow. They must have taken two days off in Ceduna, just like me. Could they be stalking me? I won't get nervous until we all arrive in Sydney together.

I'm staying in the Wirrulla Hotel for $13. Wirrulla is a small town dominated by its grain silos. There's not much in the way of tourist attractions, but the locals apparently do have a great sense of humor. On the way into town there's a sign touting Wirrulla as "A Town With A Secret." I never did find out what that secret was, but it could have something to do with the jetty that they erected next to the hotel this year. The town is 35 Km inland. Even at high tide, I can't imagine the jetty pilings getting damp. Next to the jetty is a small boat, standing at the ready in case there might be a flood of biblical proportions. Maybe the residents have extended weather forecasting information that the rest of us don't. Is that their secret?

Sunday, November 11th
Wirrulla to Wudinna - 121.82 Km

The limit of what I can comfortably ride on a perfect day is about 120 Km. Today wasn't perfect. There is still a strong southerly wind to contend with as I head south-east. More problematic than the wind are the flies. They've become such a nuisance that I can't stop for more than fifteen seconds without being swarmed over. I'm dousing myself with a repellant and wearing mosquito netting over my head. They keep attacking though. I can't wait to get out of this farmland and into suburbia where flies are not welcome and convenience stores abound.

Today may have been the first time since suburban Perth that I passed two towns of any size before reaching my final destination. I was able to stop at Poochera and Minnipa to buy Gatorade and Cheetos. I'm pretty sure that cheese snacks are an important part of Lance Armstrong's training regimen.

Monday, November 12th
Wudinna to Kimba - 104.07 Km

I was not up to snuff today. I felt like I hit the wall just 10 Km into the ride, probably because I skipped breakfast this morning. The ride just drug on, hour after hour, Km after Km. I couldn't wait to reach Kimba. Now that I'm here, I've decided to stay for a second night. Tomorrow would be difficult if I tried to do the 90 Km to Iron Knob.

I was too late for dinner at the hotel tonight. I sat down in the dining room about 7:45 PM. When I realized fifteen minutes later that they stopped serving at 8:00 PM, I got up and walked across the street to a take-away restaurant. They also stopped serving hot meals at 8:00 PM. There is no other place nearby serving meals. I loaded up on snacks, but a steak is what I really need tonight. Oh, well.

Tuesday, November 13th
Kimba - 0 Km

I went back to the take-away place this morning for a cooked breakfast. While I sat there staring out of the window, Paul from Washington cycled by. I tried to get his attention, but to no avail. After breakfast I walked down the street to the telecenter. Sure enough, Paul's bike was parked out front. I went inside and caught up with him. He told me that he and Andy, partners riding across the Nullarbor, decided to travel independently now that they're back in civilization. Besides, he said, they had different body clocks. One started and finished his riding early in the day. The other preferred to sleep in and ride later into the day. I could understand that. The freedom to set your own schedule is the best thing about solo bike touring. I have a great respect for the leaders of bike tour groups who manage to move ten to fifteen people through a region without the participants killing each other. Couples who tour on tandem bikes must be one step away from divorce court.

When I took my laundry to the laundromat near the Big Galah (a garish 30-foot high statue of a red and gray bird), I saw Paul again. I took his picture in front of the bird, and then sent him on his way with the suggestion that he shoot for Nuttbush Station tonight. It is 30 Km past Iron Knob, but had better word-of-mouth than the old mining town.

I returned to the telecenter in the afternoon to download an FTP program that would enable me to transfer pictures and website updates from my Pocket PC directly to the Internet. I even burned a couple CD's with my latest pictures and daily logs. I'll keep one CD with me and send the other home for safekeeping. I can now free up storage memory on my PC and CompactFlash cards.

I had a large pizza for dinner. All is right with the world today.

Wednesday, November 14th
Kimba to Iron Knob - 89.09 Km

I didn't follow the advice that I gave to Paul yesterday. I stopped here at Iron Knob for the night. It didn't seem to make sense to ride another 30 Km today if it meant that I would then only do 40 Km to Port Augusta tomorrow. Anyway, the Iron Knob roadhouse is under new management, so the horror stories of other cyclists may be a thing of the past.

I started the day with the obligatory photo-op in front of the Big Galah. I wonder if there's a company in Australia that makes all of these big animal statues like the Eucla Whale, the Border Village Kangaroo, and the Kimba Galah. Their brochure must be bizarre.

There was a general change of direction today. I'm heading northeast for two days, and then I'll turn south at Port Augusta. As expected, the southerlies pushed me to Iron Knob. When I pulled into the roadhouse to get a room, I saw Andy's tent set up out back. The owner let Andy set up his tent for free. She offered me the same deal, but I opted for the $20 room. I'm still not ready to start camping again.

Andy and I hung out in my room for a while, waiting for the weather forecast to come through the static of the only television station received out here. It looks like I'll have favorable winds for the next two days (NE to Port Augusta, then S to Port Pirie). He's also riding to Port Augusta tomorrow, but he's planning to hit the road around 6:00 AM. He could be there before I even leave Iron Knob.

More good news: I'm in mobile phone range again. I celebrated by downloading new e-mail.

Thursday, November 15th
Iron Knob to Port Augusta - 72.84 Km

It was an easy ride to Port Augusta. I did have to wear the mosquito netting most of the ride. And, the traffic did increase while the shoulder disappeared. Still, the weather was great, and I kept up a good pace. I'm in another Flag motel tonight.

Port Augusta is the biggest town that I've seen since Albany. In fact, I had dinner at the first McDonalds since Albany, 2,500 Km and one month ago. Before dinner I climbed to the top of the old water tower, now an observation deck, and took pictures of the town. Then, I walked down to the city center to enjoy the kick-off of their Christmas Lights Festival. They had a country and western band, line dancers, fireworks, an amusement ride, face painting for the kiddies, and lots of food booths for the big crowd. I didn't stay in the city center to see the fireworks, but went back across the river to my motel room and waited to hear the first boom after sunset. Then, I rushed outside to videotape the fireworks over the city skyline. The display only lasted about five minutes, but I got some good shots. It may not have been as loud as the fireworks that I saw outside of Bethlehem, but it was definitely more colorful. And, I didn't have to hide in the bathroom when the fireworks started.

Friday, November 16th
Port Augusta to Port Pirie - 96.4 Km

I turned due south today and was fortunate to be greeted by a strong tailwind. I don't think I've seen any northerlies since I started across the Nullarbor a month ago, so this was a pleasant change. It was a very easy 96 Km. I sat upright on the bike all day, letting the wind push me south on the Port Wakefield Road. This is still Route 1, but the Eyre Highway terminated in Port Augusta.

I'm in another Flag motel tonight. I just found out that they do have a frequent guest program. I should have signed up at the beginning of the trip. By now, I would have accumulated enough points to own one of their motels. Another opportunity lost.

I'm thinking of taking tomorrow off. There's not much in Port Pirie to keep me here, but I could use a little rest before the final push to Adelaide. The biggest disappointment about the town is that they do not have an Internet café. I had hoped to listen to the Strath Haven football team's playoff game broadcast over the web today, but it was not to be. The library offers free Internet access on their handful of PC's, but they close at 1:00 PM on Saturdays, and the Friday night game back in Pennsylvania would still be underway. Besides, all of their PC's were fully booked for the day. I wish my Pocket PC was capable of playing streaming audio, but I think that's asking too much of this tiny computer. Well, I knew that there would be hardships on this trip.

Saturday, November 17th
Port Pirie - 0 Km

It was a good day to stay indoors. The weather was lousy in the afternoon. I was content to lay about the room, watch TV, and re-design my website. I left the room once, for a McDonalds run around 7:00 PM. The "Do Not Disturb" sign has been on my door for over 24 hours now.

The "Do Not Disturb" sign is one of the most under-rated inventions known to mankind. It will stop an eager chambermaid in her tracks. It allows us to sleep past 10:00 AM without interruptions. It allows us to shower without the fear of hotel staff bursting into the room. I even think that other guests curb their conversations outside of rooms displaying the sign. I've been in many hotels/motels without the signs and have had my share of early morning intrusions. In Australia, where checkout is usually 10:00 AM and the chambermaids arrive between 7:00 AM and

8:00 AM, I'm nervous from wake-up to checkout. I'm thinking of buying a generic "Do Not Disturb" sign for the remainder of the trip.

Sunday, November 18th
Port Pirie to Crystal Brook - 31.23 Km

I had hoped to reach Adelaide in two days, but I realized as soon as I stepped out of my motel room this morning that it wasn't in the cards. I was going to have to do 130 Km to Port Wakefield today, directly into a killer wind. That wasn't possible, but I took off anyway in hopes of making tomorrow's ride to Port Wakefield more manageable. After a couple hours, I straggled into Crystal Brook. I stopped early in the day, but I couldn't see the value in beating myself up for another five hours if I still wasn't going to reach Adelaide in two days. I'll try for Port Wakefield again tomorrow and hope that the cold front from the south will have passed overnight.

I'm staying in a simple room above the pub in the Crystal Brooks Hotel for $13. It's Sunday night, so the place is quiet. That's a good thing. I slept for an hour in the afternoon and will sleep well tonight. There is no TV to distract me here. I'm listening to my little AM/FM/SW radio as I do my daily computer work. Last night I stayed up late watching *The Cider House Rules* on cable in the Flag motel. There's no chance of a repeat tonight. I need my beauty sleep.

Monday, November 19th
Crystal Brook to Port Wakefield - 102.55 Km

This had to be one of the most difficult days of the trip so far. It's at least in the top ten, all because of the wind. When I woke up this morning I thought that the cold front had passed through. The trees outside of the hotel were not being blown around as they were yesterday. But, by the time I was on the road at 9:30 AM, yesterday's southerly wind had returned.

I should have stopped after 50 Km in Snowtown, but I knew that that would push my arrival in Adelaide back another day. I'm just too anxious to get an apartment in Adelaide for a week and completely recover. I've been thinking a lot about those four weeks outside of Perth when I did nothing. I'm looking forward to doing more of the same in Adelaide. So, I punished myself today, and will probably do the same tomorrow.

In the Redhill roadhouse this morning I had a chocolate chip muffin and a gingerbread man cookie. When I was leaving, the nice elderly lady behind the counter cheerfully advised me to "stay out of the barrels" in Snowtown. When she saw the puzzled look on my face she said, "Well, it was international news last year", and then proceeded to tell me a gruesome tale of credit card fraud, murder, dismemberment, and bodies stored in barrels in the vault of a rented old bank. As horrible as the details were, the nice old lady cheerfully told the story like Aunt Bea talking about Otis, the Maybury town drunk. Bizarre.

Tuesday, November 20th
Port Wakefield to Glenelg - 113.15 Km

Finally! I didn't think that I would ever reach Adelaide. There wasn't quite as much headwind today, but I still had to work hard to get here. It was a bright, sunny day. Just north of Adelaide, at the outskirts of the suburbs, I stopped for a donut and Gatorade lunch at a BP station. They had a picnic table out back in a park-like setting. I watched the birds, studied my Adelaide city map, and relaxed for 45 minutes. That's a long lunch break for me, but it was too hard to get back on the bike and leave that spot.

The ride through Adelaide wasn't too difficult. The streets are wide and the traffic isn't suicidal. I took a few pictures of some of the gardens (with the bike in every picture, of course) as I cut through the city from north to south. Adelaide was laid out in a grid pattern, so navigation wasn't too difficult. Encircling the original grid is parkland. Beyond the parks are the suburbs. I left the city at the southwest point and continued riding out the Anzac Highway to Glenelg.

Glenelg is a coastal tourist town about six Km from Adelaide. It's been a get-away spot for city-folk for decades. There's an old trolley that still connects the two. I'll use that trolley for any trips into the city in the next week. After checking out the Visitor Information Center and cycling around town, I've decided to stay at the Buffalo Motor Lodge for the week. It's not on the water, or in the middle of town, but it's within walking distance of everything that I need. There's a bike shop, barbershop, and bakery just 100 yards up the street. One hundred yards in the other direction is a brand-new, state-of-the-art Internet café and a restaurant that offers American-style pancakes (a rarity here). What more could I ask for?

Wednesday, November 21st to Monday, November 26th
Glenelg - 0 Km

Did nothing.

Tuesday, November 27th
Glenelg to Strathalbyn - 69.03 Km

There's nothing like a day cycling in the hills after a week off to wake up the old knees. I knew that the Adelaide Hills would be difficult. I just didn't expect it to be a two-shirt day. By lunchtime the first shirt, and everything else that I was wearing, was soaked straight through. I didn't want to freeze in the afternoon during the expected downhill ride, so I put on a new, dry shirt. Public decency laws prevented me from replacing any other sweaty clothes in the parking lot of the Crafers BP gas station. On the bright side, there never was much of a downhill ride until the last five Km today.

I left the Buffalo Motor Lodge in Glenelg around 10:00 AM this morning. The first stop was the historic Gum Tree, just a few blocks away, where the state of South Australia was proclaimed in 1836. The tree is now an arch, with both the top and bottom going into the ground. I have no idea how it continues to survive. It must have a strong root system, or two.

Much of the ride up into the hills was done on a nearly abandoned old road and on bike paths. That certainly helped as I chugged along at 10 Km/hour like the little engine that could: I think I can, I think I can, I think I need oxygen.

After lunch and the quick wardrobe change in Crafers, I proceeded to get lost. Plans to pedal to Murray Bridge were quickly scuttled when I couldn't find the South Eastern Freeway. I found myself on a "scenic drive" to Strathalbyn, and then convinced myself that Strathalbyn was the better destination today, not Murray Bridge.

I broke the 11,000 Km mark today, so I celebrated by getting a motel room with a spa tub. I justified taking this room because it was only $5 more than a standard room, and my knees were sore. It's the first time I've used one of these spas. The motel information guide said to use the supplied bath gel when the jets are turned on, but not too much gel because it foams up very easily. I poured in the whole bottle of gel before I read the second half of those instructions. As soon as I turned on the jets it became a scene out of *I Love Lucy*. I had to turn off the jets after 15 seconds because the foam was already spilling out of the tub and onto the tile floor. So much for a relaxing bath. There's another $5 well spent.

Wednesday, November 28th
Strathalbyn to Meningie - 96.71 Km

I'm in a bit of a funk tonight. Just four Km from Meningie a car full of kids tried to run me off of the road. They almost did, too.

The car rushed by just inches from me. I was too busy flipping them off and waving for them to come back that I didn't get the license plate number, or even the make of car. I probably could have tried to pull out the camcorder and get the car and license on videotape. I could have called 000 (Australia's 911) and told the police to stop a white car with five or six kids entering town from the north. But, it all happened so fast that I was left with no recourse.

I cycled up and down the main street in town looking for the car. Every other car in Australia is white. I all but accused one guy getting out of his car, and then realized that his rear window had louvers. The punks who tried to kill me had a clear rear window. I went to the police station, but it was closed. This might be a nice town, but I just want to get out of it now. One incident can paint your whole impression of a town. The kids are delinquents, destined to be a burden on society. The parents are alcoholics, unable to provide structure and discipline to their children through the booze haze. The cops are incompetent Barney Fife wannabes. Right or wrong, that's the impression that I'll take away from Meningie. Attempted vehicular manslaughter can make you cranky.

Thursday, November 29th
Meningie to Policeman Point - 55.89 Km

I got back on the Princes Highway today, but kept my eyes open for a white car full of delinquents. It turned out to be a short day because, after the motel in Policeman Point, the next accommodations are 100 Km down the road. I reached this place at 1:00 PM and didn't feel like fighting the southerlies for another six hours. I'll shoot for Kingston tomorrow. I have to try to get out earlier in the day. The winds have been picking up throughout the days lately. There is also some rain predicted for tomorrow.

Friday, November 30th
Policeman Point to Kingston SE - 99.91 Km

It didn't rain, but it was a dreary day. I reached Kingston SE (the "SE" must distinguish it from another Kingston in South Australia) late in the day. The first thing to greet visitors here is Larry the Lobster, another 30-foot tall animal sculpture designed to lure in the tourist dollars. This sculpture has a "For Sale" sign in front of it. I guess Larry hasn't been pulling his weight. I've been reading a book by another cyclist who traveled much of the same route that I'm traveling, and Larry was for sale when he passed through Kingston SE two years ago. It's going to be difficult to sell a 30-foot lobster until they find a buyer with a 30-foot pot.

I had hoped to hear the Strath Haven state semi-final game over the Internet tomorrow, but this town has no Internet café. The nearest one is in Mount Gambier, 160 Km away. The library will be closed tomorrow, so I can't hear the game on the Internet there. I looked into getting a taxi or renting a car to get to Mount Gambier, but struck out. There is one bus that leaves at 9:30 PM, but that wasn't practical. So, long story short, I won't get to hear the game tomorrow morning. I wonder how people can live in places that are so cut off from the rest of the world.

Saturday, December 1st
Kingston SE to Millicent - 110.01 Km

I got a call at 4:00 AM this morning from my younger brother. The football game was postponed 24 hours due to rain back in Philly. I feel like an inmate sitting on the electric chair who just got a reprieve from the governor. I figured, if I could ride to Millicent today, it would only be a 50 Km ride to Mount Gambier tomorrow morning. I could reach the Internet café there before the game starts at 10:00 AM if I left at 7:00 AM.

Today's ride took me through pine forests and, not coincidentally, my allergies really kicked in. By the time I reached Millicent, I was a wreck. The nice lady at the front desk of the Country Haven motel gave me two of her allergy pills to hold me until I could get some of my own at the chemist. Of course, the chemist was closed by the time I went into town. And, you can't buy pharmaceuticals at the local supermarkets. So, I'll probably have to wait to buy allergy pills on Monday at some chemist down the road.

The long ride, combined with the allergy pill, really knocked me out. It could have been a longer ride if I followed the coast and cycled through Robe and Beachport. Although they're probably great towns to visit, I didn't need the extra 20 Km today. I had a steak dinner for the third night in a row, and then hit the sack.

Sunday, December 2nd
Millicent - 0 Km

I woke up to thunder and a driving rainstorm today. There was no way that I was going to be able to cycle 50 Km to Mount Gambier. The nice lady at the front desk offered to let me use her computer to hear the football game, but it didn't have the RealMedia player installed on it. I spent well over an hour attempting to download and install the player, but had no luck. I resorted to watching a high school sports message board for periodic updates of the game. It was frustrating, waiting for the message board regulars to post highlights of the game that they were listening to on their computers. In the last minutes of the game, when it could have gone either way, I was hitting the refresh button every few seconds to get the latest post. Fortunately, Strath Haven won the game.

I'm not going to have a repeat of that next weekend. When I get to Mount Gambier, I'm going to find the Internet café and test everything days before the championship game is broadcast. This game will even have video coverage streamed over the Internet. It seems crazy to take almost a full week off, after just taking a week off near Adelaide, but it's worth it. I'll take my time here in Millicent, and then ride to Mount Gambier in the middle of the week to find a nice motel and set up house. It might be nice to slow the pace down a bit.

Monday, December 3rd
Millicent - 0 Km

It was another windy and drizzly day in Millicent. So, I passed the time by meandering through the town museum. It's an excellent small town museum with a great variety of artifacts housed in a number of adjoining buildings. I spent two and a half hours checking out all of the exhibits. Millicent, by the way, was the first name of the founder's wife. The townspeople are thankful that the founder didn't marry a Gertrude.

I also made it to the chemist's shop and bought a 10-pack of Telfast allergy pills. On the way back to the motel, a one Km walk from the middle of town, I saw another solo bicycle-tourist struggling against the wind. He had just pulled into the Information Center, so I went over and introduced myself. His name was Malcolm, and he was a Scotsman who was one year into a ten-year trip. We commiserated about the weather and compared routes. He had already toured New Zealand and had lots of info to share. Since it was late in the day, I let him go to find a campground. He suggested that we meet after dinner at the pub in the middle of town to continue swapping stories. So, we did. For almost two hours we talked about our trips so far, our planned routes, our websites, and how we were supporting our travels. At the end, we exchanged e-mail addresses and agreed to keep in touch. There are so few nuts like me on the road that it's reassuring to meet another. I'm sure he felt the same.

Tuesday, December 4th
Millicent to Mount Gambier - 50.71 Km

I left Millicent at 10:30 AM today, despite a slight drizzle and some headwinds. I didn't have to leave. I didn't need to be in Mount Gambier until Saturday morning. But, if I'm going to wait around, I might as well wait in a larger town. I had already spent two hours in the Millicent Museum. What else was I to do?

The ride to Mount Gambier was only 50 Km. The winds strengthened in the last 20 Km, but it didn't really matter. I was well rested, the ride was short, and the sun was poking through the clouds by then. I rode past the big Kimberly-Clark plant and through pine forests. They weren't old growth forests but were presumably planted to be harvested years later. Each section of evenly spaced pine trees had a sign facing the road stating when it was planted. The oldest section was planted in 1926.

Mount Gambier is a large town with a McDonalds, Subway, and KFC. It also has a wealth of motels from which to choose. Based on the extensive research that I did last night, I ended up in the Avalon Motel, paying $22.50/night. The Avalon is close to the city center, but on a residential side street. I'll be comfortable staying here until Sunday. This evening I found a good Internet café in town to watch the Strath Haven game on the Internet.

Wednesday, December 5th
Mount Gambier - 0 Km

Well, I did my Christmas shopping this morning. Thank goodness for Amazon.com. Everybody back home will be getting DVD's from me this year. I spent a couple hours on-line at the Internet café choosing just the right titles for each recipient. After such a strenuous morning I spent the afternoon sleeping. I did even less tonight, if that's possible. I'm just gearing up for a big day tomorrow. I'll be doing the laundry.

Thursday, December 6th
Mount Gambier - 0 Km

Not only did I do a load of wash today, but I also went food shopping. It was a full day. I did manage to sneak in a few hours of sleep in the afternoon. The weather has turned lousy. I didn't go out for a dinner because of the rain. Fortunately, I bought enough Snickers bars and Coke to hold me until tomorrow.

Friday, December 7th
Mount Gambier - 0 Km

I spent the morning strolling around the scenic lakes formed by extinct volcanic craters at the edge of town. The Mount Gambierites are particularly proud of Blue Lake. Its claim to fame, as you might guess, is its deep blue summertime color. I happen to be in town at the right time, as Blue Lake is gray during the rest of the year. As I was sightseeing it began to rain, so I covered up the camera and raced back into town. By the time that I reached the city center, it was pouring. I popped into the Internet café for a few minutes to check my e-mail and reserve a machine for the Strath Haven game tomorrow morning. While I was there, I met Malcolm again. He told me that I had to check out the unique backpackers accommodations where he was staying. He said he was in cell 23 of The Jail, which in its former life was...a jail. He wasn't incarcerated when I stopped by later in the day, so I took a walk around. The place has an eerie ambience with barbed wire on top of the walls, an exercise yard, and two cellblocks. The cells are as Spartan as you would expect them to be, two cots and a toilet. I can't believe that people pay money to stay in a place like that.

Saturday, December 8th
Mount Gambier - 0 Km

There is no joy in Mudville, or Mount Gambier, today. Strath Haven lost the state championship game. I spent four hours in the Internet café watching the broadcast on the Internet, as planned. After the game, I did some more walking around town, had a hot dog in the Lakes Mall, then went back to the motel to rest up for tomorrow. I should be back on the road if the weather is any good. That would take me out of South Australia and into my third Australian state, Victoria.

Sunday, December 9th
Mount Gambier - 0 Km

I exercised my right to take another day off. The weather was iffy, and I attended a late mass. So, I put off the inevitable for another day. I took another long walk around town, and bought some groceries and a Sunday paper after mass. I spent the afternoon reading the paper, watching TV, and sleeping again. So, this is what it feels like to be retired.

Monday, December 10th
Mount Gambier to Nelson, Victoria - 40.93 Km

After six days off, it's difficult to get out of bed and onto the bike. I was greeted with drizzly skies when I stepped out of my motel room this morning. I decided to split the ride to Portland in half. I rode to Nelson today and will shoot for Portland tomorrow. There were intermittent showers throughout the short ride, but I had a great tailwind. I've had so few tailwinds in Australia that it was difficult to stop here. But, I had the good sense to stop rather than risk getting stuck halfway to Portland in a thunderstorm. Or, maybe it was laziness. Either way, I found a $20 motel room and I'm kicking back.

Like most towns in Australia, Nelson has an Information Board alongside the main/only road into town. All of these boards have a map of the town and coded points of interest. In addition to the churches, motels, and post office, Nelson's Information Board also points to the one spot in town where mobile phones are in range of the Port MacDonald tower. So, as soon as I got into town, I cycled to the designated spot atop a hill in a residential neighborhood. I called my brother, the coach, to congratulate him on his team's season. He was surprised when I told him that I had seen the championship game live over the Internet. He groaned when I said that people all over the world could have seen it. The world is definitely getting smaller, whether we like it or not.

Tuesday, December 11th
Nelson to Portland - 76.31 Km

I left the Princes Highway yesterday and today to ride closer to the coast. This route took me through some more pine tree forests. My allergies have kicked in again, but I have the Telfast pills to combat the symptoms now. Unfortunately, the pills zapped me of the strength needed to climb some of the hills today. I was happy to coast into Portland this afternoon and find a motel with all of the modern conveniences. I spent the night watching TV, including a new American reality program called *The Great Race* where contestants race around the globe, struggling with exotic foods, languages, and accommodations. Wimps.

Wednesday, December 12th
Portland - 0 Km

There's too much to see here in Portland, so I took another day off. Whalers founded the town in 1834 on the very large Portland Bay. Ploughers Field on the waterfront is the site of the first tilled field in Portland. It's a park now with a quaint tramline running through it. I walked up and down the waterfront to check out the lighthouse and the monuments to the early settlers. Later, I went into town to see the automobile exhibits at the Powerhouse Museum. Besides the cars, there was a large collection of antique auto memorabilia. I thoroughly enjoyed myself, and then spoke with a couple of vintage automobile enthusiasts as I was leaving the museum. They really love their antique cars in South Australia and Victoria. The biggest vintage auto rally in the country is held annually in the hills above Adelaide. The old American cars are just as popular as the old British cars. Most of the early American models were shipped down here from Canada in parts and then assembled. If I were in the market for a 1920's era Plymouth or Dodge, this would be a great spot to begin my search. But, I'm not in the market. I'm content with this bicycle as my sole mode of transportation for now.

Thursday, December 13th
Portland to Warrnambool - 100.6 Km

I felt strong today. The sun was shinning, and there were no headwinds. I met a couple of teenaged Aussies cycling from Murray Bridge to Melbourne. This wasn't their first bike tour. They seemed to be very self-reliant. They slept in a laundromat last night, and it wasn't the first time that they had done that. Many of the laundromats here automatically lock up at 8:00 PM. If you're inside before then, you're safe for the night. I filed that idea away for the next time that I have trouble finding accommodations. I rode with the guys for about five Km before splitting at Port Fairy.

I also met one of the fellows from the Powerhouse Museum while I was on the road. Just a few Km outside of Portland I was passed by a dozen or more vintage cars. A few Km farther, I saw where they had all stopped at an old church to regroup. I was waved over to meet the members of the club and get a closer look at their well-maintained Morrises, Dodges, and Fords. The club was taking some senior citizens out for a ride and was happy to show off the cars. The members were also curious about my trip. They took pictures of the bike and me in front of some of the cars. I think that I'm going to be in the next issue of the club's newsletter. The club members and senior citizens were so pleasant that I spent about 45 minutes outside the old church with them. It was a great diversion.

Warrnambool is a great cycling town. They hold a big race here every year. There is a nice bike path beside the Princes Highway as you ride into town. There's even a large sculpture celebrating cycling on the grass median strip in the middle of town. I'm very comfortable here.

Friday, December 14th
Warrnambool to Port Campbell - 73.81 Km

I'm in the middle of the most scenic coastline that Australia has to offer tonight. A variety of geological wonders with names like the Grotto, the Arch, London Bridge, and the Twelve Apostles are located on the Great Ocean Road between Peterborough and Princetown. I saw, and extensively photographed, the first three wonders before finding a motel in Port Campbell.

Early in the day I met a Dutch couple, Lisette and Giel, who had cycled from Darwin through the interior of Australia. They will be completing their travels in Melbourne in a few days. We kept crossing paths as we hopscotched from scenic lookout to scenic lookout. Later in the day I met a German couple, Peter and Andrea, on a tandem. They were already talking with Lisette and Giel. The five of us stood around for half an hour comparing equipment and routes taken. Although bicycle-tourists rarely meet like-minded travelers, we seem to congregate around scenic destinations like the Great Ocean Road.

The Bay of Islands and the Bay of Martyrs were the first two sights along the coast. There are a number of limestone stacks standing in the surf, separated from the mainland by erosion. Next is the Grotto, a small pool of still water under a stone arch, and backed by the rough surf of the Southern Ocean. It looks like one of those beachfront pools that you would see in *Architectural Digest*. After the Grotto is London Bridge. It used to be two connected arches stretching out into the surf. In 1990 the arch closest to the mainland collapsed leaving a pair of Japanese tourists stranded out on the farthest arch. It took a helicopter to get them back to the mainland. The Arch is ...just an arch.

Port Campbell is a nice little tourist town. Tonight's motel room cost me $37. I'll probably pay at least that much the next few nights along the Great Ocean Road. It's great to be back in a tourist region.

Saturday, December 15th
Port Campbell to Lavers Hill - 53.86 Km

The day started with rain as soon as I reached Loch Ard Gorge. I quickly covered all of the panniers and then pulled out the camera. The gorge must be impossible for sailors to see. It's just a narrow slot in the limestone cliffs. After passing through the slot, the gorge widens to reveal a safe harbor with a sandy beach. Nearby is the Blowhole, an open cave in the limestone where you can look down and see waves of seawater crashing through underground tunnels. The blowhole is probably 100 meters inland.

The limestone must be very porous here. Next to the Blowhole is the Loch Ard Cemetery where four victims of the Loch Ard shipwreck are buried. Fifty-four were on board. Two survived. Only four bodies were recovered. The rest were swept away. It's the most famous wreck on Australia's Shipwreck Coast. Farther up the road I reached the Twelve Apostles. They are a row of stone stacks standing out in the surf. At one time they were a part of the limestone cliffs. Now they are a tourist attraction. Every postcard in this area has a picture of the Twelve Apostles shot from a variety of angles. Never mind that there are only Eight Apostles.

After all of that sightseeing, it was time to get to work. At Princetown the road leaves the coast and heads up to Lavers Hill, 450 meters above sea level. Some stretches of road were very steep. I met Peter and Andrea again on the way up. They seemed to be doing well on the climb, despite the fact that tandems are not at their best on uphill grades. At the top of the hill I found a small motel with miniature ponies in the backyard and a great view down to the sea. I had a porterhouse steak for dinner and rested up for the big downhill tomorrow.

Sunday, December 16th
Lavers Hill to Apollo Bay - 49.33 Km

I left Lavers Hill around 10:00 AM, expecting to roll all of the way down to the coast. Unfortunately, there was at least one large uphill before reaching the coast. I used the helmet-cam on a couple of the downhills, but it fritzed out on the second one before I reached the beach. Vibrations over the rough roads disconnected the power contact.

The weather had been mostly dreary until I reached the last few Km to Apollo Bay. I never got off the main road in Otway National Park because I was anxious to get a roof over my head. I probably missed the opportunity to see koalas in the wild by skipping the park. Oh well, now I have a reason to return to the Great Ocean Road.

Apollo Bay is a very scenic town of just a few blocks nestled between the ocean and hills. The main street runs next to the beach. Although most of the accommodations are on the main street, I found a very quiet motel a couple streets back in a residential neighborhood. I'll take tomorrow off to explore the town.

Monday, December 17th
Apollo Bay - 0 Km

Apollo Bay looks like one of those great retirement towns. I'm sure Dad would love it. There's a golf course right on the water and a Catholic church next to the course. There's a harbor nearby, and everything is within walking distance of the residential neighborhood.

I took a few pictures, mailed a few postcards, and then went back to the motel to set up transfer capabilities over the Internet on my money market fund. Now, I have the ability to drain money from the down payment on my next house while half a world away. That's progress, right?

I bought a very bad take-away pizza for dinner. It's hit-and-miss with these mom and pop pizzerias. Sometimes they just don't meet up to my exacting standards. That's when it's important to have extra Oreo's on hand. Like a good Boy Scout, I'm always prepared.

Tuesday, December 18th
Apollo Bay to Lorne - 48.93 Km

As advertised, this coast is a lot of fun to cycle. But, it's not as dramatic as the French Riviera, the Amalfitano Coast, or the Pacific Coast Highway near Big Sur. Around 17 Km from Lorne I stopped for a snack at the Wye River. While I was sitting on a park bench, Peter and Andrea from Germany, and Giel and Lisette from the Netherlands cycled by. They pulled off the road and we all ate and talked for about an hour. While we were hanging out, a friend of Giel and Lisette named Barry drove up. He is an Englishman busking his way around Australia. They last saw him in Alice Springs six weeks prior. It was pure chance that they would meet up again at the Wye River. Barry pulled out a new electric/acoustic guitar that he bought in Alice Springs and Peter started playing.

Although we were having a blast, we also knew that we had to get back on the bikes and ride to Lorne. Giel took the lead and set a fast pace. We arrived in Lorne lickety-split. We stopped just outside of town and had another meal. After the two meals, I realized that it was getting a little late. It was 5:00 PM when I started looking for accommodations for the night. I was turned down at the first two motels, but the Best Western owner took pity on me. He only charged $40 for a beautiful room. I felt that I owed him something for his kindness, so I used the phone to get on the Internet, I raided the mini-bar, and I ordered a full breakfast. It was just like a business trip, except I can't expense the phone bill, mini-bar, and breakfast.

Wednesday, December 19th
Lorne to Geelong - 80.43 Km

This was my final day on the Great Ocean Road. Parts of the road today were carved out of cliffs looking out over the Southern Ocean. I reached the end (or beginning) of the GOR near Anglesea where an arch was erected across the road. At the base of the arch were plaques telling of the history of the road and its construction by the returning "diggers" (Australia's doughboys) after World War I. Farther down the road in Torquay I had a rest and a Gatorade on the well-manicured Esplanade overlooking the beach. Very scenic. I saw Peter and Andrea regrouping there, but didn't bother them. They probably think that I'm a stalker by now.

I detoured off of the main road to ride down to Bells Beach, famous among surfers for some of the world's biggest waves. It was featured in the Keanu Reeves/Patrick Swayze movie *Point Break*. They hold the Australian Open surfing championship there every year. The waves weren't too big today, but the hills sure were. They roll very steeply and are knee-killers

The road inland to Geelong is popular among cyclists around here. There are a few signs telling drivers to be on the lookout for us. The road is only one lane wide. So, when two cars pass in opposite directions, each of the outside wheels ends up on the dirt shoulder, kicking up a hail of rocks and dust. It's lots of fun to cycle through.

Geelong is an old industrial town, tied to Melbourne by train. They've had a Ford factory here since 1925. I found a motel to stay for a few days. I'll take the train into Melbourne on one of the next couple of days. I had a funny exchange with the man in the front desk as I signed in. He saw that I was from Pennsylvania and said that he was going to visit Punxetawney next February. It seems that he's a huge fan of the Bill Murray movie *Groundhog Day*. He asked a few questions about Punxetawney Phil and the weather in central Pennsylvania. I let him know that I thought he would be going a long way to see a sleepy rodent get pulled out of a tree trunk in the dead of winter.

Thursday, December 20th
Geelong - 0 Km

The groundhog lover put me in a room right next to the motel restaurant. There are obnoxious noises and smells emanating from the kitchen at all hours of the night. I guess he got the last laugh.

I took the one-hour train ride into Melbourne to do some quick sightseeing. I had been told that there was really no easy way to cycle into the city, and the train ride confirmed it. The Princes Freeway is the only direct road between Geelong and Melbourne.

My first stop in the city was the Rialto Tower, billed as the highest in the Southern Hemisphere. From the top of the tower you can see that Melbourne is just like any American city, with skyscrapers, rail yards, and a stadium or two. The Yarra River, which meanders through the downtown, looks like a working river from the tower. Down at ground level the Yarra is overrun with mozzies (Australian for "mosquitoes"). I took a few pictures of the skyscrapers hovering over the river, and then sought refuge from the bugs. Strolling around the city a few blocks back from the river did nothing for me. Melbourne isn't Perth or Adelaide. It's more like an American city. The predominant feature isn't its weather or geography or history. Melbourne is a commercial center, first and foremost. I was back on a train to Geelong after just three hours. It's probably not fair to develop an impression of such a large city in one afternoon, but I'm happy to be putting Melbourne behind me.

Friday, December 21st
Geelong - 0 Km

Today is the first day of summer, my second this year. It's also the Friday before Christmas week. Everybody and their uncle will be heading to the beach today. So, I'm staying right here. There's more to Geelong than just the Ford automobile factory. There's also the Ford Discovery Centre. It's a museum detailing the Ford Motor Company's history in Australia. I spent a couple hours strolling around the quadracycles, Model T's, and racing cars in the entertaining and informative museum. The strangest exhibit was about the safety tests done on new Fords. Beside the standard adult and child crash test dummies, there was a full-sized kangaroo dummy. The kangaroo crash test dummy is presumably not used to test the effects of a collision on a kangaroo in the passenger seat. Judging by the number of dead roo's that I saw alongside the Eyre Highway in the Nullarbor, I would guess that the boys in the safety lab had a more sinister use for the kangaroo crash test dummy. There were no bicycle-riding dummies in the exhibit, so I felt good about that.

Saturday, December 22nd
Geelong to Queenscliff - 50.47 Km

Although it was a short day, I did pass the 12,000 Km mark today. Instead of cycling directly to Queenscliff on the

Bellarine Highway, I took the beach road at the suggestion of a local. It turned out to be a good choice. The Bellarine Peninsula is very scenic along the coast. There were nearly deserted beaches where the locals walked their dogs, electric windmill farms, and a bike path from Port Lonsdale to Queenscliff. I arrived at Queenscliff too late to catch the ferry to Portsea, so I took a room here for the night.

Queenscliff has that old-timey, seaside resort feeling like Cape May, New Jersey. The main street has quaint shops, and tourists are pulled around town in horse-drawn carriages. The hotel rates are thoroughly modern, though. I'm paying $66 tonight.

Sunday, December 23rd
Queenscliff to Cowes - 74.84 Km

This was my first two-ferry day of the trip since Day One outside of Lisbon. I missed the 10:30 AM mass in Queenscliff because I wanted to catch the 10:00 AM ferry over to Portsea on the Mornington Peninsula. The guys running the ferry gave me lots of advice about cycling the Mornington Peninsula. It was welcomed because I didn't have any tourist brochures on the area.

Unless you're a captain of industry or a very successful politician, Portsea can be described as a place where the other half lives. I cycled around Portsea and Sorrento (another ritzy tourist town), and then headed out across the peninsula. I elected not to take the northerly route that crossed a high mountain or the southerly route that went too far out of the way. Instead I cycled straight across the middle of the peninsula. Unfortunately, this route had some steep rolling hills, including one Km on a gravel road. I was beat by the time that I reached the Stony Point ferry on the eastern side of the peninsula.

The resort town of Cowes, the ferry point on Phillip Island, has a number of good motels from which to choose. I decided on the Seahorse Motel where the pleasant mother and son team at the front desk put me into a one-bedroom apartment for little more than a single room. Not too shabby.

Monday, December 24th
Cowes to Inverloch - 93.2 Km

I had a brutally strong tailwind most of the day. It was certainly welcomed because I was zapped after yesterday's ride over the Mornington Peninsula. I started out the day by riding into the wind from Cowes to the Nobbies at the westernmost tip of Phillip Island. The Nobbies are eroded remnants of basalt flows just off of the coast. There were busloads of tourists and colonies of angry sea birds at the lookout, so I snapped a few pictures and got out of there.

The rest of the day I had my back to the wind. It was a fun ride with great scenery and wide shoulders on the roads. When I got to Wonthaggi I went into their Information Center to decide whether to stop there for the Christmas holiday, or to continue on to Inverloch. Both had a few motels and Catholic churches. Wonthaggi is a bigger town, but Inverloch won out because it was a beach town catering to tourists.

On the advice of a couple of locals I took the long way to Inverloch by going south to Cape Paterson and then up the Bunurong coast. The ride down to the Cape was on a bike path beside the road. I wasn't the only cyclist out there. On the way up the Bunurong coast I met a 73-year-old man from Inverloch who was out for his evening ride. We met at one of the many scenic lookout points on a cliff above the surf. We talked a while about the aboriginal history in this area. Then, he told me that he has asked his children that he be cremated when he dies and his ashes spread over this coast. That seemed a little extreme to me, but I wished him luck on his funeral plans anyway.

Tuesday, December 25th
Inverloch - 0 Km

Merry Christmas! I'm in the Inverloch Motel near the edge of town. I walked into town for the 9:00 AM mass. It wasn't as crowded as I thought it might be. All of the pews were full, but nobody was standing. And, nobody had to use the reserve seating set up in the alcove on the side of the church. It was one of the least stressful Christmas masses that I've ever attended.

It was a shame that I took the day off because there were gale force winds that would have blown me 200 Km east today. Instead, I walked around town looking for a place to eat a hot meal. No luck. Every store was closed for the holiday. I did manage to pick up some supplies at a deli. Hopefully, I can get a hot meal tomorrow, Boxing Day.

Back at the motel I got calls from home. It was still Christmas Eve back in Philly. We had all watched some of the live broadcast of the midnight mass in St. Peter's Basilica. It seems like years ago that I was in Rome. I felt the same after seeing the news reports about the mass at the Church of the Nativity in Bethlehem. It's been a long trip, and there's still a lot more left to go. I'm not tired of it yet.

Wednesday, December 26th
Inverloch - 0 Km

Happy Boxing Day, whatever that means. I spent another day locked up in the motel room in Inverloch. There was wind and wuthering throughout Victoria. They had snow last night in some town in the north of the state. They were predicting possible hale in Melbourne. There was another strong westerly, and intermittent showers throughout the day. I had to ask the owner of the motel if summer had been cancelled in Australia this year.

I snuck out between downpours to cycle into town to do my laundry and buy a couple of hot dogs. I watched a Charlton Heston movie this afternoon about the Boxer Rebellion, which apparently has nothing to do with Boxing Day. I've got to get out of here tomorrow.

Thursday, December 27th
Inverloch to Morwell - 87.93 Km

I got back on the road again, and the weather is still bad. It's cold, drizzly, and cloudy. On the bright side, I had a great tailwind all day. The route was basically one very long and gradual ascent on Route 181 to Mirboo North, followed by one very long and gradual descent on Route 182 to Morwell. I found a very nice Country Haven motel room in Morwell for $24. After showering, I went out to find a hot meal in town. Unfortunately, the town closes at 6:00 PM. Only the Coles supermarket was open, so I went in and bought iced donuts, crackers, granola bars, apple juice, and Coke. Just the staples. Thank goodness for multivitamins.

Friday, December 28th
Morwell to Sale - 71.85 Km

I'm sitting here drinking my usual post-ride Gatorade and I just noticed that it's over a month past its "Best Before" date. What ingredient in Gatorade can go bad? Sodium chloride? Potassium citrate? Food acid #330? I'm going to throw caution to the wind and chug it.

It was another easy ride today. The westerlies continued through most of the day, and the terrain was flat. I stuck to the Princes Highway, which has wide shoulders much of the way. There was no rain, and I went without the jacket in the afternoon. This is what the travel brochure promised.

In Traralgon I popped into a bike shop and asked about the availability of my Avocet Kevlar Cross tires. I've been using the same rear tire that I put on in Egypt. The clerk ripped the

Australian distributor and said that I would be better off having a couple tires sent over from the States. I'm going to take that under advisement. I had planned on cycling to Stratford today, but when I reached Sale I saw a McDonalds next to a Flag Motel. That signaled the end of another workday for me. I'm in no hurry. Stratford can wait another day.

Saturday, December 29th
Sale to Bairnsdale - 75.54 Km

The weather was near perfect today. I've had so few good weather days in Australia that it was a shame to spend some of this day repairing my first flat since Egypt. The tube was never punctured by a shard of glass or a nail. The rear tire just wore through the rubber to the Kevlar halfway between Sale and Stratford. I put on the spare tire and a new tube and continued on my way.

The sister city of Stratford, Connecticut, where I last lived, is much smaller. There is a nice park with barbecue that residents were just firing up as I passed. I stopped into the Mobile station to buy a Gatorade and Kit Kat. While there, I noticed another cycling couple going the other way. I didn't get to a chance to talk to them as they entered a gourmet food store before I could get their attention. I guess they didn't want Gatorade or Kit Kats.

Bairnsdale is a relatively large town. I got a budget room and caught a few Z's before the 7:00 PM mass. I think that the sun took a little out of me today. The church had an interesting interior, obviously modeled after the Sistine Chapel. The ceiling was covered with ornate panels of paintings, and the front wall had a version of the *Last Judgment*. Very nice.

Sunday, December 30th
Bairnsdale to Lakes Entrance - 37.23 Km

After yesterday's beautiful weather, I was surprised to find it cold and windy today. I didn't have the energy to fight headwinds all the way to Orbost, so I stopped in the tourist town of Lakes Entrance.

The day started out with some promise as I came across a sign for the Bairnsdale - Orbost Rail Trail. It was a paved, though rough, former rail bed that started out fairly close to the A1. I met an elderly local riding the path after a few Km. He told me that after the bridge over the Nicholson River, the path got rougher and went north towards Bruthen, not south to Lakes Entrance like the A1. So, at the bridge I left the path and returned to the main road.

By the time I reached Lakes Entrance, I had already decided to call it a day. The lady at the Information Center told me that the town was filling up fast and most motels were now only booking people for minimum two-day stays because of the New Years holiday. I rushed up the main street and booked a $35 two-star room for two nights. I'll be in town tomorrow night to see the fireworks display.

While I was booking my room, another guest arrived. He said to the lady at the front desk that he had been here six months before. He had heard that the motel had refurbished the rooms since then. She told him that they had almost completed a program of replacing the linens and mattresses in every room. He replied that that was a good thing because the beds were lousy six months ago. There was an awkward moment of silence from the receptionist, which only meant one thing: the room that I was just assigned had not gotten the mattress upgrade yet. Sure enough, I have a bed that's better suited for an invertebrate than a guy with a delicate spine. There's no use complaining. I'll just roll into the middle of the bed tonight and pray that I can stand upright tomorrow morning.

Monday, December 31st
Lakes Entrance - 0 Km

It's the last day of a strange year for me. So, I celebrated by sleeping late in the morning, taking a nap in the afternoon, and then relaxing in the evening. I had planned on going down to the motel pool to work on my tan, but it seemed like too much work.

Downstairs in the motel's ballroom/dining room they had a year-end party, complete with live band. I could hear the festivities loud and clear in my room, especially the ABBA medley, which I believe is a required skill to join the Australian musicians' union. Maybe if I drank the way that Australians do I would also enjoy the music of Abba. I went out to the roof to videotape the midnight fireworks show. A lone bagpiper in a kilt complimented the late showing. I think this fellow only got out to play once every year. The other guests seemed to enjoy the music, though. Once again, I don't drink like Australians do.

I'm not anxious to start cycling tomorrow. Bad weather is forecasted, and the police will still be scraping revelers off of the road. Besides, Lakes Entrance should be a quiet town tomorrow as everybody nurses their hangovers. I might even be able to get some sleep.

Tuesday, January 1st
Lakes Entrance - 0 Km

I took the day off so that I could catch up on some journal entries. I also took a shot at doing my annual net worth statement. That was impossible. All I could do was type up the State of the Finances statement. I summed up my situation this year by saying: "Dreams of a lifetime don't come cheap. I just hope it doesn't take a lifetime to pay this one off."

I watched the final show of *The Great Race*. The winners traveled 30,000 miles in six weeks. Ha! If there's a *Great Race II*, they can team me up with anybody and we would do well, assuming my partner isn't in a wheelchair or on heart medication. The $1,000,000 prize money might pay for some of this little adventure.

The forecasted bad weather did not arrive until 5:00 PM today. I could have cycled to Orbost. I'll try tomorrow, but more rain is forecasted. Happy New Year.

Wednesday, January 2nd
Lakes Entrance to Orbost - 62.37 Km

Beginning today, I am riding through a more rustic region of Victoria. That means that there are more parks and reserves, and fewer farms and towns. That, of course, means more hills. All of the flat lands were grabbed by the farmers decades ago, leaving only mountains and swamps to become state parks. This is less than ideal terrain for cycling. The cyclists' lobby must not have been too strong when the land was being divvied up.

Orbost is a very pleasant little town. The motels, all three, are kept away from the main street. The first motel had no vacancies. The second looked a little rough around the edges. I took a room in the third for $44. That's more than I expected to pay, but it did include free movies and a VCR on which to play them. I ended up watching *Shaft*, *Saving Private Ryan*, and three episodes of *Fawlty Towers*. I had to walk up to the main street to get a pizza for dinner because the motel's cook is on vacation. It had all of the elements of a cultured evening: a blaxploitation film, a sophomoric British comedy, and pizza.

Thursday, January 3rd
Orbost to Cann River - 75.09 Km

The terrain is definitely getting hillier. As I was leaving Orbost I met a couple of cyclists who were heading west. They had stayed at a little hotel in Bellbird Creek about 40 Km up the

Princes Highway. They told me that the road would roll gradually. It did just that, but the ascents and descents were very long. I had to stop halfway up a couple of the hills to catch my breath. Despite the limited gearing that my bike now sports, I haven't gotten off and pushed up any hills in Australia. Not that I pushed it much in Europe or the Middle East.

I stopped into the hotel at Bellbird Creek and had a quick snack in the restaurant. It's the only civilization between Orbost and Cann River. As is usually the case, the first topic of discussion was my rear-view mirror. From Europe to Australia, people are fascinated by my Third Eye. They always ask where I got mine and if they can buy it right off of my glasses. The lady behind the bar said that her brother, a 50-year-old touring cyclist, would love the mirror. Years ago he had cycled over 7,000 Km in Europe. When I get back to the States I'm going to have to contact Third Eye and let them know that there is a worldwide market for their rear-view mirrors. Maybe I could be their distributor.

After the snack I tried to book ahead for a room in Cann River because of the lack of availability during the school holidays. The mobile phone wouldn't work in the valley where the Bellbird Hotel was located, so I cycled to the top of the first hill and called the Hop Inn Motel. I got my room, and it was a good thing that I called. The town was filling up fast. I finished the scenic ride through the forest at a brisk pace. I had another strong westerly and a threat of rain pushing me along. I was spent by the time I reached Cann River.

Cann River isn't so much a town as a travelers' rest stop. It's at the intersection of the Monaro and Princes Highways. There are three motels, one hotel, a couple of gas stations, and a few cafés around the intersection. There isn't much else here. If there is a symphony hall or museum, I couldn't find them.

Friday, January 4th
Cann River - 0 Km

I decided at the last minute to take today off. I hadn't gotten too much sleep last night because I was working on my website. Also, my right knee was a little tender, and I knew that I would be riding through some hills today. Finally, I spent some time on the phone this morning with Delta Airlines discussing the return portion of my original flight to Europe from Philadelphia.

When I originally booked the Philly to Lisbon tickets with frequent flier miles I had to book a return flight that I knew I would never use. So, the ticket agent and I decided on Zurich to Philly tickets scheduled for January 5th. Delta called my replacement at my old work number today saying that there were problems with the Zurich flight. I didn't care because I wasn't planning on using it. But, it turns out that there is a very slim chance that I will be able to use the return ticket for one of my Pacific flights. I have the name and address of a Delta rep in Sydney who I will speak to when I arrive there, but I'm not holding out much hope. What's the worst thing that can happen? They'll say "no." It won't be the first time that I've heard that.

I spent the rest of the morning sleeping. I should be physically ready for a big day tomorrow.

Saturday, January 5th
Cann River to Eden, NSW - 112.8 Km

I crossed over into another state today, but not without some effort. The first half of the ride from Cann River to Genoa was extremely difficult and scary. The road was winding and hilly, and had no shoulder much of the way. To make matters, worse it was a Saturday morning during the summer holidays. Almost half of the cars on the road had some sort of trailer in tow - campers, caravans, and boats. I felt as if I was only inches away from ruining somebody's holiday...mine. This wasn't the time or place for an uninsured cyclist to be out pedaling.

I stopped into the store in Genoa to buy more water and unwind. I had considered stopping for the day in Genoa, but I had already booked a room in Eden. I had to give my credit card number when I called in the booking, so I knew that the payment had already been processed.

After a short chat with some of the other travelers at the Genoa store, I was back on the bike. Fortunately, the road from Genoa to Eden had wider shoulders and was not as hilly or winding. The last 10 Km was brutal, though. One of the travelers at Genoa had told me that about five Km outside of Eden I would crest a hill and a panoramic view of Twofold Bay would open up. In the last 10 Km I must have climbed over five steep hills, thinking that Eden and the bay were just on the other side. I struggled into Eden at 6:00 PM and headed right for my motel. The owners have shut down the restaurant this week, so I ordered in a pizza. I was too tired to cycle back into town for a meal. My quads are completely ripped. I'm not sure that they will recover in one night. I'll know better tomorrow.

Sunday, January 6th
Eden to Merimbula - 33.25 Km

Any hopes of putting big Km behind me today were squashed in the first five Km. The hill out of Eden did me in, even after a 10 hour sleep. I still haven't pushed the bike up any hills in Australia, but I almost did today. I stopped three or four times to rest on the way up that hill. I cycled the rest of the day with spaghetti legs.

I got a call from Dad in the morning while I was riding. I tried to carry on a normal conversation with the traffic rushing by at 50 mph, but it wasn't easy. He did ease my mind about health insurance. Although I was never covered by COBRA during my nine months on the road, I am now covered by Blue Cross. In fact, I was covered yesterday so it wouldn't have been so bad if I was hit by a caravan on the way to Genoa.

I stopped in Merimbula after only 33 Km (including a wrong turn to Pambula Beach) because it was a good-sized resort town with a number of motels and a McDonalds. At the first motel I looked into, a Flag motel, I was quoted $70 for the night. In the Merimbula Gardens Motel the elderly gentleman at the front desk quoted me $25. I was shocked, but I think he gave me a special price because I was an American. He said that he always takes care of Americans because our "boys" saved Australia during WW II. I thanked him, and we discussed the war for a little while. Then, I settled into room #1. There are still a few advantages left to being an American citizen.

Monday, January 7th
Merimbula to Tathra - 40.78 Km

I spent the morning exploring around Merimbula Point. I cycled out on the peninsula as far as the roads went. Then, I cycled another Km on a sandy track to the tip of the peninsula. I climbed down the cliff face to the rocks below and took some great pictures of the waves crashing over the rocks. The surf looked strong enough to knock a man over, so when it looked like the tide was starting to come in, I hustled back up the cliff to the bike.

It wasn't until after noon that I finally left Merimbula. I took a detour down to the beach at the next town, Tura. By the time I pedaled back up to the main coastal road my legs were useless. On the way to Tathra I finally hit the wall. I had no choice. For the first time since Turkey I had to get off the bike and push, or shrivel up and die on the side of the road. So, I swallowed my pride, pushed the bike up the hill, and stopped at the next town to rest for a day. I don't think that my legs have fully recovered from the Cann River to Eden ride two days ago.

Tathra is a very small town with a nice hotel/motel up on the hill and a nice beach down at sea level (where else?). I'm booked into motel room #1 again. I had a steak dinner in the hotel restaurant. Dinners come with a show at the Tathra Hotel Motel.

The restaurant has a wall of windows facing out to the Pacific Ocean. At 7:00 PM, Winky the mechanical whale rises up just outside of the windows for the enjoyment of the kiddies. He waves his fluke and blows his spout like a Disney animatron. He does this three or four times, each time carrying a different item on his fin ("Hi Mom!" sign, doll, etc.). Winky wowed 'em tonight, especially the all-important under-eight demographic.

Tuesday, January 8th
Tathra - 0 Km

This was a very enjoyable rest day. The weather was perfect, so I hit the beach with the rest of the citizens of Tathra. The lifeguards set up a couple of flags on the beach that all bathers must swim between. That includes the bodyboard crowd. Surfers have another slice of the beach. I think I spent over an hour in the water catching the great waves. It was a little hectic with all of the other swimmers and bodyboarders trying to catch the same waves, but it was still a blast. I worked a little on evening out my cyclist's tan, and then walked the length of the beach. I wish more of my off days were this relaxing.

Wednesday, January 9th
Tathra to Narooma - 80.35 Km

I had an inauspicious start today. After dropping off my motel room key to one of the guys behind the bar at the Tathra Hotel Motel, I cycled down the hill to the main coastal road north. After the first Km it occurred to me that I didn't pay for my room the last two nights. I didn't want to start the day by riding back up a difficult hill. My mobile phone didn't work at the bottom of the hill, so I tried to ring the motel from a phone booth. As usual, all of my efforts to use a simple payphone failed miserably. I had to go into the Reception office of a nearby caravan park to make the call. I gave the hotel my credit card number, and the issue was finally settled.

Farther down the road I had to ride over seven Km of dirt and gravel. It was, of course, all up or down hills, no flat stretches. I don't know what's harder, pedaling up a steep hill with no traction or squeezing the brakes all the way down a long hill to stay upright. I had to push the bike up one of the hills. A couple cars stopped and the drivers asked if I needed any help. I must have looked particularly pitiful because I was wearing the mosquito net head covering. I've been wearing it a lot more lately because the flies have been bad around here. No matter how much Bushman insect repellant I slather on, the little buggers still try to get in my eyes, ears, nose, and mouth.

When I reached Narooma, I saw a lot of "No Vacancy" signs. After trying a few cheaper motels, I finally gave the Flag motel a chance. It was expensive, but they did have a room available. I took the room and then started searching for a take-away dinner. They all close early in this town, so I ended up in the Woolworth supermarket trying to buy something substantial for dinner. I ended up with cereal, granola bars, and Powerade. I wonder what Mom and Dad are having for dinner tonight.

Thursday, January 10th
Narooma to Batemans Bay - 84.92 Km

I broke the 8,000-mile mark today. Yea me! It's no wonder that my right knee was sore all afternoon. One interesting sight on the ride today was a makeshift fire fighting command center set up on the sports oval in Moruya. They had four or five large air-conditioned tents set up on the grass, and three helicopters waiting to take off to survey the bush fire devastation. For almost a month the bush fires around Sydney have been the big story. I'm headed directly into them. That's not too smart, is it?

When I got off of the Princes Highway after Moruya to cycle along the coast, I found it to be tough going. I think I should have stayed on the main road and taken my chances with the heavy traffic. The secondary roads just seem to roll too steeply.

Batemans Bay is a pleasant tourist town. There was a good selection of motels from which to choose. They're getting more expensive as I approach Sydney, though. The one that I'm in tonight cost me $55. I can justify these higher motel expenditures because I saved over $3,000 by traveling without medical insurance for the past nine months. Of course, if I had been run over by a road train, attacked by wild dingoes, or shot by militant Jehovah's Witnesses in the past nine months, the lack of insurance would have been a bad thing.

Friday, January 11th
Batemans Bay to Mollymook - 55.26 Km

I can tell that I'm getting closer to Sydney because I was breathing the smoke haze from the bush fires all day. This is one of their worst seasons in years. The smoke haze has reached as far south as Batemans Bay, 225 Km away. And, I breathed in more of the toxic fumes than the locals because I was sucking wind all day as I cycled this roller coaster coast. This is a very tiring terrain. Now my left knee is sore. I'll take tomorrow off to rest both knees, but I need a good week in Sydney to give them a proper rest.

I cycled past a few lakes today. On one, there were people paddling kayaks. On another, people were fishing. A stork approached one fisherman standing in the shallow water. Like Yogi in Jellystone Park, this stork was looking for a handout. The fisherman reached into his catch box, pulled out a fish, and threw it to the stork who caught it in mid-air. It wasn't *Mutual of Omaha's Animal Kingdom* material, but it would have gone over well on Letterman's Stupid Pet Tricks. Two of the kayakers had homebuilt boats similar to the one that I had, unfinished, in the cellar for years. So, I guess it is possible to complete one of those kits. They really did look impressive gliding across the lake. Maybe when I finish this trip, and I have more time on my hands...

Saturday, January 12th
Mollymook - 0 Km

A cold front came through overnight and gave the area some badly needed rain. I was content to stay in the motel most of the day. I answered some e-mail and started researching my options after I reach Sydney this week. I'm leaning towards spending seven to ten days around Sydney, then flying to Christchurch for the New Zealand leg of the trip. This will give me more time to spend grinding over the hills there. It also gives me more time if I decide to go to Tahiti. I tried to get some airfares over the Internet but had some difficulties with the slow infrared connection between the Pocket PC and mobile phone. I'm going to have to stop into a travel agency in the next day or two.

I couldn't get the wash done today because this motel doesn't have a guest laundry room. The nearest laundromat is back in Ulladulla, a few Km away. There was no way that I was even going to touch the bike today. I need to rest both of my knees for the final push into Sydney. I did scope out the guest laundry rooms of nearby motels, but they didn't have drying machines. Now, I have to do the laundry tomorrow or risk offending anyone who would have the misfortune of getting near me.

Sunday, January 13th
Mollymook to Gerringong - 96.48 Km

As I cycled out of Mollymook this morning, I could see that it was going to be a good beach day. At 10:00 AM the beach and the nearby parking lot were already filling up. I hated leaving, but I have to get to Sydney. I'll be sure to have some productive beach time during my time off there.

I did not leave the Princes Highway for Jervis Bay, as my guidebook suggested. I wanted to put about 100 Km behind me today and be closer to Sydney for a Tuesday afternoon arrival. I did leave the highway for the coast after Nowra. The Sunday traffic on the highway had been getting to me, and the coast road looked to be flatter and calmer. I think it was flatter, but I still couldn't avoid the busy Sunday traffic. No matter. I found a nice, quiet motel room in Gerringong for $33. I got my wash done in the guest laundry room and ordered a steak from room service. I even hit the mini-bar, so this stay will cost a bit more than $33.

The highlight of the day was swimming in a rock pool at the base of a cliff in Gerringong. The pool is made of the natural stones on the beach and some cement walls to contain the seawater. While I was swimming waves were crashing over the wall, filling the pool with more seawater. Lots of fun.

Monday, January 14th
Gerringong to Clifton - 73.33 Km

Just one more day of riding and I'm done crossing my second continent. I'll be ready for a couple of weeks off the bike after tomorrow. The one-day rests don't seem to be rejuvenating my knees and quads like they used to. Between the sightseeing and administrative tasks in Sydney, I'm going to have to spend a few days vegetating on a beach. If I don't arrive in New Zealand ready for some serious climbing, I'll never make it back to America.

The portion of today's ride that went through Wollongong was a pleasure because it was all done on bike paths that hugged the coast. It looked like a good day to hit the surf, but I had to keep moving north if I wanted to be in Sydney tomorrow night. I stopped in Clifton because it had the last hotel before the Royal National Park. I'll attack the hills in the park tomorrow. This is an old pub hotel, so there's no TV in the rooms. For entertainment I've been playing Solitaire on the Pocket PC. And, the bath is down the hall. I'm really roughing it tonight.

Tuesday, January 15th
Clifton - 0 Km

I woke up to rain today. It looked bad enough at the 10:00 AM checkout time that I decided to stay in the Clifton Imperial Hotel for another night. Sydney will have to wait. I spent the entire day in the hotel, never stepping outside, even when it had stopped raining. There is nothing but a few homes around this place. To pass the time I played a little on the hotel's piano, read the local papers front to back, and did some computer work. I ate lunch and dinner in the pub. Tonight, it started raining again. I'm already regretting my decision not to ride today. If I have to stay here another day, I'm going to go nuts. I know that the rain is good for the guys fighting the bush fires. I just wish that it had waited one more day.

Wednesday, January 16th
Clifton to Brighton-le-Sands - 64.65 Km

It seems that when I'm really anxious to reach a city, like Rome or Adelaide, the weather is never in my favor. It rained again today, and will rain tomorrow morning. I did leave the pub hotel in Clifton around 10:00 AM, thinking that the overnight downpours we had gotten were the last of the wet stuff. Instead, by the time I climbed to the top of Bald Hill Lookout just outside of the Royal National Park, I could see the storm clouds over the ocean lining up like jumbo jets on final approach. The downpours came in waves as I cycled through the park, the second oldest national park in the world after Yellowstone. The park was almost completely burned in the bush fires of 1994, and was half burned in this year's fires. It needed the rain; I didn't.

At the northern end of the park I missed the ferry from Bundeena to Cronulla by four minutes. During the hour wait for the next ferry, the sun came out. That gave me the opportunity to dry everything. Of course, an hour later it was all soaked again as the rains returned in force. I was almost at the airport when they hit. I turned back, splashed into the ritzy Novotel Hotel in Brighton-le-Sands, and got a quote of $85 for a room. While a puddle formed around me on the marble floor of the Novotel lobby, the lady at the front desk was nice enough to direct me to a budget accommodation down the street where I have a room tonight for $25. It's not great, but it's dry. And, I saved $60 that I'll be sure to spend frivolously in Sydney in the next few days.

Thursday, January 17th
Brighton-le-Sands to Sydney - 33.82 Km

This was my last day of riding in Australia. I've officially crossed another continent. Two down (Europe and Australia), one to go (North America). I've also cycled in Asia and Africa on this trip. Only South America and the Antarctic will be missed. Who rides a bike in the Antarctic anyway?

On the way to downtown Sydney I got onto an elevated highway. It should have been only a short distance, but I missed the turnoff. I ended up riding shoulder-to-fender for a few Km with cars speeding into the city. It was heaps of fun, as they say here. I walked the bike through the Royal Botanic Gardens when I first hit town. It's an amazing public space. In one section there is a large number of flying squirrels hanging from the trees like bats. Very eerie. Another section is dedicated to rare and endangered plants. One tree is so rare that a locked cage protects it. Only 38 of the Wollemi Pine trees are known to exist in the wild, in a remote canyon in New South Wales. This "dinosaur tree" was thought to be extinct until it was discovered in 1994. The tree in the cage is the first to be transplanted.

At the southern tip of the park I reached Mrs. Macquarie's Point. It's the perfect spot to take photos of the famous Sydney Harbour Bridge and Sydney Opera House. While I was taking pictures, a 65-year-old Croatian guy started talking to me. He had been fishing nearby, saw my bike, and wanted to talk about bicycle touring. As a younger man, he had toured all over southern Europe. When he immigrated to Australia he did the same. He still rides and walks great distances every day. I thanked him for telling me his story and continued exploring the park.

The park is chock-a-block (another Australian expression) with statues, memorials, and fountains. It is also overrun with joggers at lunchtime. It seems as if everybody spills out of the skyscrapers overlooking the park to get some exercise at noon. I had to weave in and out of the athletes to exit the park. Before I got out, I scanned the skyline for a hotel. I found the words "Holiday Inn" on a building about a Km away. I headed in that direction and found the hotel in the Potts Point section of town. The luxury room on the seventh floor with views of the Opera House and Harbour Bridge will only cost me $45/night. It seems that in January everybody leaves the center of town for the beaches, so the rates are low. I'm going to stay at least four nights. That's a big win for me.

Friday, January 18th
Sydney - 0 Km

The bike remained safely locked away in the corner of my luxurious hotel room as I went out and toured the city on foot. I did some shopping to start the day. I bought bike shoes, a tube, a New Zealand map and guidebook, a Tahiti guidebook, postcards, and food. I searched unsuccessfully for a place that would burn a CD with all of the image files from my CompactFlash cards. I went to the Delta Airlines office to try to get something in exchange for my unused Zurich to Philly ticket. I arrived ten minutes late but did get a telephone number, so I won't have to return tomorrow. Then, I went to the top of the AMP Tower for a bird's eye view of the city.

Like the Rialto Tower in Melbourne, there is also a movie about the city at the base of the tower included in the price of the ticket. The Sydney version is much more interactive, like a cross between Disney World's *Captain Nemo* and a Lonely Planet video. The seats are on hydraulic struts that move in time with the movie. The experience is so immersive that, when the camera went underwater, I was sprayed by a mist from the seat in front of me. Or, maybe the guy in front had a perspiration problem.

Later, I took a walk around Darling Harbour. It's a fun place for kids of all ages. There was a water skiing show in the harbor, amusements, pedal boats, gardens, an IMAX theatre, and a real Russian Space Shuttle. Darling Harbour was a very popular venue for visitors during the 2000 Olympics. My busy day ended, as planned, with a haircut from a barber who had emigrated from Italy.

Saturday, January 19th
Sydney - 0 Km

I decided not to fly to Christchurch and instead bought a ticket to Dunedin. That will take me farther south and give me some more time to enjoy New Zealand. With that bit of business behind me, I enjoyed the rest of the day doing touristy things in Sydney. I rode the monorail. I rode the subway. I shopped for Australiana. I bought a pair of hand-painted aboriginal clapsticks to start my world music instrument collection. Now I'm disappointed that I didn't buy a tabla set in India.

Sunday, January 20th
Sydney - 0 Km

I joined an organized tour of the insides of the Sydney Opera House this afternoon. The guide started by telling us a little of the history of the conception, design, and construction of this Australian icon. It's a story about an idealistic architect, meddling politicians, and a slight ($50,000,000) cost overrun. Then, we were taken to the little Drama Theatre in the basement, which was originally designed to be a movie theater. Now, they put on plays there. There's a one-man play, *The Elocution of Benjamin Franklin*, running this week. The stage is so small that they probably couldn't put on an event with more than one person on stage. *Aida* would be out of the question. Then, we toured the Concert Hall where I was most impressed with the 10,500 pipe organ. They rarely use the organ because the public isn't clamoring for organ recitals, according to the guide. I wished I could sneak away from the tour, find the organ console, and play the first few bars of *Smoke on the Water*. But, the guide already had his eye on me as I had to be corrected in front of the group for attempting to photograph the inside of the Hall. Finally, we toured the equally impressive Opera Theatre. All in all, it was an hour well spent.

I didn't have time to use the free tea/coffee voucher after the tour because I had to rush up Macquarie Street to get to the 6:00 PM mass at Saint Mary's Cathedral. It too had a great organ, but probably not 10,500 pipes. I arrived a couple of minutes late, so I sat in the back with the other heathens. It's such a large cathedral that you need binoculars to follow the action on the altar. Even the sound system barely reached us in the back. Maybe they need a couple Jumbotrons and a speaker system like the Pope has in Saint Peter's Square.

Monday, January 21st
Sydney to Manly - 26.42 Km

I had planned on visiting Bondi Beach for a day or two before going to Manly, but the ladies at the Holiday Inn front desk talked me out of Bondi. They said that it was a little dirty and very touristy. So, I cycled to Circular Quay, Sydney's maritime equivalent of Grand Central Station, and took the ferry to Manly. The ferry ride took thirty minutes and offered great views of the harbor. From the Manly wharf I cycled all over the hilly peninsula to check out the views and take some pictures.

Back at Manly, the first two hotels that I approached were way too expensive. Then, I found a motel one block back from the beach for $50/night. I can stay here until Saturday morning, and then I'll have to find another place to stay. They've already booked all of their rooms for the coming Australia Day three-day weekend. That's good for me. I'll enjoy this week on the beach, and then go back into the city to see the Australia Day festivities. I would love to see fireworks launched from the Harbour Bridge.

Manly is known for its rainbow lorikeets, a bird that can best be described as visually and vocally LOUD. At night the multi-colored birds scare the tourists by making a racket in the trees on the Corso, the main pedestrian drag between the harbor and the ocean. Near the Corso tonight, I saw one standing perfectly still on the ground under a bush. Like the parrot in that Monty Python sketch, I was afraid that it might be more than "just stunned." I would have loved to stuff the beauty into a FedEx envelope and sent it back home, but I thought that FedEx and the Audubon Society might disapprove. So, I left it and moved on.

Tuesday, January 22nd
Manly - 0 Km

I hit the beach for first time today. Of course, that signaled the beginning of the rain. I did get to relax on the beach for about an hour before the rain started, but I never got into the water. The surf looked too rough and dirty. Later, I had the bike's chain cleaned at a local bike shop, stocked up at the supermarket, and took my clothes to the laundromat. Tonight I wrote some postcards for the folks back home and called the Aussie couple from New South Wales that I met at the campground in Granada. I had promised to call them when I arrived in Sydney. I'm rapidly checking items off of my to-do list.

Wednesday, January 23rd
Manly - 0 Km

It was sort of a dreary day today. I didn't even go down to the beach. Instead, I tried to visit the Manly Aquarium. I had read that divers hand-feed the sharks at 11:30 AM on Wednesdays. When I arrived at the aquarium there was a long line of children waiting to get in. It looked like a class trip for 2nd graders. Like me, I'm sure they were also there to see if the sharks would bite the hand that feeds them. Since the line was too long, I gave up and went back to the motel to do a few chores.

I cleaned the bike with a whole packet of Wet Ones moist towelettes for the first time in months. While I was going over the bike, I noticed that one of the spokes on the rear wheel was broken. With 48 spokes, when one breaks, the wheel still remains in true. I may have been riding on 47 spokes for weeks, maybe months. I took the bike back to the local bike shop down the street and had it replaced. The mechanic did the work for me in an hour. Afterwards, he explained how difficult it was to replace a spoke on my tandem-type wheel. The new spoke has to be laced through a very tight four-over pattern. He warned that more spokes could begin to fail now. I'm not looking forward to replacing any spokes on the road.

I tried booking a hotel room back at the Holiday Inn in the city for the weekend but was unsuccessful. It's going to be difficult to find accommodations in Sydney during the long holiday weekend. I'll start calling around in earnest tomorrow. I did book a room at the Airport Holiday Inn for the night before my flight. It's hard to believe that I'll finally be out of Australia one week from today. It's been a very enjoyable five months.

Thursday, January 24th
Manly - 0 Km

It was another non-beach day, so I went back to the aquarium. There was no line today, but plenty of hyperactive kids running around inside. I was a little nervous walking through the Plexiglas tunnel that goes directly through the tanks. With all of the sharks and eels floating over my head all that I could think about was, "Where do I run if one of these six year-olds breaks the glass?"

Afterwards, I broke down and bought myself a didgeridoo. I spent about 30-45 minutes with the salesman trying to find the best sounding didgeridoo in my price range. I finally settled on one that was tuned to the key of D. It wasn't the best-decorated one, but if I can get the hang of playing it, I might be able to record it, and then add some blues from my synths on a multi-track recorder. It would be a good mix of natural and artificial sounds. I got some in-store lessons and a free learn-to-play booklet from the salesman. It's surprisingly difficult to blow raspberries into a hollowed out tree root. I had it shipped back home. You just can't buy a quality didgeridoo on Philadelphia's Main Line.

Friday, January 25th
Manly - 0 Km

I had been looking forward to visiting the Taronga Zoo when I reached Sydney, and I wasn't disappointed. This afternoon, I took a ferry back to Circular Quay, and a second ferry directly to the zoo. A shuttle bus takes the ferry passengers up a hill to the zoo entrance. Since the zoo was built on a slope facing the Sydney Central Business District across the harbor, there are great photo opportunities at every turn. The exhibits that fascinated me the most are the ones that have the visitors walk straight through the enclosures with no barriers separating them from the animals. The kangaroo pen is one of these exhibits. The native birds cage is another. The big cats are kept behind glass, though. You could spend hours strolling through the zoo. And, if you plan your route correctly, you're always walking downhill. I left the zoo just before sunset as it was closing. But, it wasn't closing to everyone. Some youngsters were preparing to stay for the night. The zoo allows a limited number of people to camp out overnight on a small grass field inside the gates. You know that those kids won't sleep a wink tonight. With every growl, yelp, and grunt they'll snap to attention in their tents. There's nothing cuter than little kids afraid of being pulled from their tents by big game in the middle of the night.

Saturday, January 26th
Manly to Sydney - 6.04 Km

It was Australia Day today. The national holiday celebrates the founding of the New South Wales colony at Sydney on January 26th, 1788. So, I left Manley and took the ferry back to Sydney. I'm in another Flag hotel, this time in Darlington. I started out the day on Macquarie Street viewing an antique car rally. They had everything from Hupmobiles (3) to Messerschmidts (2). Not many Americans know it, but they often have a picture of a Hupmobile in their pocket; it's on the back of the old $10 bill. The Messerschmidts are ultra-narrow single seat cars made by the same German company that made the jets. They look a little like the fuselage of an airplane. My favorites were the Austin Healy Frogeye Sprites. I've got to buy one after I buy that house with the two-car garage.

In and around Hyde Park were a variety of bands playing live music. The one that interested me the most was a zydeco band that played a unique version of an old Robert Johnson blues song. As the festivities around the park were shutting down at 5:00 PM, I walked down to The Rocks to see some of the old neighborhood's buildings. There are lots of pubs in the area, and plenty of folks were celebrating Australia Day by getting stupid. There were police barriers around many of the pubs because the crowds were spilling out onto the sidewalks. Not feeling comfortable around the party people, I walked out onto the Harbour Bridge. The walkway took me out to one of the pylons, but I couldn't climb up the inside of the pylon to a higher viewing platform because it had already closed.

From the bridge I walked over to Darling Harbour to see the fireworks display. All sides of the harbor were packed. I bought some popcorn and sat down inside the IMAX Theater café for a half-hour. Then, I walked outside, found a prime spot to watch the show, and stood there for an hour. It was worth the effort. In addition to the fireworks, there was live music, lasers, sky searchlights, and videos projected onto large white spheres in the harbor. There were more visual effects than at a Pink Floyd concert. I knew that Sydney was famous for their fireworks displays, and I wasn't disappointed. It was well worth the price of admission, two sore feet and one aching back.

Sunday, January 27th
Sydney - 0 Km

I went back to Darling Harbour today to visit the Powerhouse Museum. The museum had a temporary exhibit on the History of Festival Records, an Australian institution. Festival Records has been in business for 50 years and has had most popular Australian singers and bands on their label at one time or another. I went hoping to see some old keyboards. They did have some of the old recording machines and a few guitars. They had a beat up Roland CR-78 drum machine, but I had to go downstairs to the permanent collection to see a couple of great old synths. The Powerhouse is a science museum, so they had a rare VCS Synthi A and a Fairlight CMI sampler on display. The Fairlight was invented by a couple of Australians in the early 1980's. It was popular with groups like the Art of Noise and Frankie Goes to Hollywood. The VCS (Voltage Control Studio) was invented near London in the early 1970's. Pink Floyd might have used this model at one time. Both synths were behind glass, unfortunately.

I had only seen half of the exhibits in the museum before I had to rush back to Saint Mary's Cathedral for 6:00 PM mass. Afterwards, I had a big Texas T-bone steak at the Hard Rock Café. There were lots of signed guitars on the walls, but only one keyboard. It was an Orla double-manual organ, supposedly used by Richard Wright of Pink Floyd. Not a bad end to a day of vintage keyboard spotting.

Monday, January 28th
Sydney to Bondi - 27.42 Km

I headed straight for Bondi Beach today and found a room with a balcony in a motel across from the beach. It was the last day of the three-day weekend, and the sun was shining. The beach was covered from end to end. The guys selling suntan lotion made good money today. I spent two hours in the afternoon on the beach. The tide was out, and the water was a little dirty. I spent most of my time lying on my new beach towel in an SPF 15 haze. It's good to veg out every once and a while.

On the way to Bondi I passed kayak rentals and seaplane rides at Rose Bay. All of the good kayaks had already been rented, and the seaplane ride would have probably broken the bank. I was content to just continue working my way through the hilly coastal suburbs to Bondi.

Tuesday, January 29th
Bondi to Sydney Airport - 36.57 Km

The day started with a few last minute chores in Bondi. I left Bondi hoping to follow the coast down to the entrance to Botany Bay at La Perouse, but I couldn't find a direct, flat route. So, I turned inland and found the Anzac Parade. That took me straight to the landing site for the British explorer Captain Cook (1770) and the French explorer Jean Francois Galaup de Laperouse (1788) at La Perouse. Once I got to the bay, it was an easy ride to the airport. Unlike Cook and Laperouse, I had to ask a few locals for directions to the airport Holiday Inn. I spent the rest of the day lounging around my corner suite on the fifth floor ordering room service. This is the life.

New Zealand

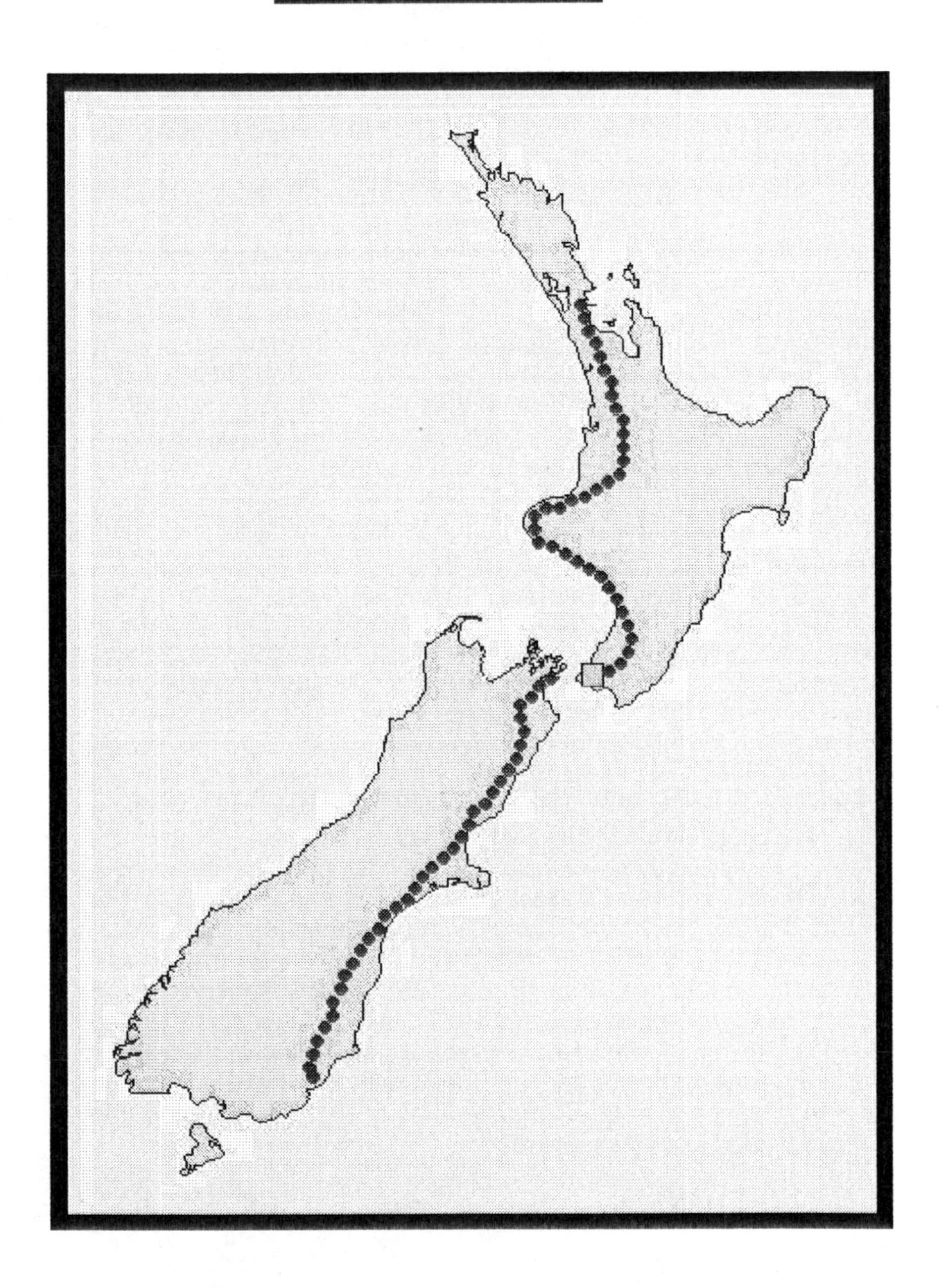

Wednesday, January 30th
Sydney Airport to Mosgiel, New Zealand - 20.85 Km

I had to get a 5:30 AM wake-up call today in order to be at the airport three hours before my flight departure at 9:45 AM. Besides the call that was programmed into the hotel's phone system last night, the front desk also gave me a personal call at 5:45 AM to make sure I hadn't gone back to sleep. You gotta love Holiday Inn.

At the airport I had the typical bike box hassles, despite assurances from the travel agent that boxes were readily available. After being told by Air New Zealand and Sydney Airport Baggage Services that bike boxes were not available, I was able to buy one from Quantas. Yea, Quantas (obscure *Rainman* reference). It was smaller than the boxes that Amtrak and many U.S. carriers supply, but I was happy to have any box at that point. I just disassembled the bike further than I normally would for transport. I think it's more difficult to get a bicycle onto a commercial airliner than it is a nuclear warhead.

The fun wasn't over then. Next, I had to check in with my one-way ticket to New Zealand. I had been told by the travel agent (a very helpful gal with all of the wrong answers) that I wouldn't need to have a ticket for my exit from New Zealand if I could show sufficient funds. Wrong, again. I am now holding a fully refundable open-ended ticket from Auckland to Nadi. The Air New Zealand ticketing agent suggested Nadi as my destination because it was the cheapest flight out of Auckland. When I get to Auckland I'll trade this in for a ticket to a real country. I might be tempted to go to the mythical land of Nadi, but I don't think Lonely Planet even has a guidebook for the place. I would definitely be the first person from my neighborhood to vacation in Nadi.

I had a three-hour flight to Christchurch, a three-hour layover, and a one-hour flight down to Dunedin. I also lost two hours due to time zone changes. That meant that I arrived in Dunedin after 6:30 PM local time. It took a bit longer to assemble the bike because it had been disassembled in Sydney into more bits to fit into the smaller box. It wasn't quite a Christmas morning type fiasco, but I wasn't on the road until 7:30 PM. Since the Dunedin Airport was the farthest point south that I would travel on this trip, I stopped to take a few pictures of the bike in front of the airport sign before hitting the road.

The city of Dunedin is 29 Km from the airport. I knew that I would be arriving late, so I booked a room at a motel in Mosgiel, halfway between the airport and the city. I struggled a bit with some headwinds and got to the motel around 8:30 PM. It was too late to get hot food in town, so I dined on ginger snaps and

Powerade. So ends another fun day traveling with a bicycle in the friendly skies.

Thursday, January 31st
Mosgiel to Dunedin - 20.80 Km

It was a short ride today into Dunedin. I started out climbing over the first of two hills on Highway 1, the main road up the coast. It has a wide shoulder most of the way, making the tough hill somewhat more bearable. A little farther down the road it became a motorway, and all bicycles were directed off just before it went over another set of hills. I followed along the hills on a parallel road, looking for an opening to cross over to the Pacific coast and Dunedin. I came across a man doing road construction and asked him for directions. He said that I was on what was supposed to be the "Highway 1 Bypass" until the government ran out of money. The way he chuckled after saying that told me that there was more to the story, and he was ready to give me the details. I wasn't interested in the politics of New Zealand road construction, so he told me just to follow this road, the Kaikorai Valley Road, until it curved right and rolled over the hills. At the top of the hill I had a great view of Dunedin and the Otago Harbor. I put on the helmet-cam and screamed down the long hill right into the center of town, the Octagon. The central streets in the middle of town form an octagonal shape, surrounding a central plaza. It was a nice bit of urban planning done by a young Scottish surveyor who was sent over in the early 1840's to lay out the street grid before plots were sold and immigrants were shipped to New Zealand.

I learned about this at the Early Settlers Museum a few blocks away. I went in mainly to see the antique cars, motorcycles, and bicycles. But, the exhibit on the birth of the city caught my attention. The early settlers were a hardy bunch. The three-month voyage from Scotland to New Zealand would have probably killed me. There was a display of the weekly rations allotted to each adult on board. It was very basic and probably not enough to last most people a full week.

I also spent a little time in front of the Dunedin railway station taking pictures. It was built with contrasting volcanic rock and sandstone in the Flemish Renaissance style, for no apparent reason. The newly planted gardens in Anzac Plaza in front of the station were in full bloom. I took a few nice snapshots of the bike in the gardens. I ended up in a Best Western motel at the northern end of the town. The exchange rate in New Zealand is even better than in Australia. I'm paying $36 for a very nice one-bedroom unit with kitchen. Not bad.

Friday, February 1st
Dunedin - 0 Km

I just hung out at the Best Western today. The weather turned ugly last night when a cold front came through around 10:00 PM. I was happy to be indoors today. I needed to catch up with my computer work anyway. I took a walk downtown for a meal at Burger King in the late afternoon.

In the evening I caught up with a few recent journal entries that were less than complete. Actually, they were random words, typed into the Pocket PC, and meant to jog my memory at a later date of all of the thrills and adventures that I had those days. Apparently I've had more thrills than I can remember because there were a few random words left over after I fleshed out the skeleton entries. Thank goodness I don't drink.

Saturday, February 2nd
Dunedin to Palmerston - 59.39 Km

For the first time in over two weeks I put in a full day of riding. Although I only covered 59 Km, it was a tough 59 Km. There was a strong headwind all day, and two difficult climbs. My first stop on the way out of Dunedin was at Baldwin Street, the world's steepest street as certified by the *Guinness Book of Records*. Near the base of the street is a shop selling Baldwin Street T-shirts, postcards, and trinkets. They sell a certificate for $.80 to anyone who wants to claim that they walked or cycled to the top. I did neither. I cycled about one-third of the way up and stopped when the road surface switched from bitumen to concrete. As the road continues it gets steeper and steeper. They use concrete on the last two-thirds of the street because they need a stronger surface at that pitch (Maximum Gradient 1 in 1.266). There was no need to blow out my knees that early in the day, so I took a few pictures and continued on my way. The first, and largest, hill of the day started just outside of Dunedin. It was a 400-meter climb over Mount Cargill. It seemed to take an hour to get to the top, but I was rewarded with some great views of the Otago Harbour. I took a few pictures and then put on the Gore-Tex jacket at the top. I was already wearing a new pullover, but the wind was picking up and chilling me to the bone.

After a second difficult hill along the coast, I rode the last 20 Km to Palmerston on Highway 1. By then, all of my energy was gone, and my allergies had begun to act up again. Fortunately, my allergy pills made it through the rigorous New Zealand customs screening. I popped one of the pills and spent the rest of the evening in a Telfast-induced haze. I'm going to sleep well tonight.

Sunday, February 3rd
Palmerston to Oamaru - 66.79 Km

It was another short ride into a strong headwind today. I hit Oamaru early enough in the afternoon to do some sightseeing. I was hoping to find a Catholic church that might have an evening mass. I found four other denomination's churches, but no Catholic church. Still, I got to see a lot of the town in my wandering. It's a well-preserved place, one of those towns stuck in a time warp. It was a boomtown decades ago due to the gold rush, and wool and mutton production. Then, it fell into an economic lull lasting decades. Now, thanks to tourism, it's on its way back.

Oamaru is called the "Whitestone City" because of the number of white sandstone public buildings built in the neo-classical style. The sandstone was quarried locally, and the town was once considered the best built in New Zealand. Until the Sydney Harbour Bridge was completed in 1932, the main bridge downtown was the widest in the Southern Hemisphere. There are some nice gardens downtown and an old steam engine to take tourists to the nearby penguin colony on its dedicated track. There are also a few museums and antique shops for the tourists to dispose of their dollars. I really like the way the past is preserved here. I probably feel that way particularly because of the two penny-farthings that I saw today. Usually you can only see these old bikes in museums. I think that there's somebody in town who makes great replicas. One was leaning against a factory building like it had just been ridden into work. The other was for sale in the window of an empty shop. For $1,000 I could have my very own penny-farthing. As impressive as it looked, I decided to stick with my Specialized Expedition for the rest of this trip.

Monday, February 4th
Oamaru - 0 Km

I took today off so that I could watch the Super Bowl on TV. I'm glad I did because it was a rare competitive Super Bowl, but I passed up the opportunity to ride on a beautiful day. I may regret that tomorrow. They're forecasting rain for the next two days.

The game broadcast had a noon start time. It was bizarre watching a pro football game on a Monday afternoon. Before the game I walked around the town again. I found the Catholic church just two blocks from my motel, back off of the main street. I did some food shopping and a load of wash. I was back in front of the TV in time to see all of the Super Bowl hoopla. It was an international broadcast, so I got to hear the color commentary from a Scottish announcer. He knew the intricacies of the game, but I just couldn't get used to the accent. If it had been Manchester United vs. Liverpool, rather than the Rams vs. the Patriots, he wouldn't have sounded so strange.

I would like to have seen the rare penguins (yellow-bellied, pink-eyed, green-lipped, something like that). I didn't go though because the rain was already threatening. Maybe tomorrow night.

Tuesday, February 5th
Oamaru - 0 Km

As expected, it rained all day. I couldn't even leave the motel room. The few times that it stopped raining I put on my shoes and jacket, and it started again. Frustrating. I finally did get out for a quick run to the McDonalds down the street. As usual, I was given a cheeseburger, despite ordering a "plain burger without cheese." I admitted defeat, sat down, and tried to eat it. It tasted awful. I threw out half of the cheeseburger. As much fun as I'm having on this trip, I think the dietary problems are finally wearing me down. I need to cook my own meals, but I don't think any restaurants will let me into their kitchen.

I still didn't get to see the blue-eyed, yellow-toed, whatever penguins because of the rain. I'll catch their act farther up the coast. I'll bet they have colonies all the way up to Wellington.

Wednesday, February 6th
Oamaru to Timaru - 87.69 Km

It's Waitangi Day! It's like New Zealand's version of Independence Day, Bastille Day, or Australia Day. On this date in 1840 the Maori and British signed a treaty that neither side liked, both sides violated, and led to the modern, dysfunctional New Zealand that we know today. They celebrate, not with fireworks, but with accusations and tears. It's great fun.

I celebrated the holiday with a fast ride to Timaru, thanks to some strong tailwinds. I averaged 22.6 Km over the 88 Km. That's a good day for me lately. The landscape today was flat, but I saw snow-covered hills to the west. The southerly winds had cooled the east coast down.

I came across a plaque, set in stone, on the side of Highway 1 near Timaru. It said that I was at 45 degrees south latitude, halfway between the South Pole and the Equator. Right next to it was a distance sign showing the South Pole 5011 Km away and the Equator 4990 Km away. That doesn't sound equidistant to me. Continental drift? Plate tectonics? It will remain an unsolved mystery for me.

I felt a little queasy during the ride, possibly from last night's burger surprise. I found a Burger King for dinner tonight. No problems. I couldn't find a cyber café after walking for an hour through a nearly deserted downtown Timaru at 7:00 PM. They roll up the sidewalks early in this town.

Thursday, February 7th
Timaru to Ashburton - 81.22 Km

Yesterday's southerly wind shifted to the east today. The road surface also got rougher. On the bright side, the terrain was flatter. It was two-shirt cold today. When it's so cold that I need to wear both the new pullover and the Gore-Tex jacket, the T-shirt underneath doesn't breathe very well. It just gets sweaty and cold. Halfway through the ride I had to put on a new, dry T-shirt because I was so uncomfortably cold. They don't have much of a summer down here.

I ordered three more Avocet Cross Kevlar tires online at an Internet kiosk in Ashburton. They'll be shipped to Mom and Dad's place, and then forwarded to me somewhere north of here. I'll be anxious to get them because my front tire won't last much longer. It's rolled almost 10,000 Km since I first put in on the bike June 8th near Follonica, Italy. That was $32 well spent.

I'm looking forward to reaching Christchurch tomorrow. I'll take at least one day off to sightsee. I also need to pick up a surprise package from an old co-worker. He assures me that the item in the package will be useful and not too heavy. I'll be the judge of that.

Friday, February 8th
Ashburton to Christchurch - 91.74 Km

The wind direction continues to shift daily. Today, it's blowing from the north. It's also another cold day. I've been getting select weather reports on my mobile phone. I see that it's warmer in Los Angeles than it is here. The road surfaces in Canterbury continue to rattle fillings loose. By the end of today's ride my head felt heavier than usual. I think my neck was weak from the bulky pullover and jacket turtlenecks. The rough roads probably didn't help either. I'm ready for that day off.

On the outskirts of Christchurch I stopped off at Dr. Heins' Classic Cars Museum. Inside was a museum/sales floor/repair shop for great vintage cars. At the front was a display with a Jaguar SS 1 and a Jaguar SS 100 side-by-side. It was a nice shop with some affordable classics, and some not so affordable.

My co-worker had agreed to send my surprise package to the American Express Travel Services office on Colombo Street in downtown Christchurch. When I got to the storefront, I saw that it was boarded up. There was a sign on the door that said, "due to changing business conditions" they had pulled out of New Zealand on January 28th, 2002. This has all of the earmarks of another Montpellier or Athens type of mail fiasco. I called Amex's help line in Australia. They will try to get me answers on Monday morning. I agreed to stay in Christchurch until then. I can spend two days sightseeing here.

I had trouble finding a motel room for three nights. Most were fully booked on Saturday night with contestants in the Coast-to-Coast race. That's a one-day cycling, kayaking, and running event that goes from the west coast of the South Island to the east coast, over the Southern Alps. Eventually, I found a Best Western with one room left for $37/night. Dinner tonight is a pizza delivery.

Saturday, February 9th
Christchurch - 0 Km

I did the town today. I walked circles around Victoria Square and Cathedral Square. I took the old-fashioned tram around downtown Christchurch. I window-shopped the souvenir shops. One shop that I went into was Fazazz - The Motorists' Shop. It's funny but, since I haven't driven a car in almost a year, my interest in vintage autos has risen. This shop had some real finds. An MG TC, a Messerschmidt, and a 1910 red REO really caught my eye. If I can scrape together $35,000, the REO could be all mine. I tried to talk my younger brother into investing in a car that's nearly 100 years old. I don't think he took the bait.

Dinner tonight? Leftover pizza. I doubt that Lance Armstrong eats like this during the Tour de France.

Sunday, February 10th
Christchurch - 0 Km

It was a day filled with a wide variety of live music, starting with the organ and full choir at the 10:30 AM mass. Then, I went down to the one-day Travel Expo at the Convention Centre. I picked up some info on Tahiti, and then watched a local Polynesian troupe dance and play their traditional music outside of the Centre. At Cathedral Square the buskers were out in force, including two kids who sang so badly that they scared the gulls away. Inside Christchurch Cathedral I paid my $1.60 and climbed the 133 steps to the top of the spire, or at least as high as tourists could go. Next, I hopped onto the tram and went to the weekend market at the Arts Centre. Most of the stalls had trinkets that didn't interest me. But, there was one stall where a lady was knitting mohair scarves, hats, and sweaters. I was very tempted to buy a tiny yellow sweater for a favorite niece, but resisted the urge to be a good uncle. They had the usual buskers, as well as a couple of stages set up for legitimate performances. I watched an old guy doing acoustic folk, a Thai group doing their traditional dance and music, and a young jazz-fusion band. It was a short walk to the Botanic Gardens where a mellow rapper and a couple of Chemical Brothers wannabes had pulled in a crowd on the lawn.

Finally, I went to North Hagley Park to catch the end of the Edwardian Festival. I wouldn't be surprised if they had a barbershop quartet or brass band playing Sousa marches earlier in the day. Unfortunately, I arrived as the festival was winding down. I did get to see a number of antique bicycles, motorcycles, and "horseless carriages." If I had arrived earlier, I probably could have ridden a penny-farthing bicycle for the first time. All things considered, it was a full, and very musical, day.

Monday, February 11th
Christchurch to Amberley - 47.49 Km

I had hoped that my contact at the American Express Travel Services would be able to tell me where the package from my co-worker was. She didn't know, so I left town without wasting any more time. I've done that waiting game before, and I never win. The package will eventually show up somewhere in the Southern Hemisphere. I sent an e-mail message to my buddy telling him to organize a search party. (*He eventually e-mailed back to me that the surprise was a Dilbert desk calendar.*)

The road out of Christchurch was flat with wide shoulders. I followed Highway 1 until it became a motorway. A parallel route for cyclists was well marked, and I followed that for about 10 Km before returning to Highway 1. I wonder how much of my ride has been on roads designated with the number 1. The afternoon brought bad headwinds. I arrived at Amberley just as they picked up. I pulled into a tearoom and had a couple of biscuits and juice while I studied the maps and guidebooks. It was too far to the next town with a motel, so I decided to stop here for the night.

I bought a hot dog at the petrol station, but threw it out down the street when I found a take-away shop selling burgers. The hot dog casing had flaked off as I picked it up with the tongs, and the bun felt stale. I thought that the burger might be a safer bet.

Tuesday, February 12th
Amberley to Cheviot - 67.62 Km

It was an easy ride day. There was only one hill, at Greta Valley. I stopped at the café/convenience store there for a juice. After about twenty minutes spent enjoying the panoramic view, I got back on my bike and coasted down into the valley.

There was a forecast of rain this afternoon, so I stopped here and got a room at the Broadview Motel. It was only 1:00 PM, and the rain didn't arrive until after dinner. I could have cycled all the way to Kaikoura in that time. Kaikoura is a bigger town with more motel options, and probably even a McDonalds. I could have used a McDonalds tonight. For the second night in a row, I threw out a dinner that I had bought. I ordered a plain burger, as usual, at the local take-away. I went through the litany of things that I did not want on my plain burger, which seems redundant but is necessary. When I got back to my motel room and opened up the bag, I found a burger smothered in either a thick sauce or thin ketchup. It was too late to return it to the shop because they were closing as I left. All I could do was throw out the offending burger and dine on the snacks that I had left in my panniers.

Wednesday, February 13th
Cheviot - 0 Km

It rained hard last night, and it looked like it would continue all day. The decision to stay here wasn't too difficult. I did dread trying to find a pizza for dinner this Ash Wednesday. I stayed inside and worked on my website while it poured outside. During a break in the rain, I walked to the supermarket and bought some supplies. Then, I asked at the café if they made pizzas. The owner told me that they normally didn't, but she offered to give it a try with some ingredients that she had in the kitchen. I took the prototype pizza back to my motel room, ate one slice, and threw out the rest. It was that bad. I've now thrown out meals three nights in a row. To make matters worse, there's a notice on the community bulletin board reminding residents to boil their water before drinking it. Not since my week in Mumbai have I been so nervous about getting sick. My gastro-intestinal defense system is now operating at Def-Con 1.

Thursday, February 14th
Cheviot - 0 Km

It rained all night and was still going strong at checkout time. I had hoped that by 10:00 AM the storm would have passed.

After a bit of hemming and hawing, I decided to stay another day. This trip is supposed to be fun, after all. Riding in the rain on a major highway is not only unsafe. It's un-fun. I stayed in the motel and watched the Olympics and *I Dream of Jeannie* reruns. Now, that's fun. I tried a different take-away shop in town and got exactly what I ordered: a plain burger, of course. I'm looking forward to getting out of here tomorrow. I'm going stir-crazy in this little town.

Friday, February 15th
Cheviot to Kaikoura - 76.91 Km

I finally got out of Cheviot, and not a moment too soon. The Chamber of Commerce had put me up for Cheviot Man of the Year. It's never good to overstay your welcome.

Although it was still cool and misty, I thoroughly enjoyed today's ride. The scenery was awesome, and I had a tailwind. For about the first 50 Km I was riding between large mountains whose peaks were obscured by low clouds. The road snaked between the mountains, and I only had a couple of minor passes to cycle over. The rest of the ride was along a very rocky coast with black volcanic sand beaches.

This town is booked solid. Luckily, the Tourist Information office got me into a nice B&B. The weather is still very iffy, so I'm happy to be indoors tonight. I thought I might have to use the tent for the first time since Greece. I don't think I have what it takes to rough it anymore. On a related note, I met a young guy from Oregon at the top of one of the passes who was cycling from Auckland to Christchurch to start a year of college there. He had been free-camping most of the way. He pointed down to a streambed below and said that it would make a great campsite. All I saw was rocks and water, and no neon sign announcing "Camp Sites Available."

I have good news to report on the dinner front. I went into a proper restaurant, ordered a Scotch fillet steak, and loved it. It was prepared just as I had requested. It's more expensive, but I'm going to have to start venturing up-market for my meals.

Saturday, February 16th
Kaikoura to Ward - 84.52 Km

I was on the road at 8:30 AM today, greeted by a light drizzle that lasted most of the morning. With another good tailwind, I got down to the business of moving north. I only stopped a couple of times to look at the scenery and wildlife. At a fur seal colony just off of Highway 1, I saw about 50 adults and pups. The pups played in rock pools, and the adults had a few territorial battles while I videotaped about five minutes of the action. I didn't stop for a meal until the last five Km, where I hit the wall. It had been a flat ride for the first 80 Km. Then, after a couple of minor hills, I ran out of steam. I ate a few dark chocolate digestive biscuits and got enough energy back to ride into town. There's nothing like a good sugar fix to get you where you need to go.

I met some more Americans cycling here today. A group of 14 college students are on a five-week course, similar to Outward Bound. I met the instructor/leader at the seal colony. I was a little nervous about competing with such a large group for accommodations at the end of the day. He put my mind at ease when he said that they would be camping. I thought, "better them than me." Camping in the cool, damp weather that the South Island has been experiencing lately is a character-building exercise for 18 year-olds, but torture for a 42 year-old like me. As it turns out, they're camping on the front lawn of the motel where I'm staying for the night. It's the only motel between Kaikoura and Blenheim, a distance of about 130 Km. My accommodations book stated that they only had six rooms here, so I called ahead in the morning and left a message on the motel's answering machine to reserve a room. In case they didn't get the message, I pushed hard all morning to reach the motel at 12:30 PM. They hadn't gotten the message, but I was the first person to arrive today. This motel has been full the past three nights, and it's getting there tonight. I don't understand why there are so many tourists during such a rainy spell.

The front tire now has 10,000 Km on it. Its replacement is back at Mom and Dad's house waiting to be shipped to Auckland or Papeete. I haven't decided yet. With American Express Travelers Service pulling out of New Zealand, I'm leaning towards Papeete. I can't believe that I'm that close to Tahiti. Tomorrow night or Monday morning, depending on the ferry schedule, I'll be on the North Island, my last stop before Tahiti. Yippee!

Sunday, February 17th
Ward to Wellington - 76.73 Km

I attended a 9:00 AM communion service in the old wooden church across the street with about 15 other people. The town of Ward is too small and remote to have a traveling priest celebrate mass every week. The gospel readings and the distribution of pre-consecrated hosts were handled by a few of the church elders this week. The 19th century pump organ in the back of the church was played by a 19th century organist. Both were well past their prime.

The last of the college group had already checked out when I returned from the communion service at 9:30 AM. I got rolling 30 minutes later. I passed most of the group as they enjoyed a snack at a café in Seddon. There were more hills on Highway 1 today, but that translated to great scenery. I shot some exhilarating helmet-cam video after traversing a 196-meter pass south of Blenheim. In Blenheim, I met the rest of the college group in front of the McDonalds. They were planning to cycle west to Abel Tasman National Park for some hiking and kayaking adventures. I said goodbye and continued north up a heavily wooded valley to Picton to catch a ferry to the North Island. I bought a $35 ticket for the 7:00 PM ferry and then called ahead to book a $40 room at the Hotel Ibis Wellington while waiting in the park near the harbor. When I finally cycled off of the ferry in Wellington, it was already dark. Fortunately, the Hotel Ibis is just a few short blocks from the ferry terminal. I'll check out the sites on foot tomorrow in New Zealand's capitol city.

Monday, February 18th
Wellington - 0 Km

Wellington is a very manageable capitol city for walkers. I spent the day strolling through the different neighborhoods. From my hotel in the central business district, I went through the Lambton Quay shopping district to funky Cuba Street. I spent some time browsing in a used record store and an antique shop there. Then, I went up Cook Hill to photograph the National War Memorial and Carillon (Bell Tower). Next, it was back down to sea level for a walk along Lambton Harbour. Near Queen's Wharf I witnessed an organized demonstration of BMX vert freestylers flipping and twisting over ramps for the afternoon business crowd. The falls that some of those young guys took had every man in the crowd cringing. My fall in Athens doesn't seem so bad now. My last stop for the day was New Zealand's new national museum, Te Papa. You could spend hours in there viewing Maori, early European, and modern New Zealand artifacts. And, I did. The Maori longboat and carved meetinghouse alone were worth the price of admission, which was free by the way. I now have a better appreciation of the country that I'm hell-bent on rushing through.

Tuesday, February 19th
Wellington to Tawa - 23.2 Km

Well, forget Athens. I had a world-class fall from the bike today as I cycled out of Wellington. A lady who had been sitting in her parked car on a local street opened her door just as I passed.

The door caught my left front pannier, the front wheel immediately turned 90° to the left, and I did a full gainer with a half-shriek over the handlebars. Whatever points I lost in style, I gained back in difficulty factor. Even the Russian judge would have been impressed with the impact that I made on the pavement. The sudden change in direction stripped the tread right off of my front tire. The handlebar mirror was also smashed beyond repair. I had to put a cheap 35 mm no-name tire on the front wheel because I have no spare 32 mm Avocet Cross Kevlars. I've already called home to have my new tires sent to Hamilton, the next big town.

After the tire was replaced, the wheel realigned, and the missing bits reattached to the bike, I continued north on Highway 1. Somehow I hurt my right knee, in addition to my back, in the fall. So, the going was slow. Then, things got worse. Wind, rain, hills, dead ends. Twenty Km into the ride, while pushing the bike up a hill on the wrong side of the highway, I came to my senses and called it a day. I know when to admit defeat. I found the nearest motel, locked myself in a room, and ordered a pizza for dinner. The pizza came with a huge fly on top. And, I wasn't surprised.

Wednesday, February 20th
Tawa to Waikanae - 46.34 Km

Despite a puffy right knee, I was back on the bike today. I have to keep moving. And, after an early morning storm, there were fresh southerlies to push me up the coast. I had the strangest feeling as I cycled north over rivers flowing from right to left under Highway 1. For the first time on the trip I am riding with a major body of water on my left. The Mediterranean, Indian, Southern, and Pacific had all been on my right. Now I look to my left and see the Tasman Sea. I'm so confused. I don't know which direction to spit.

I spent three hours this afternoon viewing the antique automobile, motorcycle, and bicycle collection in Paraparaumu's Southward Museum. Paraparaumu ("really, really faraway" in Maori?) seems a strange place to showcase the largest classic motor vehicle collection in the Southern Hemisphere, but this is the home of Sir Len Southward who started his amazing collection with the purchase of a decrepit Ford Model T for £40 in 1956. The museum is five Km from the hustle and bustle of downtown metropolitan Paraparaumu in a modern warehouse with a state-of-the-art garage in back to maintain the vehicles. Some of my favorites among the 250 cars are an 1895 Benz Velo, a 1955 Mercedes Benz 300 SL Gullwing, and a 1920 Stanley Steamer. Among the many bicycles are an 1863 Michaux Velocipede (the first commercially produced bicycle in the world) and an 1869

Hedges English Boneshaker. The motorcycle collection has a number of early Harley-Davidsons and Indians. Sir Len, who made a name for himself racing powerboats, really knows his modes of transportation.

Thursday, February 21st
Waikanae to Bulls - 90.59 Km

I had my first flat on the new dime-store front tire just as a friend called me from the States. I like to project the image that everything is going swimmingly when I get calls from friends and family. I don't want people to worry about me while I'm out here. I don't think I left that impression with Bruce today. I was pretty steamed about the flat. And, I noticed that the front axle might also be bent after yesterday's fall. I wasn't a happy camper on the phone. After we hung up, I'm sure that Bruce said to himself, "What's his problem?"

Tonight, I'm at the point on the map where I need to decide whether to continue northeast on Highway 1 up the center of the North Island, or turn northwest up Highway 3. I've decided to cycle the west coast on Highway 3 because there are fewer hills to climb in that direction. The ride will take longer, but a few extra Km won't kill me.

Friday, February 22nd
Bulls to Wanganui - 50.78 Km

As planned, my first day on Highway 3 was a short one. This is the last town with any motels before Hawera, 90 Km away. I'm glad that I didn't have to ride too far into today's wind. Between the headwind and the troubles that I'm having with the front wheel, it was a tough 50 Km. The new tires won't come soon enough. The noise of the 35 mm wide tire constantly rubbing against the fender is driving me nuts. I'm starting to think that the bent axle and the stiff caliper brakes are also making noise. Any noise means rolling resistance. It's hard enough cycling up and down hills with the wind against me. I don't need the bike to make me work any harder.

I'm glad that I got into town early enough to get a motel unit. The owners of the first motel that I visited were fully booked, but they got me into another motel a block away. The town was filling up quickly. I had hoped to catch a nap this afternoon, but ended up watching the Olympics on television. Another opportunity to sleep squandered.

Saturday, February 23rd
Wanganui - 19.86 Km

For only the second time on this trip, I had to return to a town after cycling out of it in the morning. I got about nine Km out of Wanganui, uphill and into a stiff breeze, when the rain started. I quickly covered up the panniers, tent, and sleeping bag. I considered continuing on, but the next motel was 80 Km away in Hawera. So, I turned back. It was only 11:00 AM.

The ride back into Wanganui took no time at all because I was now going downhill with a stiff breeze at my back. Almost one Km from town, as I was flying down the steepest part of the ride, I got a flat on the rear tire. Since I was so close to town and didn't want to be caught fixing the flat in the next rain cloudburst, I decided to push the bike into town and find a motel room. After a few turndowns, I realized that the town was fully booked for a Scottish Festival tonight. So, I decided to fix the flat under the awning of a closed store on the main street. It was becoming obvious that I would need to do some riding to find accommodations for the night. While fixing the flat I saw that two of the spokes on the rear wheel had broken at the hub. The beauty of having 48-spoke wheels is that they stay in true even after one or two spokes break. I cycled a few blocks to a bike shop that I had visited yesterday and paid them to fix the spokes. While the mechanic did the work, I called a few more places in town in search of a room. I finally found one at the Grand Hotel. It was their last room, and I jumped at it. It's just a block away from the bike shop, so I was at the front desk with credit card in hand within a minute. The room is extremely small, but clean. The hotel suggested that I put the bike in their garage overnight. Before I did, I worked on the caliper brakes and tires on the sidewalk out front. I found the split in the tire and put a tube patch across it on the inside.

The Grand Hotel was on the parade route of the bagpipe bands in competition for the Scottish Festival. So, I got to hear the same tune performed the same way by a dozen or more bands representing different towns in the region. There is a big show in the town stadium tonight that I elected to miss. There's a limit to how much bagpipe music a person can take in one day.

Sunday, February 24th
Wanganui to Waverley - 45.29 Km

Lately it seems as if I've had one difficult day after another. Today, I had some of the worst headwinds of the trip. There was a cold front blowing in all day. At one point it suddenly dumped a good bit of rain on me before I had the chance to cover up my tent and sleeping bag stuff sacks. By the time that I got my jacket on, the damage had already been done. I was soaked. Making matters worse, the terrain rolled over a number of river valleys. The steep hills up from the rivers really slowed me. I averaged a little over 12 Km/hour for the day. Not a personal best.

The mobile phone was out of coverage down in some of the river valleys. Dad tried to call me a few times but was unsuccessful. I knew that he was trying to reach me because it was the time for his weekly scheduled phone call. When I got to the little town of Waitotara, I bought a Coke and called home. It doesn't pay to let Mom worry about me for too long. While I drank my Coke in Waitotara, I answered the standard questions from three local kids. What was unique about this encounter was that they were extremely courteous. Normally, when a group of kids approach me, they get a little hyper and bratty. These three showed a genuine interest in the trip and in life in America. I think that they may have been starved for some conversation with an outsider.

I stopped at Waverley this afternoon hoping to choose between the town's two hotels, but only one is open on Sundays. For $10 I have a little room above the pub. It's a quiet night in town, so I'll get lots of sleep. I don't imagine they have too many unquiet nights here.

Monday, February 25th
Waverley to Stratford - 77.79 Km

I hit the 9,000-mile mark today. I think that I also started to get back into the groove. A lot of that had to do with a change in the weather. It was a sunny day, and the headwinds were not quite as fierce. The terrain was still a bit difficult, but not as bad as it has been the past few days. The scenery even picked up. The towns of Patea and Hawera were very nice, and the view of Mount Egmont was pretty amazing. In Patea I sat down in a garden behind the library and soaked up some rays while downing a lemonade and chocolate chip cookie. In Hawera I walked around the well-maintained King Edward Park for an hour, taking pictures of the duck pond, flower gardens, and Wendy statue. The Wendy (of Peter Pan fame) statue is one of only two in the world. The other is in England. While I was smelling the roses, literally, a fellow told me a funny story about Hawera. Years ago some locals got drunk, fired off the retired cannon in the middle of the park, and almost hit the statue of one of the town's forefathers. The moral of that story is that alcohol and heavy artillery do not mix. If you stand behind the cannon you can see that it is aimed about one degree to the left of the statue 100 yards away. That's smart landscape design.

Mount Egmont is a dominant feature on the west side of the North Island. It's an extinct volcano over 2,500 meters high, visually similar to Japan's Mount Fuji. I first noticed it from 30 Km away. The top quarter of the mountain was above the clouds today. Very imposing. Stratford is the base of operations for people who explore the Egmont National Park. Stratford's other claims to fame are that it has the only glockenspiel in New Zealand, and it's movie theatre showed the first talkies in the Southern Hemisphere. This must be the cultural center of the bottom half of the world. That's why I stopped here for the night. I want to head down to the clock tower at 10:00 AM tomorrow and see the glockenspiel in action.

Tuesday, February 26th
Stratford to Mokau - 108.51 Km

For the first time since January 5th, I've cycled over 100 Km for the day. That would explain why I had trouble walking up the hill to my motel tonight. Even the owner commented on how tired I looked. I should have taken my business elsewhere after that remark, but I couldn't move anymore. In my defense, an allergy pill took a little out of me today. At 190 meters high, Mount Messenger took the rest out of me. My right leg actually fell asleep as soon as I got into the motel room. I'm going to sleep well tonight.

I had hoped to see der glockenspiel werk das morgen, but I missed it by five minutes. Oh, well. Que sera, sera. That's life. I had my usual New Zealand breakfast (orange juice in an apple juice base, and a big chocolate chip cookie) and then hit the road. Most of the ride was over rolling farmland, but Mount Messenger at the 80 Km mark was straight up and down. I stopped once on the way up to catch my breath. I did the same at the top, then put on my jacket, and enjoyed the quick ride down the other side. After that, I had another 21 Km before reaching my destination for the day.

Wednesday, February 27th
Mokau to Te Kuiti - 79.31 Km

The guidebooks may describe the terrain that I covered today as "gently rolling", but I say it's a series of hills, one after another. After nine straight days in the saddle, my legs don't have the strength to breeze over these hills. I need a day off. I think that after tomorrow's ride to Hamilton, I'll do just that. The forecast is for rain in two days, so that's a good time to take a day off and recover. I'll put on the new tire on the day off. That should make my final day to Auckland much easier.

The first five Km today took me up the coast to Awakino, and then I turned inland. It was almost 50 Km before I reached the next store at Piopio. I ran out of water in the last 10 Km, and I still had some climbing to do. The riding, though difficult, was through some scenic areas. The Awakino Gorge was very impressive. There's only enough room in the gorge for a river and the two-lane highway. At one point the road narrows to one lane as it passes through a short tunnel carved out of stone. I had been out of mobile phone range since yesterday afternoon. I was told that there would be coverage in Piopio. For the last 10 Km to Piopio I listened for the sound of the incoming message beep on my phone. When I heard the telltale beep (scheduled weather and stock reports), I knew that I was only a couple of Km from town. I spent at least 30 minutes at the first gas station in town, drinking Powerade and eating snacks.

The final push into Te Kuiti was dull by comparison. The town itself is a bit depressed. I found a new motel literally on the wrong side of the tracks. But, I was happy to find it because the only other motel worth its weight was back a couple of Km, and up a steep hill.

Thursday, February 28th
Te Kuiti to Hamilton - 84.05 Km

This would have been a fairly easy day of cycling, but it was the tenth in a row. So, I struggled. In this country of 60 million sheep, I saw a cute baby lamb today having a sneezing fit. Poor kid. He's going to spend the rest of his life in fields, and he's allergic to grass. When I see such cute little lambs, I invariably think, someday he'll grow up and make somebody a very nice rug.

I got another flat on my dime store front tire today. I got to Hamilton just in time to pick up the new tires from home. I'll give the bike the once over tomorrow. I'm staying in the King's Court Motor Lodge on the city's north side motel and fast food strip. I ran down to the Pizza Hut for dinner.

Friday, March 1st
Hamilton - 0 Km

This was a long overdue day off. I spent the day exploring the city, visiting music stores, looking for that elusive mint 1967 3C Moog Modular synthesizer collecting dust in a backroom. They have a few very nice music stores here, but none selling instruments from the LBJ era. I strolled a bit through the downtown mall, had a tea and muffin, and watched the Hamiltonians go about their chores. Airline tickets for Tahiti and Hawaii have now been purchased. I got caught out in the rain returning to the motel from the mall.

Tonight, I attended the opening pro rugby match at the new stadium behind the motel strip. It was a two-minute walk and a $6 ticket. The rain even held off. The local Hamilton Chiefs were playing the Canterbury Crusaders. The place was packed and ready for a party. Unfortunately, the Chiefs lost. Worse still, they ran out of booze with two minutes left in the first half. That two-minute warning was not well accepted by the locals. They didn't care that the new stadium was still a construction site. But, they were ready to string the concession manager up for "poor management." Secretly, I was more than a little happy that they weren't going to pump more liquid aggression into the fans.

One of the more terrifying episodes of the night was the introduction of the "crowd wave" early in the second half. The fans here have a custom of throwing more than their hands into the air when the wave passes over their section. They throw debris. I was sitting at one end of the stands watching a hail of beer bottles flying through the air at the other end and moving toward me. I cowered under the seat while the wave passed me two times. On the third pass a bottle hit my leg. It was plastic. They don't sell glass bottle beer at these matches. Now, I call that good management.

Saturday, March 2nd
Hamilton - 0 Km

Plans to get back on the road were scuttled when I took a look outside today at ominous skies. I had heard reports of worse weather possible in Auckland. So, I went shopping instead. I bought a lens cloth, a blank Mini DV tape, and an adventure magazine with an article on Bora Bora. And, that was the highlight of these past 24 hours.

Sunday, March 3rd
Hamilton to Auckland Airport - 122.54 Km

Most of today's ride was flat, not Nullarbor-flat, but flat enough to make 122 Km seem easy. Only the Bombay Hills offered any resistance. It was Sunday, so there were a few events that I passed along the way. A horse jumping show. A drag race competition. I worked up a good sweat crossing the Bombay Hills, then got off of State Highway 1 and onto the Great South Road.

SH1 becomes a motorway after the hills. And, the Great South Road parallels it without any traffic. It was a fun road to cycle.

I had decided not to ride into Auckland, but to find a motel near the airport, set up shop for two nights, and take a bus into the city to see the sights. It took a lot longer to get to the airport than I expected. Then, I had to cycle out of the airport five Km north to find the nearest motel. I had my choice of motels, so I took the Travelers International. After almost a year on the road, and traveling halfway around the world, I guess that I can consider myself an international traveler.

Monday, March 4th
Auckland - 0 Km

If it's Monday, this must be Auckland. I signed up for a city sightseeing bus tour last night. So, at 9:10 AM today I hopped onto the bus with my fellow elderly tourists to experience Auckland as God intended, behind glass and at 50 mph. I only regret that I didn't have a matching white shoes and belt set like the rest of the men on the bus. The bus that picked up my sartorially-challenged friends and me from the airport motel strip took us to Auckland's War Museum, the first stop on the city loop tour. From there, a number of buses make hourly loops around the city with about a dozen stops. For $10 I could hop on and off anywhere I wanted. I just had to be back at the War Museum by 4:30 PM for the return to my motel.

My first stop was Queen Street in the center of town to burn a CD with my latest digital pictures. I also did some souvenir shopping and mailed home a package of stuff. Then, I was back on the bus for the short ride to the Sky Tower. Completed in 1999, it's a 1,000-foot tall tower, similar to the AMP and Rialto Towers in Australia. There is a bunch of broadcasting thingies on the top part, called the whip. Below that are the observation decks where you can have a meal, look out over the city, or jump to a certain messy end. Well, the Sky Jump isn't advertised like that, but it sure didn't look safe to me. From one of the observation decks the Sky Jump operators walk you out along a plank, clip your harness to a wire, and encourage you to jump. The central wire slows your descent to about 50 mph and two guide wires keep your lifeless body from swaying back into the tower and doing any real damage. Of course, they get the money up front.

The main observation deck wasn't much safer than the Sky Jump. In all of their wisdom, the architects replaced some of the cement flooring with 38 mm glass panels. The apparent benefit is that tourists no longer have to go to the effort of leaning out over a railing to look down on the city below. Now they can just stand still, hang their head, and look straight down. There's a sign posted above the panels stating that they are as strong as the cement flooring. I don't doubt that, but I question how strong the nuts and bolts holding the glass to the cement are. Who's to say that some laborer didn't torque his wrench too much, stripping the bolt threads, when he attached those glass panels. I showed some respect for gravity and held onto a railing as I gingerly stepped out onto the glass and took some pictures.

Then, I walked over to Victoria Park Market to browse the crafts and souvenirs. For almost 100 years the building was an incinerator for the city's trash. The brick smoke stack still stands. Now you can buy trashy T-shirts and incense in the touristy shops. I had no burning desire (pun intended) to buy any scented candles, so I moved on to the America's Cup compound. The docks where contenders for the Cup are based are a little like a naval base, only with tighter security. I suppose I could have climbed the eight-foot high cyclone fence to get a better look, but I was afraid of being shot.

So, I got back on the city loop bus and rendezvoused with the other elderly tourists at the War Museum for the trip back to the motel. I ordered a steak from room service and got on the phone to book my first night's accommodations in Tahiti. I'm ready to say goodbye to New Zealand.

French Polynesia

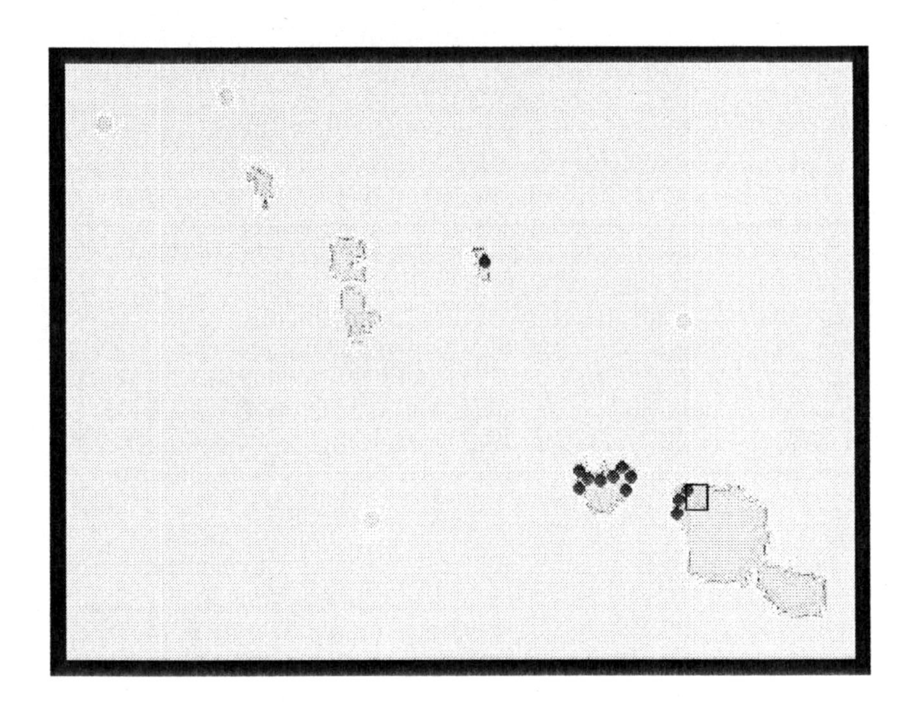

Tuesday, March 5th
Auckland to Papeete, Tahiti, French Polynesia - 4.6 Km

There was no need to rush out today. The flight to Tahiti didn't depart until 6:00 PM. I hung around the motel until noon, and then cycled the five Km to the international terminal. First, I bought a used bike box from the baggage office. I took my time disassembling the bike outside the terminal at one of the two stations set up expressly for that purpose. The folks in Auckland had the foresight to set up two bicycle stands under an overhang outside of one of the doors into the terminal. That's a good sign for anyone arriving in Auckland to cycle. The town respects the rights of cyclists. After boxing the bike and taping it airtight, I checked in. In the long wait until my flight departure I exchanged money, composed e-mail messages, and had a couple meals.

The flight was quicker than expected because of a strong tailwind. We touched down around 11:30 PM, Tahiti time. The bike arrived unscathed and I assembled it in record time. I got out of the airport around midnight and headed up the hill to Chez Sorenson. The guesthouse was only a hundred yards from the terminal entrance, but it was up a dark alley with a lot of angry dogs. There's also no neon sign on top of the house. I saw a small placard for Chez Fifi, and I knew that I was close. I looked into the open window of Chez Fifi and saw a guy from my flight just settling in. I got his attention and asked where my guesthouse was. He directed me to the Chez Fifi owner who was asleep on a lounge chair outside. The owner directed me to the house next door. Everyone was asleep at Chez Sorenson except for the guard dog. Besides scaring the daylights out of me, its barking also woke up the owner. He showed me to my room and then went back to sleep. Even in the dark I could tell that this place was a dive. The windows are left open because of the intense heat and humidity. That lets in the bugs and the noise from the airport, dogs, and roosters. For the first time since Greece, I used my silk sleeping sack. I hoped it would keep the bugs from eating me alive over night, while not melting me like the Wicked Witch of the West.

Tuesday, March 5th (2)
Papeete - 16.9 Km

If it's Tuesday *again*, it must be Papeete. I crossed the International Date Line last night. So, like Bill Murray in *Groundhog Day*, I have the pleasure of experiencing Tuesday, March 5th all over again. Today is a national holiday in French Polynesia. It marks the arrival of the first London Missionary Society missionaries in 1824. The streets of Papeete were empty, so it was easy to do some exploring on the bike. Unfortunately, most of the stores were closed for the holiday. I was hoping to get an answer from one of the phone stores why my mobile phone wouldn't work. I also wanted to get an electrical adapter to keep all of my gadgets charged. After getting a flat in front of the Tourist Information building, I needed to find a bike store to pick up tubes. I had no luck with any of these problems.

The nice lady in the Information office took pity on me and booked me a room at the Hotel Sofitel Maeva Beach at the resident, not tourist, rate of $108. I cycled back out of Papeete, past the airport in Fa'aa, to the hotel complex at Maeva Beach. The air-conditioning in the room alone was worth the $108. I didn't want to leave it, but I did take a dip in the large pool near the hotel's beach. Then, it was back to the air-conditioned room for the evening. I even ordered up a burger from room service. I could stay here the full 10 days and be happy. I just need to refresh my limited French skills.

Wednesday, March 6th
Papeete to Moorea - 36.26 Km

I didn't want to leave the Sofitel Maeva Beach and its mega-sized bed this morning. They didn't post a checkout time in the room, so I was tempted to stay until noon. But, I did want to take care of a few details before catching the 12:15 ferry to Moorea. So, I packed up the bike and headed out into the heat, humidity, and carbon monoxide of Greater Papeete. The ride was much different today, a day after the public holiday. I had to do battle with le trucks (local mini-buses) and other trucks. Traffic gets a little hairy after passing the airport at Fa'aa, and then it comes to a standstill in downtown Papeete. The drivers were all very courteous, but I resorted to guerilla cycling tactics. Sidewalks, one-way streets, construction sites - none of these were off-limits as far as I was concerned.

My first chores in town were to buy the electrical adapter and stamps for the obligatory postcards from paradise. Then, I searched unsuccessfully for tire tubes. Next, I got the lowdown on my mobile phone situation. It seems that VINI, the GSM monopoly in French Polynesia, will not allow travelers to register. We must buy one of their SIM cards to put into our phones. I didn't even ask the price from the shopkeeper. It sounded like a rip-off scam. I've decided to go native for 10 days, and leave the phone packed away. I'll communicate with home via e-mail and mental telepathy. I just pray that the e-mail service is reliable because I've been told that my mental capabilities are severely limited.

Finally, I rushed to the ferry quay and bought a ticket on the new Ono-Ono ferry to Moorea. "Ono-Ono" seems a funny name for a public transportation vehicle, but I felt safe throughout the entire 30-minute trip.

I had considered staying at the Sofitel resort on Moorea because of the great time that I had at the Sofitel Maeva Beach, and because it was just a couple Km from the Vaiare quay on Moorea's east coast. That's where the other ferry service docks. The new Ono-Ono service goes to the northern side of the island and down into Cook's Bay. That was a surprise to me. I don't know how small the Vaiare quay is, but the Paopao quay has a café, a boutique, and a 20-car parking lot. Nothing else. I had definitely left the congestion of downtown Papeete behind.

I was already 10 Km away from the Sofitel la Ora to the east, so I decided to cycle west to the strip of hotels around the Club Med on the northwest corner of the island. The Club Med is about 17 Km away from Paopao at Hauru Point. I cycled out of Cook's Bay (where Capt. Cook never dropped anchor) and around Opunohu Bay (where Cook did drop anchor) to the Club Med strip. Along the way I saw a number of loose dogs. They didn't give chase, but they did give it consideration. I could tell. I also saw one of the more remote phone booths in my journeys at the nearly uninhabited base of Opunohu Bay. It's also one of the most scenic places on earth from which to make a crank call: "Is your refrigerator running? By the way, what's a refrigerator?"

Like the rest of the paved world, the Club Med strip seemed to be booked solid when I arrived. I thought that I might be camping tonight, but the last hotel to reject me suggested that I try the Hotel Fare Viamoana. They had a semi-detached fare (bungalow) available tonight and could move me to another, slightly more expensive, single fare tomorrow night. I jumped at the offer. I set up house in the fare, and then walked down the strip to the shops at Le Petit Village to e-mail home. I finished up the day by kayaking out into the lagoon in front of the hotel. It was a great end to a busy day.

Thursday, March 7th
Moorea - 0 Km

It was "just another day in paradise", as the song goes. I did get moved from one fare to another. No sweat. In fact, the fan in this one works better. That's an important fact here in French Polynesia where humidity is measured in fathoms. I find myself wishing I had gills instead of sweat glands.

I took a walk this morning to Le Petit Village to buy a Powerade and check my e-mail. I inhaled the Powerade in 30 seconds, but spent 30 minutes reading and sending e-mail. Everyone back on the home front now know that I am telephonically-deprived due to French Polynesia's "Cousin VINI" plan - "youse pay us up front, or fugetabouddit." I'm no patsy; only one phone company at a time can bully me. Back at the Hotel Fare Viamoana I spent some quality time working on my tan, and then took out the kayak for a nice paddle around one of the three motu's on this section of coastline. This trip was even more fun than yesterday's. The narrow passage between two of the motu's had schools of fish to view in clear water. There were a few snorkelers, probably from the Club Med, enjoying the view as well.

I took another walk back to the village to mail postcards and buy essentials (USA Today Tuesday and Wednesday copies, Powerade, Coke, Arnott's cookies and crackers). I tried to have a meal there, but they don't start serving dinner until 7:00 PM. So, it was back to the fare where I booked a table for one at the hotel restaurant at 7:00 PM. I ordered the steak natural, well done, and a Coke. You're probably snickering, just like the waiter did. I couldn't be more of a stereotypical American if I wore a Stars and Stripes jacket and a 10-gallon hat. The French try to turn food into art, while we just want to turn it into calories. I had the last laugh because the steak was a little gristly. At least, I think I had the last laugh.

Friday, March 8th
Moorea to Tahiti - 45.36 Km

Despite the limited opportunities to cycle in French Polynesia, I managed to hit a milestone today. In my ride from the Club Med strip to the ferry quay I surpassed 15,000 Km. The next big milestone will be 10,000 miles. I'm only 768 miles short today.

I missed the 10:30 AM Ono-Ono ferry at the Paopao quay in Cooks Bay. My schedule showed it departing at 10:45AM. I was on the other side of the bay when I saw the ferry heading out to sea. I wasn't too upset because it gave me a reason to explore further and take the other ferry from Vaiare.

The coastal road was more of the same, scenery-wise. Just perfect views across the water to Tahiti. At one point the road even rises a bit to a lookout over the Sofitel la Ora and Temae Beach. Then, I coasted down to Vaiare. The town is a bit bigger than Paopao, and the ferry quay is much larger. The ferry had just arrived from Tahiti, and dockhands were pulling out a 40-foot container using two forklifts, one at the front and one at the back. It was a delicate operation, but they pulled it off as if they do it every day. And, they probably do. I bought tickets for the bike and myself and got on board. I went to the top deck and stood outside without a hat for 30 minutes, watching the activity on the quay below. That was a mistake. My slightly bald spot is now slightly red.

Back in Papeete, I had a load of wash done for $12. Ouch! I also looked into flying to Bora Bora and Maupiti. No luck. Bora Bora is booked solid for an international canoe race. Flights to Maupiti are also booked solid. I'm disappointed. It seems a shame to come all this way and not see the famous Bora Bora lagoon. This just means that I'll have to return some day.

The travel agent in Papeete suggested that I give Huahine a try. So, I booked a flight for tomorrow with a return three days later. She also got me back into the Sofitel Maeva Beach tonight. I'll try to book myself in Sofitels for the remaining six nights in French Polynesia. I hope to get a better rate by staying with one chain exclusively. I also like what I've seen so far on their Tahiti and Moorea properties.

Saturday, March 9th
Tahiti to Huahine - 0 Km

The front desk at the Maeva Beach hotel put me on the phone to Sofitel's central booking in French Polynesia so that I could book the rest of my nights here in their hotels. I booked three nights in a beach bungalow on Huahine, two nights in an over-water bungalow on Moorea, and my final night back at the Maeva Beach hotel near the Fa'aa Airport. Although these are extremely pricey digs for someone on a bicycle-tourist budget, I justified the expense because of the drastic discounts that I was given. I think that I may have even gotten prices better than the residents get. Overseas business must really be down. I'm happy to take advantage of the downturn.

I left the bike in storage and packed up just enough stuff to last me a few days on the outer islands. It all fit into my two front panniers, which conveniently snap together to act as one carry-on bag. I checked out at noon, but hung around the pool and beach until 3:30 PM.

The flight at 5:10 PM to Huahine was uneventful. It was the first time that I boarded a plane with festival seating (no assigned seats). While most of the passengers bum-rushed the front "crumple zone", I took a seat in the last row, the "safety zone." I was also closest to the exit. You can never be too careful. My only regret is that I didn't get a window seat. The pilot took us almost completely around Huahine while he was landing. I could have shot some great video. I'll keep that in mind for the return flight.

The private bungalow that I'm in tonight is something that would make Robin Leach's jaw drop. It's in the style of a

Polynesian fare, but very up-market. The bed is sumo-sized, with a mosquito net above. All of the furniture is bamboo/wicker/rattan. The floors are a heavily varnished hardwood. The bathroom décor is heavy on the seashells. And, the piece d'resistance, loose flower petals are placed everywhere. On the bed. On the desk. In the sink. Even on the toilet lid. Martha Stewart would have approved.

Saturday nights they offer a Polynesian feast and show in the hotel restaurant. The pig is roasted all day in an underground oven, and then offered up at the 7:00 PM meal. There is also traditional music and dance performed for the guests. That's not my scene, man. So, I hung out in the bungalow, writing postcards, and sniffing flowers.

Sunday, March 10th
Huahine - 0 Km

I skipped the 8:00 AM transfer to a local church, not knowing if it was even going to a Catholic church. Most of the locals are Protestant. The London Missionary Society took care of that almost 200 years ago. Instead, I had the continental breakfast out by the pool. They had Frosted Flakes, a real rarity for me lately. I got my daily sugar fix first thing this morning.

Since I have been unable to communicate with the folks back home, I went back to my room and initiated the weekly Sunday telephone chat session with Mom and Dad. Since money means nothing to me these days, I didn't even watch the clock. If I had an accountant, he would be in a coma by now.

I'm not much for organized activities like eel feeding and nature walks to archeological sites, so I grabbed a kayak and headed out into the lagoon. I probably did about five Km around the nearby motu, into the Faie Bay, and back. I saw trumpet fish and a couple of dead baby sharks. It might have been the hot water in the shallow lagoon that did the sharks in. I finished off the afternoon's activities with some quality time in the pool. That sure beats handing out chum to eels or swatting away mosquitoes at old stone piles.

Like Melville and Michener before me (how's that for a pompous lead-in?), I decided to do some writing in this island paradise <Pomposity Mode Off>. Actually, I decided to punch up a few lackluster journal entries. Like the entries from April 5th through yesterday. It wasn't even a punch up. It was more like a grammar check. Anyway, most of the nouns and verbs are now in their correct positions. A couple of participles may still be dangling, but that's just human nature.

Monday, March 11th
Huahine - 0 Km

I bought a little black pearl and silver dolphin pendant for my godchild's birthday at the boutique on the compound. If you're not willing to leave the Sofitel compound, as I am not, your gift choices are limited to what can be found in the boutique. Straw hats and beach towels don't say "Happy Birthday" as well as jewelry, so the decision was easy. The salesgirl explained that what I purchased was not really a black pearl because it did not have the nucleus around which pearls are formed. I've forgotten all of my high school chemistry but, without a nucleus, I think that makes it an isotope. Either way, it looked good to me and the price was right. We wrapped it up and I was on to my next task for the day. I took out the camcorder and walked around the compound shooting heaps of video and digital photos. It's hard to take a bad shot in this setting; the lush mountain dominating the mainland; the blue-green waters of the lagoon; the palm trees swaying on the motu; the waves crashing out beyond the reef. Even someone like me, who actually took Photography 101 in college, can turn out stunningly beautiful tropical images.

I repeated yesterday's activities with a paddle around the motu by kayak and a swim in the pool. I also tried my hand at paddling an outrigger canoe. The guy who hands out the paddles suggested that I try the three-man canoe because it's more stable. It also handles like an ocean liner. I couldn't get it to track a straight line to save my life. Thirty minutes of paddling in circles in front of the compound was all the humiliation that I could take. The folks on shore must have thought that they let a one-armed man out onto the water.

I finished up the afternoon with an HTML session. Although I can't upload any changes to my web page, I updated the code on my Pocket PC. As soon as I hit civilization again (Hawaii), I'll post the changes.

I skipped dinner, but still enjoyed the live Polynesian music from the comfort of my fare. There's a little lizard crawling along the walls tonight that has me a bit concerned. I hope that the mosquito net over the bed will deter him from attacking me at 4:00 AM.

Tuesday, March 12th
Huahine to Moorea - 0 Km

It was the best of days; it was the worst of days. Jeez, that sounds vaguely familiar. Anyway, I had an up and down day today. The good news is that I'm staying in one of the greatest accommodations on earth, an over-water bungalow on the island of Moorea. The bad news is that I passed a kidney stone here tonight.

This morning I flew directly from Huahine to Moorea. I took a $7.50 taxi ride from the airport to the Hotel Sofitel la Ora, one Km away. That seemed a little frivolous at the time, but it proved to be a worthwhile investment as I employed the very helpful, bilingual driver later in the day.

The resort is set on a beach facing Tahiti, with spectacular mountains behind it. I am in one of the twenty over-water bungalows. We elite travelers are set apart from the riff-raff in the beach and garden bungalows by means of a causeway stretching out into the lagoon. We only come ashore to spill our money in the boutiques and restaurants. The rest of the time we enjoy life to the max on our own private islands. Our bungalows have all of the basic amenities (A/C, cable TV, mini-bar) plus a few items not found in most hotel rooms. In the middle of the room is a glass topped coffee table that has a view clear through to the lagoon below. There's a spotlight below the bungalow to facilitate nocturnal fish spotting. We can even lift the glass tabletop and drop food to the fish below. For what it's worth, Polynesian fish do not like Cheetos or sugary French confections.

The double glass sliding doors that face Tahiti open up to a spacious bi-level deck. And, from the deck there are steps down to the lagoon. Snorkels and masks are provided for our little swims around the lagoon. They've thought of everything at the Sofitel la Ora. The best thing about my bungalow may be that I got it for half the published price because I booked it at the same time as my stays at the Sofitel hotels on Tahiti and Huahine.

I promised myself that I would buy one flashy Polynesian shirt before I left the islands, so I bought a blue and white one with flowers and ukuleles at the boutique. An elite traveler must look the part at all times.

In the afternoon I took another kayak out for an hour, and then had a late lunch/early dinner. That's about the time when I knew that I was in for a long and painful night. Having had kidney stones twice before, I am familiar with the symptoms. In the past the pain came on very quickly, so I left dinner and went back to my bungalow to take my one emergency Percocet. The rest of the pills were back on Tahiti with most of my luggage. Then, I asked the front desk for help with a local doctor and a taxi. I spoke on the phone with the doctor that the hotel recommended about getting more pain pills. Instead, he suggested a pill that widens the canal through which the stone would pass. He said it could be gotten at the Moorea Hospital, about five Km away.

When my taxi arrived, I saw that it was the same driver that I had this morning. On the way to the hospital I told her what was going on. She told me that her father suffered from kidney stones as well. She went into the tiny hospital with me to act as interpreter. I got eight of the Spasfon pills that the doctor recommended, plus two pain pills. They didn't charge me, and I didn't think to offer. I wasn't in a great state of mind. I was sent back to the hotel with the advice to "drink lots of water, but not too much." Moderation in everything, I guess.

I took two Spasfon and one pain pill immediately, on top of the one emergency Percocet. Around 10:00 PM I entered the Pain Zone. I immediately took the second pain pill from the hospital. For the next two hours I laid on the bathroom floor writhing in pain and breathing like a Lamaze class on speed. Every muscle in my body contracted completely. I couldn't grip anything because my thumbs folded into my palms. My lips involuntarily pursed. I could barely move my limbs.

All things must pass, and at midnight I vomited from the pain. That's when the stone passed. My body immediately went limp. I took a quick shower and fell into bed. Another successful day on the bike trip completed.

Wednesday, March 13th
Moorea - 0 Km

As another day in paradise dawned, I could barely get out of bed. The two hours in a full body clench last night had really weakened me. I hobbled over to the restaurant for breakfast, only because I had already paid for it. I hardly ate any of it. I hobbled back to the bungalow to get in some more horizontal time. I couldn't do much of anything, so I did nothing. It rained most of the day, so I didn't miss any of the hotel's exciting activities.

I skipped lunch, and then went over to the Bar Molokai in the compound around 5:00 PM for a burger and fries. It took an hour, but I finished the burger. I didn't even attempt to eat the fries. I only struggled through the burger because I knew that I needed to get my strength back for the trip to Hawaii in two days. At the bar I watched some young Polynesian dancers put on a show for the tourists. Very entertaining. Then, I went back to my bungalow and collapsed.

Thursday, March 14th
Moorea to Papeete - 0 Km

I was healthy enough to eat a full breakfast this morning. I caught a taxi to the quay a couple Km south of the Sofitel compound. I missed the slow ferry to Papeete, but caught the fast one thirty minutes later.

My first stop in town was at the local Internet café to catch up with e-mail. Then, I took a walk through the central market to see what sort of musical instruments were for sale. There were a variety of four and eight string ukuleles. Every one of them had the same price, 18,000 CFP. It looks like there may be price collusion in the Tahitian crafts market. I considered buying a rain stick, shakers, and a variety of other percussion instruments. In the end I walked out empty-handed.

My final stop of the day was at the Cardella Clinic to verify that I had no more stones floating around inside me, waiting to appear as soon as I reached 30,000 feet tomorrow. I first made the mistake of walking into an office across the street from the hospital to ask for a consultation. I thought that it was part of the hospital because there was a sign outside that read, "Clinique." The receptionist did not understand me, so she took me into an office to speak with a man who knew some English. I assumed that he was a doctor. I told him about my stones, then drew him a schematic of the urinary tract to make sure that he understood the point. It turns out that the man was not a doctor, and the place that I walked into just sold medical equipment. The man, who I now think was a salesman, directed me across the street to the hospital, but kept my schematic. I have a feeling that copies of my drawing have already been faxed to the rest of the sales force along with a funny story about an American with kidney stones.

Like most hospitals, there was a lot of waiting involved. After two hours, two x-rays, and a sonogram, I was declared stone free (Insert 1960's flashback moment here). A quick taxi ride back to the Sofitel Maeva Beach had me in bed by 8:00 PM, ready for a 3:00 AM wake-up call. Hawaii awaits.

Hawaii

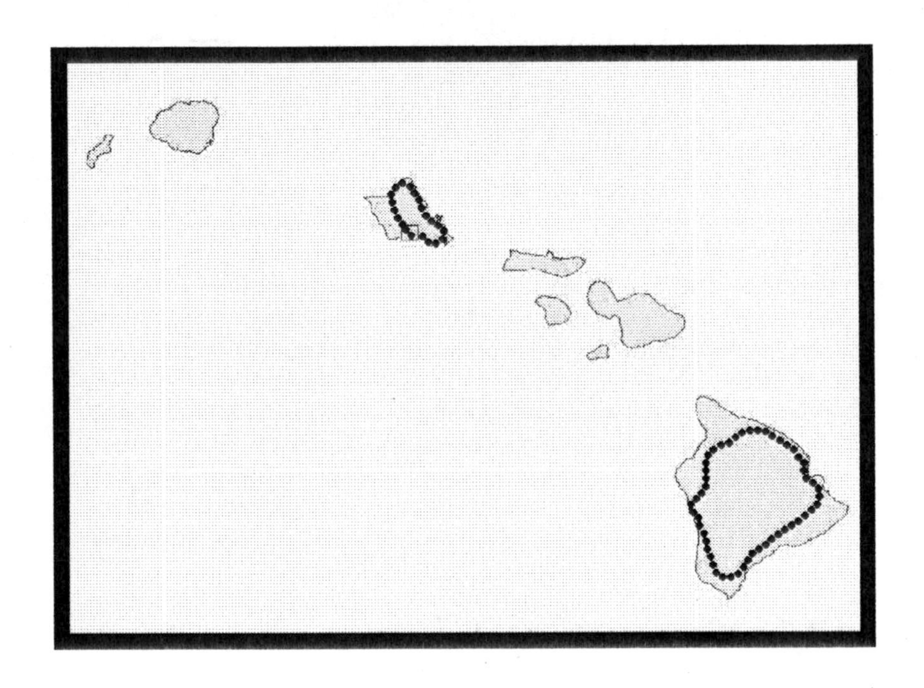

Friday, March 15th
Papeete to Waikiki, Hawaii - 0 Miles

I just spent 15 hours flying over the Pacific. Since I was unable to book a direct flight from Papeete to Honolulu, I had to connect through Auckland. That meant that I flew six hours east to Auckland, and then nine hours west to Honolulu. I crossed the International Date Line twice and the equator once. I arrived in Hawaii at 10:30 PM on the same day that I departed, but I did travel back to the future (March 16th) during the Auckland layover. I'm happy to report that the future looks bright, assuming I get through today.

My biggest fear today wasn't falling out of the sky in the middle of the Pacific Ocean. I was most afraid of another kidney stone making that slow and painful journey through my urinary tract in the middle of the Pacific Ocean. Fortunately, no stones materialized en route. I arrived at Honolulu International Airport unscathed. My bike didn't fare as well. The headset would not lock, leaving my handlebars to face north while my front wheel faced west. Not being of circus stock, I was unable to ride the cockeyed bike. So, I hailed a taxi, threw my bike into the trunk, and asked to be taken to Waikiki. The hotel that I selected in the airport lobby was less than I had hoped for. I ended up in a $49 high-rise flophouse. At 2:00 AM I had the obligatory wakeup call from a drunk pounding on my door, thinking it was his room. At this point, I'm still waiting for that Aloha Spirit to kick in.

Saturday, March 16th
Waikiki - 0 Miles

The first order of business today was to get the bike's headset repaired. That required a few phone calls to find a shop to do the work, and a taxi to get me there. By noon I was back on the repaired bike again. Another care package from home was scheduled to be in the Honolulu AmEx office, so that was my next stop. Posted on the door in front of the empty AmEx office was a sign stating, "CLOSED - From March 18, 2002 we are relocating to 677 Ala Moana Blvd. Suite 1025." I'm not paranoid by nature, but I now believe that the American Express Company is toying with my sanity. Montpellier, Athens, Christchurch, and now Honolulu. Their operatives must have gathered intelligence indicating that I would arrive in Honolulu late last night, so they shut down the office and stripped it of all its equipment by 5:00 PM yesterday. That's OK. They won't stop me. I'll go to 677 Ala Moana Boulevard on Monday morning, though I doubt that there really is a Suite 1025. In 48 hours that package could be anywhere. It's just as likely to be in a bunker under Red Square as it is to be in downtown Honolulu.

I met another cyclist outside of the old AmEx office, and we talked for a while about riding in Hawaii. When I told him that I was looking for another hotel he suggested the Pagoda. It's far from the beach, but reasonably priced. It was also just a few blocks away. That was enough to convince me. I took a room above the gardens and koi pond. This hotel is very popular with Japanese tourists. I watched as a couple of Japanese wedding parties had their formal photos taken in the gardens this afternoon.

The International Car Show is in town today, so I took a walk over to the Convention Center to drool over the Lamborghinis and Maseratis. The rest of the evening was spent in front of the tube watching VH1 and eating Hot Tamale candies. You don't realize how much you miss when you're overseas until you return home.

Sunday, March 17th
Waikiki - 0 Miles

What a lazy day. I hardly left the hotel. I did attend mass at a nearby church this evening. After mass, I stopped by a burger joint for dinner. The rest of the day was spent updating my website and speaking with family on the phone.

Monday, March 18th
Waikiki - 10.90 Miles

I tracked down the latest elusive care package at the new AmEx location. The search wasn't without its drama today, but I'm just happy to now have all of the maps that I need to get from here to Texas. A new Visa debit card was also included in the package. Take that, AmEx.

Although doctors at the Clinique Cardella in Papeete have already told me that I do not have any more kidney stones, I decided to get a second opinion. I'm sure that the Tahitian doctors didn't misinterpret the test results, but I may have misinterpreted their French. At the Queen's Medical Center I was referred to a nearby urology specialist who, for $92, concurred with his French-speaking colleagues. My kidneys are good for another year, or 10,000 miles.

Things were going so well today that I stopped into The Bike Shop and bought myself new gloves, water bottles, and tubes. The shop clerk gave me some info about cycling around Oahu and a free "The Bike Shop" T-shirt. Then, I was off to the post office to mail home old maps. I finished up the day cycling along the famous Waikiki beach where the Sidewalk Patrol issued me a warning for not riding on the street. Even that couldn't upset me today. I had my first Denny's dinner in over a year near the beach. I'm a happy man tonight.

Tuesday, March 19th
Waikiki - 24.88 Miles

I made a half-hearted attempt to start cycling around the island today, but stopped before I even reached Diamond Head. Another cyclist told me that there were no accommodations on the windward side of Oahu. There are campgrounds, but permits would be needed to stay at one of them. I decided that further research needed to be done before I took off for the other side. Instead, I rode leisurely down the coast to Maunalua Bay, checking out the nice homes in the upscale neighborhoods. On the way back to Waikiki I cycled through a 500-foot tunnel into the extinct crater of Diamond Head. There's a military base and popular state park within the crater now. I was anxious to get back to Waikiki and find another hotel, so I decided not to walk the .8-mile hiking trail to the summit. As soon as I got back to Waikiki I found a nice room at the Aston Waikiki Grand facing the Honolulu Zoo. That left me time to ride down to Ala Moana Park to take a few pictures of the Waikiki skyline and Diamond Head. A few miles farther put me in front of the famous Aloha Tower for my final photographs of the day.

Wednesday, March 20th
Waikiki - 0 Miles

I explored the shopping district of Waikiki today. I didn't buy much, but I did enjoy walking through the malls behind the hotels. Despite a preponderance of evidence to the contrary, I am still trying to convince myself that I am on a budget. All that I purchased were a Hawaiian cycling book and a Pocket PC magazine. I paid for the reading material after exchanging the last of my French Polynesian francs for dollars. At sunset I photographed the lighting of the torches on the beach in front of the Waikiki Grand.

Thursday, March 21st
Waikiki - 0 Miles

I took a nice, long walk around Waikiki today. The most interesting site that I visited was the Father Damien Museum. It's housed in a small building behind St Augustine's church, just a few steps from the beach. Father Damien was a Belgian missionary sent to the Hawaiian Islands in the 1860's. In 1873 he requested, and received, permission from his order to work with the lepers in an isolated corner of Molokai. In those days the people who contracted leprosy, or Hansen's disease, were sent to the colony to live out their days away from the general population. The only way in or out of the colony was by sea because it was at the base of a 2,000-foot cliff. Father Damien treated the lepers with compassion and dignity for sixteen years, eventually contracting the disease himself and dying on April 15, 1889. He is currently only one miracle away from being canonized a saint by the Catholic Church.

I saw on a local news broadcast tonight that I missed the concert of the season while I walked around town. Jimmy Buffet played a surprise solo show on the deck of Duke's Canoe Club, just a few blocks down from the Waikiki Grand this afternoon. If I had walked down to that end of the beach I could have been eating cheeseburgers in paradise while Jimmy played his hits, acoustically and barefoot. Don Ho, Bruce Willis, Glen Campbell, and approximately 2,200 Parrotheads all saw the show from the club and the beach. I'm disappointed that I missed it.

I've heard of a Hilton hotel on the North Shore of Oahu that I could probably shoot for tomorrow. That would get me half way around the island. I'll call tomorrow for a reservation.

Friday, March 22nd
Waikiki to Laie - 62 Miles

I don't know the exact distance that I cycled today because the cyclometer was temporarily dislodged in the middle of the ride. According to my map, the ride was probably 62 miles. I have to switch from the metric to imperial measures now that I'm back in the States. Everything is measured in miles, pounds, and gallons, except for the two-liter bottle of Coke that I'm chugging tonight.

I started out the day by calling the Hilton Turtle Bay Resort to check on the availability of rooms tonight. They only had $350 bungalows left, and those needed to be booked for two nights. I was ready to give up on cycling around Oahu when the lady at the front desk of the Waikiki Grand suggested the Laie Inn on Oahu's windward coast. She made the call and got me a room for $79. So, at almost 11:00 AM I took off from Kapiolani Park for a counterclockwise ride around the island.

The scenery around the southeastern tip of Oahu is fairly dramatic. There was some hill climbing, but none of it was too taxing. I shot some video of the little islands off of Makapu'u Point, and then cycled through the neighborhood where *Magnum PI* was filmed. After a quick lunch at the Subway in Kailua, I continued up the coast. Although this area of the island is sparsely populated, it has its fair share of state parks. At Kualoa Park I took some pictures of the little cone-shaped island off the coast called "Chinaman's Hat" (Sino-personage headgear, in PC). By 4:30 PM I was at the Laie Inn. It's situated next to the Polynesian Cultural Center and a McDonald's, a perfect location. Unfortunately, I can't eat a hamburger on a Lenten Friday, and the Cultural Center appears to be closed. So, I spent the evening on the phone with a friend, eating a Domino's pizza. Tomorrow, I should complete the trip around Oahu, ending up near the airport and Pearl Harbor.

Saturday, March 23rd
Laie to Waikiki - 36.11 Miles

Well, that was a fun day. After years of watching world-class surfers at the Banzai Pipeline on ABC's *Wide World of Sports*, I finally saw the infamous North Shore surf spot in person this morning. The waves weren't too big today, but it was obvious that you could do some damage if you were a novice out there. When the waves break, it appears to be at a very shallow spot close to the shore. I sat and watched the surfers for a few minutes, and then got back on the bike path and continued cycling to Waimea Bay. For entertainment on the beach at Waimea Bay, teenagers leap from an enormous lava rock into the surf. It's about a 35-foot drop. The kids on the North Shore are fearless.

After the bay the Kamehameha Highway turns inland and over the central hump of Oahu to Honolulu. It's a long, gradual climb up from the North Shore with wide-open vistas behind. I stopped a few times to photograph the coastline, and catch my breath. At the apex of the hump I passed the Dole Plantation Visitors Center and Schofield Barracks. The world's largest maze and a soon-to-be-built amusement park are adjacent to Dole's Visitor Center. They had a good crowd this Saturday afternoon. Schofield Barracks, which played a part in the defense of Pearl Harbor in 1941, has a number of retired Army helicopters on display just inside the gate. Despite the increased security, I was allowed to roll over to the field and photograph the old helicopters. The remainder of the ride was downhill through residential neighborhoods to Pearl City, where I picked up a bike path to the Airport Hotel.

Sunday, March 24th
Waikiki to Kailua-Kona - 10.69 Miles

I cycled into the airport this afternoon and bought a First Class ticket for a 6:45 PM flight to the Big Island of Hawaii. That left me with a few hours to ride over to Pearl Harbor to tour the U.S.S. Missouri. Launched in 1944, "Mighty Mo" is the last battleship ever built. She participated in World War II, the Korean War, and the Gulf War. The Surrender Deck on the Mighty Mo was the site of the signing of the Instrument of Surrender by Japan on September 2, 1945. It's fitting that the ship that represents the end of WW II is permanently docked so close in Pearl Harbor to the ship that represents the beginning of the war, the U.S.S. Arizona. Although I was able to tour the nearby U.S.S. Bowfin submarine, I didn't have enough time to visit the Arizona Memorial. I had to get back to the airport for my flight to Kailua-Kona on the Big Island.

Kona International Airport is about 12 miles from the town of Kailua-Kona. Since I arrived on the Big Island after dark, I decided to take a taxi into town. The driver suggested that I try for a room at the Seaside Hotel. Success. I have a comfortable room for a reasonable price tonight. I'll explore Kailua-Kona on foot tomorrow.

Monday, March 25th
Kailua-Kona - 0 Miles

This was one of those lazy days that I just love spending in tourist towns. Kailua-Kona is famous as the site of the annual Ironman Triathlon every October. Even though it's March, there are still a lot of serious jocks running and cycling around here. The town caters to the athletes, so I had no trouble finding a bike shop to replace my old handlebar wraps and brake hoods. They didn't have my standard black wrap, so my usually staid stead is now sporting a fire engine red accessory. Until now, my dark gray Specialized Expedition only had black racks, black panniers, a black saddle, a black pump, a black cyclometer and black handlebar wraps. It's no wonder that I'm nervous about cycling after dark.

Tuesday, March 26th
Kailua-Kona to Captain Cook - 12.98 Miles

A bicycle-tourist at rest tends to remain at rest. Had Sir Isaac Newton been a cyclist, I'm sure that he would have added this statement to his Laws of Motion. It's so hard to get back on the bike after a day off. For the past 24 hours, all that I did was study maps, read guidebooks, and worry more and more about the upcoming ride around the Big Island. Never mind that I've already cycled over the Pyrenees and Apennines, or across the Negev, the Sinai, and the Nullarbor. Today I was worried about accommodations, weather, and hills on the Big Island.

I didn't leave the hotel until almost noon. Before I did, I called ahead to the Manago Hotel in the town of Captain Cook for a room. I thought that it was close to 30 miles away. I was way off. The ride was only 13 miles. That's all right. I gained almost 1,500 feet in those 13 miles, so I had a nice workout. I know it was a good workout because I had to stop a couple of times to wring the sweat out of my gloves and do-rag. I was sopping wet when I stopped at a gas station for a Gatorade at the end of the ride. I'm surprised that they didn't kick me out of the mini-mart.

Routes 19 and 11, which form the Hawaii Belt Road, do not hug the coast. They are inland a mile or so. That means that they are also well above sea level. So, coming out of the port towns of Kailua-Kona and Hilo, I knew that I would be doing some climbing. I think the trip over Kilauea Volcano at 4,000 feet will be the most difficult day here on the Big Island. I'm anxious to get that behind me. The short ride down to Hilo after that should be fun.

Wednesday, March 27th
Captain Cook to Waiohinu - 44.7 Miles

It's been dreary on the Big Island since I arrived. Even on the Kona Coast, which is supposed to be a very dry and sunny place, the weather has been lousy. It spritzed on me a bit yesterday, but today it rained on me. If I had gotten an earlier start, I might have been able to avoid it because the rain showers began around 3:00 PM. I got on the road around 11:00 AM because I knew that it would be a relatively short ride. I stuck to the Belt Road the entire way. I could have taken a short detour to see a church whose interior is painted to look like a cathedral, but I've already been to St. Peter's and seen the Sistine Chapel. No need to stop.

As the scenic views thinned out, I entered Hawaiian Ocean View Estates. The sign on the road said that it was the world's largest subdivision. The landscape had a lunar quality to it, and it smelled of sulfur. Levittown it ain't. No need to stop.

Near the end of the ride was a turnoff to take travelers down to South Point, the spot farthest south in the United States. It was 12 miles away and down at least 1,000 feet. No need to stop.

Finally, at 3:30 PM I reached my destination, the Shirakawa Motel in Waiohinu. It's the farthest south motel in the United States. I know that because they sell T-shirts with that slogan emblazoned across the front. That would make me the farthest south bicycle-tourist in the United States tonight. After checking in, I ran across the street for supplies (Gatorade, pretzels, Haagen-Dazs bar). I spent the rest of the night munching and lightening the load that I have to haul up to Volcanoes National Park. I'm hoping to hit a post office before I start climbing tomorrow. I have a few items ready to mail back home. I threw out eight AA batteries from my helmet-cam, the free T-shirt that I got back in Honolulu, a beach towel that I won't get much use out of now, and hundreds of pages from a couple of guide books. I'm as ready as I'll ever be for the big climb tomorrow.

Thursday, March 28th
Waiohinu to Volcanoes National Park - 38.8 Miles

It took six hours to cycle almost 39 miles, but I made it without destroying my knees or having a heart attack. The road to the summit is graded so that it's just a very long, gradual climb.

I began the day by riding one mile to Naalehu and mailing home some excess baggage from the farthest south post office in the United States. Then, the road dropped farther down towards the coast. I cursed every foot of altitude lost, knowing that I would have to regain it during the climb to the summit. I probably got down to about 300 feet before the road turned inland and began to head uphill. I turned off at the regional hospital in Pahala to fill up my water bottles from their water fountain. There is nothing between Pahala and Volcanoes National Park, just mileage and altitude markers. Every 500 feet in elevation gained brings another sign. In a cruel twist, the road crew placed a 1,500-foot sign at 1,000 feet. It wasn't until I reached the real 1,500-foot sign that I realized their mistake. Aaargh!

In the last half-hour the skies opened up on me. I was riding through a thick fog, soaked to the bone, wondering why my Gore-Tex jacket wasn't working anymore. I pulled into the park entrance, paid the $5 fee, and rode up to the Volcano House hotel. There were two tour busses parked in front. That immediately made me nervous. I didn't have a reservation, and the next hotel is probably down in Hilo, 40 miles away. Fortunately, rooms were still available, so I chose a garden view (i.e., basement) room for $85. I rewarded myself with a filet mignon for dinner. The view from the restaurant looks out over the Kilauea Crater, at least that's what the guidebooks say. The fog was so thick that I couldn't see anything.

There's been a Volcano House, in some form, on the rim of Kilauea since 1846. Mark Twain stayed here in 1866. For a state that has very little history pre-Don Ho, this is an impressive site. It's part museum, part resort. If the weather weren't so lousy, I might consider staying a second night. But, I won't. Tomorrow, I drop 4,000 feet in altitude on my way to Hilo. Wheeee!

Friday, March 29th
Volcanoes National Park to Hilo - 39.09 Miles

Today was F-U-N, FUN. For over 20 of those 39 miles I did not need to pedal once. Most of the ride down the northern slope of Kilauea I was in a tuck position, resting on my aero bars. The highway was very straight and had clean, wide shoulders. It almost made the ride up Kilauea yesterday worthwhile. Almost.

Before I left Volcanoes National Park, I took a quick spin over to the steam vents a half-mile from Volcano House and the Visitor Center on Crater Rim Drive. It was a great spot to take panoramic photos of the crater. The steam rising up from the edge of the crater here also made for some great photos of the bike. When you're traveling solo, you don't get too many pictures of yourself, but the bike appears in front of every natural and man-made wonder that you photograph. Eventually, you find yourself thinking, "What a lucky bike."

On the way down to Hilo I passed the Mauna Loa Macadamia Nut Visitor Center at a high rate of speed. In fact, all that I could read of the sign out front was, "Mauna Loa Mac———————————". It could have read, "Free Gold Bricks" and I wouldn't have stopped. When momentum and gravity are working for you on a bike, you don't stop.

I reached Hilo lickety-split, cycling past a few shopping centers until I reached the Waiakea Peninsula. It's just a little spit of land jutting out into Hilo Bay, but it has most of the hotel rooms in Hilo. In addition, it has a golf course, the Liliuokalani Gardens, and some waterfront parks. The only drawback to staying in one of the high-rise hotels is that you are in the landing pattern of the nearby Hilo International Airport. I took a room in the Hilo Hawaiian Hotel on Banyan Drive. Dignitaries and celebs from the 1930's planted the very mature banyan trees that now line Banyan Drive. About the only names that I recognized on the little plaques in front of the trees were Bobby Jones, Babe Ruth, and Amelia Earhart. My hotel is behind the Babe Ruth tree.

Hilo is known as the wettest city in the US. It's also famous for its occasional deadly tsunamis. There is even a Tsunami Museum downtown. It's a wonder that anyone visits here. But, I had great weather today, and more sunshine is predicted for tomorrow. The one thing that I couldn't help but notice, and it probably has a lot to do with the bad weather here, is that Hilo has more than its share of obese people. The residents are probably cooped up in their homes so many days that they can't get out and exercise. They can't do any gardening or take their kids to the playground. They're left with only indoor, sedentary activities to keep them busy. It's pretty sad.

Saturday, March 30th
Hilo - 0 Miles

Since Hilo is the largest city on the Big Island, and since I just cycled over Kilauea, I decided to take a day off. It might turn out to be a bad decision because it was a good day to ride, weather-wise. They don't get too many good weather days on the windward side of Hawaii. I read in my guidebook that they get measurable amounts of rain on 280 days in an average year. So, it rains four out of every five days. I don't like those odds. I definitely don't want to be stuck in my hotel room for the next four days, at least not without room service.

It was a typical rest day for me. I did a load of wash, updated my website, and spoke to family on the phone. Hilo doesn't have much in the way of tourist attractions other than the Tsunami Museum (possible slogan - "You'll Be Swept Away by Our Exhibits"). So, I watched the NCAA men's semifinal basketball games on the tube. It felt good to just kick back. I only hope that I don't regret it tomorrow.

Sunday, March 31st
Hilo to Honokaa - 43.5 Miles

I asked for a 6:00 AM wake-up call so that I could ride into town and attend the 7:00 AM Easter mass. Either the call was an hour late, or I fell back to sleep for another hour, but I arrived at the church at 8:00 AM. The mass must have started late because they were only half way through mass when I arrived. Stackable chairs and an awning were set up outside the church for the overflow crowd. A large screen TV on an A/V cart showed the outsiders what was going on inside. I stood behind the chairs, almost in traffic, for the final half-hour of mass. I'm happy to report that I survived another Easter Sunday mass.

During the 42-mile ride up the Hamakua Coast to Honokaa I gained 1,200 feet in elevation while still staying close to the ocean. There are a number of scenic waterfalls and steep drops along the way. There are no stores along this stretch of road from which to buy water, so I had to be careful with how much I drank near the end of the ride. I wish that I hadn't stopped to take so many pictures of the waterfalls because in the last five miles the skies just opened up and drenched me. I had to take my wet and fogged glasses off to blindly find my way to Honokaa.

The hotel that I had reserved a room in earlier in the day was one mile off the main Belt Road. After settling into my room, I rode down to the local supermarket for supplies. I spent the rest of the night indoors because of the intense rain. This is one soggy town. Even a rolling stone would gather moss here.

Monday, April 1st
Honokaa - 1.75 Miles

I'm still in Honokaa. It might be time to start building that ark. After raining hard all night, there was a brief moment this morning when it appeared to stop. Nature was toying with me because, as soon as I packed up the bike and stepped outside, it started to rain again. I got as far as Tex's Drive Inn restaurant back on the Belt Road before turning around. I realized the futility of cycling on such a rainy and foggy day. I couldn't see the cars, and they probably couldn't see me. I would have to cycle 20 miles, most of it uphill, to get over to the dry side of the island. And, there was no guarantee that it would be dry over there today.

So, I'm back at the Hotel Honokaa Club. Its been pouring all day. I know that I made the right choice to turn back. I'm just nervous about how long I'll have to wait here until there's a dry window of opportunity to get off this coast. I just hope that it's not 40 days and 40 nights.

Tuesday, April 2nd
Honokaa to Kailua-Kona - 59.77 Miles

It rained hard all night again. I was determined to get off this side of the island if it was at all possible. The five-day forecast mentioned rain for all five days in varying amounts. So, when it slowed down to a drizzle in the morning, and visibility through the fog increased to about a quarter mile, I went for it. I had to climb from 1,200 feet to 2,800 feet at Waimea. It was a gradual climb, and I had a good shoulder most of the way. I had to go without my glasses and rear-view mirror because of the rain and fog. I stopped a couple of times to wring the sweat and rain out of my gloves and do-rag. Farms bordered the road most of the way up. As soon as I came across the first couple of stores, the weather changed dramatically. I got the feeling that I crossed the threshold from windward to leeward right there. Did the rain from the east always stop right at that point? The people with businesses to the west of that point probably think so.

My front caliper brakes had frozen a bit in all of the rain. Fortunately, I came across a bike shop as soon as I entered Waimea. The shop mechanic greased the cable, no charge. I thanked him and headed off for what I thought would be a 2,800-foot descent to the Kona Coast. First, I passed Parker Ranch, the largest privately owned ranch in America at 225,000 acres. Then, I passed a large wood and stone sculpture that signaled the turnoff for Waikaloa. That's where I made a slight navigational error. I should have turned right at the modern art. Instead, I continued on

Route 190, the Belt Road. The next turnoff down to the coast was probably 15 to 20 miles down the road. So, instead of cycling through the Ironman lava fields, at sea level, along the coast, from luxury resort to luxury resort, I stayed on the very desolate Belt Road at 2,500 feet, looking down to where I wished I were. The Belt Road just rolled, and there were no stores to buy food or water. Of course, I ran out of water. I know that I could have gotten water at the luxury resorts down the hill.

At the first opportunity to hang a right and get down to sea level, I went for it. But first, I bought water, Gatorade, and a muffin in the market at the intersection. The ride down the steep slope was exhilarating, to say the least. I was using the brakes liberally and sitting upright to catch the wind, yet I still hit 45 mph. The crossroad dropped me off at the new airport. For the last eight miles from the Kona International Airport to downtown Kailua-Kona, I got to ride on some of the Ironman racecourse. It was the widest (at least 10 feet wide) and cleanest shoulder that I've ever seen. It's the perfect road for recreational riding and training.

I rolled into Kailua-Kona around 3:30 PM and got a room at the same hotel that I stayed in seven nights earlier. I checked my e-mail, called home to discuss my finances, took a quick shower, and then hustled over to a nearby travel agency to work out flight plans for tomorrow. I got there just as they were closing, so I'll return tomorrow. But, it looks like I'll be taking a direct red-eye to LAX. I can't wait.

Wednesday, April 3rd
Kailua-Kona to Honolulu - 13.48 Miles

I returned to the travel agency first thing this morning to book my flight. I got a different agent than last night. Tiger got me on a Hawaiian Airlines flight to Honolulu, and then a flight to LAX. She booked it for $475 through a consolidator. I just had to stop by the agency in an hour to confirm that the consolidator could deliver. At 4:00 PM I got the green light to start cycling to the airport.

I was able, after some investigation at the airport, to get a new bicycle box from United Airlines. From that point on everything went smoothly. I'm in the air now, over the Pacific, not watching the in-flight movie, *Ocean's Eleven*, because I didn't want to pay $5 for a headset. It's time to go to sleep.

Western United States

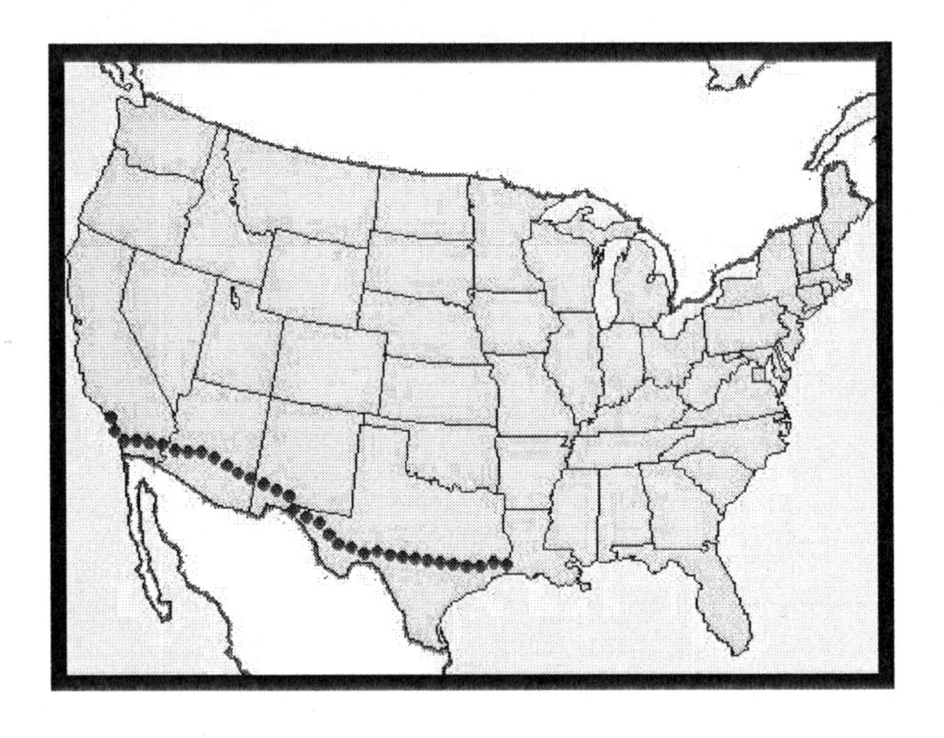

Thursday, April 4th
Honolulu to Sunset Beach, CA - 40.03 Miles

One year to the day after leaving the continental United States, I touched down at LAX at 5:30 AM today. I had considered spending a day or two in Los Angeles, but when I stepped out of the terminal I just wanted to start riding home. It was a cool Spring morning, and I was still sleepy from the flight. But, the pull from home is noticeably stronger now that there are no oceans in my way. There's just one more continent to cross, just a few thousand more miles.

I cycled this way before, on a trip from San Francisco to Tijuana in 1990. I have no maps until I reach San Diego, so I'm winging it. I'll just have to keep the Pacific Ocean on my right. That strategy worked fairly well today. Getting from the airport exit to the bike path along the beach may have been the trickiest part of the day. Once on the path, riding through Manhattan, Hermosa, and Redondo Beaches is a blast. I inadvertently took a zigzag inland route through Palos Verdes. West of Long Beach the ride took me through some rough areas, just as I remember from 1990. Workers were setting up for the Grand Prix in downtown Long Beach as I passed by. At Seal Beach, I stopped to take a picture of the bike in front of Clancy's Bar. If we Clancy's aren't cops ("Alright, Clancy. Take the boys and surround the house"), we're bartenders. The owner's son told me that they've been in business since 1957. By the time that I came across this Ramada in Sunset Beach, my lack of sleep last night finally caught up with me. Knowing that I'm on familiar territory, I'll sleep well tonight.

Friday, April 5th
Sunset Beach, CA to Dana Point - 36.38 Miles

It was another unimpressive mileage day, but I thoroughly enjoyed myself. Today's ride was mostly along SR 1, the Pacific Coast Highway, or "PCH" to the locals. In Huntington Beach I rode on a nearly empty bike path. The path along Newport Beach was much livelier. The day had warmed up, and there were people walking their dogs, running, rollerblading, and cycling on the path. Newport Beach is an extremely wealthy community. It's where the Republican Party has all of its money printed. The local Porsche dealership appears to be doing very well, also. I spent some time riding up and down the back streets, ogling the million dollar properties, before taking the short ferry ride back to the PCH.

At Laguna Niguel I stopped to look over the Ritz-Carlton property. I stayed there for a national sales meeting two years ago. It was a week of opulent living on the company's dime. The

Holiday Inn Express at Dana Point, where I'm staying tonight, is a little less opulent. There is no chandelier in the bathroom, and not even one private balcony. In keeping with the austerity of this evening, I had dinner at a 1950's themed Denny's diner down the road. Of course, I can order burgers and fries from here to Philadelphia, and I'll still come in over budget. Only a Newport Beach fundraiser could save the budget now.

Saturday, April 6th
Dana Point to Carlsbad - 45.5 Miles

I had trouble re-tracing the route that I cycled in 1990 today. It's not possible to get on a road along the beach and follow it all the way from Los Angeles to San Diego. There are inlets and peninsulas and dead-ends all the way. Add to that, a closed bicycle path through Camp Pendleton, and you soon realize that cycling here without a map is an exercise in frustration. I wasted eleven miles and almost one hour of riding due to the closing of the Camp Pendleton path. The Marines are running some serious exercises this weekend. I ended up cycling over ten miles on I-5, the major north-south thoroughfare on the West Coast, and the scene of most of America's best televised police chases. That was an exhilarating ten miles, to say the least. Just after pulling off I-5, I stopped into a gas station for a snack. The young clerk had seen me exit the interstate and asked why I was riding there. I told him about the Camp Pendleton path closing, and then about the extent of my trip. I had to laugh when he asked me if the trip around the world was "some kind of Forrest Gump thing." I'm going to remember that the next time I'm asked "why." It's as good as any explanation that I've given so far.

I had spent four nights at the La Costa Resort and Spa in Carlsbad a few years ago on business. It's one of the best spa resorts in the world. It has two championship golf courses, 21 tennis courts (hard, clay and grass), an awesome fitness center, and four restaurants. But, tonight I'm staying at the Carlsbad Surf Motel. It has a mini-pool and a vending machine.

Sunday, April 7th
Carlsbad - 0 Miles

It was a typical day off. I did a load of wash. I worked on the journal. I ate lots of stuff that wasn't healthy. The highlight of the day was watching the Carlsbad 5,000 Road Race that was run right in front of my motel. I missed the earlier heats, but the last two were the world-class men's and women's races. They drew a nice crowd along a couple of the main streets, and the spectators weren't disappointed. An American woman broke the world record in 14:14. It was nice to see other people working hard while I sat back and enjoyed a hot dog and Coke.

Monday, April 8th
Carlsbad to San Diego - 44.09 Miles

It's been a cool spring here in SoCal. I've been wearing my Gore-Tex jacket everyday. And, there are very few people on the beaches. Of course, the surfers are still out there. As I learned during my winter in Scarborough, Western Australia, a little chill in the air won't deter surfer dudes from catching the perfect wave. I probably passed more surf shops today than exist in the entire state of South Dakota. I also passed a lot of bicycle stores. At each store I pulled in looking for a replacement Gore-Tex jacket. I had no luck. I'm wearing a mail-order jacket that no longer repels water or breathes. In fact, it now does the opposite. I'm thinking of wearing it inside out tomorrow.

The first half of the ride today, from Carlsbad to Del Mar, was spent on the "Historic Route 101." The road stayed within a block or two of the ocean most of the way. At Torrey Pines State Reserve and Beach the road turned inland and up. It was a nice little climb up to the Torrey Pines Golf Club. Somewhere around there I missed a turn back down to the coast. I ended up cycling farther inland, over I-5. Eventually I found a road that took me back down to La Jolla. The village of La Jolla was established to house Southern California's lottery winners and professional athletes. I passed more vintage Porsche 356's here than exist in the entire state of South Dakota. I actually stopped into an upscale car dealership to ask about the availability of the Lotus Elise in the US. I had seen one farther up the coast, and I thought that they weren't legal. The salesman said that they still aren't legal, but will be next year. I've resolved to start playing the lotto more religiously and work on getting a tryout with the Chargers.

After cycling past all of the manicured properties of La Jolla, I entered the neighborhood where La Jolla's gardeners live. Surprisingly, the lawns aren't as well kept. I went through Pacific Beach and Mission Beach until I finally made it to downtown San Diego. There's an Oracle convention in town, so the hotels have jacked up their rates. I settled on a Super 8 motel at the edge of downtown for $69/night after passing on two hotels that were $129 and $189. That's probably more expensive than any hotel in the entire state of South Dakota.

Tuesday, April 9th
San Diego - 0 Miles

I slept late today, missing the free continental breakfast at the Super 8. Dang! I had to go out in search of a convenience store for my breakfast. I walked around the neighborhood last night looking, but I seem to be in a 7-11 free zone. I'm right at the edge of Little Italy, but I typically don't like foods that end in a vowel. The motel's front desk pointed me in the direction of a mom and pop mini-market that stocked Gatorade and mini chocolate donuts just two blocks away. Bingo! After a healthy breakfast, I took a ride into the heart of downtown to have the photo image files on my CompactFlash cards burned onto CD's. I looked for a bike shop with no luck. I didn't do much else today, other than sleep. I did have my first Jack in the Box hamburger tonight. Man does not live by McDonalds hamburgers alone.

Wednesday, April 10th
San Diego to Alpine - 32.38 Miles

I began my push east today, leaving the Pacific Ocean behind. Throughout almost this entire trip I've been able to get my bearings by keeping a large body of water to my right. Now, all that I'll have to my right is Mexico. I enjoy riding along a coast because the scenery and weather are usually very good, and because accommodations and services are easy to find.

The ride out of San Diego is uphill, way uphill. It will top out at over 4,000 feet above sea level near Pine Valley. I got a noon start today, so I only got 32 miles in. There are some nice suburban and exurban areas outside of San Diego as you make your way uphill. On the bike path in Mission Trails Regional Park I stopped to shoot some videotape when one of the dog walkers approached me to ask about my trip. It turns out that she was a bike trip leader with Backroads in Italy for six years. She made it sound like a great job. I'll have to keep that in mind when I finish this trip, assuming I ever want to touch a bicycle again. I probably could have gone farther today, but I liked the look of Alpine. I was also a little worried about the sun setting before I reached the next town with accommodations. I'm in an upscale motel next to a bike shop, a fast food restaurant, and a donut place. Why go any farther?

I surpassed 16,000 Km today. I'm closing in on 10,000 miles. I also found out that my state tax return was just deposited in my checking account last week. Unfortunately, half of that money will go to pay last month's phone bill. Voicestream just announced that I would now be charged for calls that I receive, not just calls that I place. The free calls that I received this past year while overseas had been a "gift" while they got their systems upgraded. I don't know whether to complain or thank them.

Thursday, April 11th
Alpine to Pine Valley - 23.98 Miles

I slept well last night, getting another late start. The climbing seemed more difficult today. My quads did not fully recover from yesterday's ride. The services are also becoming fewer and farther between. The one spot of civilization along the route was the casino and factory outlet center on the Viejas Indian Reservation. The casino looks like an oversized adobe house. And, the factory outlets included Nike, Reebok, and Eddie Bauer. The Viejas Indians don't need my money, so I kept moving.

I was stopped at Pine Valley for a quick snack when I noticed that my tire pump was missing. It must have fallen off of the frame's top tube earlier in the day. I immediately booked myself into the local motel. My cell phone won't work up here, so I borrowed the front desk's phone to call for a new pump. Unfortunately, the mail-order bike shops cannot ship overnight to this zip code. A bike shop in Alpine has what I need, but it's 18 miles back down the hill. The only taxi service in the area says they would charge $60 just to pick me up. There is a bus leaving for San Diego tomorrow at 8:40 AM, returning late in the day. I didn't want to waste a whole day for a new pump. Someone suggested that I cycle back two and a half miles to an Ace Hardware store, and I did. Ace has pumps, but only for tubes with schraeder, not my presta, valves. Returning back from that wasted five-mile roundtrip, I saw a cyclist just finishing a training ride. Jan, a triathlete from Phoenix, grew up in this area. He said the nearest bike shop east of Pine Valley is in El Centro. He offered me his CO2 cartridges, and I forced $10 on him. I'm about to ride into an area where self-reliance is critical, so it's comforting to know that I have air if it's needed.

Friday, April 12th
Pine Valley to El Centro - 73.08 Miles

I broke 10,000 miles today. And, it wasn't easy. I had to climb a few hills in the high desert before a long ride across half of the Imperial Valley. The only enjoyable part of the day was the 20-minute amusement ride down the In-ko-pah Gorge on I-8. Most of the route in the high desert was on the Olde Highway 80. I have no idea why they spell "Olde" with the "e". Maybe there's somebody employed by Caltrans with a sense of humour. The highway parallels I-8 through the desert. There's not much of interest to see up there, other than the Golden Acorn casino on one of the Indian Reservations. I didn't stop. Instead, I tried my luck on the ride through the Gorge, coasting at over 40 mph. I was too nervous to get into an aero position. I videotaped half of the ride with the helmet-cam. I'm disappointed that I didn't tape the entire ride because the camera was off when I screamed past the Border Patrol arresting about 20 illegal immigrants. I came within a few yards of the Mexican border back at Jacumba and wondered if I would see any illegals. Jacumba, by the way, has the smallest airport terminal I have ever seen. It looks like a tool shed.

I probably could have stopped at Ocotillo for the night, but I continued across the Yuha Desert to Seeley and El Centro in "the center" of the Imperial Valley. The map that I bought from the Adventure Cycling organization suggests taking SR 98 and S 29 to get to Seeley. The map addendum states that S 80 through Plaster City is 10 miles shorter but "in very rough shape." I can confirm that. The bike and I took a real beating on S 80. For the first time in ages I came across a loose dog that didn't like me in Seeley. I got over to the other side of the road, hopped off the bike, and walked for about 50 yards. The dog lost interest in me after that. I'm in a Super 8 motel tonight, and ready for a day off tomorrow. My quads are completely ripped.

Saturday, April 13th
El Centro - 0 Miles

I had a full day here in El Centro. I got the wash done. I hung out by the motel pool. I bought another pump in town. I updated my web page. I bought California and Arizona maps to help me decide if I want to follow the Adventure Cycling route, or try a few detours. I had a steak at Sizzler's. Yeah, it was a full day.

Sunday, April 14th
El Centro to Brawley - 18.93 Miles

The distance from El Centro to Brawley is only 14 miles. The next town after Brawley with a motel is Palo Verde, 70 miles away. I didn't want to cycle 84 miles in 100-degree heat over a 1,500-foot hill today, so I've split the ride in two. I went to the 10:30 AM mass at Saint Mary's in El Centro. That meant that I wasn't on the road until noon. No problem. Like most of the roads in the Imperial Valley, SR 86 is straight and flat, and has very few distractions. The only picture that I took during the ride was that of a sugar refinery silo. About 40 or 50 feet up the silo was a line marking sea level. I've been below sea level since Seeley. That may make this the low point of my trip, though it could be argued that my hospital visit in Mumbai was really the low point.

I celebrated my arrival in Brawley with a small Slurpee, then scoped out the available motels. The nicest one ran $69/night. I decided to stay at a less-luxurious motel for $49. I've just realized that I can't take a shower here tonight because the drain is clogged. You get what you pay for.

Monday, April 15th
Brawley to Palo Verde - 69.23 Miles

The Adventure Cycling map says that there are very few services between Brawley and Palo Verde, and they aren't kidding. Other than the little market in Glamis, it was just desert wasteland. In case the store in Glamis wasn't open today, I filled all three water bottles and strapped another liter of water to the bike before leaving Brawley. Thank goodness the market was open. That's where I stopped to have lunch.

Before I got to Glamis, I had to cycle through 10 to 15 miles of sandy desert. There were plows patrolling SR 78 to push the wind-blown sand off of the road. They weren't keeping up. The stinging sand was viciously sideswiping me. I probably still have sand in my right ear tonight. A few times I had to cycle clear over to the shoulder on the other side of the road just to avoid the encroaching sand drifts. I also had a near fall riding through one sand drift that was deeper than it appeared. Still, I didn't mind because I knew that, as I turned northeast to Palo Verde, I would have a strong tailwind. The slight change of direction occurred right after lunch in Glamis. For about 10 miles, I gradually climbed to 1,200 feet. The road rolled for a few miles after that, and then the real fun began. I dropped almost 1,000 feet to Palo Verde with a stiff breeze pushing me the entire way. I hardly had to pedal the last 30 miles. It was getting a bit late when I reached Palo Verde, so I took a room at the Lagoon Lodge motel. I probably could have stayed on the bike and sailed another 20 miles to Blythe, but I just wanted to get inside at that point. The strong winds were the big story on the local news broadcast. I guess today's tailwind was more the exception than the rule. I'm still keeping my fingers crossed for tailwinds tomorrow, though.

Tuesday, April 16th
Palo Verde to Quartzite, AZ - 44.3 Miles

I passed into my third state today. Only 14 more to go before I'm back in Pennsylvania. After an uneventful ride through Greater Blythe, California, I crossed over the Colorado River into

Arizona at 12:30 PM today. I had expected the Colorado to be much grander, but between the Grand Canyon and the I-10 Bridge I guess it's probably been dammed a few dozen times. It's legal to bicycle on I-10 in Arizona from the California border all the way to Phoenix, 120 miles away. I would love to do this, but after 13 miles on the highway today, I realize that it would kill me. The Arizona Department of Transportation cut rumble strips every 20 yards clear across the wide shoulders. Rumble strips are deep cuts in the asphalt designed to wake up sleeping drivers and paralyze cyclists. They loosen nuts, screws, and dental fillings. I can't endure another two days of that torture. I'll follow the Adventure Cycling route, which takes me north of I-10 and adds another day's riding.

Quartzite has the look and feel of a temporary town, as if it could be disassembled in a couple days and re-assembled down the road, just like a circus. It's a town known for its rocks, not for grapefruits or beef. There are no public gardens or manicured lawns. If there is any grass in town, it's probably in a museum. I couldn't help but think of the lines from Emerson, Lake & Palmer's *Karn Evil 9 - 1st Impression*: "There behind the glass lies a real blade of grass. Be careful as you pass. Move along. Move along."

Wednesday, April 17th
Quartzite, AZ to Salome - 41.1 Miles

I didn't expect today's ride to be as difficult as it was. The first part, on I-10, was alright. It was a gradual climb, and the Arizona DOT got the rumble strips right here. They don't cut clear across the shoulder, but stay next to the "out-of-bounds" line. At the US 60 turnoff, a long, gradual descent into the Ranegras Plain began. That's a funny name for a place that probably hasn't seen rain or grass in decades. During the entire 20 miles across the Plain, strong side winds and headwinds tortured me. It wasn't until I got over the Granite Pass at 1925 feet that I finally got some tailwinds. I sailed the rest of the way into Salome, but the damage had already been done. I was toast.

As I arrived in town I noticed a couple of touring cyclists right on my tail. They were a father and son, cycling from San Diego to Phoenix in six days. They started today at Blythe. We commiserated about the wind, and then asked at the Visitors Center about accommodations. There's not much of a choice in downtown Salome, so we're all booked into the same motel. I'll probably see them the next two days as we're all following the same Adventure Cycling route. Once again, it's good to know that I'm not the only idiot out here cycling through the Arizona desert.

Thursday, April 18th
Salome to Wickenburg - 56.62 Miles

I didn't see the father/son cycling team today. I think they got on the road early like most hard-working, God-fearing bicycle-tourists do. I, on the other hand, started my day with the slothful heathens after 10:00 AM. The ride today was more than a little bit boring. I stayed on one road, US 60, all the way to Wickenburg. Not that I had any choice. There are no parallel roads or alternate routes between towns out here. There are train tracks, but that's not an option for a cyclist who wants to retain his sanity.

If it weren't for the RV parks, this place would be empty. All of the old folks from the northern states descend on Arizona in the winter. They're called snowbirds. It's thought that since it doesn't snow down here, they're less likely to fall and break a hip. I'm passing through at the end of the snowbird season, so the RV parks look deserted.

At Wickenburg, I passed a number of motels as I cycled through town to the eastern edge. It was getting a little late, so I had a quick dinner at Burger King. Back in town I found a Super 8 motel a mile north of US 60, close to a Denny's restaurant. I kicked myself for not waiting until I checked into the Super 8 to have dinner. I'm never disappointed with a Denny's meal. The food is bland and inexpensive, just what I look for in a restaurant.

Friday, April 19th
Wickenburg to Mesa - 71.47 Miles

I didn't follow the Adventure Cycling route exactly today. Instead of leaving US 60 at Morristown, I continued on for a more direct ride into the Phoenix suburbs. It turned out to be a good move because I saved some miles, and I got to ride on a newly built road not yet open to traffic. They're doubling the capacity of US 60 around Whitmann. That's where I rode for about ten miles on the new asphalt without worrying about cars or trucks bearing down on me from behind.

After passing through Surprise (very nice) and Peoria (not as nice), I got onto the Arizona Canal Bike Path. It was a great way to enter the sprawling city. The path goes under most intersections and is perfectly flat. I was hoping to ride into downtown Phoenix and find a motel near the action (historical sites, shopping, entertainment). I just had no idea where that was in Phoenix. They don't have a Times Square or Sunset and Vine. Where did the Phoenicians gather on V-J Day? Where do they hold their parades? I had no idea. So, I ended up in Tempe.

Saturday, April 20th
Mesa - 0 Miles

There are people hooked to life-support machines who were more active today than me. Thank goodness the motel room came with a TV remote. Otherwise, I might have had to get out of bed to change channels. I just sat around the room, watching traffic go by on I-10. Hopefully, the lack of activity helped me recover fully. I've got some serious cycling to do in the coming week.

Sunday, April 21st
Mesa to Apache Junction - 29.07 Miles

Metropolitan Phoenix spreads as far east as Apache Junction. I took the easy ride out here to set myself up for tomorrow's ride to Globe. The roads around Metro Phoenix are laid in a grid pattern so, despite my best efforts, it's impossible to get lost. After only two hours on the bike, I arrived at the Super 8 motel in Apache Junction. The Super 8 is about a mile from downtown Apache Junction (i.e., the Wal-Mart). The only restaurant within walking distance is a Blimpie's. Dinner tonight was a 6" Three Cheese Sub with a bag of Sun Chips on the side. If an army travels on its stomach, I should have lost this war a year ago.

Monday, April 22nd
Apache Junction to Globe - 56.26 Miles

I really did not want to ride today. It took some real willpower to get out of the motel, and I didn't do that until 11:00 AM. The route elevation profile showed an almost 3,000 foot climb today. Temperatures were forecast for the high 90's. It would have been so easy to put that off for another day, but I knew that I would eventually have to do it. Why delay the inevitable?

Five miles into the ride I got a flat on my rear wheel. An inch long nail got through the tire's Kevlar belt. It occurred near the site of this weekend's "Country Thunder" music festival. I saw a poster for the festival yesterday. It looks like the "Monsters of Rock" tour, but with more pedal steel guitars and less spandex. They're working to prepare the site for the crowds, and the shoulder of US 60 was filled with debris for a few miles leading up to the parking lot turnoff. I took the opportunity to use the CO2 canisters given to me by Jan, the triathlete that I met in Pine Valley, California. They worked like a charm.

After passing over the Gonzales Pass at 2,651 feet, I cycled into Superior. The whole way I stared at the massive cliffs just beyond Superior wondering how I was going to get over, through, or around them. Usually I can see where a pass between mountains naturally rises. This just looked like an impenetrable wall. But, somehow a road was laid along the Queen Creek Gorge. The road included a large arched bridge and a long, uphill tunnel. It was 10 miles of climbing from Superior to the next pass at 4,600 feet.

Two miles from the pass I saw a couple who had pulled their minivan to the side of the road. They called me over as I approached to offer me water and Dr. Pepper. They explained that they had cycled this route last year on a trip from California to Memphis, and they knew that I would be thirsty. They did the 2,100-mile ride to attend the woman's 50th high school reunion. I quickly did the math and realized, "Hey, these folks are old!" I told them that I would have my 25th reunion this year, and that I hoped I was half as healthy as they were for my 50th. To paraphrase those old Honda motorcycle ads, "You meet the nicest people on a bicycle." That pleasant encounter gave me the energy I needed to go the last two miles over the pass.

The last ten miles on US 60 were through the Miami-Claypool-Globe tri-cities metroplex corridor. That was sarcasm. I was back in civilization, though. I took a room in the last motel at the eastern edge of Globe to cut down the number of miles that I would have to ride to the next motel in Pima. The Best Value Inn has a Ramada sign (used to be) and a Motel 6 sign (soon to be) out front, but no Best Value Inn sign. I'm sure there's an interesting story there, but I didn't ask. I just wanted to take a shower and crash. The lady at the front desk asked if I was claustrophobic when she gave me an "internal" room. That means that there are no windows. My room is off an internal hallway. The downside is that I don't know when the sun rises or sets. On the upside, I'm completely protected from nuclear detonations. I'll sleep well tonight.

Tuesday, April 23rd
Globe - 0 Miles

There hasn't been much to write about on my off-days lately. There are very few crusader castles or medieval cathedrals to investigate around these parts. My enthusiasm for small town museums has definitely waned. The local curators seem intent on beating their plowshares into my brain. I could write a book on the history of farm implements. So, I hang around my motel for the day, swimming in the pool, channel-surfing, sleeping. I won't touch the bike. With the terrain becoming more difficult, I need to give my body time to fully recover. I need to be fresh when I attack the mountain passes and great distances between towns out here.

So, although I'm cycling around the globe, I didn't even take a walk around Globe today. There's no need to expend that energy here, especially with some very tough riding expected in the next three or four days. I did study the maps today, and I'm a little concerned. I may actually have to camp out for the first time since Paros, Greece. There is a way to avoid camping, but I'll have to do 90 miles on the day that I cross the Continental Divide. I'm not sure if I'm up to that task. In the meantime, I have enough to worry about with tomorrow's ride. I would like to concentrate on one day at a time, but route planning is a bit like playing chess. You have to think three or four days ahead. I try to even out the daily efforts and still finish each day in a town with good facilities. I don't want to do 80 miles one day and 20 the next if it's at all possible to do 50 miles each day. I also try to schedule these off-days just before a day requiring a big effort. I'm hoping that by the time I reach the Gulf Coast, I'll be able to relax a little. The towns should be closer together and the terrain much easier. Famous last words.

Wednesday, April 24th
Globe to Safford - 75.81 Miles

The day off yesterday really helped. This ride today should have hurt much worse than it did. I felt strong on the hills, and I kept up a good pace. I hope this general feeling of invincibility lasts for a few more days. Once I get past the Continental Divide, it's all downhill. That, by the way, is pretty much how they define the Continental Divide. It's the locus of points on the map where bicycle-tourists can no longer complain about hills. Of course, there are still dozens of other hardships that we can complain about.

Today, I obsessed on the extremely low humidity in Arizona. It was 7% last night in Phoenix. When I wake up in the morning, my mouth is so dry that I almost gag. I'm beginning to get nosebleeds. I haven't had them since the Nullarbor. This may not compare with the Scott Antarctic Expedition or Donner Party hardships, but I still exercise my right to complain.

I almost had company on US 70 today. At Peridot I saw a large group of cyclists arriving at what appeared to be a pre-defined rest stop. They were heading west and had a support crew handing out drinks from a van. Then, in the little post office at Bylas on the San Carlos Apache Reservation, the postmaster asked me if I was part of the organized tour that had passed through town today. When I told him that I was going east he said there were two groups that passed through Bylas, one going east and one going west. He thought they were both on the Disney cross-country tours, going from Orlando to Anaheim and vice-versa. I was anxious to talk to anybody on the Disney tour because I wanted to know what his or her route through the Rockies would be. I never did catch them. I think I arrived after them in Safford. I took a room in the Best Western. They were probably a mile up the road in one of the other motels. Maybe I'll see them tomorrow.

Thursday, April 25th
Safford to Lordsburg, NM - 78.22 Miles

The Disney group must have left Safford at 7:00 AM, well before I fell out of bed. I know this because I asked a construction crew flag lady five miles out of Safford if any cyclists had passed before me. She said a large group passed around 7:30 AM. I also saw one of the motivational notes written in chalk on the road by the group's support crew nearby.

I couldn't decide whether to follow the Adventure Cycling route north on US 191, or to continue heading east on US 70. From information gathered from locals, which is always suspect, I thought that the ride to Lordsburg, New Mexico via US 70 would be flatter and would ensure me a motel room for the night. I didn't find out until later in the day, but the Disney group followed the standard Adventure Cycling route north on US 191 into the hills. When I arrived at the fork in the road, you could say that I took the route less traveled by, and it made all the difference. My apologies to Robert Frost.

US 70 did rise and fall, but very gradually. There were no steep grades to completely zap my strength. The one downside to choosing this lonely stretch of road was the limited services. The only place to get supplies was the town of Duncan, about 40 miles from Safford. I underestimated my water needs and ended up rationing the water before arriving in Duncan. I arrived bone dry and bought three liters of water and a Gatorade. Things went swimmingly after that.

I'm in a Holiday Inn Express tonight. It's just off the entrance ramp of I-10. I did not see a sign prohibiting cyclists, so I'm planning on riding the 58 miles to Demming entirely on the interstate tomorrow. I-10 has to be the best road to use to avoid the mountains. I think I made a smart decision to come this way. Let's hope my luck holds out for the next couple of days.

I saw one of the funniest road signs of the trip this morning. It said, "Prison Ahead. Do Not Pick Up Hitch-hikers." It sounds like they have a little problem with prison security around these parts. There were no hitchhikers in orange jumpsuits as I passed. It's my policy not to pick up hitchhikers on my bike, anyway.

Friday, April 26th
Lordsburg, NM to Deming - 59.59 Miles

I rode almost 60 miles on I-10 without receiving any warnings from the state police. And, I wasn't the only unconventional traveler on the interstate today. Shortly after leaving Lordsburg, I came across a guy who was rollerblading while pushing all of his gear in a three-wheeled jogger's carriage. Stacy told me that he was rollerblading cross-country to raise money for his infant nephew who was born with serious medical problems that required expensive treatments. Stacy was averaging 40 miles per day, but the rough surface on the shoulder of I-10 was slowing him down. He had to switch out of the skates and into sneakers on some stretches of the road. I was impressed with the way that he packed all of his camping gear on the baby carriage. Traveling cross-country by rollerblade seems an impossible task, but this guy is well prepared and motivated. He's already reached the Continental Divide, which we crossed over today. He'll complete his trip successfully.

The wind picked up throughout the day. It blew me right over the Continental Divide. I was making great time, and then the wind swung around from the south. It started to kick up more and more dirt devils. Eventually, I found myself in a full-blown dirt storm. The visibility was about 100 feet, and I was taking on dirt in the gears and various orifices. When you mix 45 mph winds with a flat, parched landscape, this is what you get. The cars on I-10 had slowed down, and their headlights were on. But, I still felt uneasy because of the poor visibility. To make matters worse, I had to repair a flat a few miles from Deming. The motel and restaurant strip of Deming was a sight for sore, and dirty, eyes.

Saturday, April 27th
Deming to Las Cruces - 68.91 Miles

I was a little reluctant to get on the bike today, after the effort that I had to put in the last three days. I was also a little nervous about cycling without any spare tubes. I used my last spare yesterday. I searched around Deming in the morning, but no stores carried tubes with presta valves. I knew that I could find a bike shop in Las Cruces, so I decided to go for it. Besides, there was a huge tailwind building up, and I-10 was flat to descending. It turned out to be a good decision. I had great weather the entire ride, including one of the best tailwinds of the trip. I sat upright and let the wind push me east to Las Cruces.

I'm in a nice motel tonight. It's the weekend, and there's a youth soccer tournament in town. Many of the players and their parents are guests here tonight. The kids are burning off a lot of excess energy around the pool and the common areas. I, on the other hand, had to struggle to find the energy to ride to the local bike shop for the new tubes. I'm feeling old tonight. It doesn't help that all of the soccer parents are younger than me. I need a day off.

Sunday, April 28th
Las Cruces to El Paso, TX - 55.02 Miles

Yee-Haw! I'm in the Great State of Texas. I reached El Paso after a leisurely ride from Las Cruces on a couple of shoulder-less roads that parallel I-10. Since it was Sunday, there were probably more drivers on State Routes 28 and 273 than usual. There were quite a few motorcyclists out for a Sunday spin. Everybody seemed to be heading to a Pepsi-sponsored wine tasting event. I didn't realize that Pepsi had gotten into the wine business while I was out of the country.

I didn't stop at the wine tasting event, but I did spend a little time in La Mesilla, a town dating back to the 1500's. At one point, La Mesilla was the capitol of the Arizona and New Mexico Territories. The main square, Old Mesilla Plaza, looks like many of the squares that I've seen in Spain. The most interesting building on the square is the old courthouse where Billy the Kid was sentenced to hang. It's now the Billy The Kid Gift Shop. A lifetime of dedicated banditry is immortalized in trinkets, tripe, and trash for the tourist trade. Billy must be rolling over in his grave.

I saw more inspirational messages written in chalk on the road by the Disney riders' support crew today. Once again, we're on the same route. I'm sure that I'm just a few hours behind them. Don't those people ever sleep in? I would love to discuss the route to Florida with them, but that would mean that I would have to wake up early one of these days. That's not going to happen.

On my way into El Paso I crossed over the Rio Grande, headed up the hill to Mesa Street, and then started looking for the perfect motel to spend three nights. I passed quite a few for a variety of reasons (not near a bike shop, no good fast food nearby, not a chain that I have a club card with). I was too picky. Before I knew it, I was in downtown El Paso. I ended up in the Presidential Suite of the Travelodge, just a few blocks from Juarez, Mexico. Up here on the ninth floor I should be able to watch smugglers wade across the Rio Grande in the moonlight. The Mexican influence is very obvious in this town, especially in the choice of television stations. About all that I can get is Spanish-language stations. I like *Sabado Gigante* as much as the next hombre, but *Matlock* just doesn't seem right in Spanish. There are more Spanish-language stations broadcasting here than in Madrid, no kidding.

I'm going to rest here for two days before heading out into the urban sprawl of West Texas. I won't enjoy cycling through the congestion, but at least I'll know that I won't be far from the next Starbucks.

Monday, April 29th
El Paso, TX - 0 Miles

The highlight of this day was getting a haircut. That tells you how active I was. I slept in even later than usual, and then took a walk around downtown El Paso. It amazes me how few people can be seen walking in the center of many large cities, especially outside of work hours. I think I stunned the three employees at the Burger King on the main square in downtown El Paso when I came in for a dinner at 7:00 PM. The place was empty. They probably hadn't seen a customer in well over an hour. I think they were preparing to shut down at 7:30 PM. I didn't have the nerve to eat in. I ordered take-away and walked back to the hotel to eat my burger and fries.

The room in the Travelodge is great. There's space to spread out. I have a bird's eye view of the city. The balcony is a nice place to relax. My only complaint is that the cold water is coming out hot. I told the front desk. The response from the maintenance department was that it had something to do with the limited number of guests in the hotel, and that I should let the water run for a minute or two before hopping in the shower. After five minutes of running both the shower and sink faucet, the water temperature finally approached tepid. There's nothing like a bracing tepid shower after walking around a city in 95-degree heat. If it's possible to work up a sweat in the shower, I did today.

Tuesday, April 30th
El Paso, TX - 0 Miles

I updated the web site for the umpteenth time today. I also hung out on the balcony reading the newspapers and soaking up the sun. More important than what I did do, was what I didn't do. I didn't get my clothes washed. I didn't replace the tubes on my front and rear wheels. I didn't get my chain cleaned. All that I can say about that is, "mañana." Being so close to Mexico, that should be an acceptable excuse. The knees and quads feel good after the two days off. I don't remember when I last had two days in a row off, but I should do it more often.

Wednesday, May 1st
El Paso, TX to Fabens - 33.41 Miles

I took advantage of the noon checkout time at the Travelodge by having a leisurely breakfast, washing my clothes, and replacing both front and rear tubes on the bike. This put me on the road too late to do a 60-mile day. It wasn't going to be a big mileage day anyway. State Route 20 heading southeast out of El Paso was a little rough, and had construction delays in some parts. There were also some intense dirt storms. I decided to call it a day when it became unsafe to ride because of low visibility. The late afternoon winds kicked up so much dirt that I felt that I wasn't being seen by the traffic. I found a small motel about two miles north of SR 20 at exit 76 of I-10. I'm happy to be indoors. I'll shoot for Sierra Blanca tomorrow.

Thursday, May 2nd
Fabens to Sierra Blanca - 61.38 Miles

I encountered more road construction crews today as I left SR 20 and turned due east on I-10 at Esperanza. It didn't matter much because I was able to cycle on a frontage road the last 17 miles up to Sierra Blanca. Although the road rose well over 1,000 feet, the grade was gentle. On roads like that, it's possible to get into a steady rhythm and avoid too much pain. I just get into a comfortable gear and go on autopilot. Occasionally, I get up out of the saddle to crank a bit harder. That keeps me from cramping up, and also relieves the pressure caused by the saddle. I change my grip on the handlebar every few minutes to avoid carpal tunnel problems. I am constantly monitoring my physical condition. There is any number of stress injuries that could sideline me. So far, my ankles, knees, hands, neck, and butt haven't failed me.

The rest stop at Esperanza was an interesting place. They had a row of wooden Indians out front, and a couple of live tigers in a cement cage out back. Political Correctness is a concept unknown to the people of Esperanza.

In Sierra Blanca I chose to stay in the less expensive of the two motels. The bed is a bit uncomfortable, I can't dial out on the phone, and I can still hear the trains passing through town. But, this old motel has a lot of character. The whole town seems to be in a time warp. It still gets its water pumped in from Van Horn, 35 miles away. That'll be my destination for tomorrow.

Friday, May 3rd
Sierra Blanca to Van Horn - 34.97 Miles

This was certainly an easy day in the saddle. Twenty of the 35 miles were cycled on another frontage road adjacent to I-10. A psychological boost was provided when I passed into the Central Time Zone just outside of Van Horn. There is only a one-hour time difference between Philadelphia and me now. With every milestone I feel closer to home.

Van Horn is one of the bigger crossroads in West Texas. State Route 54 and US 90 meet I-10 here. So, there are 17 motels for weary travelers to choose from. There are, in fact, two Best Western motels in town. I chose the Best Western farthest east in preparation for my next day of riding. Also, I had a coupon for this place. This is the beginning of the Cinco de Mayo weekend, so I have to be careful about finding accommodations. The guy at the front desk tells me that rooms are scarce around here this weekend. The cowboys will be coming into town for some fun.

Even in West Texas I'm on the lookout for antique autos. Across from my Best Western is the burnt out shell of an automobile museum. Among the cars still covered in dirt was a Stanley Steamer. The Stanley brothers' cars run on steam and take a half-hour to warm up before they can go anywhere. It's no wonder that I am drawn to these old Steamers.

Saturday, May 4th
Van Horn - 0 Miles

I couldn't decide whether to continue following the Adventure Cycling route out I-10 and over the Davis Mountains, or turn southeast on US 90 to Marfa. So, I did neither and slept in. Whichever route I do choose to follow, it's going to be a difficult ride tomorrow. So, this is a good day to take off.

Sunday, May 5th
Van Horn to Marfa - 75.56 Miles

When you have a day as tough as today, you spend most of your time on the bike mentally ranking the difficulty of the day with other tough days. This day was probably in the Top 10. I spent nine hours on the bike and only went 75 miles. I decided to deviate from the Adventure Cycling route. This time it may have been a mistake. I took US 90, which parallels the main rail line, to avoid the Davis Hills near the McDonald Observatory. Instead of hills, I got headwinds. The terrain was gradual, but the winds never seemed to ease up.

I knew that it was going to be a bad day when I was considering turning around just five miles into the ride. I thought that I had prepared well enough by filling all three water bottles with ice water and strapping another one-liter bottle of water on the back rack. Well, the temperature was in the high 90's, and the water didn't stay cool for long. I passed the abandoned town of Lobo at 25 miles. Then, at 38 miles I rolled into Valentine (pop. 217). The only store in town was closed, and I needed water badly. I walked the bike over the train tracks to the other side of town and found a church where I could draw water from the spigot in the men's room. The water was cool, but didn't taste great. And, it had to hold me for another 35 miles.

I struggled the rest of the way into Marfa. My legs were jelly by then. All afternoon I had been dreaming about that first Gatorade when I arrived in town. It never tasted so good. I found a reasonably priced motel in town, and then went back out for dinner at the Dairy Queen. I took advantage of the free refills on my Coke, and then bought three more large Gatorades at the Texaco station mini-mart. I was a human sponge, soaking up all of the liquid that I had lost throughout the day. My kidneys and I have survived another drought emergency.

Monday, May 6th
Marfa to Alpine - 28.35 Miles

I probably should have pushed on to Marathon today, but I didn't have it in me. I continued cycling US 90, watching the trains and antelope pass me. The only two sites of interest between Marfa and Alpine are the Marfa Mystery Lights viewing stand and the Paisano Pass. Marfa is famous for the eerie lights that often appear in the night sky southwest of town. Nine miles east of town, in ranch country, the state has built a very nice viewing stand and cyclist-friendly rest stop. Farther to the east is Paisano Pass, high point on the old Chihuahua Trail at over 5,000 feet. Surprisingly, I didn't see any of those little Mexican dogs on the trail today.

On the way into Alpine I met up with a local cyclist who offered to lead me in. He taught mathematics at the local college and was out for a quick spin. He gave me a great orientation around town. On his recommendation, I ended up in a very nice Best Western motel. I had the hotel pool to myself this afternoon. Tonight, I grabbed dinner from the Pizza Hut across the street.

Tuesday, May 7th
Alpine to Marathon - 31.11 Miles

I don't know where I got the idea that I would have tailwinds all the way from California to Florida. I had more of those southerly winds today. They were very strong and slowed me down a good bit. I'm glad I only had to cycle 31 miles to reach Marathon. Even though it was a short ride, I surpassed 11,000 miles for the trip.

There are two places to stay in Marathon, the motel at the western edge of town and the Gage Hotel downtown. The Gage Hotel was originally built in 1927 for a cattle rancher who came down to Texas from Vermont in 1878 to make his fortune. It's an historical site now, complete with metal plaque on the front wall and inflated room rates. I could get a room without bath in the main building for $69. The prices went up steeply from there. I decided to go back to the Marathon Motel for the night. It's $54, but the setting is very scenic. They have a series of two-room cabins placed around a central Spanish-style courtyard. The cabins have porches with comfortable rocking chairs to set a spell and enjoy the views of the newly renovated courtyard and the mountains beyond. It's a nice place, originally built in 1940. It was featured in the 1984 movie *Paris, Texas*. I think I'm passing through an area where a few movies were filmed. *Giant*, with Rock Hudson, Elizabeth Taylor, James Dean, and Dennis Hopper was filmed back at Marfa.

I saw a few more inspirational chalk markings on the road today from the Disney group. They're a little more faded, which tells me that I'm many days behind them now. While I was taking a few pictures in the middle of town I met Pat, a touring cyclist going the other way. He was going from the Carolinas to San Diego on a Moulton foldable bike. We spoke for a while, comparing bikes and routes. There seems to be a very small, and mobile, community of cross-country cyclists out here on the Adventure Cycling route. When two cyclists traveling in opposite directions meet, there is a great interest from each in what lies ahead. The topics of discussion usually center on road construction, sources for food and water, and motel/campground quality and cost. I always ask the other cyclists if dogs have chased them, and where. You can never have too much information.

Wednesday, May 8th
Marathon to Sanderson - 58.81 Miles

Boy, was it windy last night. I thought that the windows in my motel room would be blown in. I woke up a few times during the night because of the noise, the last time at 6:00 AM. I slept for another two and a half hours after that, only to be awakened by the chambermaid at 8:30 AM. On the way out of town I stopped at a cafe to check my e-mail. Then, I stocked up on groceries for the day (cheese peanut butter crackers and bottled water). Before leaving Marathon, I had to pump up the front tire. I seem to have a slow leak. The new self-sealing tubes worked well throughout the day. On the way to Sanderson I met two guys and a gal crossing from Florida to San Diego. They're doing it the hard way, into the prevailing wind. Westerlies were forecast for this afternoon. Of course, I got easterlies. Go figure.

I had planned on staying in Sanderson for an extra day to prepare for the 89-mile ride to Comstock. There's not much to see or do in Comstock, so I think I'll try to cycle out of here tomorrow. I'm expecting headwinds, according to the Weather Channel, and road construction. It should be a fun day. I need to get up early, but there's no alarm clock in this motel room. Aaargh!

Thursday, May 9th
Sanderson to Comstock - 88.15 Miles

I am no longer "west of the Pecos." I crossed over Pecos Gorge around mile 80. "Crawled over" is more like it. I'm happy doing 60 to 65 miles per day. Anything more than that and I feel like I'm pulling a train over the Rockies. I ended up spending 11 hours in the saddle today. I was on the road at 8:00 AM, and got into my hotel room at 7:00 PM, in time to catch NBC's "Must See TV" shows. It's strange that they get the Denver stations for their news and network programming here. They're not even in the same time zone.

The first 30 miles out of Sanderson was on newly paved road, but it was stones-over-tar paving. That slowed me down. Throughout the day the easterlies grew stronger. That slowed me down. The temperature was in the high 90's again. That slowed me down. And, all day I worried about the forecast of late afternoon thunder showers. Texas weather can be extreme, and there are no places to duck into if the skies suddenly open up. Fortunately, the storm held off until 10:00 PM tonight. It was a Duesey, too. I was happy to be inside watching *ER*, and not outside slogging my way up to Comstock.

I was so concerned about getting to the motel before the storm hit that I didn't take a one-mile detour off of US 90 to see Judge Roy Bean's place in Langtry. He was known as the "Law West of the Pecos", and was apparently quite a character. I did stop at the gas station/grocery store/Visitors Center right on the highway at Langtry to have a few Gatorades and cheese peanut butter crackers. I talked to a half-dozen touring motorcyclists while I had my well-balanced lunch. They told me that they average 500 miles per day. I was more than a little envious. On my next trip around the world I will probably ride a Harley.

Friday, May 10th
Comstock to Del Rio - 30.95 Miles

Despite being only a 30-mile day, I had to work to reach Del Rio. There were 30 mph headwinds the entire way. And, the mile long bridge across the Amistad Reservoir was downright scary. The blasts of air from passing tractor-trailers buffeted me right and left across the minimal road shoulder. Add to that a puncture to my front tire and a pair of weak knees, and you get a feel for how miserable this day was. There was, however, a pot of gold at the end of US 90 in Del Rio. This is a very tourist-friendly town. There are many hotel and restaurant choices for the road weary. And, I can definitely be described as road weary at this point.

My last care package, a FedEx envelope full of maps, was delivered to the Ramada on US 90. I felt a little guilty going in to retrieve a package addressed to "Michael Clancy – Guest", and then riding next door to book a room in the Motel 6. But, I saved a few bucks due to a promotion at the Motel 6. The folks in the Ramada were nice about it, though. I think they had a full house for an air show at the nearby Laughlin Air Force Base this weekend anyway. Dinner tonight was a sirloin steak at Appleby's in the mall. It's good to be back in suburbia.

Saturday, May 11th
Del Rio - 0 Miles

With six good days of cycling behind me, I decided to rest on the seventh. It was probably a good choice. The temperature reached 100 degrees, and yesterday's easterlies returned in full force. I only left my air-conditioned motel room to walk over to the air-conditioned mall. That 100-yard walk was enough exercise for me today.

Sunday, May 12th
Del Rio to Brackettville – 34.88 Miles

Monday, May 13th
Brackettville to Uvalde – 42.81 Miles

Tuesday, May 14th
Uvalde to Hondo – 42.9 Miles

Wednesday, May 15th
Hondo to San Antonio – 43.77 Miles

Thursday, May 16th
San Antonio - 0 Miles

Friday, May 17th
San Antonio – 3.42 Miles

Saturday, May 18th
San Antonio to Seguin – 38.17 Miles

[*All journal entries were saved to original and backup files in groups of seven days. The two files for these entries were both lost during a bout of sleep-depraved dementia on March 19th. Here's what I think happened this week.*]

US 90 served me well as I crossed West Texas, so I continued to ride it all the way into San Antonio. The Adventure Cycling route veers north into the Hill Country after Del Rio, but US 90 appeared to be a more direct route with fewer hills and more motels. I met a few other cyclists on the road who obviously felt the same way. One westbound cyclist gave me encouraging information about US 90 beyond San Antonio to just west of Houston. This fellow had cycled from Florida to Galveston along the Gulf Coast, and then went inland on US 90. We spoke for about 20 minutes, and afterwards I had a good feeling about the road ahead. There seemed to be no more insurmountable obstacles in my way. The mountains and deserts and bad roads were all behind me. So, I cycled the 160 miles from Del Rio to San Antonio without a care in the world. In Fort Clark Springs I stayed in the decommissioned fort's old officers barracks that have now been converted into a motel. My room was in Patton Hall. Originally built in 1870, Patton Hall is named after General George S. Patton who was stationed here as a Colonel in 1938. In Uvalde and Hondo I stayed in modern motels with all of the necessary conveniences.

When I arrived in San Antonio I cycled straight through the city to the east side where I found accommodations in the Red Roof Inn hard up against I-37. The next two days were spent enjoying the sights of the U.S.'s ninth largest city. First, and foremost, I photographed the loaded bicycle in front of the Alamo. Built in 1724, the famous front façade of the former Misión San Antonio de Valero was a photo-op that I couldn't pass up. Afterwards, I toured the grounds, listened to a lecture in the Cavalry Courtyard, and watched Alamo – The Price of Freedom at the nearby IMAX Theater. I'm not yet an expert on the struggle for

Texas' independence from Mexico, but I'm much more knowledgeable than I was a week ago. Besides the Alamo, I'll also remember the Tower of the Americas and Riverwalk in downtown San Antonio. The former is similar to the other towers that I ascended in Melbourne, Sydney, and Auckland. The latter is the shopping and entertainment district that runs along the banks of the San Antonio River. I thoroughly enjoyed my time in San Antonio. I found it difficult to leave on Saturday morning for the short ride to Seguin, but I had to keep moving.

Sunday, May 19th
Seguin to Flatonia - 56.99 Miles

Immediately out of the gate this morning I cycled on the frontage road alongside I-10, hoping to follow it all the way to Houston. One-quarter mile later it petered out, and I found myself pushing the bike up a cement bridge embankment to get on I-10. It's a difficult and un-graceful operation to lift a fully loaded touring bike over a guardrail. Once I was on the interstate's shoulder, I didn't leave it until I reached Flatonia. For the first thirty miles the shoulder had a rough surface that slowed my progress. After that, my pace increased noticeably. By the end of the day I think the constant headwinds of the last two weeks might have become tailwinds.

I'm staying in Grumpy's Motor Inn in Flatonia (Land of the Flat People) tonight. I'm not sure why it's called Grumpy's. The Indian owner doesn't look like Grumpy, or any of the other dwarves. Still, the rooms are clean. And, I'm 100 feet from a McDonalds and attached Shell mini-market. In honor of the Flat People, I'm going to have pancakes tomorrow morning.

Monday, May 20th
Flatonia to Weimar - 20.87 Miles

Aaargh! I realized this morning that I deleted the last seven entries in my daily journal on the Pocket PC last night. I wanted to crawl back into bed at that point. I've been feeling a little tired lately. I shouldn't have been working with the computer while I was so sleepy. You would have thought that I had learned my lesson after the blunder in Paros, Greece. Don't operate heavy equipment or computers while drowsy.

I might as well have stayed under the covers. I was so miserable that I only cycled 20 miles before throwing in the towel. Besides the usual headwinds and rough road surface, my allergies also kicked in. I took an allergy pill for the first time since New Zealand. I was cycling along the shoulder of I-10 when I saw the sign for a new Super 8 motel at the next exit in Weimar. It was no use soldiering on, so here I am. Hopefully things will go better tomorrow.

Tuesday, May 21st
Weimar to Sealy - 39.42 Miles

It was another sub-par performance today. Of course, there were more headwinds. I've also had one broken spoke on my rear wheel for days now. Today, a second spoke broke. I replaced one spoke while on the frontage road along I-10. That was a first for me. I've been lugging those spare spokes and spoke wrench around the world. I'm happy that I finally had a chance to use them.

I'm in an expensive Holiday Inn Express tonight. I should have shopped around. The motel rooms are a lot more expensive in the US, compared to the rest of the world. A strong dollar doesn't help me here.

Guess what Sealy, TX is famous for. Mattresses and high school football. There's a sign on the highway calling Sealy "Titletown, Texas" and listing all of their state 3A championship teams. I think there's also a Sealy Mattress factory outlet store here. I would love to buy a new mattress and box spring, but I don't think I could strap them on the bike's rear rack. Too bad. Another opportunity to pick up local souvenirs missed.

Wednesday, May 22nd
Sealy to Houston - 33.43 Miles

I finally arrived in Houston, and I have a problem. That sounds familiar, doesn't it? I woke up three or four times last night with intense pain below one of my molars. It's one of the teeth on which I've already had root canal surgery. I had planned on taking tomorrow off after reaching Houston, so in the morning I gritted my teeth (not a good idea) and packed up for the short ride into the city.

I took I-10 and its frontage road the whole way to the outer ring of the city at State Highway 6. The cycling was difficult, with bumpy and non-existent shoulders. The tooth didn't bother me until I reached my destination, Motel 6. This is a very busy neighborhood, but there are no dentists within walking distance. I had to call a taxi to take me to a dental clinic with late hours. The clinic took me as a walk-in and X-rayed me from all angles. They confirmed what I suspected. I have an infection at the base of the root canal. The dentist wanted to set me up for two visits, one tomorrow and the other in three weeks. When I explained that I can't stay anywhere for three days, let alone three weeks, he prescribed an antibiotic and a painkiller. I had the prescriptions filled immediately, and then took another taxi back to the Motel 6. The pain returned again tonight, so I took two painkillers just an hour apart. I should have waited four hours, but I needed that second pill.

Thursday, May 23rd
Houston - 0 Miles

Those painkillers can really knock you out. I slept like a baby last night and was drowsy all day. I can see why they don't want you to operate heavy equipment after popping one. Even operating the TV remote is a struggle. I barely left the motel room. I did walk across the street to the Jack in the Box for a burger. Other than that excursion, I just laid around the room all day, conserving my energy (sleeping).

I hope these antibiotics work. I won't be able to take care of any dental problems until I reach Philadelphia in six to eight weeks. When I finally do arrive in Philly, I'm going to make some lucky dentist a very rich man. It will be 18 months since my last visit. I usually have a check-up every four to six months. My mouth must be a disaster area by now.

Friday, May 24th
Houston - 43.86 Miles

Houston is a big city. It took me all day just to cross it. It didn't help that I kept changing routes to get across. Every time I stopped and asked somebody for the best way to get over to the east side I got a different opinion. I probably did 10 to 15 miles more than I needed to do.

I enjoyed cycling through Terry Hershey Park on a bike path. I also enjoyed cycling through the Bunker Hill area. It reminded me of the Main Line outside of Philadelphia. After that, the scenery went downhill. At one point, a cop pulled over and asked me where I was headed. He told me that I was in the most dangerous neighborhood in Houston. He gave me his suggestions for getting east, and I pedaled off with a little more vigor than usual.

I found a bike shop to have the other broken spoke replaced on my rear wheel. They told me that I was due for a rebuild of the wheel. They also pointed out that the axle is not spinning freely. Like my teeth, which are still giving me trouble, I may have to endure that discomfort until I reach Philly. The closer I get to home, the harder this trip is going to be.

Saturday, May 25th
Houston to Baytown - 20.63 Miles

I had more trouble with my teeth today. A different molar is causing me pain now. It's on the left side again, but on the top, not bottom. Any time I let the teeth touch it sends a sharp pain. That's what happened today. It's not easy to keep the top and bottom teeth apart when you're riding a bike over poorly maintained road surfaces. There is always a lot of teeth-chattering.

The pain got to be a bit too much after 20 miles, so I stopped at a Motel 6 here. The next motel appeared to be too far away. I needed to take one of the painkillers, and I knew that it would knock me out. Better to be lying in a motel bed than out on the shoulder of I-10 when the drowsiness kicks in. As it turns out, I slept for almost four hours this afternoon after taking the pill. I obviously needed the sleep.

I only ever get sick at the beginning of long holiday weekends. That means that I'll be in pain for three, rather than two, days before I can see a doctor or dentist. That's just the way my luck runs. After this long weekend is over, I'll visit another dental clinic to see if they can do anything to alleviate the pain. It's killing my daily average miles. I want to get back on track and start pushing out 60-65 miles daily. I can't wait to reach Philly.

Sunday, May 26th
Baytown to Winnie - 32.84 Miles

Once again, I've stopped short of my intended destination for the day. Beaumont was definitely within reach, just 25 miles down the road. But, the skies looked threatening early in the afternoon, so I stopped here in Winnie. There has been more talk of possible thunderstorms on the Weather Channel lately. I guess I psyched myself out, because the afternoon turned out to be beautiful. I spent it relaxing in my suite at the Holiday Inn, eating soft foods, and watching TV. The teeth are still a problem that I'll have to address on Tuesday. In the meantime, I'll keep moving east. I should be in Louisiana on Tuesday. I hope dentists there use Novocain.

I had another first today. I put my bike in the back of a pickup truck for a short ride over a bridge. I cycled on I-10 or a frontage road all day. At this one river, nine miles into the ride, the frontage road stopped and the I-10 bridge had no shoulder. It was fairly steep and about a half mile long. The traffic was what you would expect on a Memorial Day weekend. If I attempted to ride over the bridge I was going to make a lot of motorists very unhappy. I would also be putting myself at risk. I cycled under the bridge to look for a ferry. There was only a boat-launching ramp for the local fisherman. I explained my predicament to one of the guys, and he offered to take me over the bridge in his truck. I reluctantly agreed when he told me that otherwise I would have to ride about 25 miles to backtrack and cross at the next bridge upstream. This is what happens when you don't follow the researched routes by Adventure Cycling. Sometimes you run into roadblocks.

I figure that this ride over the bridge is the same as a ferry ride across the river. I don't want to get into the habit of accepting rides in pick-ups. I still want this to be an unassisted bike tour. But, I guess that I'm more of a pragmatist than a purist when it comes to touring.

Monday, May 27th
Winnie to Orange - 50.99 Miles

I felt a little better today. I had something like a tailwind for much of the ride. I didn't bite down hard on the painful molars while on the road. The shoulder of I-10 was smooth, although littered with Kevlar-piercing debris. I had one flat on the front tire. Most importantly, I'm just about three miles from the border. Tomorrow, I'm finally going to say "Adios" to Texas and "Bonjour" to Louisiana. If I push hard and don't take a day off, this time next week I could be in Florida, "Oy Vey." I'm not making any promises, though. I may stop tomorrow or Wednesday to have the teeth re-evaluated.

I spent almost all of the day on I-10 or its frontage road. I'm disappointed that I didn't make it to Beaumont yesterday. There was a nice place to stay just 20 miles from Winnie, on the southern outskirts of Beaumont. There are motels, fast food joints, and a Cineplex. I had a quick lunch there today. Beaumont was much nicer than I expected. I stayed close to I-10, but what I saw was clean and modern. The town of Orange doesn't look that bad either. I hope that trend holds as I ride through Louisiana. I'm thinking of staying on I-10 for a few more days. I'll decide tomorrow after I talk to someone in the Louisiana Visitors Center.

I haven't taken many pictures or shot much videotape in the past week. East Texas isn't too photogenic. There are no dramatic scenes, just flat landscapes. I'm not disappointed, though. Those flat landscapes are easy to cycle. And, that's just what I need right now.

Eastern United States

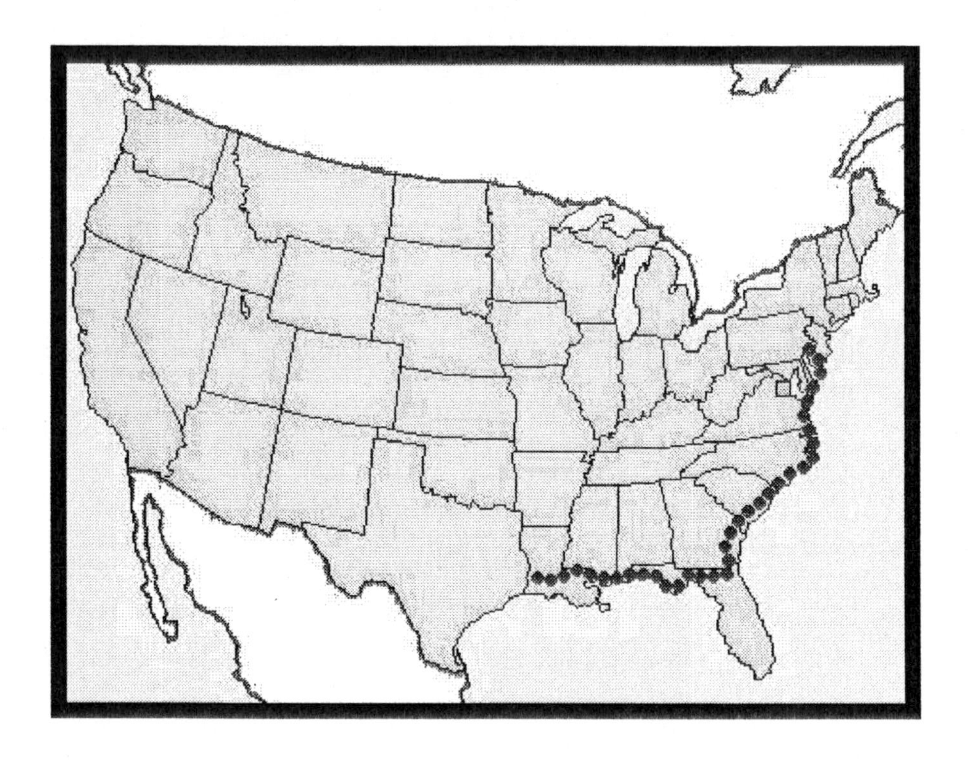

Tuesday, May 28th
Orange to Lake Charles, LA - 41.5 Miles

I crossed over the Sabine River into Louisiana on a brand new bridge. It isn't even opened yet. The bridge is fairly high, so I had a nice view of the surrounding countryside. Just over a mile past the bridge I rolled into the Visitors Center to get some information on road conditions. The lady working behind the counter suggested that I cycle on US 90, rather than I-10. No other information was offered. I got the impression that she was anxious to get me out of there. Then, on the way out, I noticed a sign on the door that stated that visitors should be properly dressed to enter the Center. My cycling shorts with the large posterior rip probably weren't acceptable. After 14 months in the saddle, it's only natural that I would appear a bit ragged. I'm something of a sartorial freak show now. It's going to take months for me to re-enter civilized society at the end of this trip.

I cycled US 90 to Westlake, just west of Lake Charles (the city) on Lake Charles (the lake). The only way across the lake was over a tall and long I-10 bridge. The 4-lane bridge had no shoulders, just a narrow, elevated sidewalk between the speeding tractor-trailers on the left and a low iron railing, leading to certain death, on my right. I gripped the handlebar so tightly as I slowly peddled across that I had sore hands when I reached the other side.

I took a few pictures on the lakefront before it started to rain. Then, I cycled a few more miles east to find a motel. I'm in the Days Inn on Martin Luther King Boulevard. Generally, I try to stay off of MLK Boulevards. I feel more comfortable on Poplar Place's or Whippoorwill Lane's, but that's where the motels are in Lake Charles.

Wednesday, May 29th
Lake Charles, LA - 0 Miles

As I was slowly preparing to get on the road today, I noticed that the weather outside was dreary. I turned on the Weather Channel to see the latest satellite image of Lake Charles. Sure enough, there was a storm fast approaching. My procrastination paid off. The rain started at 11:30 AM and continued all day. It could have been a miserable afternoon slogging it through Louisiana in the rain. Instead, I extended my stay here. Thank you Weather Channel.

Thursday, May 30th
Lake Charles, LA - 0 Miles

Well, the rain never really stopped. It rained all last night and all day today. I've developed a bad case of cabin fever. I have to get out of here tomorrow. There may be a window of opportunity in the morning. I'm setting the alarm clock for an early departure tomorrow.

Friday, May 31st
Lake Charles to Jennings - 34.14 Miles

Even though it was a short distance to Jennings, I got in a good workout today. The forecast for this area included rain and possible thunderstorms around noon. Around 25 miles into the ride the skies grew ominous. There were a few spritzes of rain, too. I did the last nine miles as fast as I could. I did not want to be stuck out on the interstate in a thunderstorm. I reached the Holiday Inn (with attached Denny's) just in time. As I checked in, the skies opened up. There never was thunder, and the downpour stopped within thirty minutes, but I was still happy to be inside looking out.

I tried riding on US 90 for some of the ride, but without shoulders it was more dangerous than I-10. In some stretches I-10 wasn't so hot either. The shoulder was crumbling. I bounced around for a few miles on those ragged shoulders until my hands, wrists, elbows, and shoulders were numb. That took my mind off of my numb feet, knees, and butt.

I had a sirloin at Denny's tonight, my first sit-down meal in ages. I even wore long pants and a collared shirt to dinner. I almost felt civilized. That's in contrast to my lunch today, peanut butter crackers and Gatorade eaten while sitting on a curb at a gas station. Very dignified.

Saturday, June 1st
Jennings to Lafayette - 52.42 Miles

"Standing on a corner in Lafayette, state of Louisiana" - Paul Simon on *That Was Your Mother* (*Graceland*). Actually, I'm sitting in a motel in Lafayette. I'm just happy to be indoors. I don't think any more dogs can terrorize me in here. This was the worst day of the trip, so far as dog attacks are concerned. I had three run-ins with five separate dogs on US 90. I spent the last half of the day on I-10, although I think that it may be unlawful to do so now. Who cares? If the police don't enforce the dog control laws here, they probably won't enforce the bicycle traffic laws either. I'll take my chances with the 18-wheelers on I-10 rather than Bubba's dogs on US 90. I can't wait to get out of Louisiana and back into a first world country.

Another minor annoyance is that I'm ready to do a load of wash and none of the motels in Lafayette have guest laundry facilities. At least that's what a couple of motel receptionists told me tonight. I had to hand wash a few items that will not be dry tomorrow morning. I'm already looking forward to putting on soggy clothes tomorrow. It's a great way to start the day.

I'm shooting for Baton Rouge tomorrow. Should be interesting. Fifty-two miles. Entirely on I-10. No parallel roads. Possible construction work for many miles. Twenty-five miles on a causeway over swampland. A trucker told me that there was a wide shoulder on the causeway. I'm keeping my fingers crossed.

Sunday, June 2nd
Lafayette to Livonia - 54.37 Miles

It was another tough day at the office. Halfway across the 20-mile swamp on I-10, a state trooper pulled me over. He took my license and went back to the squad car to check for prior bicycle infractions. When he returned he asked if I was carrying any firearms. "No. I'm from out of state" was my first thought. Then, he told me that it's illegal to bicycle on any interstate in Louisiana. I had to get off at the next exit. That exit put me on a gravel road 18 miles from any other roads. It also took me back northwesterly. As soon as I got on US 190 and headed east again, toward Baton Rouge, I found myself on another causeway, similar to the I-10 causeway through the swamp. Only this one was seven miles long and had no shoulder. The state trooper had ordered me onto a far more dangerous road. My water bottles were empty by then. Halfway across the US 190 causeway a trucker blasted his horn just as he passed me, trying to shake me up. I've been coming across more yahoos like this lately. I take comfort in the fact that they will soon be candidates for the Darwin Awards.

I was fed up when I finally reached a motel in Livonia, 24 miles from Baton Rouge. As Dennis Miller would say, "I don't want to get off on a rant, but..." Louisiana sucks. I say we should give their star on the flag to Puerto Rico and sell the state back to France. I'm willing to start the petition. Of course, France may not want it back. Maybe Haiti would want to colonize Louisiana. The funny thing is that the slogan on their license plates says "Sportsman's Paradise." If you can remain upright in a flat-bottomed fishing boat after your sixth beer they consider you a sportsman. But, bicyclists are treated like intruders. They might as well put signs up at the borders that say, "Cyclists Not Welcome." I just want to get out of here before I catch rickets.

Monday, June 3rd
Livonia to Denham Springs - 42.38 Miles

I had a better day today. It only rained a little as I arrived at the Holiday Inn here, just off of I-12. The big event of the day was that I finally crossed the Mississippi River. There is no documentation of that feat because, once again, Louisiana saw fit to squeeze four lanes of traffic over a bridge suitable for two lanes. It was 100 feet up and a mile across. I think they even raise the speed limits on their bridges, just to make it interesting. There was no shoulder or curb to stop and take pictures. I hardly looked left or right, or even straight ahead, while I screamed across the bridge in my biggest gear. I spent most of the bridge crossing looking through the rear view mirror, searching for twitchy drivers, trying to decide when to ditch the bike and grab for the railing.

I didn't get as far as I had hoped, but I did put 42 miles behind me. I'm still on target for getting out of here in two days. East of Baton Rouge, US 190 was OK to ride. I hope that holds up until I hit the border. Then, I'll just have one more Louisiana bridge crossing adventure before I'm on the Gulf Coast. After that, it's just casinos and oilrigs all the way to Florida.

Tuesday, June 4th
Denham Springs to Hammond - 29.54 Miles

My average daily miles have really taken a hit lately. I didn't even reach 30 miles today. There are, of course, many good reasons for the downturn in productivity (business-speak). I spend my hours on the bike collecting and cataloging the excuses. That's probably a counter-productive exercise, but it's comforting to believe that I was only able to ride 29 miles today because of friction in my right pedal's axle.

The first 25 miles on US 190 had no shoulder. I shared the narrow road with many pick-ups and beer trucks. Most of the drivers on the 55 mph road were nice enough to take their foot off of the accelerator as they squeezed past. One driver in a pick-up encouraged me to "get a job." I didn't hear the rest of his statement as he flew by me. Just before I arrived in Hammond there was finally a shoulder. A state government car had pulled over and the driver got out to flag me down. For a split second I thought that I was about to be kicked off another road in Louisiana. It turns out that the driver works for the Department of Agriculture, and is a local cyclist. I was shocked to hear that there are local cyclists in Louisiana. For a good 10 minutes Ray gave me excellent directions for the most enjoyable ride to Mississippi. He also told me where the bike shop in Hammond was located so that I could buy a couple more spare tubes. With Ray's directions, I should be in Slidell tomorrow afternoon before the rain hits, assuming I get out of bed early enough. That will eliminate one of my best excuses.

Wednesday, June 5th
Hammond to Slidell - 62.99 Miles

I went over 12,000 miles for the trip today. I almost didn't. I had a late start and got stuck in a noon downpour. I waited out the downpour at a Wal-Mart Distribution Center, talking with the workers as they took their breaks. They asked the usual questions. I've started telling people that I started in Los Angeles. It easier to explain and it cuts the number of questions in half. One of the guys asked how many miles it was from Los Angeles To Louisiana. I was stumped. I know the mileage from Portugal, but not Los Angeles. I said it was around 2,000 miles. I hope that's right. The workers on break were almost all black men. When one of the guys said, "You would never catch a black man doing that", we all had a good laugh.

It was still very overcast as I cycled to Covington. I took some time there, trying to decide weather to find a motel or to continue on to Slidell. While I was thinking it over, I went into the library, got on their Internet, and transferred more money into my checking account. Outside of the library a local told me about the Tammany Trace, a 25-mile bicycle path that would take me from nearby Abita Springs to just outside of Slidell. He was also encouraging about the afternoon weather. So, I decided to shoot for Slidell. It turned out to be a good decision, although I did get stuck in a downpour in the last five miles. The Trace is well maintained. It was an easy ride, and there were no dogs allowed. It wasn't until I was forced off of the Trace due to a bridge outage that I met another angry dog. Later, I met a father and son out for some exercise on their bikes. I picked up my pace with these two. Still, I didn't reach my Days Inn until 6:30 PM. I am ready to sleep tonight.

Thursday, June 6th
Slidell to Biloxi, MS - 56.51 Miles

I have two reasons to feel good today. I'm finally out of Louisiana, and I've finally reached the Gulf Coast. I could see an immediate improvement in the quality of the roads when I crossed the border. It was a cloudy morning, but I didn't mind. By the time I reached the white sandy beach at Pass Christian, after the long ride over the bridge from Bay St. Louis, the day turned beautiful and sunny. I stopped to take pictures beside the beach. I even sent SMS messages home with the good news. I was on top of the world, Ma.

The rest of the Mississippi coast was built up. I passed some historic mansions on the waterfront in Pass Christian, and then some casinos in Biloxi. It felt good to be riding along a coast again. As long as I kept the beach on my right I couldn't get lost. The traffic was a little heavy, but there was still enough room on the road for a loaded bicycle. With every passing day the trip gets easier.

Friday, June 7th
Biloxi to Bayou La Batre, AL - 51.21 Miles

I didn't make it to Dauphin Island as I had hoped, but I'm satisfied with my progress today. The temperature was 100 degrees at noon, and the humidity was so high that a person would need gills to breathe. I was sweating this morning even before I got on the bike. I replaced the rear tube and swapped out the rear tire for the reserve. There was a shard of glass and a small nail causing slow leaks in the tube. In places, the rubber on the tire had worn through to the cord.

On the ride out of Biloxi I saw the famous lighthouse on a median strip between four lanes of traffic. It must be bizarre to be the keeper for that lighthouse. Instead of supplies being shipped out once a week, he can just run across a couple lanes of traffic for a Slushee anytime he wants.

I saw more casinos on the Mississippi coast today. Musical acts playing in the big rooms down here in the near future are Styx, Jethro Tull, and Blondie. I guess Wayne Newton can't leave the desert. John Tesh, on the other hand, is playing at one of the casinos tonight. He can play Mississippi in the summer because of his alien gills.

The skies were extremely threatening late this afternoon. I had already gone about eight miles past Pascagoula when I took refuge at a roadside stand on the Mississippi/Alabama border. The little store was attached to the owners' house. The lady of the house just opened up a window with attached counter and took my order. I drank my Coke and stepped out from under the overhang every two or three minutes to see if the huge black cloud had disappeared. It never really moved, but I could see that it was pouring back towards Pascagoula, so I got back on the bike and headed into Alabama. The first town, Grand Bay, didn't have any accommodations. I should have known that ahead of time because I got back onto the Adventure Cycling route here. Their maps show where all of the hotels, motels, and campgrounds on the route are located. I saw that there was one motel in Bayou La Batre, nine miles farther on. I called ahead and booked a room, after some area code hassles. I'm settled in now, and for the second night in a row I had my dinner at a Sonic Drive-In. I'm hoping to be near Pensacola tomorrow night. That would put me in four states in four days. I may take a day off after that.

Saturday, June 8th
Bayou La Batre to Orange Beach - 48.32 Miles

August comes early in Alabama. It was a tad humid today. I may have even perspired a smidgen. That is to say, I left a 48-mile trail of sweat on the Alabama roadways. I missed the ferry that travels across the mouth of Mobile Bay by 10 minutes. Two hours later I caught the next ferry. It had been delayed by an hour. It was a frustrating feeling, waiting to take the 40-minute crossing. I kept thinking that if I hadn't stopped for a Gatorade at the convenience store on my way onto Dauphin Island, I might be on the other side of the bay, riding towards Pensacola.

The cycling on the other side of the bay was enjoyable, but it was too late to reach Florida tonight. It's Saturday night, and there are no rooms until Pensacola. I checked everywhere, but to no avail. If only I didn't buy that Gatorade. Now, for the first time since Paros, Greece, I am camping out. And, I am not a happy camper. I'm being eaten alive by the bugs every time I leave the tent. What the bugs don't get, the gators will probably devour while I sleep. Dinner was lemonade and peanut butter crackers. No Gatorade.

Sunday, June 9th
Orange Beach to Pensacola, FL - 29 Miles

I had visitors at my tent site last night. I didn't hear them, but my bag of food was taken. I suspect it was raccoons. I put the unopened bread and crackers into a large black trash bag and rested the bag onto my aero bars last night. The bike was leaning against a picnic table, so I guess the thieves climbed up onto the table and grabbed the whole bag. The area looked undisturbed, so the raccoons must have drug the big bag into the woods and had a feast.

It rained very hard this morning. Being that it was my first time in a tent in a year, that was bound to happen. I noticed that the rain fly and tent floor are not as watertight as I would like. Fortunately, the rain stopped around 9:00 AM because I had run out of dry spots in the tent to stack all of my stuff. I took the tent down and laid it out in the sun to dry, and then spent the next half-hour doing battle with the local insects. After loosing a pint of blood to the mosquitoes and gnats, I packed up everything and hit the road. The weather was less humid, but the headwinds were strong after the morning storm had passed.

The big event of the day was crossing into Florida. I took the obligatory photo of the state "Welcome" sign, and then continued on towards Pensacola. I should have checked out the Naval Air Museum, but I was too anxious to get to a motel and take a shower. I think my days of camping out for days at a time are well and truly behind me. I've become soft in my old age. I ended up at a Super 8 a few miles off-route on Naval Boulevard. It looks like a nice neighborhood to dry out and relax for a couple of days. There's a laundromat across the street and a bike store a couple of blocks away. What more could I ask for?

Monday, June 10th
Pensacola, FL - 0 Miles

Another day off, another load of wash done. In fact, I washed everything including the tent, sleeping bag, and sleeping pad. Then, I went across the street and bought a bottle scrubber and some dish detergent for cleaning my water bottles. God only knows what was breeding in those bottles. They were like three petrie dishes on wheels. I could have sent them back to one of the nephews for their Science Fair project. I'm amazed that my weak constitution hasn't suffered more on this trip. Other than the Mumbai and Moorea incidents, I've managed to keep my insides inside.

I continued my shopping spree this afternoon when I cycled down the road to a local bike shop. I bought a ventilated triathlete's hat and CO2 canisters to pump up the tires in a roadside emergency. I was really hoping to find a new pair of shorts to wear over my padded shorts. I've worn my current shorts clear through. I won't be arrested for indecent exposure, but I could be picked up for vagrancy. I've got to find a new pair before I end up on Mr. Blackwell's list.

Tuesday, June 11th
Pensacola, FL to Destin - 57.36 Miles

I officially started riding the "Redneck Riviera" today. The beaches on the Florida Panhandle are popular vacation spots for Southern families. I cycled through downtown Pensacola before I hit the beaches. If you can put up with the occasional fighter jet roar, it seems like a great place to live. It was the site of one of the earliest European settlements in the New World in 1559. It's amazing that it's not more built up. The best thing about the town is that it's only two easy bridges away from the beach.

Pensacola Beach and Navarre are both very laid-back summer resort communities. The houses are not lined up along the few streets in an orderly fashion. Rather, they appear to be haphazardly dropped on the thin strip of sand between the Gulf and the bay behind. Maybe they just get moved around with every passing hurricane.

I managed to get another flat on the rear wheel. The tires are definitely on their last bit of rubber. Baldness works for me, but not my tires. It's not safe. I need to find a couple Avocet K/Cross tires soon.

I had a funny encounter with the young girl at the Tourist Information Office in Destin. She asked about my trip, and when I told her that I was cycling around the world she asked me, "Have you slept?" She thought that I had undertaken some sort of endurance test. If I had gone 14 months without sleep, I probably wouldn't have responded so politely. I quickly got out of there, realizing that any information that I got from her was bound to be suspect.

Wednesday, June 12th
Destin to Panama City Beach - 50.8 Miles

I found a bike shop in Destin with one Avocet Cross/K tire. It was pure luck. It was the owners last, and he gave it to me at a discount. That may be the last tire that I need to reach Philly.

There is a lot of construction underway on US 98, so I stayed off of it as much as I could today. There were a few scenic routes that stayed close to the coast. I even spent about 20 miles on a bike path/sidewalk. I went through a couple of brand new towns as well. This looks like a growing area with all of the new home and road construction. I had a tailwind for most of the afternoon. I don't know how long it's been since my last westerly. I hope it continues for a few more days until I reach the Atlantic Ocean. Then, I'll be ready for some more southerlies to push me up the coast.

I'm in Panama City Beach tonight. This is Party Central on the Redneck Riviera. They have the largest disco/dance club in the U.S. here, Club La Vela. It can hold up to 7,000 Tony Manero's. I saw a few tonight out on their rented scooters, cruising the strip, honking their horns. As Dan Akroyd said in the SNL sketch that sent up Saturday Night Fever, "to be young, stupid, and have no ambition." That's the life.

Thursday, June 13th
Panama City Beach to St. Joe Beach - 55.7 Miles

The route today was not as scenic as I had hoped. Panama City has some rough sections, and I rarely saw the beach as I rode through Tyndall Air Force Base. The road through the base, US 98, does have wide shoulders and smooth blacktop. It's lined with tall pine trees on either side for miles. There is a lot of jet fighter training activity behind the trees and overhead. Unfortunately, I couldn't enjoy the air show because I ran out of water near the north end of the base. I was parched by the time I reached the southern edge of the base. I re-supplied and relaxed at Mexico Beach, and then continued on.

After Mexico Beach, I finally reached the Eastern Time Zone. I was last in this time zone 14½ months ago. I realized that I wasn't going to reach Apalachicola today at that point. I had been slow going through Panama City and Tyndall Base, and I was loosing an hour on the clock. So, I decided to ride to Port St. Joe, the last stop before a 24-mile inland ride to Apalachicola. At Port St. Joe I found the only motel under reconstruction. I had to cycle back three miles to the Dixie Belle Motel north of town. There I found that the last room had been given away 15 minutes before I arrived. That meant another five mile backtrack to Saint Joe Beach and the Gulf Sands Motel. That means I wasted 16 miles of cycling today. I'm frustrated, so I'm going to bed early. A good sleep should ease my disposition.

Friday, June 14th
St. Joe Beach to Carrabelle - 56.78 Miles

I started out today by re-tracing the eight miles to Port St. Joe. If I were ambitious, I would have left US 98 then and cycled out to Cape San Blas and the St. Joseph Peninsula to see the best beaches in the continental US, according to "Dr. Beach." But, my reserves of ambition have all been depleted. I only have one focus now - Philadelphia.

So, I stayed on US 98 to historic Apalachicola. The town has a very interesting cemetery where casualties of the Civil War are interred. There's also an old church, originally manufactured in New York State and shipped down here in pieces to be assembled. But, the historical fact that caught my attention was that John Gorrie invented the modern refrigeration process here in 1851. This place is so hot that they must have canonized the guy. There is a museum in his honor in town. Of course, I didn't enter the museum, the church, or the cemetery. I had to stay focused.

After crossing another long bridge between Apalachicola and Eastpoint I stopped to call ahead for a motel room in Carrabelle or Lanark Village. Five motels turned me down. They fill up fast here on summer weekends. To make matters worse, there's a big fishing tournament taking place this weekend. Finally, the Georgian Motel in Carrabelle said they had a cancellation, but they could only offer the room for a minimum of two nights. I didn't need the rest, but I took the room anyway.

I passed 20,000 Km today. I celebrated with a grilled American cheese sandwich from Subway. I'm seeing tiny lizards on the wall of my room tonight. I hope that's not a bad reaction to the cheese.

Saturday, June 15th
Carrabelle - 0 Miles

Today would have been a nice day to ride, but these days are also good for relaxing. So, I spent some time in the motel pool. I worked a little on evening out the weird cyclist tan. I took a walk around downtown Carrabelle. I called home to wish Dad a Happy Father's Day. The day wasn't totally unproductive. I did get the laundry done.

One of the town's big events is the annual Father's Day weekend saltwater fishing contest. This afternoon I witnessed some of the awards ceremony outside of a local restaurant. On the way back to the motel I saw the town's real claim to fame, the world's smallest police station. It's a phone booth. That's not a punch line. They really have a phone booth painted blue with the police logo on the windows. It's been Guinness-certified, so it must truly be the smallest. There's an old police cruiser parked next to the station/phone booth to add authenticity. But, there's hardly enough room to swing a billy club, so I think it might just be a tourist trap. The real police work probably takes place a block away at a more solid police station. I'm not hanging around to find out. Tomorrow morning I'm back on the road.

Sunday, June 16th
Carrabelle to Tallahassee - 67.52 Miles

I took a couple pictures of the world's smallest police station before leaving Carrabelle this morning. Then, I followed US 98 along the coast up to Saint Mark's. Since it's Sunday, there was more traffic on the road than usual. Lots of folks were pulling boats. They were all very courteous as they sailed past me. At Saint Mark's I got onto a rail/trail that took me over 10 miles to the outskirts of Tallahassee. You gotta love the rail/trails. They shoot right through forests, fields, and neighborhoods with hardly a reason to stop. They're like interstates for cyclists. I did stop at one point to watch one of Florida's protected turtles feeding near the path. Mesmerizing. I took a few pictures and continued on.

Tallahassee is a fairly compact capitol city. It's also very clean. I took a few more pictures downtown, including shots of the imposing State Capitol building. Then, I went north towards I-10 to find a motel. I found a Super 8 near a Boston Market restaurant and settled in for the night. I had a Chicken Carver sandwich at the Boston Market, my first in 14 months. I went to bed a happy man.

Monday, June 17th
Tallahassee to Monticello - 34.9 Miles

I was not as successful today as yesterday. I had hoped to reach Madison, 30 miles farther to the east. But, I stopped here in historic Monticello because of the threat of afternoon thunderstorms. The meteorologists predict possible bad weather every afternoon this week. I was afraid of being stuck 15 miles from any lodgings if the skies opened up.

I feel like I may not be making great route decisions lately. I probably should not have cycled through Tallahassee to the north side yesterday. I think I would have done better to veer east, south of the city. I wasted too many miles. I'm getting a little lazy with my pre-ride planning every night. I need to plan my route based on the availability of accommodations for the next two or three nights. It's not easy to plan 60-mile routes that day after day end on the doorstep of a Super 8 motel.

Most of the day was spent on US 90, where the conditions seemed to change every mile. In some sections it was four lanes with special bicycle lanes. In other sections it was two lanes with absolutely no shoulder. I got the horn from a few drivers in those spots. It's no wonder. When you jam too many bodies into a tight space, tempers rise. I wish the guys at the DOT realized this. If they would just set a standard of two-foot shoulders on all federal roads, everybody would be a whole lot safer and happier.

For the first time in weeks I encountered rolling hills today. That added to the unsafe nature of today's ride. Tonight, I received e-mail from the cyclist that I met in Louisiana. He wrote about a couple of cyclists who were killed this past week in Baton Rouge in a head-on collision with a pick-up truck. I'm definitely not going to be careless these last few weeks of the trip. I'll err on the side of caution and sacrifice some speed. I'll reach Philly eventually. And, of course, it didn't rain this evening.

Tuesday, June 18th
Monticello - 0 Miles

I awoke to a rainy, dreary morning. The forecasted afternoon rains came early today. At checkout time, 11:00 AM, it had slowed to a drizzle but was still very overcast. I decided to spend another day here. It wasn't an easy decision because I'm in a motel with only eight channels on the television. My concept of "roughing it" has gone from camping in a muddy field to staying in a motel without Animal Planet on cable TV.

I spent most of the day stuck in the motel room. I pulled two AA batteries out of the razor and popped them into the radio. I found a classic rock station and rocked out for the first time in months, not a pretty sight. The incidental music that you hear in stores and other public places is usually current pop hits. If that's not your cup of tea, you can go home and listen to your LP, tape, and CD collection. But I can't do that. There was no way that I would lug tapes or CD's over every hill between Lisbon and Philadelphia. I just suffer in silence as the music industry's flavor of the month publicly assaults my eardrums. The expense and hassle of downloading MP3's to my Pocket PC made that an impossibility. One of the first things that I'll do when I reach Philly is get my CD's out of storage. Then, I'll rock out like an epileptic Pete Townsend. God help the neighbors.

Wednesday, June 19th
Monticello to Live Oak - 66.8 Miles

I put in a good day of riding before the rain kicked in. I cycled on US 90 just about the entire way. Lately, at the start and finish of the days, I have had to ride from and to a motel at an exit on the parallel I-10. The road today was less rolling than yesterday. Most of the way I was riding directly alongside a rail line. That's always a good thing. Railroads always follow the easiest path through regions. Madison looked like a nice town. A few of the historical markers in town and surrounding it made reference to U.S. wars in the early 1800's with the Seminole Indians. There seems to be lots of history in this section of Florida. There's also lots of logging and farming. I was passed by a number of logging trucks today. More intriguing than the loggers were the produce haulers. They transported their watermelons and greens in modified school buses. The seats, back walls, and side windows of the old yellow buses were removed and the produce stuffed inside. I gave the produce buses a wide berth.

Two miles off of US 90 I found a Best Western motel. I had hoped to do the laundry here, but the dryer is out of order. It's raining hard tonight, and there's some thunder. I hope that this is a system that clears out overnight. I would like to do 60 miles again tomorrow. I could be in Georgia by Friday morning.

Thursday, June 20th
Live Oak to Lake City - 41.44 Miles

I wasted 20 miles of cycling today. Ten miles past Lake City I rounded a bend and saw a wall of rain just ahead. I immediately threw on my pannier covers and turned back. The rain clouds caught up with me after five miles. I pulled into an ugly old motel. The clientele was a little shady, and they didn't have a guest laundry. That was enough to convince me to continue riding another five miles in the rain to the I-75 exit where all of the chain motels are located. It's frustrating to backtrack like that, but at least I dried out and got a load of wash done.

I was slowed down around Lake City because I was forced to do a lot of sidewalk riding. That'll test your riding skills and rattle the fillings out of your mouth. I'm still shaking.

Friday, June 21st
Lake City - 0 Miles

It's summertime and I'm still in Florida. That wasn't part of the plan. I'm hooked on the Weather Channel. I watched the satellite images this morning as a wall of rain clouds headed towards Lake City from the Atlantic Ocean. I would have ridden right into it if I checked out. So, here I sit, locked up in my motel room, waiting for the rain to stop. I would rather be making progress toward Philadelphia, but I'm happy not to be stuck out in the rain. That can be dangerous, as well as uncomfortable. I can see from the Weather Channel that there will be a window of opportunity tomorrow morning to get in some miles before the rain kicks in again. I've got to remember to set the alarm clock tonight.

Saturday, June 22nd
Lake City to MacClenny - 37.49 Miles

I woke up early, but I didn't get out early enough. About 10 miles into the day it started to rain again. There was no thunder or lightning, so I continued on. I knew that the first motels that I would come across were in MacClenny. That meant that I would have to ride about 25 miles in the rain. It was just as much fun as I had imagined. I got soaked through my porous Gore-Tex jacket. Despite the rain covers, some items in the bottom of my front panniers got wet because I rode through a few deep puddles. The bike chain picked up a lot of road gunk. And, I couldn't see through my glasses. At least I'm back on the move again.

I did a little sightseeing at Olustee Battlefield State Historical Site. One of the deadliest battles of the Civil War was fought there, near the rail line. One thousand Confederate and two thousand Union soldiers died. Except, down here, the Union soldiers are called Federalists. The Southerners were intent on maintaining states' rights and minimizing the federal government's power. Judging by the number of Confederate flags flying down here, some of them are still fighting the war.

Sunday, June 23rd
MacClenny to Yulee - 53.87 Miles

I'm about one mile from Georgia, and about 10 miles from the Atlantic Ocean. I successfully skirted Jacksonville and have begun moving northward. If I don't start getting tailwinds now, I'll know that the weather gods have it in for me. They've certainly been socking it to me the past few days with all of the rain falling on northeastern Florida. This state is just one big puddle. Now, I remember why I chose a route around the world that stuck mainly to deserts. I would much rather ride in the Negev, the Sinai, the Nullarbor, and the Desert Southwest than in rainy, tropical regions like Florida.

Within seconds of stepping out of my motel this morning it began to rain. No kidding. For the first 15 minutes the rain increased, and I thought that I was in for another long day. Miraculously, a few minutes later the rain stopped. By the time I left US 90 in Baldwin and headed north on US 301, it was sunny. It ended up being a great day of riding. The temperature was cool. The shoulders were wide. The drivers were courteous. Only one loose dog came out to greet me, and he was easily avoided. I hope this is a portent of things to come. As a card-carrying pessimist, I know it isn't.

One thing that could go wrong is that the slight pain in my right knee could become worse, slowing my progress. More likely, the pain will shift back and forth between the two knees as I overcompensate for the tender knee, hurting the opposite one. My wrists and hands are also beginning to act up. I guess that putting all of the weight of my upper body on a thin metal tube for 15 months is not a good thing. On the bright side, my butt isn't sore.

Monday, June 24th
Yulee to Darien - 66.41 Miles

I'm finally out of Florida. If all goes well, I'll only be in Georgia for two days. I'm halfway up the Georgia coast already. Barring any bad weather, I should be in Savannah tomorrow night and South Carolina on Wednesday morning. With the exception of the last mile today, I rode US 17 all day. As usual, I had to ride over to an interstate to find decent lodging at the end of the day. Highway 17 is one of the original colonial roads used by the Spanish and British. It was called the St. Mary's Road because it led down to the St. Mary's River in Florida. It was important for the early U.S. army and postal service. Now, the bulk of the north-south traffic is handled by I-95, which weaves in and out with US 17. That makes US 17 a great road for bicycle-tourists.

As soon as I crossed over the St. Mary's River I could see that the Georgia DOT cared about cyclists. There were signs indicating the route that would take me north as Bike Route 95. There were also neon yellow signs before each bridge alerting motorists to the presence of cyclists on the road. And, for the most part, there were wide shoulders. They did make one mistake, though. They dug rumble strips clear across the shoulders, forcing cyclists to ride on the road anyway. Well, at least they tried to help us.

It started to rain halfway into the ride, but I was able to stop the rain by putting covers on my panniers and throwing my tent and sleeping bag into a waterproof trash bag. In the last 15 miles, the skies became threatening. I pushed hard in an effort to reach Darien before the deluge. I did get into the Super 8 in time, but I tore right past a few historical markers. Being a history buff, that was difficult. But, better to be dry and ignorant than wet and informed. I wonder if I could get that embroidered onto a pillow?

Tuesday, June 25th
Darien to Savannah - 64.83 Miles

I'm storming through Georgia faster than Sherman. I've made it to Savannah, the state's birthplace. The history quotient increased dramatically today. There seemed to be historical markers at every corner. The towns along US 17 played important roles in the Revolutionary and Civil Wars. In particular, the town of Midway was fascinating. On one corner, across from the old cemetery, there were eight markers highlighting the town's place in American history. Two of Georgia's three signers of the Declaration of Independence came from this small town, Lyman Hall and Button Gwynett. Lyman and Button. Tell me they didn't get beat up at recess. I also passed the smallest church in America, near Riceboro. How small is it? It's so small that God would have to step outside to change His mind. That's my version of Divine Comedy, folks.

I filmed with the helmet-cam as I rolled down Bull Street in Savannah. It's the main street, with small squares every block. It's the best way to capture the feel of a city, without stopping at every corner and pulling out the camera to shoot another thirty seconds of tape. After settling into the Best Western near the Savannah River, I took a walk along the revitalized riverfront to see the fancy stores and restaurants. It's no wonder that James Oglethorpe decided to start his colony here. The base of the bluffs near the river is a natural place to exploit the tourist trade with designer chocolate, artsy candle, and hip T-shirt shops.

Tomorrow should be an adventure. I don't have a map of North Carolina or a catalog of motels. I'm not sure if I'll be allowed on the bridge over the Savannah River. I have another broken spoke on the rear wheel. And, the front tube has a slow leak. Also, I'm out of clean clothing. In the army this would be called SNAFU. I just call it Tuesday.

Wednesday, June 26th
Savannah to Hardeeville, SC - 23.93 Miles

The day started out poorly, but then it got worse. From 8:30 AM to 11:00 AM I watched storm clouds roll up the coast in waves on the Weather Channel. It's amazing how accurate those satellite images are. The images are updated every 10 minutes. And, when a band of clouds crossed over Savannah, I could look outside and see another round of showers start. I prefer those images to the forecasts typed on the screen by one of the channel's meteorologists. Throughout the morning downpours it still read "Cloudy." But, I could see that a couple of inches of "Cloudy" had already been dumped on Savannah by 11:00 AM, checkout time.

After a final check of the satellite image, I decided to hit the road. I went through my morning routine of pumping up the tires to 95 PSI. Today, the leaky front tube gave out completely. I had to change the tube right there, outside of the motel. Then, I set off to find an entrance ramp for the Talmadge Bridge, which crosses the Savannah River. It's a modern, enormous suspension bridge that seems to start somewhere back near Jacksonville and presumably ends in Charleston. While I cycled away from downtown Savannah searching for an entrance ramp, I also looked for a store to get a map of South Carolina. Of course, I never found a map.

I finally found an entrance ramp and cycled past the sign that says, "no pedestrians, cyclists, or farm animals allowed." By the way, now would be a good time for one of those disclaimers that say, "*Do not attempt this cross-country route. The author is an experienced bicycle-tourist who has been misreading maps for years.*" Anyway, I broke the law on a good day because orange cones for a bridge maintenance crew blocked off an entire lane. I sped up and over the bridge behind the cones, giving an apologetic wave to the crew.

I rode another 15 miles through the boonies before I reached I-95 at Hardeeville. There, I was able to get a map, a lousy one as it turns out. I determined that I needed to get from Exit 5 to Exit 8 on I-95 to get onto US 278. So, I rode the three miles in my top gear on the shoulder of I-95. (Insert disclaimer again here). On my sprint up I-95, the skies opened up again. I was soaked by the time I pulled off the exit ramp. There was one motel at this exit, a Ramada Limited, and I headed right to it. I had only done 20 miles, but I really needed to get inside, dry out, study my map, replace the broken spoke, and do a load of wash. I completed all of my chores this afternoon, and I'm ready for a new day tomorrow. To quote 80's synth-wizard Howard Jones, "Things can only get better. Whoa. Whoa. Whoa."

Thursday, June 27th
Hardeeville to Walterboro - 51.32 Miles

I am really having trouble deciding which route to take up the East Coast. My original intention was to hug the coastline all the way up the Outer Banks to the Delmarva Peninsula. Lately, I've been considering staying as close to I-95 as possible. Or, I could compromise and follow the Adventure Cycling route between the coastline and I-95. Today, I stayed near I-95 when I realized, 25 miles into the ride, that I was still 60 miles from Charleston. I didn't want to get stuck in the swamps of South Carolina overnight, so I continued farther north on US 17A. That left me within a mile of motels and restaurants at Exit 53 on I-95.

The weather was great today. Lots of sun and a slight tailwind. In a section where there did not appear to be a parallel road to I-95 on the map, I found that there was a frontage road. With I-95 fifty feet to my right and a rail line fifty feet to my left, for much of the day I was comfortably in my element. There were a few houses with potentially angry dogs to pass, though. Tomorrow, as I cycle out of the Best Western's parking lot, I'll probably decide which route to take. At least, it will be my route for the next 24 hours. Thank goodness I'm traveling alone. My indecisiveness might have caused a cycling companion to tip over, physically and emotionally.

Friday, June 28th
Walterboro to Mount Pleasant - 60.46 Miles

Well, I think I've left I-95 for good. I won't leave the Atlantic Coast until I hit South Jersey and turn towards Philadelphia. The deciding factor? I don't think I'll be chased by as many dogs near the water. I'm not sure how I reached that conclusion, but I'm sticking by it now.

I left Walterboro on SR 64, hooking up with US 17 fifteen miles later. US 17 is a four lane divided highway with no shoulders. It's aimed directly at Charleston and the beaches beyond. That makes it an unsafe place to ride a bicycle on Friday afternoon in the summer. I pushed hard through this stretch of road, knowing that the traffic would only get worse as the afternoon wore on. Before crossing the bridge over the Ashley River into Charleston, I stopped in a bike shop to search for a book on cycling the Atlantic Coast. Although he didn't have the book, the owner imparted some local knowledge. He told me that the bridge out of Charleston, over the Cooper River to Mount Pleasant, was closed to bicycles. He said that the police constantly monitor the bridge, and I would be ticketed if caught. There is a water taxi that I should take instead.

I am so burned out from sightseeing that I just followed a horse-drawn tourist carriage for a few blocks in the old section of the city, and then took off for the docks. I arrived too late for the last water taxi to Mount Pleasant. The water taxi operator said that I could probably ride over the newer of the two US 17 bridges. He had seen people walk to Mount Pleasant on that bridge. It turned out to be another two miles of extreme exertion and fear. There was a raised sidewalk on the bridge, but it was barely wide enough for the jumpers to walk out on. So, I was left to fend for myself with Charleston's NASCAR-wannabe's. By the time the bridge over the Cooper River spit us out on the other side, I was spent. I coasted to my motel about a half-mile farther on US 17 and crashed in my room. On the up side, no dogs chased me on the bridge. Apparently, dogs realize that playing in traffic on a tall, narrow, long bridge is dangerous. I'm still working on that concept.

Saturday, June 29th
Mount Pleasant to Georgetown - 60.31 Miles

I broke the 13,000-mile mark today. That should be the last big milestone before I reach Philadelphia. The ride started out slowly as I searched a few stores along US 17 in Mount Pleasant for that Atlantic Coast cycling book and another Mini-DV tape for my camcorder. I got a tape, but the book wasn't available anywhere. Those wasted minutes at the beginning of the day would turn out to haunt me in the afternoon.

I stayed on US 17 the entire day. A good portion of the ride was through Francis Marion National Forest. Francis Marion, aka, the Swamp Fox, was the Revolutionary War hero portrayed by Mel Gibson in the movie, *The Patriot*. I could see how Marion and his men would be hard to find in the dense forests around Charlestown. You can't help but gain a better understanding of the past as you cycle through regions that are as rich in history as the Low Country of South Carolina and Colonial Georgia.

About eight miles from my hotel in Georgetown I could see and hear the beginnings of a thunderstorm ahead. I picked up my pace to Mel Brooks' "ludicrous speed." Despite the effort, I fell three miles short of the Hampton Inn. I was at the base of the bridge over the Sampit River when a big storm hit. I found shelter under the overhang of an equipment rental store. The heavy rain, thunder, and lightening continued for 90 minutes while I stood there, waiting for a break to make my run for the hotel. It looked like it would never stop, so I had to ride over the high bridge with lightening flashing all around me. No doubt, I'll have nightmares about that scene tonight. I arrived in the stately lobby of the hotel dripping from head to toe. I felt a little guilty about rolling my wet and muddy bike over their beautiful carpet, but I got over it pretty quickly. Now, I'm a prisoner in my room. My only pair of shoes is soaked, and the rest of my gear is spread throughout the room so that everything can dry out overnight. I had a pizza delivered for dinner. All of this could have been avoided if I left Mount Pleasant ten minutes earlier. Dang!

Sunday, June 30th
Georgetown to North Myrtle Beach - 66.42 Miles

I almost made it to North Carolina, but I ran out of roadway. Throughout the second half of the day I was riding almost exclusively on beachfront roads. In North Myrtle Beach the beachfront road dead ends just before the North Carolina border. I had to turn around and head back two miles to the main intersection in town where I could leave the coastal community and take an inland route to my next state. I'm in a motel near the intersection, ready to cycle out of South Carolina first thing tomorrow morning. When I say first thing, I mean eleven-ish in the morning. There's no need to be fanatical.

I think that I can officially say that I've crossed my third continent today. I've been close to the Atlantic Ocean since reaching Jacksonville, but I've never actually been on the beach. Well, today I stepped onto the beach just south of Myrtle Beach. There were no marching bands or tickertape, but I shot some videotape to mark the occasion anyway.

It was a different type of riding today, but still very enjoyable. Cycling through beach resorts on a hot Sunday afternoon in the summer can be a little crazy. You have to be aware of all of the different obstacles that could get in your way. It can be a madhouse on the roads. I had a few hairy moments, but no one was able to tag me. Another successful day.

Monday, July 1st
North Myrtle Beach to Southport, NC - 50.37 Miles

I'm out of the Deep South, and just in the Regular South now. My crossing into North Carolina was inauspicious because I crossed on a back road, not US 17. At least there was a "Welcome" sign for me to photograph for my collection. They do a nice job in North Carolina, sign-posting recommended bicycle routes. I am on Bike Route 3 now. I hope that route continues up the Outer Banks. It'll make the navigating easier for me.

I stayed off of US 17 much of the day, following the backroads of Bike Route 3 instead. It was a fun day to ride. The weather was great. I didn't get any headwinds until I turned directly towards Southport. I decided to stay about five miles outside of town, thinking that I might save some money on a room. Where NC 211 and NC 87 meet, there were two nice motels, a Comfort Inn and a Hampton Inn. The Comfort Inn, because it is brand new, quoted me a price of $126. I told them that I didn't want to stay the week, just one night. That was the daily rate (for smelly cyclists with greasy bikes) in their pristine motel. The folks at the Hampton Inn weren't much cheaper, but they gave me the AAA rate of $102. These last two weeks on the road are going to bankrupt me.

Tuesday, July 2nd
Southport to Sneads Ferry - 70.08 Miles

I took the first of many ferries in North Carolina this morning. It was a 30-minute ride from Southport to Fort Fisher. Then, I began meandering up the coast. I didn't want to take the Adventure Cycling route because it went straight through Wilmington. I also didn't want to stay on US 17 because it didn't have a shoulder. So, I took some backroads near the coast. I wish I had one of those GPS units that track your movements throughout a day. It would be comical to see the zigzag route that I took to get past Wilmington. It would probably look like a toddler's doodling. I'm sure that I easily went five miles out of my way. Eventually, I met up with two local cyclists who took pity on me and offered to get me out of the maze. It's been so long since I've cycled with anybody. It was fun. I rode with Al and Greg for about 30 minutes until they had to veer off. But, they got me to a road that eventually fed into US 17 above Wilmington. I was home free from there.

I still had many more miles to go until I reached my hotel, the Holiday Inn Express in Sneads Ferry. I'll be booking ahead throughout this holiday week, if possible. I did it today, and am happy that I did. It's one less thing to worry about while on the bike. The rooms have gotten very expensive lately. This evening I'm paying $103, before tax. It looks like a nice place. It's on a golf course, and it has a nice big pool. I was so hungry and tired and late when I got here that I just wanted to eat and sleep. Since the hotel is not near any other businesses, I had to order a Domino's pizza. I could really use a steak dinner one of these nights. I need the protein. My legs are like jelly now. A good meal might restore some of that lost strength.

Wednesday, July 3rd
Sneads Ferry to Morehead City - 60.84 Miles

Once again, I think I wasted a few miles by making a wrong turn today. Somewhere in Camp Lejeune I must have missed a turnoff to take me off the base to the east. I went too far north before getting out. When I eventually reached the gate that I should have exited from, I got a flat on my rear wheel. Doesn't that just figure?

I stayed inland on NC 24 to reach my motel in Morehead City. On the way I passed a bike shop where I picked up another tube and some CO2 cartridges. Just before reaching my motel, a man pulled his pickup over and asked to speak with me. He had his son with him and was interested in my trip. He's a Marine, one year from retirement, and he planned on trekking in the Himalayas with the boy in a few years. He was interested in the adventure aspect of bicycle touring. I gave him the condensed version of my ride and then wrote out the address to my web site. All told, it was about a 15-minute encounter, and he was very thankful. I seem to be having more and more encounters like this lately. Traffic on the web site has probably increased dramatically. I'm getting more e-mail from people that I've met on the road. They often say that they've passed the web address on to friends. It's amazing to think that 15 months ago only the immediate family knew I was going around the world. The secret's out now.

Thursday, July 4th
Morehead City - 6.15 Miles

I made a half dozen phone calls this morning, trying to find an available motel room near Cape Hatteras. The Cape is booked solid. I could have cycled there and set up the tent, but the weather didn't look promising. And, I needed to do the laundry. After 12 straight days in the saddle, I thought it was OK to take a break here today. Besides, it's a national holiday. Why not relax? That was my thought process this morning. So, I called the front desk at the Hampton Inn and found out that they were already fully booked tonight. I packed up and headed out. On my second attempt I found a motel with vacancies in Morehead City. I've spent the day in the EconoLodge, working on my tan and my web page. It's been a productive day on both counts.

Friday, July 5th
Morehead City to Ocracoke Village - 45.85 Miles

I'm back on the road again. I hope that's my final day off. I'm so close to Philadelphia that I can taste it. In fact, I had a Tastykakes snack after dinner tonight.

Before leaving Morehead City I called the same motels to try to reserve a room. I got the same responses as yesterday. Still, I packed up and headed out. I knew that I was going to have to hit a campground tonight. I rode through Beaufort, and then continued on US 70 up to the Cedar Island National Wildlife Refuge. Before getting on the 3:00 PM ferry to Ocracoke Island, I checked to see if any rooms were available at the motel next to the ferry dock. Once again, no luck. On to the ferry I went. The ride across the Pamlico Sound took two hours and fifteen minutes. By the time I reached Ocracoke Village, it was too late to do the 14 miles up the island to the Hatteras Inlet ferry. I cycled straight through the touristy village, past all of the "No Vacancy" signs, to the Beachcomber Campground. I'm paying over $31 to camp out here tonight, a new record. Congratulations Beachcomber Campground. You have risen holiday price gouging to a new level. To cap off the day, one of the local cats marked his territory on my tent's rain fly. That would be a metaphor, I believe. I wonder when it will start to rain tonight.

Saturday, July 6th
Ocracoke Village to Rodanthe - 50.00 Miles

The rain started around 1:00 AM last night. Then, the winds shifted to the northeast this morning. I feel as though I can control the weather. If you need rain, I just have to pull out the tent. If you want wind from a certain direction, I just have to point the bike in that direction. Mother Nature is having a good laugh at my expense.

Because of the strong headwinds I did not get as far as I had hoped. I took the 10:30 AM ferry from Ocracoke Island to Hatteras Island. While struggling through Hatteras, Frisco, and Buxton, I met up with a local cyclist. When I told him how far I had come, he wanted to stop and have lunch, presumably to hear all of the gory details. I had to decline. I felt bad about it, but I still had too many miles to ride into a stiff breeze. When I didn't even pull off to see the famous Cape Hatteras Lighthouse with him, he must have thought I was real jerk. But, I didn't even want to cycle a mile off of NC 12 to see that landmark for fear that it would slow me down.

I stopped at the KOA campground in Rodanthe. There were no vacancies in the few motels. The next town was about 30 miles north, and I didn't have the strength in my legs to fight the wind for another three hours. I got lucky at the campground when I asked about the availability of one of their Kabins. I was in luck. One became available today when a Kabin-holder had to leave for a family emergency. I took it for $64. That was actually a good price, considering a tent site costs $31. So, since I'm under a roof tonight, this means that the forecasted rain for tonight will hold off.

Sunday, July 7th
Rodanthe to Barco - 76.25 Miles

Two of the reasons that I chose to closely follow the coastline up the Atlantic were, 1) I knew the winds would be stronger near the water and 2) I knew the winds would come from the southwest. Well, I was half right. For the second day in a row I was faced with northeasterlies. When that happens, there's nothing to do but put your head down and pedal...hard. It's tough to sightsee when your head's down. I passed right by the Bodie Lighthouse without noticing it. I did see lots of sand, though. The dunes on my right obscured my view of the beach. On my left I had a constant stream of traffic. It's the end of a long 4th of July weekend, and everybody is rushing home.

I'm also rushing home. There are very few things that could stop me now. A broken saddle would be one of those things.

I always knew that the saddle would give out before my butt did. The two metal rails that support the saddle snapped just outside of the Wright Brothers National Memorial at Kill Devil Hills. It was fortunate that it happened when and where it did. I peddled back a couple of miles, cautiously, to the KDH Cycle & Skate store that I had just passed. I bought a new Specialized saddle, attached it, and was back on my way in no time.

Kill Devil Hills, just south of Kitty Hawk, has a monument to a couple of bicycle mechanics named Orville and Wilbur. I pedaled up the hill to get some pictures of the park below. I don't know how many times the Wright's pedaled up that hill, but once was enough for me. In the park, a kite flying competition was taking place. The spectators were treated to large flying teddy bears and octopuses. Looking out over the sea of festive kites, all that I could think was, "That must be a strong northeasterly to float a bear and an octopus."

I left the Outer Banks after Kitty Hawk and continued on US 158. The accommodations are few and far between on this stretch of road. At a motel near Grandy I was turned away because they had a broken water pipe last night. They weren't accepting customers tonight. The owner was nice enough to call the Palmer Inn B&B to get me a room in Barco, just a few more miles north. The owners of the B&B hadn't planned on accepting customers after a very busy weekend, but they too felt sorry for me. Like Blanche DuBois, I've had to rely on the kindness of strangers whenever accommodations were scarce. I thanked the owners profusely and settled in for a quiet night.

Monday, July 8th
Barco to Cape Charles, VA - 47.77 Miles

I'm on the southern tip of the Delmarva Peninsula tonight, and it feels like I'm almost home. I could reach the finish in four more days, so I did the laundry and now have four clean shirts to get me home.

I left the B&B around 8:00 AM this morning and rode the four and a half miles to the Currituck ferry, and then waited around for over a half-hour. The only paying passengers were two motorists and I. The 45-minute ride over the Currituck Bay was very relaxing. On the other side I made it through quiet, rural towns and the Mackay Island National Wildlife Refuge until I unceremoniously rolled into Virginia. There wasn't even a state welcome sign, just a "Welcome to Virginia Beach" sign. That'll have to do for my collection of state welcome photos.

Virginia Beach became more and more congested as I pushed north to the Chesapeake Bay Bridge-Tunnel entrance. I called ahead to the Authority for a pick-up truck to be available for a 1:30 PM arrival. Then, I developed trouble with my rear wheel. The spokes were making nasty noises whenever I exerted a great deal of pressure. I thought that the spokes on the left side needed to be tightened a bit. After some roadside maintenance, I realized that I had overdone it. The wheel now rubbed against the brake pads and was out of true. I had to call back to the Authority and tell them that I would be late. A half-hour later the wheel was back in decent shape. This is not the type of maintenance that should be done on the road. The wheel still needs further tensioning and truing by a mechanic in a shop. I just need it to work four more days.

At the entrance to the Bridge-Tunnel I waited a short time, and then got a lift in one of the Authority's pick-up trucks. I threw the bike in the back, over a bunch of orange traffic cones and stop signs. We stopped once to rescue a driver on the bridge who had frozen with fear. The guy had pulled off into a breakdown area and called for help. My escort said that this sort of thing happens quite a bit. I guess the bridge just seems too narrow for some folks. It's 17.6 miles long, and that's a long way to grip a steering wheel in fear. Once a year they shut down the Bridge-Tunnel to let pedestrians and cyclists take over. Unfortunately, they don't let anyone into the tunnels, so you can't cycle from end to end. I would pay to do that.

At the northern terminus of the Bridge-Tunnel is a Best Western. I decided to call it a day here. I can attack the Delmarva Peninsula tomorrow. I'm almost home.

Tuesday, July 9th
Cape Charles, VA to Pocomoke, MD - 73.69 Miles

I finally had one of those tailwinds that I've been waiting for the entire trip. It pushed me right up US 13 in no time. The road had very good shoulders most of the way through Virginia. The shoulders only seemed to disappear when the road passed through some of the bigger towns.

I didn't stop to do any sightseeing today, and this region has a lot to offer for someone interested in Early American history, or bird-watching. I barely slowed down when passing roadside historical markers. I am just too excited, being so close to home.

I'm staying in my last motel of the trip tonight, the Pocomoke City Holiday Inn Express. I'm livin' large one last time. Tomorrow night I stay with a former co-worker at his house in Lewes, Delaware. The next night I stay with my younger brother and his family at their summer rental in Sea Isle City, New Jersey. The day after that, I'm home. That means I'll sleep in six different states on successive nights. Is it too much to ask for three more days of tailwinds?

Wednesday, July 10th
Pocomoke, MD to Lewes, DE - 68.89 Miles

A weather front blew in overnight. It rained and got cooler. The winds are now blowing from the north. I hate when that happens. Of course, a little wind is not going to stop me now. I was on the road by 10:15 AM, riding up US 113. This road is even better than the stretch of US 13 that I cycled yesterday. There were wide shoulders. Much of the road is recently paved. And, the road passes through scenic forestland. The Delmarva Peninsula gets my seal of approval for bicycle touring. I even passed a couple of bicycle-tourists heading south during the day.

I did get some rain around 1:00 PM and went into full cover-up mode. The rain stopped 10 minutes later. That figures. I rode the rest of the day with my less-than-vibrant orange pannier covers on. At this point in the trip, everything is faded from constant exposure to the sun. The backs of my shirts and cycling shorts are faded. I'm actually getting a tan on my back, through the shirts. And, I haven't been wearing suntan lotion on my arms, legs, or head. I've become a dermatologist's worst nightmare. I'm afraid that the weird bike glove tan on my hands will leave me scarred for life. It will be difficult to explain that tan when I start interviewing for a new job.

I'm now in the guest wing of my co-worker's mansion in Lewes, DE. John graciously invited me to stay with his family in his new house, if I passed through Lewes on the trip. He lives just six miles from the Cape May ferry. I couldn't pass that up. John grilled a great steak on the barbecue, which we ate on the back deck with corn from some of the fields that I had just passed today. Then, he drove me around Lewes to see the sights in this historic and scenic area on Cape Henlopen. Finally, he treated me to homemade ice cream from King's Ice Cream downtown. I felt like visiting royalty. It certainly is great to be the king.

Thursday, July 11th
Lewes, DE to Sea Isle City, NJ - 29.31 Miles

Strong headwinds made what should have been an easy ride, very difficult. I left John's house just after 7:00 AM to catch the 8:00 AM ferry, seven miles away. The crossing of the Delaware Bay took 90 minutes, 20 minutes longer than advertised. If the headwinds slowed the massive ferry, what would it do to me when I reached Cape May? I pushed hard up US 9, and then turned off for Avalon. From Avalon I cycled over the $.50 bridge connected to Sea Isle City. Bikes cross for free. I'm spending the night with my younger brother's family at a beach rental on 87th Street.

Friday, July 12th
Sea Isle City, NJ to Havertown, PA - 80.21 Miles

Wow! I made it. After 15 months and nearly 14,000 miles, I arrived back on the Main Line unscathed. I even managed to remember some of the shortcuts through the old neighborhood. It's great to be home.

Although the family often spent summer vacations in Sea Isle City, the only route that I knew back to Philadelphia included the Garden State Parkway and the Atlantic City Expressway, not bicycle-friendly roads. So, at breakfast this morning I found a direct route through New Jersey to Camden and the Ben Franklin Bridge. The roads that I chose (NJ 50, 557, and 555) were great cycling roads. Of course, I did have one last flat tire and one more dog scare, but that stuff doesn't faze me at this point. It turned out to be a beautiful day. Even the ride through Camden was tolerable.

The last major bridge crossing of the trip was from Camden to Center City Philadelphia on the Ben Franklin Bridge. There's a wide pedestrian walkway on the bridge that I leisurely pedaled over. I stopped to talk to another cyclist on the walkway, and then took a few pictures of the Philadelphia skyline. I crossed the city in the bike lane on Spring Garden Street. Then, I stopped in front of the Art Museum for more photos. I resisted the urge to run up the steps of the Art Museum like Rocky Balboa. I had a few more miles to go, up the West River Drive, through Fairmount Park, past Saint Joseph's University, and out the Main Line. For the final quarter-mile I used the helmet-cam, recording my last pedal strokes, just as I had recorded my first pedal strokes outside of the Lisbon Airport. I was greeted with American flags and a "Welcome Home" sign on the front lawn of Mom and Dad's place. I stood for the obligatory pictures in front of the house, and then went inside and started to regale the folks with tales of my derring-do. The ride may be over, but the story telling has just begun. God help everyone who has the patience to sit through these stories.

Appendix

Daily Mileage Chart

Date	Miles	From	To
4/5/01	0.93	Lisbon	Lisbon
4/6/01	50.65	Lisbon	Carvalhal
4/7/01	51.27	Carvalhal	Vila Nova de Milfontes
4/8/01	33.67	Vila Nova de Milfontes	Odeceixe
4/9/01	42.84	Odeceixe	Sagres
4/10/01	11.84	Sagres	Cape St. Vincent
4/11/01	43.03	Cape St. Vincent	Praia da Rocha
4/12/01	50.28	Praia da Rocha	Olhao
4/13/01	28.33	Olhao	Monte Gordo
4/14/01	0.00	Monte Gordo	Monte Gordo
4/15/01	0.00	Monte Gordo	Monte Gordo
4/16/01	41.04	Monte Gordo	Huelva, Spain
4/17/01	55.80	Huelva, Spain	Seville
4/18/01	0.00	Seville	Seville
4/19/01	48.76	Seville	El Cuervo
4/20/01	31.02	El Cuervo	Cadiz
4/21/01	50.66	Cadiz	Tahivilla
4/22/01	46.74	Tahivilla	Gibralter
4/23/01	0.00	Gibralter	Gibralter
4/24/01	0.00	Gibralter	Gibralter
4/25/01	60.03	Gibralter	Torre Real
4/26/01	41.46	Torre Real	Malaga
4/27/01	27.88	Malaga	Villanueva del Rosario
4/28/01	67.36	Villanueva del Rosario	Granada
4/29/01	4.09	Granada	Granada
4/30/01	53.28	Granada	Baza
5/1/01	75.71	Baza	Puerto Lumbreras
5/2/01	71.86	Puerto Lumbreras	Cartagena
5/3/01	24.74	Cartagena	Los Alcazares
5/4/01	44.30	Los Alcazares	Santa Pola

Date	Miles	From	To
5/5/01	38.81	Santa Pola	Benidorm
5/6/01	0.00	Benidorm	Benidorm
5/7/01	80.40	Benidorm	Mareny de Barraquetes
5/8/01	72.54	Mareny de Barraquetes	Benicasim
5/9/01	41.71	Benicasim	Peniscola
5/10/01	0.00	Peniscola	Peniscola
5/11/01	61.80	Peniscola	Montroig
5/12/01	71.30	Montroig	Gava
5/13/01	8.55	Gava	Barcelona
5/14/01	37.50	Barcelona	Pineda de Mar
5/15/01	74.62	Pineda de Mar	le Boulou, France
5/16/01	38.19	le Boulou, France	Torreilles
5/17/01	0.00	Torreilles	Torreilles
5/18/01	64.97	Torreilles	Beziers
5/19/01	31.00	Beziers	Sete
5/20/01	33.93	Sete	Clapiers
5/21/01	11.00	Clapiers	Lattes
5/22/01	15.34	Lattes	Lattes
5/23/01	33.37	Lattes	Aigues Mortes
5/24/01	60.21	Aigues Mortes	Salon-de-Provence
5/25/01	60.24	Salon-de-Provence	Brignoles
5/26/01	49.82	Brignoles	St. Raphael
5/27/01	49.03	St. Raphael	Villeneuve-Loubet
5/28/01	38.02	Villeneuve-Loubet	Menton
5/29/01	36.59	Menton	Diano Marina, Italy
5/30/01	47.34	Diano Marina, Italy	Albissola Marina
5/31/01	49.71	Albissola Marina	Santa Margherita Ligure
6/1/01	0.00	Santa Margherita Ligure	Santa Margherita Ligure
6/2/01	61.31	Santa Margherita Ligure	Ameglia
6/3/01	42.62	Ameglia	Pisa
6/4/01	60.18	Pisa	Florence
6/5/01	0.00	Florence	Florence
6/6/01	56.38	Florence	Pisa
6/7/01	70.49	Pisa	Follonica
6/8/01	32.85	Follonica	Grosseto
6/9/01	23.95	Grosseto	Albinia

Date	Miles	From	To
6/10/01	41.51	Albinia	Tarquinia
6/11/01	59.50	Tarquinia	Rome
6/12/01	0.00	Rome	Rome
6/13/01	0.00	Rome	Rome
6/14/01	36.46	Rome	Ostia
6/15/01	62.30	Ostia	Sabaudia
6/16/01	48.14	Sabaudia	Formia
6/17/01	49.46	Formia	Isola d'Ischia
6/18/01	0.00	Isola d'Ischia	Isola d'Ischia
6/19/01	0.00	Isola d'Ischia	Isola d'Ischia
6/20/01	26.82	Isola d'Ischia	Salerno
6/21/01	58.50	Salerno	Picerno
6/22/01	85.21	Picerno	Metaponto
6/23/01	79.22	Metaponto	Brindisi
6/24/01	0.00	Brindisi	Patras, Greece
6/25/01	5.83	Patras, Greece	Patras
6/26/01	67.77	Patras	Xilokastro
6/27/01	75.14	Xilokastro	Athens
6/28/01	0.00	Athens	Athens
6/29/01	0.00	Athens	Athens
6/30/01	12.40	Athens	Naousa, Paros
7/1/01	6.20	Naousa, Paros	Naousa, Paros
7/2/01	6.20	Naousa, Paros	Naousa, Paros
7/3/01	0.00	Naousa, Paros	Naousa, Paros
7/4/01	0.00	Naousa, Paros	Naousa, Paros
7/5/01	0.00	Naousa, Paros	Naousa, Paros
7/6/01	9.76	Naousa, Paros	Naousa, Paros
7/7/01	0.00	Naousa, Paros	Naousa, Paros
7/8/01	17.64	Naousa, Paros	Athens
7/9/01	10.83	Athens	Pireus
7/10/01	9.07	Pireus	Rhodes
7/11/01	54.03	Rhodes	Ortaca, Turkey
7/12/01	37.44	Ortaca, Turkey	Fethiye
7/13/01	49.20	Fethiye	Patara
7/14/01	25.47	Patara	Kas
7/15/01	0.00	Kas	Kas

Date	Miles	From	To
7/16/01	0.00	Kas	Kas
7/17/01	49.69	Kas	Finike
7/18/01	52.30	Finike	Kemer
7/19/01	32.90	Kemer	Antalya
7/20/01	10.06	Antalya	Antalya
7/21/01	63.05	Antalya	Manavgat
7/22/01	32.54	Manavgat	Alanya
7/23/01	3.73	Alanya	Girne, N. Cyprus
7/24/01	52.51	Girne, N. Cyprus	Gazamagusa
7/25/01	1.07	Gazamagusa	Mersin
7/26/01	44.99	Mersin	Adana
7/27/01	21.43	Adana	Tel Aviv, Israel
7/28/01	70.63	Tel Aviv, Israel	Haifa
7/29/01	37.44	Haifa	Nazareth
7/30/01	0.00	Nazareth	Nazareth
7/31/01	69.75	Nazareth	Netanya
8/1/01	65.54	Netanya	Jerusalem
8/2/01	0.00	Jerusalem	Jerusalem
8/3/01	0.00	Jerusalem	Jerusalem
8/4/01	7.70	Jerusalem	Bethlehem
8/5/01	6.18	Bethlehem	Jerusalem
8/6/01	44.65	Jerusalem	Tel Aviv
8/7/01	0.00	Tel Aviv	Tel Aviv
8/8/01	0.00	Tel Aviv	Tel Aviv
8/9/01	48.92	Tel Aviv	Nir Am
8/10/01	72.21	Nir Am	Nitzana
8/11/01	60.52	Nitzana	Al-Arish, Egypt
8/12/01	0.00	Al-Arish, Egypt	Al-Arish, Egypt
8/13/01	125.69	Al-Arish, Egypt	Al-Ishmailya
8/14/01	0.00	Al-Ishmailya	Al-Ishmailya
8/15/01	86.30	Al-Ishmailya	Cairo
8/16/01	0.00	Cairo	Cairo
8/17/01	26.13	Cairo	Cairo
8/18/01	0.00	Cairo	Mumbai, India
8/19/01	0.00	Mumbai, India	Mumbai
8/20/01	0.00	Mumbai	Mumbai

Date	Miles	From	To
8/21/01	0.00	Mumbai	Mumbai
8/22/01	0.00	Mumbai	Mumbai
8/23/01	0.00	Mumbai	Mumbai
8/24/01	0.00	Mumbai	Mumbai
8/25/01	0.00	Mumbai	Perth, Australia
8/26/01	14.48	Perth, Australia	East Perth
8/27/01	18.40	East Perth	Scarborough
8/28/01	0.00	Scarborough	Scarborough
8/29/01	0.00	Scarborough	Scarborough
8/30/01	0.00	Scarborough	Scarborough
8/31/01	0.00	Scarborough	Scarborough
9/1/01	0.00	Scarborough	Scarborough
9/2/01	0.00	Scarborough	Scarborough
9/3/01	0.00	Scarborough	Scarborough
9/4/01	0.00	Scarborough	Scarborough
9/5/01	0.00	Scarborough	Scarborough
9/6/01	0.00	Scarborough	Scarborough
9/7/01	0.00	Scarborough	Scarborough
9/8/01	0.00	Scarborough	Scarborough
9/9/01	0.00	Scarborough	Scarborough
9/10/01	0.00	Scarborough	Scarborough
9/11/01	0.00	Scarborough	Scarborough
9/12/01	0.00	Scarborough	Scarborough
9/13/01	0.00	Scarborough	Scarborough
9/14/01	0.00	Scarborough	Scarborough
9/15/01	0.00	Scarborough	Scarborough
9/16/01	0.00	Scarborough	Scarborough
9/17/01	0.00	Scarborough	Scarborough
9/18/01	0.00	Scarborough	Scarborough
9/19/01	0.00	Scarborough	Scarborough
9/20/01	0.00	Scarborough	Scarborough
9/21/01	0.00	Scarborough	Scarborough
9/22/01	0.00	Scarborough	Scarborough
9/23/01	0.00	Scarborough	Scarborough
9/24/01	53.07	Scarborough	Mandurah
9/25/01	71.03	Mandurah	Bunbury

Date	Miles	From	To
9/26/01	38.15	Bunbury	Busselton
9/27/01	30.93	Busselton	Margaret River
9/28/01	0.00	Margaret River	Margaret River
9/29/01	0.00	Margaret River	Margaret River
9/30/01	0.00	Margaret River	Margaret River
10/1/01	33.86	Margaret River	Augusta
10/2/01	56.54	Augusta	Nannup
10/3/01	49.39	Nannup	Pemberton
10/4/01	22.05	Pemberton	Northcliffe
10/5/01	62.44	Northcliffe	Walpole
10/6/01	42.25	Walpole	Denmark
10/7/01	43.34	Denmark	Albany
10/8/01	0.00	Albany	Albany
10/9/01	0.00	Albany	Albany
10/10/01	0.00	Albany	Albany
10/11/01	66.17	Albany	Borden
10/12/01	54.94	Borden	Jerramungup
10/13/01	73.67	Jerramungup	Ravensthorpe
10/14/01	0.00	Ravensthorpe	Ravensthorpe
10/15/01	0.00	Ravensthorpe	Ravensthorpe
10/16/01	121.59	Ravensthorpe	Esperance
10/17/01	0.00	Esperance	Esperance
10/18/01	68.16	Esperance	Salmon Gums
10/19/01	62.89	Salmon Gums	Norseman
10/20/01	0.00	Norseman	Norseman
10/21/01	0.00	Norseman	Norseman
10/22/01	0.00	Norseman	Norseman
10/23/01	121.64	Norseman	Balladonia
10/24/01	0.00	Balladonia	Balladonia
10/25/01	115.94	Balladonia	Caiguna
10/26/01	41.97	Caiguna	Cocklebiddy
10/27/01	58.06	Cocklebiddy	Madura
10/28/01	71.30	Madura	Mundrabilla
10/29/01	49.40	Mundrabilla	WA/SA Border Village
10/30/01	0.00	WA/SA Border Village	WA/SA Border Village
10/31/01	23.47	WA/SA Border Village	WA/SA Border Village

Date	Miles	From	To
11/1/01	114.70	WA/SA Border Village	Nullarbor
11/2/01	0.00	Nullarbor	Nullarbor
11/3/01	57.18	Nullarbor	Yalata
11/4/01	32.55	Yalata	Nundroo
11/5/01	0.00	Nundroo	Nundroo
11/6/01	49.31	Nundroo	Penong
11/7/01	49.77	Penong	Ceduna
11/8/01	0.00	Ceduna	Ceduna
11/9/01	0.00	Ceduna	Ceduna
11/10/01	57.49	Ceduna	Wirrulla
11/11/01	75.53	Wirrulla	Wudinna
11/12/01	64.52	Wudinna	Kimba
11/13/01	0.00	Kimba	Kimba
11/14/01	55.24	Kimba	Iron Knob
11/15/01	45.16	Iron Knob	Port Augusta
11/16/01	59.77	Port Augusta	Port Pirie
11/17/01	0.00	Port Pirie	Port Pirie
11/18/01	19.36	Port Pirie	Crystal Brook
11/19/01	63.58	Crystal Brook	Port Wakefield
11/20/01	70.15	Port Wakefield	Glenelg
11/21/01	0.00	Glenelg	Glenelg
11/22/01	0.00	Glenelg	Glenelg
11/23/01	0.00	Glenelg	Glenelg
11/24/01	0.00	Glenelg	Glenelg
11/25/01	0.00	Glenelg	Glenelg
11/26/01	0.00	Glenelg	Glenelg
11/27/01	42.80	Glenelg	Strathalbyn
11/28/01	59.96	Strathalbyn	Meningie
11/29/01	34.65	Meningie	Policeman Point
11/30/01	61.94	Policeman Point	Kingston SE
12/1/01	68.21	Kingston SE	Millicent
12/2/01	0.00	Millicent	Millicent
12/3/01	0.00	Millicent	Millicent
12/4/01	31.44	Millicent	Mount Gambier
12/5/01	0.00	Mount Gambier	Mount Gambier
12/6/01	0.00	Mount Gambier	Mount Gambier

Date	Miles	From	To
12/7/01	0.00	Mount Gambier	Mount Gambier
12/8/01	0.00	Mount Gambier	Mount Gambier
12/9/01	0.00	Mount Gambier	Mount Gambier
12/10/01	25.38	Mount Gambier	Nelson, Victoria
12/11/01	47.31	Nelson, Victoria	Portland
12/12/01	0.00	Portland	Portland
12/13/01	62.37	Portland	Warrnambool
12/14/01	45.76	Warrnambool	Port Campbell
12/15/01	33.39	Port Campbell	Lavers Hill
12/16/01	30.58	Lavers Hill	Apollo Bay
12/17/01	0.00	Apollo Bay	Apollo Bay
12/18/01	30.34	Apollo Bay	Lorne
12/19/01	49.87	Lorne	Geelong
12/20/01	0.00	Geelong	Geelong
12/21/01	0.00	Geelong	Geelong
12/22/01	31.29	Geelong	Queenscliff
12/23/01	46.40	Queenscliff	Cowes
12/24/01	57.78	Cowes	Inverloch
12/25/01	0.00	Inverloch	Inverloch
12/26/01	0.00	Inverloch	Inverloch
12/27/01	54.52	Inverloch	Morwell
12/28/01	44.55	Morwell	Sale
12/29/01	46.83	Sale	Bairnsdale
12/30/01	23.08	Bairnsdale	Lakes Entrance
12/31/01	0.00	Lakes Entrance	Lakes Entrance
1/1/02	0.00	Lakes Entrance	Lakes Entrance
1/2/02	38.67	Lakes Entrance	Orbost
1/3/02	46.56	Orbost	Cann River
1/4/02	0.00	Cann River	Cann River
1/5/02	69.94	Cann River	Eden, NSW
1/6/02	20.62	Eden, NSW	Merimbula
1/7/02	25.28	Merimbula	Tathra
1/8/02	0.00	Tathra	Tathra
1/9/02	49.82	Tathra	Narooma
1/10/02	52.65	Narooma	Batemans Bay
1/11/02	34.26	Batemans Bay	Mollymook

Date	Miles	From	To
1/12/02	0.00	Mollymook	Mollymook
1/13/02	59.82	Mollymook	Gerringong
1/14/02	45.46	Gerringong	Clifton
1/15/02	0.00	Clifton	Clifton
1/16/02	40.08	Clifton	Brighton-le-Sands
1/17/02	20.97	Brighton-le-Sands	Sydney
1/18/02	0.00	Sydney	Sydney
1/19/02	0.00	Sydney	Sydney
1/20/02	0.00	Sydney	Sydney
1/21/02	16.38	Sydney	Manly
1/22/02	0.00	Manly	Manly
1/23/02	0.00	Manly	Manly
1/24/02	0.00	Manly	Manly
1/25/02	0.00	Manly	Manly
1/26/02	3.74	Manly	Sydney
1/27/02	0.00	Sydney	Sydney
1/28/02	17.00	Sydney	Bondi
1/29/02	22.67	Bondi	Sydney Airport
1/30/02	12.93	Sydney Airport	Mosgiel, New Zealand
1/31/02	12.90	Mosgiel, New Zealand	Dunedin
2/1/02	0.00	Dunedin	Dunedin
2/2/02	36.82	Dunedin	Palmerston
2/3/02	41.41	Palmerston	Oamaru
2/4/02	0.00	Oamaru	Oamaru
2/5/02	0.00	Oamaru	Oamaru
2/6/02	54.37	Oamaru	Timaru
2/7/02	50.36	Timaru	Ashburton
2/8/02	56.88	Ashburton	Christchurch
2/9/02	0.00	Christchurch	Christchurch
2/10/02	0.00	Christchurch	Christchurch
2/11/02	29.44	Christchurch	Amberley
2/12/02	41.92	Amberley	Cheviot
2/13/02	0.00	Cheviot	Cheviot
2/14/02	0.00	Cheviot	Cheviot
2/15/02	47.68	Kaikoura	Kaikoura
2/16/02	52.40	Ward	Ward

Date	Miles	From	To
2/17/02	47.57	Wellington	Wellington
2/18/02	0.00	Wellington	Wellington
2/19/02	14.38	Tawa	Tawa
2/20/02	28.73	Waikanae	Waikanae
2/21/02	56.17	Waikanae	Bulls
2/22/02	31.48	Bulls	Wanganui
2/23/02	12.31	Wanganui	Wanganui
2/24/02	28.08	Wanganui	Waverley
2/25/02	48.23	Waverley	Stratford
2/26/02	67.28	Stratford	Mokau
2/27/02	49.17	Mokau	Te Kuiti
2/28/02	52.11	Te Kuiti	Hamilton
3/1/02	0.00	Hamilton	Hamilton
3/2/02	0.00	Hamilton	Hamilton
3/3/02	75.97	Hamilton	Auckland Airport
3/4/02	0.00	Auckland Airport	Auckland Airport
3/5/02	2.85	Auckland Airport	Tahiti
3/5/02	10.48	Tahiti	Tahiti
3/6/02	22.48	Tahiti	Moorea
3/7/02	0.00	Moorea	Moorea
3/8/02	28.12	Moorea	Tahiti
3/9/02	0.00	Tahiti	Huahine
3/10/02	0.00	Huahine	Huahine
3/11/02	0.00	Huahine	Huahine
3/12/02	0.00	Huahine	Moorea
3/13/02	0.00	Moorea	Moorea
3/14/02	0.00	Moorea	Papeete
3/15/02	0.00	Papeete	Honolulu
3/16/02	0.00	Honolulu	Honolulu
3/17/02	0.00	Honolulu	Honolulu
3/18/02	10.90	Honolulu	Honolulu
3/19/02	24.88	Honolulu	Waikiki
3/20/02	0.00	Waikiki	Waikiki
3/21/02	0.00	Waikiki	Waikiki
3/22/02	62.00	Waikiki	Laie
3/23/02	46.11	Laie	Honolulu

Date	Miles	From	To
3/24/02	10.69	Honolulu	Kailua-Kona
3/25/02	0.00	Kailua-Kona	Kailua-Kona
3/26/02	12.98	Kailua-Kona	Captain Cook
3/27/02	44.70	Captain Cook	Waiohinu
3/28/02	38.80	Waiohinu	Volcano
3/29/02	39.09	Volcano	Hilo
3/30/02	0.00	Hilo	Hilo
3/31/02	43.50	Hilo	Honokaa
4/1/02	1.75	Honokaa	Honokaa
4/2/02	59.77	Honokaa	Kailua-Kona
4/3/02	13.48	Kailua-Kona	Honolulu
4/4/02	40.03	Honolulu	Sunset Beach, CA
4/5/02	36.38	Sunset Beach, CA	Dana Point
4/6/02	45.5	Dana Point	Carlsbad
4/7/02	0.00	Carlsbad	Carlsbad
4/8/02	44.09	Carlsbad	San Diego
4/9/02	0.00	San Diego	San Diego
4/10/02	32.38	San Diego	Alpine
4/11/02	23.98	Alpine	Pine Valley
4/12/02	73.08	Pine Valley	El Centro
4/13/02	0.00	El Centro	El Centro
4/14/02	18.93	El Centro	Brawley
4/15/02	69.23	Brawley	Palo Verde
4/16/02	44.30	Palo Verde	Quartzite, AZ
4/17/02	41.10	Quartzite, AZ	Salome
4/18/02	56.62	Salome	Wickenburg
4/19/02	71.47	Wickenburg	Mesa
4/20/02	0.00	Mesa	Mesa
4/21/02	29.07	Mesa	Apache Junction
4/22/02	56.26	Apache Junction	Globe
4/23/02	0.00	Globe	Globe
4/24/02	75.81	Globe	Safford
4/25/02	78.22	Safford	Lordsburg, NM
4/26/02	59.59	Lordsburg, NM	Deming
4/27/02	68.91	Deming	Las Cruces
4/28/02	55.02	Las Cruces	El Paso, TX

Date	Miles	From	To
4/29/02	0.00	El Paso, TX	El Paso, TX
4/30/02	0.00	El Paso, TX	El Paso, TX
5/1/02	33.41	El Paso, TX	Fabens
5/2/02	61.38	Fabens	Sierra Blanca
5/3/02	34.97	Sierra Blanca	Van Horn
5/4/02	0.00	Van Horn	Van Horn
5/5/02	75.56	Van Horn	Marfa
5/6/02	28.35	Marfa	Alpine
5/7/02	31.11	Alpine	Marathon
5/8/02	58.81	Marathon	Sanderson
5/9/02	88.15	Sanderson	Comstock
5/10/02	30.95	Comstock	Del Rio
5/11/02	0.00	Del Rio	Del Rio
5/12/02	34.88	Del Rio	Brackettville
5/13/02	42.81	Brackettville	Uvalde
5/14/02	42.90	Uvalde	Hondo
5/15/02	43.77	Hondo	San Antonio
5/16/02	0.00	San Antonio	San Antonio
5/17/02	3.42	San Antonio	San Antonio
5/18/02	38.17	San Antonio	Seguin
5/19/02	56.99	Seguin	Flatonia
5/20/02	20.87	Flatonia	Weimar
5/21/02	39.42	Weimar	Sealy
5/22/02	33.43	Sealy	Houston
5/23/02	0.00	Houston	Houston
5/24/02	43.86	Houston	Houston
5/25/02	20.63	Houston	Baytown
5/26/02	32.84	Baytown	Winnie
5/27/02	50.99	Winnie	Orange
5/28/02	41.50	Orange	Lake Charles, LA
5/29/02	0.00	Lake Charles, LA	Lake Charles, LA
5/30/02	0.00	Lake Charles, LA	Lake Charles, LA
5/31/02	34.14	Lake Charles, LA	Jennings
6/1/02	52.42	Jennings	Lafayette
6/2/02	54.37	Lafayette	Livonia
6/3/02	42.38	Livonia	Denham Springs

Date	Miles	From	To
6/4/02	29.54	Denham Springs	Hammond
6/5/02	62.99	Hammond	Slidell
6/6/02	56.51	Slidell	Biloxi, MS
6/7/02	51.21	Biloxi, MS	Bayou La Batre, AL
6/8/02	48.32	Bayou La Batre, AL	Orange Beach
6/9/02	29.00	Orange Beach	Pensacola, FL
6/10/02	0.00	Pensacola, FL	Pensacola, FL
6/11/02	57.36	Pensacola, FL	Destin
6/12/02	50.80	Destin	Panama City Beach
6/13/02	55.70	Panama City Beach	St. Joe Beach
6/14/02	56.78	St. Joe Beach	Carrabelle
6/15/02	0.00	Carrabelle	Carrabelle
6/16/02	67.52	Carrabelle	Tallahassee
6/17/02	34.90	Tallahassee	Monticello
6/18/02	0.00	Monticello	Monticello
6/19/02	66.80	Monticello	Live Oak
6/20/02	41.44	Live Oak	Lake City
6/21/02	0.00	Lake City	Lake City
6/22/02	37.49	Lake City	MacClenny
6/23/02	53.87	MacClenny	Yulee
6/24/02	66.41	Yulee	Darien, GA
6/25/02	64.83	Darien, GA	Savannah
6/26/02	23.93	Savannah	Hardeeville, SC
6/27/02	51.32	Hardeeville, SC	Walterboro
6/28/02	60.46	Walterboro	Mount Pleasant
6/29/02	60.31	Mount Pleasant	Georgetown
6/30/02	66.42	Georgetown	North Myrtle Beach
7/1/02	50.37	North Myrtle Beach	Southport, NC
7/2/02	70.08	Southport, NC	Sneads Ferry
7/3/02	60.84	Sneads Ferry	Morehead City
7/4/02	6.15	Morehead City	Morehead City
7/5/02	45.85	Morehead City	Ocracoke Village
7/6/02	50.00	Ocracoke Village	Rodanthe
7/7/02	76.25	Rodanthe	Barco
7/8/02	47.77	Barco	Cape Charles, VA
7/9/02	73.69	Cape Charles, VA	Pocomoke City, MD

Date	Miles	From	To
7/10/02	68.89	Pocomoke City, MD	Lewes, DE
7/11/02	29.31	Lewes, DE	Sea Isle City, NJ
7/12/02	80.21	Sea Isle City, NJ	Havertown, PA

In the Baggage Claim area of Lisbon Airport with my luggage / panniers and bike in the Delta box.

Standing in the middle of a new road under construction near Los Alcazares, Spain.

Looking to the Rock of Gibraltar from La Linea, Spain.

Outside the walls of the medieval city of Aigues Mortes, France.

The Field of Miracles in Pisa, Italy with the Cathedral and Leaning Tower in the background.

St. Peter's Square as seen from the roof of St. Peter's Basilica in Vatican City.

Camping on the sandy shore of Surfing Beach near Naousa, Paros, Greece.

Posing after lunch at a BP gas station on the Lycean Coast of Turkey.

A wide shoulder on Route 4 between Tel Aviv and Haifa, Israel.

A "Worning" road sign on Highway 55 between the Rafah border crossing on the Gaza Strip and Al-Arish, Egypt.

The Sphinx and two of three of the pyramids at Giza, Egypt.

Friends from my stay at the Best Western Emerald hotel in Mumbai, India. My bike traveled to the airport on the roof of this taxi.

Approaching the Stirling Range National Park in Western Australia.

A sign at the Border Village between Western Australia and South Australia warning of camels, wombats, and kangaroos crossing the Eyre Highway.

A spontaneous bicycle-tourist summit on the Great Ocean Road in Victoria, Australia.

The Sydney Opera House and Harbour Bridge as seen from Mrs. Macquarie's Point in Sydney, Australia.

Anzac Plaza in front of the railway station in Dunedin on New Zealand's South Island.

The "Whitestone City" of Oamaru on New Zealand's South Island.

At Postal Kilometer 1 on the ring road around Moorea, French Polynesia. The island is shaped like the road markers.

Updating my website on the deck of my over-water bungalow on the island of Moorea.

The Waikiki skyline and Diamond Head as seen from Ala Moana Park on Oahu, Hawaii.

The widest and safest shoulders of the trip were on the Ironman route near Kailua-Kona, Hawaii.

In front of the Alamo in San Antonio, Texas.

A pair of pachyderm posteriors in Hardeeville, South Carolina.

Maintaining my daily journal on the Pocket PC with foldable keyboard in a campground on Ocracoke Island, North Carolina.

A red, white, and blue welcome on the completion of my trip.

Please visit www.oncearoundonabicycle.com to learn more about my round-the-world bicycle trip. Dozens of color photos, maps, videos, and other information can be found at the website. Thank you for your interest.

Printed in the United States
20012LVS00002B/264